Strategic HRM:
Contemporary Issues in the Asia Pacific Region

1st edition

Julia Connell & Stephen Teo
Editors

Strategic HRM: Contemporary Issues in the Asia Pacific Region
1st edition, 2nd printing

Editors
Julia Connell & Stephen Teo

Cover designer
Christopher Besley, Besley Design.

ISBN-13: 978-0-7346-1080-5

Copyright

Text copyright © 2010 by The Tilde Group
Illustration, layout and design copyright © 2010 by The Tilde Group.

Under Australia's *Copyright Act 1968* (the Act), except for any fair dealing for the purposes of study, research, criticism or review, no part of this book may be reproduced, stored in a retrieval system, or transmitted in any form or by any means without prior written permission from The Tilde Group. All inquiries should be directed in the first instance to the publisher at the address below.

Disclaimer

All reasonable efforts have been made to ensure the quality and accuracy of this publication. Tilde University Press assumes no responsibility for any errors or omissions and no warranties are made with regard to this publication. Neither Tilde University Press nor any authorised distributors shall be held responsible for any direct, incidental or consequential damages resulting from the use of this publication.

Published in Australia by:
Tilde University Press
PO Box 72
Prahran VIC 3181 Australia
www.tup.net.au

FOREWORD

The current phase of globalisation is characterised by a number of features including: increased global economic competition and international trade; the rise of powerful new economies, for example China and India; tremendous advances in information and communication technologies; and increasing demands for highly skilled workers. All of these impact directly on the global value chain relating to the nature of work, where work is carried out, and by whom. Clearly, this increasingly complex environment creates enormous challenges for international management in general and for human resource management in particular. Hence, we need to continuously reassess our understanding of the world of work, the nature of the contemporary workplace, and the impact on individual workers and their families.

One perspective from which to view these developments is to focus on organisations – and in particular multinational enterprises or MNEs – as they are at the forefront of the movement of capital, productive capacity, knowledge and employees across borders and within international supply chains. The success of MNEs is dependent on how well they manage the performance of their global workforce. Increasingly, this workforce is located not only in their home country but also in different host countries across the world, often creating a global–local tension that is not only of tremendous importance it is also a potential great source of knowledge.

Another consideration is to explore the impact of globalisation on institutional arrangements in different countries, for example changes in labour market legislation or workforce policy. Over the past twenty years there have been enormous changes in the Asia Pacific region as countries struggle to compete in an increasingly dynamic global environment. While there are some similarities between some countries, these changes have not been uniform across the region and depend on history and culture as well as on politics and economics.

The great strength of this book is that it includes both of these perspectives. It focuses not only at the organisational level but also situates organisations within the broader context of the Asia Pacific region. The editors are to be congratulated for having brought together some of the leading contemporary HRM academics in the region, an experienced set of authors who are carrying out cutting edge research in contemporary topics. By showcasing their work, the book demonstrates some key challenges that are faced by practitioners and scholars in the current context. Hence, this is a valuable book for practitioners and scholars. By embracing up-to-date cases and examples from throughout the region – including India, China,

Singapore, Korea and Vietnam – the book captures a global flavour that is essential for a 21st century readership. In essence, this book is well structured, clearly focused, timely and valuable. I recommend it wholeheartedly.

Professor Pauline Stanton
Victoria University, Melbourne Australia
April 2010

CONTENTS

Chapter 1: Strategic HRM in Context: An Overview 1
    Introduction 1
    The outer context 2
    The inner context 3
    HRM—an organisation-wide responsibility 4
    Strategic management 4
    Matching organisational competencies with strategic capability 4
    Generating strategic capability 5
    Conclusion 13
    References 14

Part I: Outer Context—
Political, Economic, Socio-Economic, Technical, Legal, Environmental 17

Chapter 2: Contemporary Issues in HRM in the Asia Pacific Region:
An Explanatory Framework 19
    Introduction 19
    Contextual factors 20
    Korea after World War Two 20
    Role of the state 21
    Ethnic and linguistic homogeneity 21
    Religion, beliefs and customs 21
    The core ideology of HRM 22
    Korean economy 22
    Labour market factors 23
    Shifting patterns of gender and demographics 23
    HRM practices and key issues 27
    The war for talent 28
    Recruitment at Samsung 28
    Annual pay 29
    Retention strategies in Korea post 1997 30
    Corporate venture programs (CVP) 31
    CVP modes 31
    Dismissals and redundancies 32
    Labour laws 32
    Outplacement programs 32
    Possible directions for HRM 33
    Why HRM changes might occur 35
    Environmental turbulence 35
    Strategic choice 35
    Institutional influences 36
    Similarity versus distinctiveness 36
    Constraints on convergence 37
    Macro variables v. micro variables 38

Key issues for HRM 38
Focus on managing change 38
Focus on organisational performance... 38
Focus on professionalism.. 38
Paradoxes in HRM functions 39
Best practice 39
Multiple modes of employment.. 39
Conclusion.. 40
The war for talent... 40
References.. 41

Chapter 3: Developments in Employee Relations in the Asia Pacific........... 45
Introduction.. 46
States, trade unions and markets in Asia 47
China, Vietnam, Malaysia, and Indonesia 49
Japan and South Korea... 49
Forces for and against protective labour law.. 49
China... 50
The Labour Contract Law 51
The Employment Protection Law... 51
Dispute resolution.. 52
Japan 53
Singapore 54
Conclusion.. 56
Discussion questions 58
References.. 58

Chapter 4: Managing Globalisation and International HRM........................ 60
Introduction.. 61
Case study 63
The changing global landscape 63
China and India 64
Demand for goods, services and natural resources 64
Sovereign Wealth Funds... 64
Global terrorism 65
What does globalisation mean?... 65
Globalisation of the economy.. 65
Globalisation of culture.. 66
Globalisation of politics 66
The positive view of globalisation 66
The negative view of globalisation 67
The 'nothing new' view of globalisation 67
Geographical fragmentation of production chains 68
Regime shopping 68
Delocalisation... 68
Regime competition... 69
Globalisation and multinational enterprises (MNEs)................................. 69
Role of MNEs in the process of globalisation 69
Managing globalisation in Australia and New Zealand.............................. 70

The tyranny of distance v. the power of proximity 71
Performance of MNEs in New Zealand 72
Economic interdependency of Australia and New Zealand 72
Performance of MNEs in Australia 73
Globalisation and the SIHRM challenges 73
Cross-cultural studies 74
Comparative HRM research 74
Strategic HRM in the multinational context 74
Strategic international human resource management 74
Global integration v. local differentiation 75
The scope and content of the corporate HR function 75
Strategy and structure v. domestic, institutional and political pressures 75
The war for talent 76
Scope of global talent management 76
Attraction of talent a strategic priority 77
International migration 77
Career management 78
Conclusion 78
References 81

Chapter 5: Sustainability in Strategic Human Resource Management 86
Introduction 87
Contemporary trends 88
International consensus 89
Intergenerational equity 89
Isolation of non-sustainable companies 89
The GRI and the DJSI 90
SHRM 91
Social and human objectives 92
Internal benefits 92
External benefits 92
Economic outcomes 93
Interrelationship between SHRM and environmental sustainability 93
Stakeholder relationships 94
Building relationships with stakeholders 94
Facilitating culture change 95
Values statements 95
Westpac's code of conduct 95
Role of leaders and managers 96
SHRM and the development of skills towards furthering sustainability
and stakeholder management 96
Understanding values and assumptions 97
Critical thinking 97
Affective competence 98
Collaborative learning 98
Participation in partnerships and decision making 98
Visioning and imagining 98
Systemic thinking 99

Living systems 99
Learning journeys 99
Ethical leadership 100
Conclusion 104
Discussion questions 105
References 105

Chapter 6: The Business Case for Human Capital Metrics 110
Introduction 112
Temporal limitations of accounting figures 112
Need for human capital indicators 112
Economic value of intangible assets 112
Employee engagement scores and the value of the firm 113
Pressures for changing the nature of the human capital metrics debate 113
Non-financial factors in investment decisions 115
Three views on human capital measurement principles 115
Need for both quantitative and qualitative measures 117
International perspectives on the context for human capital metrics 118
Irrelevance of traditional HR metrics 118
Need for systems to analyse how human capital creates value 119
Failure of traditional approaches to human capital analysis 119
Traditional approaches to human capital metrics 120
Watson Wyatt's Human Capital Index 120
European Business Excellence Model 120
Malcolm Baldrige Criteria for Performance Excellence 120
William Mercer's Human Capital Wheel 121
Measuring ROI of Human Capital 121
The Balanced Scorecard 122
The Skandia Navigator 123
The HR Scorecard 123
The Intangible Assets Monitor 124
The Human Capital Monitor 124
Intellectual Capital Index 125
Systems-based approaches to human capital metrics 127
Tool 1: Mapping human capital using drivers of the value of human capital ... 128
Tool 2: Analysing human capital systems using the Human Capital Wheel 128
Tool 3: Rating the organisation's human capital using a star rating system 128
Tool 4: Change Management Matrix 129
Summary 134
Discussion questions 134
References 135

Chapter 7: Human Resource Outsourcing and Shared Services: An Asian Pacific Perspective 139
HR outsourcing in the changing business context 140
ROI of HR interventions 140
HRO on the increase 140
Categories of HR service providers 141
To outsource or not: A strategic decision 141

Continuity of skill supply 142
Core v. periphery activities 142
Transaction cost economic model (Williamson 1985) 142
Lack of in-house expertise 142
To perform one-time tasks 143
To overcome cultural differences... 143
Cost efficiency 143
HR activities that can be outsourced 143
Core and non-core HR activities 143
Outsourcing in large and small organisations 144
Alternatives to HR outsourcing 144
Back-office processes 144
Call-centre technologies and approaches to work organisation 144
Main tasks of shared services centres 145
Advantage of the shared services model 145
Trends in HR outsourcing... 146
Growth in HR outsourcing... 146
Differences between countries 146
Predicted growth 147
Growth in single process outsourcing.. 147
Differences between Europe and North America for multi-process HRO 147
Europe's share in the global HRO market 147
The North American market for HRO.. 148
Latin America 148
HR outsourcing in Asia Pacific region... 149
India as an HR outsourcing destination 149
Major services and strengths 150
Recruitment process outsourcing 151
Complete HR delivery.. 151
Potential for global growth 151
Cost and confidentiality 152
Sentiment against offshoring.. 152
Cultural and psychological mindsets 152
New models of industry-specific solutions 152
Ready availability of HR skills 152
Conclusion 155
Benefits of HRO... 155
Cost-cutting v. transactional activities.. 155
Growth of HRO in India... 156
References.. 156

Chapter 8: The Transfer of HRM Policies and Practices in Multinational Companies **159**
Global perspectives.. 160
Pluralistic industrialism 161
A globalised economy 161
Denationalisation of MNCs 162
Criticism of the globalisation thesis 162

Comparative perspectives 163
Dimensions of cultural difference 163
Problems with the cultural approach 164
Country perspectives 165
Corporate identity 165
The dominance effect 166
Open v. closed environment of host country 166
Internal strength and economic power 166
Developing countries 167
Sector perspectives 167
Multidomestic industries 167
Global industries 168
Organisational perspectives 168
Business strategy 169
Administrative heritage 169
Nature of the subsidiary 169
Low power host countries 170
Dynamics of influence 170
Reverse diffusion 172
The transfer process 172
The adaptive approach 173
The exportive approach 173
The integrative approach 173
Direct mechanisms 173
Indirect mechanisms 173
Conclusion 176
The role of nationality in the global market 176
Perspectives on HRM transfer 176
Mechanisms of transfer 177
References 177

Part II: Inner Context–
Organisational Culture, Structure, Politics/Leadership,
Task-Technology, Business Outputs 183

Chapter 9: Work–Life Management 185
Introduction 186
Research in the work–life concept 187
Collectivist cultures v. individualistic cultures 187
Links between work–life and nationality 187
Defining work–life issues 188
Early studies 188
The whole person—interacting spheres of work, family and life 189
Role-related expectations and responsibilities 190
Emphasis on integration and harmony 190
Work–life v. work–family 190
Global trends 191
Urbanisation 191
Women in the workforce 192

Dependent care 192
Aged care 193
Other pressures 193
The Australian perspective 194
Women in the workforce 194
Generational values 194
Working hours 194
Work–life initiatives 194
Discrimination on the basis of parental or carer responsibilities 196
Parental leave 196
Requests for changes in working arrangements 196
The business case for work–life initiatives 197
A strategic approach to work–life implementation issues 198
Diversity/inclusion 199
Talent management 199
Culture change 199
Health and wellness 200
Employee relations 200
Total rewards 200
Corporate citizenship 200
Human resource policies 201
Strategic human resource management 202
Conclusion 202
Discussion questions 205
References 206

Chapter 10: Managing Talent:
Exploring HR Strategies in a Dynamic Environment 212
Introduction 213
Defining talent 214
Managing talent—a theoretical perspective 215
Attraction and retention of employees 216
Long-term organisational renewal 216
Skilled employees 216
Managing talent—a practical perspective 217
Knowledge workers 219
Motivating essential employees 219
Job-hopping 219
The move to a contingent workforce 220
Need for high-calibre managerial talent 221
Strategies to regenerate the knowledge base 221
Training and development the top benefit 222
Embracing a new mindset 222
Managing talent—a research perspective 224
Contradictions in organisational focus 224
Employment v. employability 226
Conclusion 227
References 229

Chapter 11: An Ageing Workforce: HRM Challenges 233
Introduction 234
The trend to an ageing workforce 234
Retention of older workers 234
Growing diversity of the workplace 235
Population and workforce ageing 235
Workforce participation and gender 236
Workforce participation and education 237
Racial differences and workforce participation 237
Global perspectives 237
Tienen 239
Implementing job security post-tienen 239
Age discrimination 240
The 2007 amendments 240
The HREOC enquiry into age discrimination in Australia 241
The *Age Discrimination Act* 2004 242
The *Fair Work Act* 2009 242
The 'National Ageing Strategy' and the 'Intergenerational Report' 242
The pension eligibility age 243
Tax incentives 243
The national policy agenda 243
An ageing workforce—an issue of human rights or economics? 243
A focus on economic goals 244
Industry issues and organisational responses: Australia 244
Early retirement 244
Increase in average age of public servants 245
Consequences of an ageing public service workforce 245
Recognising organisational commitment to engaging an older workforce 246
Managing diversity—the business case argument 246
Ageing, public policy, and strategic HRM 249
Economic focus of policy initiatives 249
Changes in the characteristics of older workers 250
Government motivations 251
Employer motivations 251
References 254

Chapter 12: Managing Diversity, Social Inclusion and Change in the Workplace 256
Introduction 258
Managing diversity 260
Social inclusion 260
Need for a holistic, lifespan perspective 260
Organisation benefits 261
Employee benefits 262
Country perspective on diversity – diversity in Australia 262
Challenges for managing diversity 264
Hourly earnings 264
Salaries of top earners 265

The *Workplace Relations Act* 1996 265
Needs and preferences of mature-age workers 265
Collectivist cultures v. individualist cultures... 266
Social exclusion 266
Organisational responses to the management of diversity 267
Diversity in teams 267
No 'one best way'... 268
Flexible work design 268
Differential work design 268
Need for both flexible work design and differential work design................... 269
Establishing workplace diversity programs... 269
Managing organisational change in diverse cultures 271
Diversity in single cultures 271
Diversity between cultures 271
Resistance to change 272
PDI, UAI and IDV 272
Differences between countries 273
Correlation between cultural dimensions and change management 273
Need for change management to be adapted to culture............................... 274
Public policy and legislation on diversity 274
Equal opportunity 274
Direct discrimination.. 275
Indirect discrimination 275
Workplace Relations Act 1996 276
Identified criteria 277
Special measures.. 277
Workplace diversity coordinator.. 277
Conclusion 278
Discussion questions 278
References... 279
Appendix 1—Acts related to diversity in the workplace.............................. 283

Chapter 13: Performance Management of Expatriates in China 284
Introduction.. 285
A country perspective: HRM in China 287
HRM in China... 288
Strategic integration of HRM and firm performance in China 288
Performance appraisal in non-foreign firms in China 289
Global perspectives on performance management....................................... 290
Growth of Chinese MNEs... 291
IPM of non-expatriate and 'third-country' staff.. 291
Performance appraisal... 291
IPM v. domestic PM... 292
PM in Chinese MNEs v. Western MNEs 292
PM in Chinese MNEs v. domestic organisations 293
Reverse diffusion... 293
EPM and level of internationalisation 294
Methodology 295

Findings 295
Conclusion 300
References 302

Chapter 14: The Ethics of Workforce Drug Testing and HRM 307
Introduction 308
Global perspectives 308
Workforce drug testing in the USA 308
Workforce drug testing in the Asia Pacific region 309
Workforce drug testing in the UK 309
Rhetoric and evidence 309
Links between drug use and high-risk employees 309
Evidence for negative effects of employee drug use 310
Effectiveness of workforce drug testing 310
The testing process 310
Personal privacy 310
Other privacy issues 311
Recency of drug use 311
Recreational drug use 311
Random drug testing 312
Behind the momentum for testing 312
Preservation of rational order 312
Managerial anxiety 313
Country and sector perspective: Australia 314
Legal obligations 314
Position of the Australian Industrial Relations Commission 315
Management 'fads' and 'fashions' 315
Tainted evidence 316
Summary 320
Discussion questions 322
References 322

Glossary 327
Index 335

About the Editors

Julia Connell, Dip RSA, Dip Ed, MA Dist (Reading), PhD (Newcastle), FAHRI, is Professor and Dean of Graduate Studies, Australian Catholic University, North Sydney. Prior to this Julia was Associate Dean Postgraduate Programs, UTS Business; Chair of Research, University of Wollongong in Dubai; and Associate Dean International, University of Newcastle. Julia worked in various public and private sector organisations in the UK before joining The Henley College, Oxford. Julia has co-edited four books, published over 40 refereed journal articles, and co-edited nine special issue journal editions.

Julia is a Fellow of the Australian Human Resources Institute and is on the editorial board of the British journal *Personnel Review*. Her research areas include HRM, organisational change, networks and clusters, and organisational and management effectiveness. Julia has designed and delivered a number of management programs for various organisations including the RAAF, Macquarie Generation, Newcastle City Council, Maitland City Council, Energy Australia, ANI Comsteel, The Victorian Meat Council, Ampcontrol, the NSW Police Service and QBE.

Stephen Teo, BEc (Monash), Grad Dip Bus (Monash), Grad Dip Japanese (Professional) (Swinburne), MBA (Int Bus) (Monash), PhD (QUT), is Professor and Associate Dean (Academic) at the University of Western Sydney. He previously worked in the banking and public sectors before holding academic positions at QUT, MGSM, the Chinese University of Hong Kong, and the University of Technology Sydney.

Stephen is a member of the editorial boards of the *Journal of Small Business Management*, the *Public Management Review*, *Research and Practice in Human Resource Management*, *Career Development International*, *Sports Management Review*, and the *Deakin Business Review*. He is a Fellow of the Australian Human Resources Institute and a Senior Associate of the Australian Institute of Banking and Finance.

His research and consulting interests lie in the evaluation of HRM effectiveness, focusing on the status and influence of the HRM function in strategic decision-making processes. He has consulted for organisations such as the NSW Department of Environment and Climate Change, and the Australian Defence Force.

About the Contributors

Anne Bardoel (MBA, Melbourne; PhD, Monash) is Associate Professor in Management at Monash University in Melbourne, Australia. Anne currently heads the Work Life Research Program which is part of the Australian Centre for Research in Employment and Work (ACREW). She has developed a national and international reputation as a researcher in the work and family area, and has published a number of articles in academic journals in the area. She is also a member of the Victorian Government's Working Families Council.

John Burgess (PhD, Newcastle) is Professor of International Human Resource Management at Newcastle Business School, the University of Newcastle in Newcastle, Australia. His research interests include job quality, HRM practices of multinational enterprises, and the development of industry clusters.

Noelle Donnelly (PhD, Warwick) is a Senior Lecturer in Human Resource Management and Industrial Relations at Victoria University of Wellington in New Zealand. A graduate of Warwick Business School in the UK, her current research interests include IHRM and small country MNEs. Previously Noelle taught at the Graduate Business School at University College Dublin, Ireland, where she was awarded a post-doctorate scholarship in IHRM. Noelle also has international team-based experience, working on the EU-funded Industrial Relations in the European Community (IREC) project.

Peter J Dowling (PhD, Flinders) is Professor of Human Resource Management at La Trobe University in Melbourne, Australia. His current research interests are concerned with international HRM, international management and strategic management. Peter is the lead author of a number of texts, and has published over seventy journal articles and book chapters. He serves on the editorial boards of the *International Journal of Human Resource Management*, *Journal of World Business*, *Management International Review*, the *Journal of International Management*, the *Journal of Management & Organization*, *ZfP-German Journal of Human Resource Research*, the *Asia Pacific Journal of Human Resources*, and *Thunderbird International Business Review*.

Anthony Fee (MBA, Bond University) is a Lecturer in International Business at the Faculty of Economics and Business, The University of

Sydney in Sydney, Australia. His research focuses on expatriate development and training.

Kerry Grigg (BCom, MCom) is currently researching employee perceptions of work-life balance policies and practices as part of her PhD candidature at Monash University in Melbourne, Australia. Her other research interests include employer branding, psychological contracts and talent management. Kerry has disseminated her research at Australian and International Management Conferences and has presented workshops to industry and professional groups including the Australian Institute of Police Management and the National Local Government HR Association.

Zeenobiyah Hannif (PhD, Newcastle) is a Lecturer in the School of Management, University of Technology, Sydney in Sydney, Australia. Her doctoral research examined the quality of work life in the Australian call centre industry. Her recent research activity has centred on the human resources practices of MNCs in Australia, and the quality of work life in the call centre industry.

Charmine EJ Härtel (PhD, Colorado State) is Professor of Human Resource Management and Management Cluster Leader (Research Development and Training) in the UQ Business School, University of Queensland in Brisbane, Australia. Her current research areas include workforce diversity, emotions, leadership development and employee well-being. Her publications have featured in the *Academy of Management Review*, the *Journal of Applied Psychology*, *Leadership Quarterly*, the *Journal of Management* and *Human Resource Management Review*.

Rob Hecker (PhD, Tasmania) is a Senior Lecturer and Director of the MBA program at the University of Tasmania in Australia. His research interests are focused on understanding the place of the individual within and outside the organisation – both from a human resource development and from consumer behaviour perspective. His background in psychology and as a working manager informs these research and teaching interests.

Peter Holland (PhD, Tasmania) is Associate Professor in Human Resource Management and Employee Relations in the Department of Management, and Deputy Director of the Australian Centre for Research in Employment and Work at Monash University in Melbourne, Australia. Peter has worked in the Australian Finance Industry and consulted to the private and public sector in a variety of areas related to human resource management and employee relations. His current research interests include human resources development, talent management, employee voice and monitoring and surveillance in the workplace. He has co-authored seven books and numerous journal articles, monographs and book chapters on a variety of human resource management and employee relations issues.

Ajay K Jain (PhD, IIT Kanpur) is Associate Professor in Organizational Behaviour at the Management Development Institute in Gurgaon, India. He is Visiting Professor to the University of Free State, South Africa, to the Aarhus School of Business, and to the Denmark and Indian Institute of Management in Lucknow, delivering courses in the area of organisational design and research methods. Professor Jain has been widely published in national and international journals – including the *International Journal of Stress Management*, the *Leadership and Organization Development Journal*, and *Psychological Studies* – in the areas of leadership, executive stress, emotional intelligence, self management and organisational citizenship.

Grant Jones (PhD, Canberra) is a Senior Lecturer at the Macquarie Graduate School of Management, Sydney, Australia where he teaches organisational behaviour and human resource management. Grant has taught strategic management and organisational behaviour throughout Asia, including guest lectureships at the University of Nanjing, the East China University of Science and Technology (Shanghai), and the University of Ningbo. He is the author of three books, one in the area of environmental management and two in the area of organisational dynamics. He is also a company director and Chair of the Academic Board of the Australian Institute of Higher Education.

Christina Kirsch (DPhil, Potsdam) is Senior Researcher at ChangeTracking Research (CTRE) in Sydney, Australia, and is an active researcher and practitioner in the area of organisational psychology and corporate sustainability. Christina has extensive experience as a lecturer, academic writer and consultant, and has been published in numerous international journals. Her research interests include organisational change, cross-cultural industrial psychology, organisational analysis and work design, and corporate sustainability.

Robin Kramar (PhD, Sydney) is Professor, Deputy Dean and Director of Accreditation at MGSM, Macquarie University, Sydney Australia. She has had a long-term interest in managing people in the workplace and the consequences for organisations, society and individuals. Robin has co-authored numerous books, articles and chapters on human resource management, diversity, equal employment opportunity and change. She is Editor of the *Asia Pacific Journal of Human Resources*, and is also on the Editorial Board of *Human Resources*. In addition, she is researching the relationship between corporate social responsibility and diversity.

Susan McGrath-Champ (PhD) is Associate Professor in Human Resource Management and Industrial Relations at the School of Business, University of Sydney, Australia. Her recent research areas include international human resource management, the geographical aspects of work and employment, and skill and training in the construction industry. She has previously worked in industry, consulting and research in Australia and Canada, and in 2004 was awarded an International Exchange for research in China by the Australian and Chinese Academies of Social Science. Susan has published widely in employment relations and social science journals. She is Chief Editor of the *Handbook of Employment and Society: Working Space*, and was guest editor of special editions of *Economic and Industrial Democracy* (August 2005) and *Labour and Industry* (December 2002).

Loretta O'Donnell MBA (AGSM), PhD, is the Director of the AGSM Graduate Certificate in Change Management, Australian School of Business, University of New South Wales, Sydney, Australia. Her research incorporates systematic tools for human capital analysis in financial markets and human capital links to corporate performance. Dr O'Donnell has advised senior management in the US, UK and Europe on strategic change management, including evaluating Board performance, for corporations in investment banking, performing arts, building products, tertiary education, the public sector and not for profit organisations. She previously occupied senior consulting roles in a global consulting firm, with roles in Chicago and in Sydney.

Chris Rowley (DPhil, Oxford) is Subject Group Leader and the inaugural Professor of Human Resource Management at Cass Business School, City University, UK. He is the founding Director of the multi-disciplinary and internationally networked Centre for Research on Asian Management, Editor of the leading journal *Asia Pacific Business Review*, and Series Editor of the *Working in Asia* and *Asian Studies* book series. Professor Rowley is well known and highly regarded in the area, with visiting appointments at leading Asian universities and several journal editorial boards. Professor Rowley researches in a range of areas, including international and comparative human resource management, and Asia Pacific management and business. He publishes widely, including in leading US and UK journals such as *California Management Review*, the *Journal of World Business*, *Human Resource Management*, the *International Journal of HRM*, the *British Journal of Management*, and *Human Relations*, with over 330 articles, books, chapters and other contributions.

Carol Royal (PhD, UNSW) is Director of the Masters in Technology Management and a Senior Lecturer at the Australian School of Business, University of New South Wales in Sydney, Australia. Her research evaluates publicly listed companies through human capital analysis and its links to corporate performance. She also researches in the areas of corporate sustainability and human capital, and organisational change management systems. Carol has provided research and advisory services to numerous industries including investment banking, retailing, manufacturing, tertiary education, and the public sector.

Debi S Saini (PhD, GPHR) is Professor of HRM at the Management Development Institute (MDI) in Gurgaon, India. His areas of interest are strategic HRM, global HRM, new industrial relations, and employee relations law. He has authored 65 papers, book chapters and cases that have been published, among others, in the *Journal of World Business, Human Resource Management, Asia-Pacific Business Review, ACRC Hong Kong Case Series*, the *Indian Journal of Labour Economics*, and *Economic & Political Weekly*. He is Editor of *Vision-The Journal of Business Perspective*, and has consulted for the ILO, GTZ (Germany), and SHRM (USA).

Anne Vo (PhD, De Montfort UK) is a Lecturer at the School of Management and Marketing, University of Wollongong in Wollongong, Australia. Anne researches and publishes in the areas of international and comparative HRM (focusing on Asian countries), the transfer of multinational companies' HRM/IR policies and practices across borders, and the transformation of HRM systems in developing countries.

Peter Waring (PhD, Newcastle) has qualifications in commerce, law and management and is Deputy CEO, University of Newcastle, Singapore where he is also a Senior Lecturer in Business. Peter's teaching and research interests extend to the fields of corporate governance, human resource management and employment relations. He has also published more than fifty refereed book chapters and academic articles in leading international journals such as *The Journal of Business Ethics, Corporate Governance: An International Review, Employee Relations*, and *Corporate Governance and Personnel Review*. He has also co-authored three best-selling books in employment relations and human resource management.

Jennifer Waterhouse (PhD, QUT) is a Senior Lecturer in the Newcastle Business School, University of Newcastle in Newcastle, Australia, teaching in the areas of diversity management and negotiation. She researches and has published in the areas of employment policy, human resource management, public policy and organisational change.

Edward Wray-Bliss (PhD, UMIST) is a Senior Lecturer in the School of Management at the University of Technology, Sydney in Sydney, Australia. He teaches in the fields of HRM, management and organisation studies. His research, examining the specific topics of drugs and drug testing, has been published in the journals *New Technology, Work and Employment*, in *Culture and Organisation*, and in *Tamara*, as well as and in Hancock and Tyler's reference work *The Management of Everyday Life*. In addition, Edward's expert commentary on drugs and drug testing at work has appeared in a range of national and international media, including the *Sydney Morning Herald*, *ABC Canberra*, *The Dominion Post*, and the *Nottingham Evening Post*.

Xiaohua Yang (PhD, Kansas) is Associate Professor of International Business in the School of Business and Professional Studies at the University of San Francisco. Her work in the areas of international strategic alliances, the internationalisation of firms, expatriate management, international firms' practices of corporate social responsibility, and foreign market entry strategies has been published and presented in international journals and conferences. She also co-edited the *Asia Pacific Journal of Management Special Issue on Varieties of Asian Capitalism* (vol. 26, 2009). Dr Yang serves on the editorial board of the *Asia Pacific Journal of Management* and on the executive committee of the International Association for Chinese Management Research. She has taught International Business subjects in the US, Australia, China and Taiwan, and has lectured in Europe and directed overseas study programs for nearly ten years.

Acknowledgements

We would like to express our thanks to several people who made this book possible.

Firstly, thank you to our publishers: Rick Ryan who has been so enthusiastic, friendly and helpful right from the creation and signing of the contract and to Sally Keohane in the UK who has been amazingly responsive, professional and thorough during the final stages of publication preparation.

Secondly, thank you to all of the authors who contributed. Without you, there would be no book. We believe your collective effort has contributed to a very special outcome.

Last, and definitely not least, we would like to thank Virginia Furse our wonderful research assistant. Virginia's exceptional organisational skills, endless patience and ability to track missing references have contributed enormously to our ability to finalise this book.

Julia Connell & Stephen Teo
April 2010

Chapter 1

STRATEGIC HRM IN CONTEXT: AN OVERVIEW

Julia Connell & Stephen Teo

OBJECTIVES

This chapter provides an overview of what is meant by strategic human resource management (SHRM) and a rationale for the choice of topics included in the book. It also outlines the framework utilised for each chapter before providing a brief glimpse into their content and argumentation.

Chapter two provides an explanatory framework for HRM in the Asian Pacific, setting the scene for the chapters that follow. In addition it provides a number of models and frameworks that HR practitioners and researchers can utilise in order to explore more fully the issues discussed in the book.

Introduction

Researchers have generally agreed that the ability to sustain competitive advantage is the crucial factor distinguishing a successful firm from one that is less successful, especially through the strategic management of its human resources.

Rationale

Recent changes in the global and domestic external environment, along with changing role expectations, have led to different demands from human resources specialists (BCG 2008). Focusing on SHRM in the Asia Pacific region (a region which despite recent economic and organisational failures remains attractive for developing economies), this book aims to provide insight into how such demands can be supported.

Our intention was to create a book that is unique in terms of both structure and content—while being useful and appealing to HR scholars, HR practitioners and industry leaders.

While there is a growing body of literature on SHRM, researchers have urged the conduct of more research into HRM in the Asia Pacific region (De Cieri & Dowling 1997). It is evident that in a world economy increasingly shaped by the emergence of China and India as major powers, SHRM challenges relate to global labour markets and complex environments generated by offshoring and other multi-country strategies (BCG 2009).

Although we recognise the increasing volume of literature published on HRM and SHRM we believe that with this volume we have created a distinctive product:

- firstly, by identifying some of the key topics associated with SHRM; and
- secondly, by bringing together leading researchers in the field to share their work with you.

The Warwick model of strategic change and HRM

The range of topics chosen under the umbrella of SHRM was guided by the Warwick model of strategic change and human resource management (Hendry & Pettigrew 1990). This model considers the outer context of an organisation through a strategy which is similar to that of a PESTLE lens, recognising that the political, economic, socio-economic, technological, legal and environmental contexts influence the inner context of the organisation with regard to:

- organisational culture;
- structure;
- leadership;
- technology; and
- business results (see Figure 1.1).

The model was selected as it identifies strategic change as both a dynamic and iterative process while taking into account the role of contextual factors in the shaping of strategic decisions over time (Huczynski & Buchanan 2007).

The outer context

Topics included in Part I of the book (the outer context) include SHRM and:

- employee relations;
- managing globalisation;
- sustainability;

- human capital metrics;
- shared services and outsourcing; and
- the transfer of HRM policies in multinational companies.

Figure 1.1 The Warwick model of human resource management

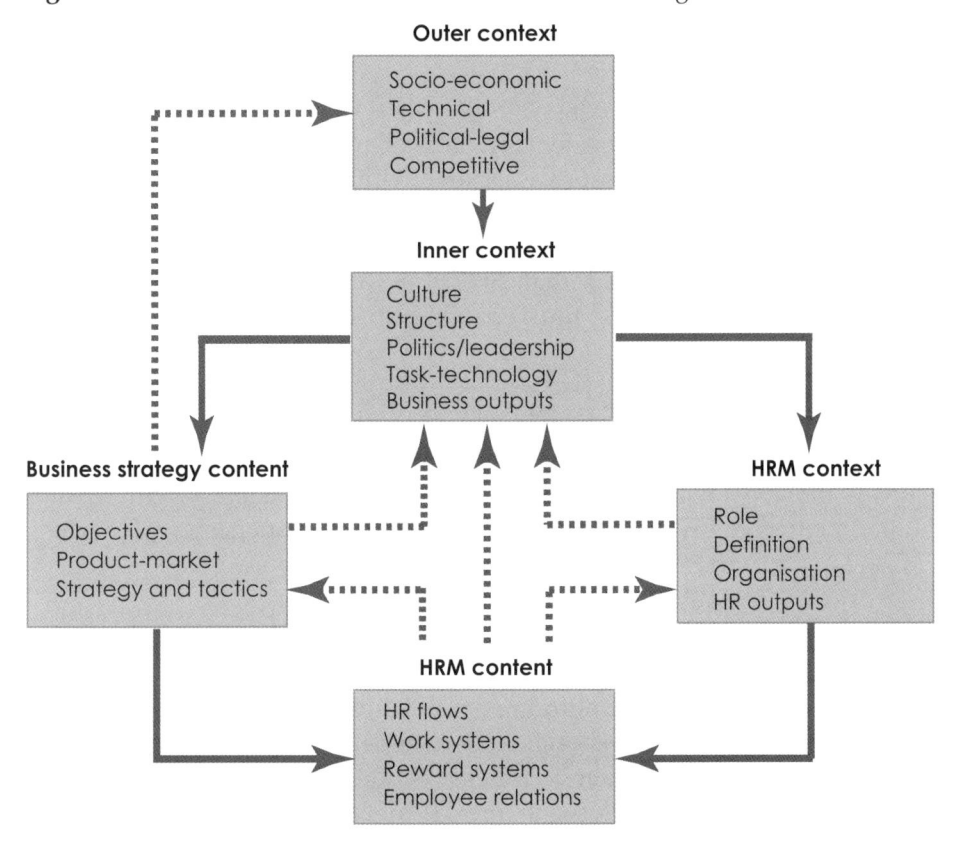

Outer context
- Socio-economic
- Technical
- Political-legal
- Competitive

Inner context
- Culture
- Structure
- Politics/leadership
- Task-technology
- Business outputs

Business strategy content
- Objectives
- Product-market
- Strategy and tactics

HRM context
- Role
- Definition
- Organisation
- HR outputs

HRM content
- HR flows
- Work systems
- Reward systems
- Employee relations

Source: Hendry & Pettigrew 1990.

The inner context

According to the Warwick model, the inner context influences, and is influenced by, the HRM content. This refers to the way in which an organisation defines the role and structure of the HRM function and the outputs expected of it. Human resource policies are, of course, considered dependent on organisational strategy.

In this context the chapters comprising Part II examine SHRM and:

- factors that influence an organisation's culture;
- the effective deployment of human resources; and
- its business outputs.

Specifically, the chapters in Part II encompass an analysis of:

- work–life management;
- talent management;
- the challenges and opportunities presented by an ageing workforce;
- the case for the need to manage diversity and develop a socially inclusive culture;
- the performance management of expatriates in China; and
- the increasingly prevalent practice of workforce drug testing and consequent ethical issues associated with SHRM.

HRM and competitive advantage

It is commonly understood that SHRM is an approach to HRM that supports business strategies thus enabling an organisation to achieve its goals (Armstrong 2008).

HRM—an organisation-wide responsibility

The requirement for HRM policy to support business strategy indicates that HRM is moving towards an organisation-wide responsibility with greater commitment and involvement from all levels of management (Sheehan, Holland & De Cieri 2006).

Strategic management

Strategic management offers firms a systematic framework for managing their internal and external environments, affecting both short and long-term organisational decision making and competitive advantage. Gaining competitive advantage through strategic action has become an important focus of research and analysis in the HRM field (Delery & Shaw 2001; Dunford, Snell & Wright 2001).

A basic principle underlying the concept of strategic intention is that firms cope with external environmental changes through the choice and application of appropriate strategies. It has been consistently pointed out, however, that the notion of adopting a strategic approach to HRM requires:

- senior management support for HR policies, processes and systems; and
- the integration of people management issues with the process of strategic management (Kane, Crawford, & Grant 1999; Ulrich 1997).

Matching organisational competencies with strategic capability

In order to build competitive advantage, an organisation needs to align its capabilities and resources with the opportunities and challenges occurring within the external environment. This refers to the matching of organisational competencies (i.e. resources and skills) with strategic capability (i.e. the ability to develop and implement strategies that will achieve sustained competitive advantage. This requires consideration of the factors examined in Part I of this book (The outer organisational context).

Generating strategic capability

In Part II (The inner organisational context) the focus is on SHRM with regard to the generation of strategic capability—that is, enabling the organisation so that it has the skilled, engaged, motivated employees it needs to achieve sustained competitive advantage.

By shifting the emphasis in the strategy literature from external factors (i.e. industry) to the internal resources of the firm as a source of competitive advantage (Barney 2001), the resource-based view of a firm (mentioned in several chapters in this book) provides a basis for emphasising that it is the strategic importance of people *within* organisations that makes the difference in gaining competitive advantage.

The need for a global outlook

A GLOBE study of leadership and culture in 62 societies (Javidan and Dastmalchian, 2009) supported the necessity for the development of a global outlook—whether the reference point was HR managers or other leader managers. The researchers further point out the need to mobilise global resources and meet the needs of global stakeholders. These claims have implications for:

- leadership development;
- managing uncertainty;
- cultural sensitivity;
- the selection of high performing individuals; and
- performance management.

These topics and more are examined in the context of the Asia Pacific, focusing in some chapters specifically on Korea, Singapore, Australia, China and Japanese companies in Vietnam.

Chapter structure

Each chapter (apart from chapter two) follows the following structure:

1. chapter objectives;
2. definitions;
3. a case study addressing the issues outlined; and
4. discussion questions.

Part I: The outer organisational context—political, economic, socio-economic, technical, legal and environmental factors

As pointed out earlier, a key element of SHRM is the need for organisations to align their HR strategies with what is occurring in the external environment (De Cieri & Dowling 1997; Hendry & Pettigrew 1990; Jackson & Schuler 1995). In Part I, the contributions from various scholars provide evidence of how organisations in the region adopt SHRM as a result of a changing external environment, taking into account the various political, economic, socio-economic, technical, legal and environmental influences.

Chapter 2 Contemporary issues in HRM in the Asia Pacific Region

Chapter 2 by Chris Rowley provides an explanatory framework for HRM in the Asia Pacific region. Rowley begins by pointing out that the 'Asian miracle' of the post-1960s involved both people and HRM practices. He focuses on Korea where, up until the 1990s, the term 'insamansa' referred to the understanding that human resources (HR) were the most critical assets for corporate success.

Conversely, following the 1997 Asian financial crisis, Rowley points out that the term reversed to 'insamangsa' meaning that people spoil everything. In this vein the post-2008 credit crunch and its impact on economies has had, Rowley argues, an indisputable influence on HRM. Hence, Rowley claims that there has been some shifting in the role of people from a strategy of 'sweating the assets' to 'managing scarce resources' with an accompanying move from 'imitation to innovation' in terms of corporate strategy.

Through historical and political, social and cultural, economic and labour market contexts, Rowley explores:

- HRM practices and possible future directions;
- implications for theory; and
- some traditional and emerging HR practices.

In this way Chapter 2 helps to set the scene for the chapters that follow, in addition to providing a number of models and frameworks that HR practitioners and researchers can utilise in order to explore the topics discussed in this book more fully.

Chapter 3 Developments in employee relations in the Asia Pacific

In Chapter 3, Peter Waring, a Singapore-based academic, explores developments in employment relations in the Asia Pacific. Waring proposes that the early part of the twenty-first century could be described as belonging to the Asia Pacific, particularly as the period from the turn of the millennium until 2007 was characterised by strong global expansion.

In turn, this period of growth was associated with a number of employment relations challenges which Waring examines in more detail with a focus on recent employment relations developments in China, Japan and Singapore. Waring explains that these three countries were selected for closer analysis as they are highly significant and interdependent trading economies in Asia. In addition, all three countries have introduced new labour laws and policies in recent years. Finally, Waring concludes the chapter by commenting on the impact of the global financial crisis on the region's employment relations.

Chapter 4 Managing globalisation and IHRM

Chapter 4 examines the impact of globalisation on the management of HRM within multinational enterprises (MNEs).

Authors Noelle Donnelly and Peter Dowling argue that MNEs currently 'compete with everyone from everywhere for everything'. Consequently, they identify some key imperatives for International HRM (IHRM) that contribute to a more strategically significant role in the global context. These are:

- the utilisation of a different focus for the corporate HR function;
- global talent management;
- diversity and cross-cultural management.

Further, they explore the impact of some of the large, developing economies — particularly India and China — on global trade and competition as they claim that the entry of these emerging players has set a new transnational agenda. The chapter concludes with a short case study on milk contamination in the Chinese joint venture partner of a New Zealand-based MNE — a case that highlights a number of the IHRM issues and challenges that MNEs face.

Chapter 5 Sustainability in Strategic Human Resource Management

Chapter 5 links SHRM to sustainability. The authors, Robin Kramar and Grant Jones, propose that while a sustainable approach to SHRM provides mindful stewardship of all resources, this approach centres on HR as it exploits the talents of people while at the same time renewing their skill base and sense of vocation.

Elements of human capital associated with sustainability include a focus on:

- outcomes and longer-term visioning;
- organisational resilience;

- adaptability; and
- a capacity for resource renewal.

In this sense the factors inherent in managing for sustainability support SHRM in delivering economic viability for the organisation at the same time as nurturing social, environmental and human outcomes. These themes are explored in this chapter in relation to how SHRM impacts on economic, social and environmental outcomes, and the capabilities required to further sustainable environmental, economic, social and human outcomes.

Chapter 6 The business case for human capital metrics

Chapter 6 by Loretta O'Donnell and Carol Royal argues the case for gathering organisational level data in order to calculate HR metrics.

The authors claim that a key challenge is for HR professionals to choose appropriate human capital metrics which provide both valid and useful information for both internal use by the firm and for the broader investment community. Human capital (HC) metrics are analysed from the perspective of financial markets and the investment community, as it is argued that HC has an impact on future financial performance.

O'Donnell and Royal point out that a subset of intangible assets is HC, and that this can be analysed more systematically for both managers and employees to provide investors in the financial markets with more transparent ways to make investment decisions.

To date, there is no clear agreement on measurement principles and no standards equivalent to accounting standards. Hence, they argue that it makes sense to consider more qualitatively based approaches to HC metrics given that financial metrics have not served investors well — as demonstrated by the collapse of the Lehman investment bank in late 2008. The challenge for the HR profession is to utilise HC metrics which are rigorous, simple and able to be understood by markets. In this chapter, the authors provide ideas and frameworks to assist with that process.

Chapter 7 Human resource outsourcing and shared services: An Asian-Pacific perspective

Chapter 7 by Ajay Jain and Debi Saini centres on human resource outsourcing (HRO) and shared services.

Jain and Saini maintain that HRO is being used more frequently in recent times as an increasing number of organisations explore its potential. They claim that HRO helps an organisation to focus on its core competencies while freeing up ability to utilise internal resources more effectively and control the bottom line. As a result, HRO has become an integral part of the business process outsourcing (BPO) industry with its scope rapidly evolving to include areas such as:

- payroll, benefits administration;
- training;
- recruiting;
- performance management;
- compensation management and more.

These issues are examined in this chapter with regard to:

- HR outsourcing and the decision whether or not to outsource;
- HR activities that may be outsourced;
- alternatives to HR outsourcing;
- trends in HR outsourcing; and
- HR outsourcing in Asia.

Chapter 8 The transfer of HRM policies and practices in multinational companies

Chapter 8 by Anne Vo and Zeenobiyah Hannif has a particular focus on the practice of Japanese companies in Vietnam.

The aim of the chapter is to investigate some important questions relating to the key forces influencing the nature and implementation of multinationals' (MNCs) HRM practices within their subsidiaries and the possible constraints and opportunities associated with these practices.

The authors maintain that the recent trends of:

- regional integration;
- the removal of trade barriers;
- the deregulation and opening of closed national markets to international competition;
- the rise of Asian countries; and
- the integration of Central and Eastern Europe and China into the world economy,

have led to an increasing number of companies spreading their activities outside the borders of their home countries. The authors use a number of lenses to examine HR transfer practices within MNCs before concluding with a framework for examining the interaction of different forces in the shaping and implementation of MNC practices into subsidiaries across borders.

Part II: The inner organisational context—organisational culture, structure, politics, leadership, task-technology and the outputs of a business

A key element of SHRM relates to the internal context of organisations. For example, the chapters in Part II of this edited text highlight how a strategic approach to HRM can be operationalised by HR practices which are aligned to an organisation's external environmental factors. The various authors have drawn upon empirical data from both primary and secondary research to demonstrate how organisations in the Asia Pacific region have engaged in SHRM. These chapters are consistent with the view of SHRM from a resource-based view (RBV) (Barney & Wright 1998). As Dunford, Snell and Wright (2001) point out, the RBV shifted emphasis in the strategy literature away from external factors (such as industry position) towards internal firm resources as sources of competitive advantage.

Chapter 9 Work–life management

Chapter 9 is contributed by Anne Bardoel and Kerry Grigg who examine work–life management through three key themes which they refer to as barriers in reconciling work and personal lives. The three barriers comprise:

- a lack of flexible work policies and practices;
- the availability and affordability of dependent care; and
- the negative impact of work over-load and long working hours.

In turn, the authors argue that these three factors form the foundations that can lead to an understanding of how organisations operating in different countries in the Asia Pacific region may respond. Hence, they propose that the strategic challenge for HR professionals is to ensure that the significant changes in work patterns and in family structures that have occurred in Australia and other parts of the Asia Pacific region over the last thirty years are also matched by changes in organisational culture and practice. The chapter adds value to current literature by providing a business case for work–life initiatives and an identification of the major roles for HR in the process.

Chapter 10 Managing talent: Exploring HR strategies in a dynamic environment

Despite the recent global financial crisis, Peter Holland and Rob Hecker argue that, in an environment that is characterised by increasing volatility in organisations, there is a need to prioritise talent management. In particular they argue that organisations need to focus on the design of employment systems that prioritise

- attraction;
- retention; and
- development,

identifying such strategies as key elements of retaining competitive advantage in order to be competitive. In common with Chapter 5, Holland and Hecker draw on the resource-based view of the firm as the theoretical perspective underpinning the argument for developing talent management strategies in a dynamic environment.

Over the latter half of the 20th century, population trends across OECD countries revealed almost static populations and declining birth rates. The authors maintain that this is of concern as it is clear that, in Australia at least, organisations are not responding to the changing labour market as might be expected as they are failing to invest in human capital. They argue that this will make it more difficult for individual firms to 'understand the supply and demand of the critical workforce segments' necessary to maintain competitiveness in an increasingly globalised market. Finally, they conclude that it has become increasingly evident that the war for talent is heating up, irrespective of the global financial crisis.

Chapter 11 An ageing workforce: HRM challenges

Chapter 11 by John Burgess and Jenny Waterhouse explores the policy and human resource implications of an ageing workforce with a specific spotlight on Australia and Japan.

The authors identify significant policy implications related to an ageing workforce in a number of areas. These include:

- adjustments to the supply and demand of social services (such as child care, elderly and dementia care);
- immigration policy; and
- labour policy.

This chapter begins by outlining the global perspectives of an ageing workforce before proceeding to an exploration of policy initiatives and organisational implications of an ageing workforce with regard to HRM. Burgess and Waterhouse argue that if the main motivation for the employment of older workers by government and employers is to address labour, knowledge and skills shortages, then the employment of older workers is a response to an organisational need that is aligned with SHRM objectives. Further they stress that under this scenario there may be a greater valuing of older workers, although past evidence has demonstrated that where labour market conditions loosen and there is a ready availability of labour, it is often older workers who are laid off—bringing the focus of HR back into play.

Chapter 12 Managing diversity and social inclusion in the workplace

Chapter 12 by Christina Kirsch and Charmine Härtel considers workforce diversity, change and HRM practice.

The authors contend that for organisations to be fair and productive, it is essential to ensure that a firm's workplace culture and practices value and encourage contributions from people with different backgrounds, experiences and perspectives. In order to facilitate such practices the authors provide examples of potential HR strategies and practices that can support inclusion of these differences.

Kirsch and Hartel draw upon research conducted by ChangeTracking Research concerning a 2009 cross-cultural study of over 111,000 responses to an employee survey across a large variety of cultures and industries. The survey investigated the relationship between Hofstede's (1993) cultural dimensions and the characteristics of change projects in order to identify the ways in which change is managed in various countries and how these relate to cultural dimensions.

The authors present a summary of the key findings from these surveys. They conclude that the relationship with one's direct supervisor and the emotions experienced during organisational change showed hardly any difference between cultures. However, they did find that there were significant differences between countries in:

- the amount and pace of change;
- the availability of resources provided during change;
- the level of employee involvement; and
- the responsiveness of the teams.

Chapter 13 Performance management of expatriates in China

Chapter 13, by Susan McGrath-Champs, Anthony Fee and Xiaohua Yang identified that, despite the global financial crisis, economic change and growth in China has been both fast and vast. In this climate, issues of work, employment and people management — the strategic management of human resources — are vital.

As a result this chapter provides an overview of the role of international human resources with regard to strategic management within contemporary China. The core of the chapter addresses the management of expatriates, connecting expatriate performance management with firm internationalisation, and the strategic role of the HRM function in a global context.

The empirical findings provide insights of potentially wider relevance. As Tung (2007) suggests, in its transformation to the fastest growing economy in the world and its quest for global expansion, China has had to confront one of the biggest business challenges—i.e. effectively deploying human resources. The authors suggest that foreign MNEs may contribute to the build-up of a human powerhouse in China and could be an effective means through which performance management 'best practices' might be diffused within China.

Chapter 14 The ethics of workforce drug testing and HRM

Chapter 14 by Edward Wray-Bliss examines the practice of workforce drug testing and the ethics of the widening managerial prerogative embodied in contemporary HRM. The chapter explores:

- international evidence concerning drug usage;
- alleged associations with workplace accidents;
- the positioning of HR with regard to ethical issues and workplace drug testing.

Wray-Bliss argues that for some people there is, in certain aspects of contemporary HR practice, an attempt to redraw the boundaries of the employment relationship so as to render the employee an object of management discipline both in work and out of work.

Furthermore, the author maintains that while human resource management has long attracted questions with regard to its efficacy and ethics, the movement into areas such as workforce drug testing, which brings into focus the out-of-work choices of employees, generates some of the most pressing questions yet regarding the scope of the managerial prerogative embodied in contemporary HRM.

Conclusion

In conclusion, this volume of edited chapters highlights the contribution that SHRM can make with regard to the strategic issues and challenges facing organisations and countries in the Asia Pacific region. The 13 chapters present HR strategies and practices that address the various complexities evident in the external environment, both globally and domestically, and their consequent impact in the workplace. Changes to the internal environment of organisations, together with a variety of HR processes and practices provide evidence of how the HRM function can be strategically managed in order to address the implicit and explicit challenges and complexities of the external business environment in the Asia Pacific region.

References

Armstrong, M 2008, *Strategic Human Resource Management*, Kogan Page, London.

Barney, JB & Wright, PM 1998, 'On becoming a strategic partner: The role of human resources in gaining competitive advantage', *Human Resource Management*, 37(1): 31-46.

Barney, J 2001, 'Is the resource-based view a useful perspective for strategic management research? Yes', *Academy of Management Review*, 26, 41-56.

Boston Consulting Group 2008, *The Future of HR in Europe Key Challenges Through 2015* http://209.83.147.85/publications/files/ES_Future_HR_Europe.pdf, accessed 15/2/2010.

De Cieri, H & Dowling, P 1997, 'Strategic international human resource management: an Asia-Pacific perspective', *Management International Review*, Vol. 37 No.1, pp. 21-42.

Delery, JE & Shaw, JD 2001, 'The strategic management of people in work organizations: Review, synthesis, and extension' in GR Ferris (Series Ed.) & PM Wright, LD Dyer, JW Boudreau & GT Milkovich (Sup. Eds.), *Research in personnel and human resources management: Supplement 4, Strategic human resource management in the 21st century*, pp. 167–197, Stamford, CT, JAI Press.

Dunford, B, Snell, S & Wright, P 2001, 'Human Resources and the Resource Based View of the Firm', *CAHRS Working Paper Series*, http://digitalcommons.ilr.cornell.edu/cgi/viewcontent.cgi?article=1065&context=cahrswp, accessed 15/2/2010.

Hendry, C & Pettigrew, A 1990, 'Human resource management: an agenda for the 1990s', *International Journal of Human Resource Management*, Vol 1, No 1. Pp. 17-43.

Hofstede, G 1993, 'Cultural constraints in management theory', *Academy of Management Executive*, 7(1), 81-94.

Holland, C, Sheehan, P & De Cieri, H 2006, 'Current developments in HRM in Australian organisations', *Asia Pacific Journal of Human Resources*, Vol. 44, No. 2, 132-152.

Jackson, S & Schuler, R 1995, 'Understanding Human Resource Management in the Context of Organizations and Their Environments', *Annual Review of Psychology*, 46:237-264.

Javidan, M & Ali Dastmalchian 2009, 'Managerial implications of the GLOBE project: A study of 62 societies', *Asia Pacific Journal of Human Resources*, Vol. 47, No. 1, 41-58.

Kane, B, Crawford, J & Grant, D 1999, Barriers to effective HRM. *International Journal of Manpower*, 20(8), 494-515.

Tung, RL 2007, 'The human resource challenge to outward foreign direct investment aspirations from emerging economies: the case of China', *International Journal of Human Resource Management*, 18 (5): 868-889.

Ulrich, D 1997, *Human resource champions: The next agenda for adding value and delivering results,* Harvard Business School Press, Boston.

Part I: Outer Context—
Political, Economic, Socio-Economic, Technical, Legal, Environmental

Chapter 2

CONTEMPORARY ISSUES IN HRM IN THE ASIA PACIFIC REGION: AN EXPLANATORY FRAMEWORK

Chris Rowley

Introduction

The management of people, or human resource management (HRM), its latest lexicon, has been forged in the crucible of both its long- and short-term backgrounds and events. This formative context includes developments in:

- historical and political;
- social and cultural;
- economic and labour market

factors which have impacted on HRM practices and issues. The key aspects of HRM in the contemporary business environment focus on:

- resourcing;
- rewarding; and
- developing people.

This is the case for the Asia Pacific region. Hence, this chapter develops a framework to examine HRM in Asia, exemplified with some examples from South Korea (referred to as 'Korea' from now on).

One issue is that, even with the more narrow 'Asia Pacific' label, it still refers to a vast range of countries that differ in terms of:

- size;
- population;
- religions;

- economic resources;
- development; and
- key sectors.

For example, the nomenclature covers North East Asia with its developed economies of Japan and Korea and the rapidly developing economy of China. Moreover, South East Asia is not only different from these countries—it is also internally diverse, ranging from Singapore, Malaysia and Thailand to Vietnam, amongst others.

The 'Asian miracle' of the post-1960s involved both people and HRM practices. For example, in Korea up until the 1990s the term 'insamansa' (people and personnel affairs are everything) was coined to stress that human resources (HR) were the most critical assets for success. However, after the 1997 Asian financial crisis the term reversed to 'insamangsa' (people spoil everything).

The post-2008 credit crunch and impacts on economies (especially export dominated ones) will be another influence on HRM. Nevertheless, there is some shift in the role of people. The shift is from a strategy of 'sweating the assets' to 'managing scarce resources'. In Kim's (1997) terms it is from 'imitation to innovation' and in Krugman's (1994, p. 62–78), from 'perspiration to inspiration'.

Contextual factors

This chapter will now detail the influential and operating context of HRM using some examples of Korean data.

Historical and political factors

The historical and political context of HRM is important. In Asia it includes long histories of:

- peace/war;
- colonial and military occupation/civilian, independence governance; and
- statist/laissez-faire stances on economic direction and involvement.

Recent examples include political and government reforms in China and Vietnam; changes in Malaysia, Korea, and Japan; and challenges in Thailand.

Korea after World War Two

Korea has a long history involving periods of war, colonisation and occupation. The Japanese and US impacts of World War Two included:

- infrastructure development and imitation of industrial policy;

- technology application and operations management techniques; and
- HR practices including lifetime employment and seniority-based pay.

The military influence permeated widely as many executives were ex-officers who applied their military experience in companies. Additionally, many male employees had served in the military and had received regular military training. Some companies even maintained reserve army training units.

Indeed, the army staged a coup in 1961. The coup was followed by authoritarian, military rule until in 1987 when the new constitution revived presidential elections. Civilian control was re-established in 1992. As the state in Korea integrated and strengthened, it became a crucial component for growth, owning banks and, in turn, creating reliance on government for capital.

Role of the state

A key aspect of HRM is the state and its role. In Korea, state policy often promoted strategically important sectors, large companies, and 'national champions'. It provided protection and support as a development strategy, intervening directly to maintain quiescent workforces.

The rapid development of Asia with its 'Tigers' and 'Dragons' was often based on a model of industrialisation that was a powerful mix of a developmental, state-sponsored, export-oriented and labour-intensive initiatives.

Social and cultural factors

The social and cultural edifice of a country is important for HRM. It includes factors like ethnicity, language, religions, and beliefs.

Ethnic and linguistic homogeneity

Country to country, the ethnic homogeneity of populations varies enormously. In Japan and Korea, for example, the populations are relatively homogeneous; in Malaysia much less so (Table 2.1). Korea's population is one of the most ethnically and linguistically homogenous in the world. Except for a small Chinese community (about 20,000), virtually all Koreans share a common cultural and linguistic heritage.

Religion, beliefs and customs

Another set of critical influences comprises religion, beliefs and customs. In Asia the religions can include Buddhism, Islam, Christianity, Confucianism, Taosim, Shinto and Caodoism (see Table 2.1 for examples). These religions, beliefs and customs have powerful, early, and continuing impacts on family, social life, outlook, society and, consequently, business (see Rowley & Bae 2003).

The core ideology of HRM

A major issue is the core ideology of HRM. In Asian HRM the core principles are:

- organisation first;
- collective equality; and
- community orientation.

Lately, however, the ideology has been changing to principles geared more to:

- individual respect;
- individual equity; and
- market principles (Bae & Rowley 2001).

Economic and labour market factors

The economic and labour market background is critical to HRM. The issues include:

- geography;
- people; and
- organisational aspects such as size, ownership patterns, and product markets. Table 2.2 provides some Asian examples.

Korean economy

In the post-1960s Korea moved speedily from a rural backwater with limited natural resources into a world-renowned industrial powerhouse. It became an exporter, overseas investor, and manufacturer with phenomenal growth rates.

The Korean economy shifted from agricultural to industrial. The shift was driven by large indigenous firms, with varied amounts of state encouragement, protection and support. Korea's large, diversified business conglomerates, the *chaebol*, with myriad affiliates and cross-shareholdings, dominated the economy. Chaebol growth was based on a variety of elements (Rowley & Bae 1998), explained by a range of theories—for example:

- neo-classical economics,
- Marxist perspectives;
- culture;
- network analysis;

- transaction cost economics;
- resource dependence; and
- power theory (Oh 1999).

Some argue the state–military interactions with the *chaebol* were the most important external factor, creating politico-economic organisations that substituted for trust, efficiency and the market.

Labour market factors

The labour market is also important to HRM. Some Asian countries had abundant, cheap, hardworking labour to draw on. From the early stage of industrialisation, governments also made special efforts to create enough jobs for new entrants. In some countries, such as Japan and Korea, this was accompanied by extensive investment in HR development (HRD) through formal and informal routes. Thus, these countries built capable human capital (Kim 1997). Often strong internal labour markets developed, stemming from factors ranging from labour and skills shortages and the need for retention to organisation-specific training returns.

Shifting patterns of gender and demographics

Adding to these labour market factors are issues of gender and demographics and their shifting patterns. These include:

- emigration and immigration;
- population growth;
- stagnation and decline—such as falling birthrates and ageing populations in some Asian countries, especially Japan and Korea. Some examples are given in Figure 2.1.

Korea has experienced large rates of emigration, with ethnic Koreans residing primarily in China (2.4 million), the US (2.1 million), Japan (600,000), and the countries of the former Soviet Union (532,000). Moreover, Korea has one of the world's lowest birthrates—below replacement level, with the expected commensurate projections impacting on future workforce levels.

It is within this broad background and context that the key elements of HRM can be placed to see the contours of their development.

Table 2.1 Social and cultural comparative contextual factors

	Japan	Korea	China	Malaysia	Thailand	Vietnam
Ethnic groups	Japanese 98.5%, Koreans 0.5%, Chinese 0.4%, other 0.6% *note:* up to 230,000 Brazilians of Japanese origin migrated to Japan in 1990s to work; some returned (2004)	Homogeneous (except for about 20,000 Chinese)	Han Chinese 91.5%, Zhuang, Manchu, Hui, Miao, Uyghur, Tujia, Yi, Mongol, Tibetan, Buyi, Dong, Yao, Korean, and other nationalities 8.5% (2000 census)	Malay 50.4%, Chinese 23.7%, Indigenous 11%, Indian 7.1%, others 7.8% (2004 est.)	Thai 75%, Chinese 14%, other 11	Kinh (Viet) 86.2%, Tay 1.9%, Thai 1.7%, Muong 1.5%, Khome 1.4%, Hoa 1.1%, Nun 1.1%, Hmong 1%, others 4.1% (1999 census)
Religions	Shintoism 83.9%, Buddhism 1.4%, Christianity 2% other 7.8% *note:* total adherents exceeds 100% as many belong to both Shintoism and Buddhism (2005)	Christian 26.3% (Protestant 19.7%, Roman Catholic 6.6%), Buddhist 23.2%, other or unknown 1.3%, none 49.3% (1995 census)	Daoist (Taoist), Buddhist, Christian 3%–4%, Muslim 1%–2% *note:* officially atheist (2002 est.)	Muslim 60.4%, Buddhist 19.2%, Christian 9.1%, Hindu 6.3%, Confucianism, Taoism, other traditional Chinese religions 2.6%, other or unknown 1.5%, none 0.8% (2000 census)	Buddhist 94.6%, Muslim 4.6%, Christian 0.7%, other 0.1% (2000 census)	Buddhist 9.3%, Catholic 6.7%, Hoa Hao 1.5%, Cao Dai 1.1%, Protestant 0.5%, Muslim 0.1%, none 80.8% (1999 census)

Table 2.2 Economic and labour market comparative contextual factors (2009, est.)

	Japan	Korea	China	Malaysia	Thailand	Vietnam
Geography						
Size (sq km)	377,915	99,720	9,596,961	329,847	513,120	331,210
People						
Population (million)	127.08	48.51	1,338.61	25.71	65.90	86.96
Age structure (%) 0-14 years	13.5	16.5	19.8	31.7	20.8	24.9
15-64	64.3	72.3	72.1	63.6	70.5	69.4
65+	22.2	10.8	8.1	5.0	8.7	5.7
Median age (years)	44.2	37.3	34.1	24.9	33.3	27.0
Growth rate (%)	-0.191	0.266	0.655	1.723	0.615	0.977
Birth rate (per 1,000 pop)	7.64	8.93	14.00	22.24	13.40	16.41
TFR* (children per women)	1.21	1.21	1.79	2.95	1.65	1,83
Urban population (%)	66	81	43	70	33	28
Education expenditure (% GDP)	3.5 (2005)	4.6 (2004)	1.9 (2006)	6.2 (2004)	4.2 (2005)	1.8 (1991)
Economy						
GDP ppp** (US$ 2008)	4,329 trillion	1,335 trillion	7,973 trillion	354.3 billion	547.4 billion	241.7 billion
Real growth rate (% 2008)	-0.7	2.2	9.0	4.6	2.6	6.2
Per capita ppp (US$ 2008)	34,000	27,600	6,000	15,200	8,400	2,800
By sector (% 2008) - Agriculture - Industry - Services	1.5 26.3 72.3	3.0 39.5 57.6	11.3 48.6 40.1	10.1 43.7 46.3	11.6 45.1 43.5	22 39.9 38.1

	Japan	Korea	China	Malaysia	Thailand	Vietnam
Labour market Labour force (million 2008)	66.5	24.35	807.3	11.09	37.78	47.41
By occupation (%) - Agriculture - Industry - Services	4.4 27.9 66.4 (2005)	7.2 25.1 67.1 (2007)	43.0 25.8 32,0 (2006)	13.0 36.0 51.0 (2005)	42.6 20.2 37.1 (2005)	55.6 18.9 25.5 (2005)
Unemployment (% 2008)	4.0	3.2	4.0	3.3	1.4	4.7
Inflation (CPI % 2008)	1.4	4.7	5.9	5.4	5.5	24.4

* Total fertility rate; ** Purchasing power parity.

Source: Adapted from CIA *The World Factbook* (online).

Figure 2.1 Change in youth labour force, selected Asian economies 1996-2006 and 2006-2016 (%)

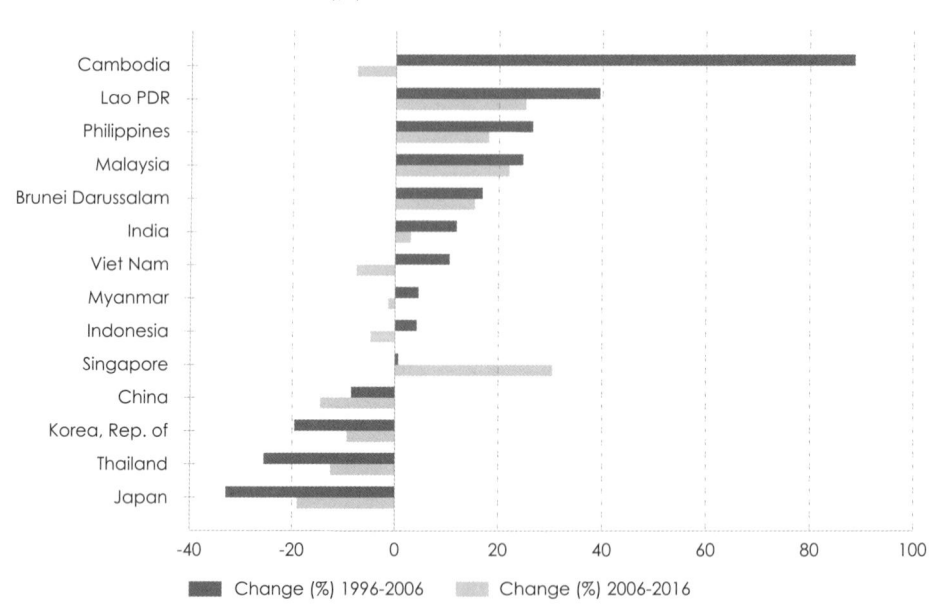

Source: ILO, Laborsta, Economically Active Population Estimates and Projections (Version 5).

HRM practices and key issues

The context discussed thus far allows for the location of HRM issues in a more grounded fashion. The fundamental assumptions of traditional Asian HRM from its core ideology are reflected in lifetime employment and seniority-based pay—the key HRM practices. These interrelate with the HRM functions of recruitment, remuneration and development. These areas of HR practice can be categorised as the '4Rs':

(1) Recruiting competencies;
(2) Reinforcing competencies;
(3) Retaining competencies; and
(4) Replacing competencies (Bae & Rowley 2003).

Their characteristics in 'traditional' and 'emerging' HRM practices are compared in Figure 2.2.

Figure 2.2 HRM issues: traditional and emerging HRM practices

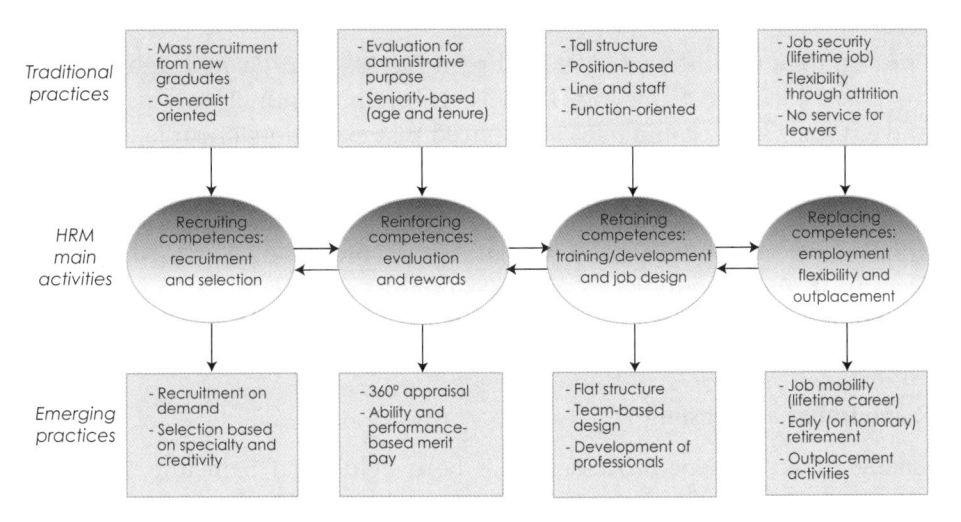

	Recruiting competences: recruitment and selection	Reinforcing competences: evaluation and rewards	Retaining competences: training/development and job design	Replacing competences: employment flexibility and outplacement
Traditional practices	- Mass recruitment from new graduates - Generalist oriented	- Evaluation for administrative purpose - Seniority-based (age and tenure)	- Tall structure - Position-based - Line and staff - Function-oriented	- Job security (lifetime job) - Flexibility through attrition - No service for leavers
Emerging practices	- Recruitment on demand - Selection based on specialty and creativity	- 360° appraisal - Ability and performance-based merit pay	- Flat structure - Team-based design - Development of professionals	- Job mobility (lifetime career) - Early (or honorary) retirement - Outplacement activities

R1 Recruiting competencies: resourcing and selection

The traditional form involved the annual, mass recruitment of new graduates with generalist orientations. The newer form shifted towards greater recruitment on demand with a focus on specialists with general ability to be creative. Thus, as noted in Table 2.3, recruitment strategy has evolved in terms of focus, methods, scope, size and time.

Table 2.3 Trends in resourcing

Area	Traditional	Trend	New
Focus	General purpose	→	Professionally specialised
Method	Net casting	→	Fishing type
Scope	Local	→	Global resource pool
Size	Mass	→	Small
Time	Regular	→	Anytime

Source: Adapted from Bae & Rowley 2003.

The war for talent

From the late 1990s we had the so-called 'war for talent' with strategies for attracting skilled staff becoming an increasingly prominent concern. Firms became actively concerned with, and involved in, recruitment (and retention) of such employees.

For example, from the late 1990s Korean *chaebols* that dashed into the war for talent included Samsung, LG, SK, Hyundai Motor, Hanwha, Doosan and Kumho. These companies announced that exceptional people would be recruited regardless of their nationality and ethnicity.

To facilitate this more inclusive approach, fast-track systems, signing-on bonuses, stock options and similar, were provided. Furthermore, for Samsung the recruiting (and retaining) of talent accounted for approximately 40% of the evaluation of affiliates' CEOs and, importantly, CEOs were personally responsible for this issue.

Recruitment at Samsung

Changed recruitment processes have been evident at Samsung (Pucik & Lim 2002; Woo 2002). For instance, Samsung established a new 'injaesang' ('ideal image of HR') relating to the core competences of:

- professionalism (professional ability and motives);
- creativity (thinking and critical reasoning);
- leadership (leading change and challenging the future); and
- humanity (innate personality and organisational adaptability).

Based on this, a new interview process was developed. This process evaluated candidates on their innate personality and ability (both competence and adaptability). In order to evaluate these, structured tools and methods were used.

- For evaluating personality, structured interview questions and observations were used to analyse such factors as personal

background, past behaviours and perceptions with regard to future situations.
- Evaluation tools for personal competence included task assignments for problem solving, case analysis and simulations.
- To examine adaptability, group-based discussions, problem solving and behaviour observations, were used.

R2 Reinforcing competencies: performance-based approaches

This has seen the de-emphasis of seniority and a consequent increase in importance of performance and ability. However, it is not just a simple question of either 'pure' seniority, or performance. Rather, there can be four more nuanced scenarios (Bae 1997). These comprise:
- traditional seniority-based progression;
- seniority-based progression with performance factors;
- performance-based with seniority factor;
- purely performance-based progression.

Annual pay

One example of a performance-based system is annual pay. Here, annual salary is determined in advance based on individual ability or performance, which is similar to merit pay. Greater emphasis on performance may also be encouraged via other reward practices, such as employee shareholding and profit sharing.

In Korea, performance management has spread more widely (Yang & Rowley 2008). Financial flexibility rose via wage freezes and the reduction of bonuses, benefits and base pay (Park & Ahn 1999). Cases of these include LG Chemical's performance-related pay at its Yochon plant (*Economist*, 1999), while Samsung also made reward changes (Pucik & Lim 2002).

Korean examples of annual pay can be seen in surveys and individual cases. These include Samsung, Doosan, Daesang, Hyosung and SK (Korea Ministry of Labor 1999; Rowley & Bae 2002). The Korean government moved to stimulate firm performance with tax incentives such as employee stock ownership plans. Examples of employee share options and profit sharing can be seen in the cases of:
- Hyundai Electronics, which introduced share options; and
- Samsung Electronics, which used profit sharing (Labor Ministry in *Economist* 2000).

R3 Retaining competencies: development and job design

In traditional HRM this 'R' was not a focus of HR managers. Indeed, strong internal labour markets, career ladders and seniority, with limited ports of entry, meant inter-company employment mobility was very limited in some

Asian countries. Whereas in some countries labour supply was copious and seemingly endless, others had greater problems, such as growing or declining demand for labour and indigenous workforces with economic and demographic changes, such as low birthrates (see Table 2.2 and Figure 2.1).

In Korea, in the post-1997 context, there was a huge outflow of large company core employees to growing numbers of venture firms. Behind this movement lay both 'push' (i.e. dissatisfaction with labour market rigidity) and 'pull' (i.e. attractive incomes and entrepreneurial cultures) factors. For instance, venture firms started to scout for experienced engineers from large corporations. Younger employees streamed to venture firms and 'dot com' companies in anticipation of instant and easy wealth (Bae & Rowley 2001). Thus, firms soon realised that employee retention was an increasingly critical task.

Retention strategies in Korea post 1997

Corporations in Korea responded to these changes in labour markets with a variety of strategies. Examples include companies that divided employees into three groups, each with different employment strategies.

- First, for core employees, firms took attraction and retention strategies (i.e. in relation to the talent war).
- Second, for full-time employees who were considered to be poor performers, companies used replacement (i.e. dismissals) and outplacement strategies (i.e. providing information and training for job switching).
- Third, for contingent workers, companies employed transactional and outsourcing strategies (i.e. a contract-based and short-term approach).

The above implies that companies used a more commitment-maximising strategy (expecting outcomes related to long-term attachment for core employees) and a numerical flexibility strategy for contingent workers.

Companies offered large rewards to retain core employees who wanted to quit. HR managers recognised, however, that these employees left regardless of the counter offers. Firms saw that they could not compete with venture firms in monetary incentives. They found, in fact, that these offers actually generated internal disharmony among other employees. Even more problematic was the fact that some ex-employees subsequently returned when the venture bubble burst. Therefore, a critical issue for some firms was the perception of equity in the workplace.

In order to encourage the of retention core employees, Samsung provided:

- a mentoring system;

- the assignment of competent employees as top talent;
- dual-ladder career paths;
- succession planning; and
- fellowships for R&D staff.

By providing more opportunities for development, mentoring, personal growth and employability, companies were making clear efforts to retain their talent.

Corporate venture programs (CVP)

Other retention strategies of large corporations such as LG CNS, KT and SDS were their adoption of internal corporate venturing programs (CVP) which provided challenging jobs. Thus, CVP strategies assisted in the retention of staff who would otherwise leave for more entrepreneurial opportunities. At the same time, these corporations were building fresh mechanisms for the creation of new market opportunities (Kim & Bae 2003).

Indeed, CVP can exploit the strength of corporations through resource sharing while simultaneously indicating appreciation of entrepreneurial initiatives. Core employees can participate in CVP and develop their entrepreneurial initiatives through internal venture projects.

CVP modes

The two modes of CVP comprise:

- new venture units (NVU); and
- corporate venture capital (CVC).

NVUs are directly related to retention strategies. To overcome the constraints and inefficiencies of existing units of large companies (e.g. differences in business models, bias for exploitation, bureaucratic structures and short-term orientations), LG CNS had a CVP that launched several venture projects. For example, it incubated an NVU program to develop a new business model reflecting the requirements of the target market (subsequently spun-off as Nexerve). Considering the differences in cost structure and decision-making style, it would have been difficult for existing units at LG CNS to have nurtured the new business targeting medium-sized firms.

R4 Replacing competencies: flexibility and outplacement

The general direction here has been away from lifetime employment towards more numerically flexible employment. It is not, however, a simple choice between lifetime employment and flexibility: there is a range of degrees between them.

Dismissals and redundancies

While labour adjustment can be achieved through reduced hiring, there are difficulties with this in lifetime employment systems. Here annual employee inflow can be young and cheap compared to existing groups of progressively more expensive employees paid by seniority. Companies, therefore, have also used dismissals and redundancies via so-called 'honorary retirement plans' to reduce labour.

Labour laws

To enable easier adjustments, labour laws have been changed (sometimes as a condition of post-crisis IMF bailouts, as in Korea). Thus, economic and legal changes created more conducive environments for employment adjustment. Indeed, the usage of a contingent labour force (e.g. part-time and temporary workers) increased.

In Korea, for example, the *Law on Protecting Dispatched Workers* 1998 regulated and controlled the use of contingent workers. The ratio of contingent workers to the total employed population rose.

Outplacement programs

Some firms adopted outplacement programs. Samsung (Life Insurance and Electronics), for instance, opened a Career Transition Centre (CTC) to help with re-employment or self-employment. Staff used its facilities and rooms (PC, consulting, conference reference, and resting). The CTC provided a range of services, including:

- *Candidate Management System*, with access to hidden job information data (no information to the public so institutions need to provide this to job searchers);
- *Job-Lead Assistance* to provide information by region, for both open and hidden jobs;
- *Self-Diagnosis Program* to elicit competences, values and occupational orientations in order to identify career goals and job preferences;
- *Self-Marketing Strategy* to assist in preparing résumés and self-introduction statements;
- *Self-Employment* to check core competences, financial conditions, market research and critical procedures; and
- *Self-Development Assistance* to provide educational and training programs to enhance language and computer skills.

This chapter has now considered key HRM practices and their development. Discussion will turn next to what the future direction of these HR practices might be.

Possible directions for HRM

We can now use the two key dimensions (employment and reward basis) shown in the framework in Figure 2.3 to predict possible directions for HRM. Possible consequences of previous changes and future scenarios using these factors are shown in Figure 2.4 using the Korean exemplar. This shows that until the mid-1980s HRM was characterised by seniority-based lifetime employment systems. Post-1987, labour cost increases along with greater international competition and the 1997 crisis encouraged and pushed companies to adopt more flexible, performance-based systems.

So what might occur in the future? As we have seen, future configurations depend on:

- historical and political contexts;
- social and cultural contexts; and
- economic and labour market contexts.

Five different scenarios are presented in Figure 2.4.

Figure 2.3 Possible directions for major issues in HRM

		Numerical flexibility		
		Low	Medium	High
Reward basis	Pure seniority based			
	Seniority and performance mixed			
	Pure performance based			

Source: Adapted from Bae & Rowley 2003.

Figure 2.4 Major issues in HRM: Korea examples

Numerical flexibility

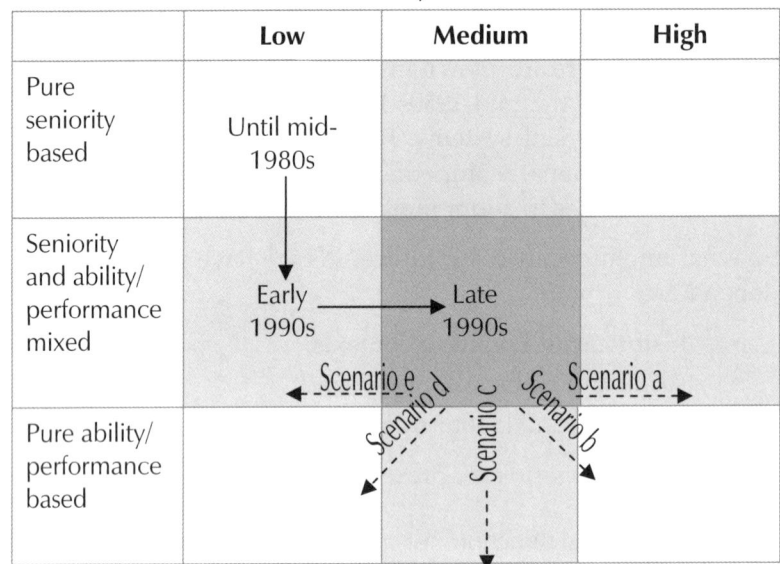

	Low	Medium	High
Pure seniority based	Until mid-1980s		
Seniority and ability/ performance mixed	Early 1990s →	Late 1990s	
Pure ability/ performance based			

Reward basis

Scenario e ← Scenario d · Scenario c · Scenario b · Scenario a →

Note:
- Light grey represent the positioning of some firms' HRM systems.
- Heavy grey represents the positions of many firms' HRM systems at this point.

Source: Adapted from Bae & Rowley 2003.

It is unlikely that the reward basis will return to seniority. We may assume that while the current reward basis remains focused on performance, flexibility systems could change. This allows three options:

- scenario 'a';
- scenario 'e'; or
- remaining the same.

When we assume the reward basis could change to pure performance, this brings another three options:

- scenario 'd' (decrease in flexibility);
- scenario 'c' (remaining flexibility); and
- scenario 'b' (increase in flexibility).

LG CNS, for example, changed its reward system towards pure competence- and performance-based annual pay systems, which can, if we assume medium-level flexibility, be seen as scenario 'c'.

Of interest here, however, is a survey (Lowe, Milliman, DeCieri & Dowling 2002) which included Korean respondents (237 managers and engineers, mainly from manufacturing, but with some services, in a mix of medium and large, private organisations). A five-point Likert type scale on the dimensions of:

- current state (CS) and
- desired future state (FS) of HR practices

was used. The questions and scores included:

- pay incentives (CS 2.94, FS 3.90); and
- seniority is important (CS 2.92, FS 3.50).

One result concerned 'performance as the basis for pay rises', where CS was 1.83, labelled 'exceptionally low', and FS was 3.27, labelled 'lowest'. On such evidence, performance in reward practices may not be as universally desired for the future as many assert.

Why HRM changes might occur

We categorise the reasons for HRM changes into three main areas:

- environmental turbulence;
- strategic choice; and
- institutional influence.

These relate to some of the wider convergence and divergence debates.

Environmental turbulence

Under the first category are the 1997 crisis and IMF bailout conditions when different thinking, ways, methods and activities were more easily formulated and accepted as their influence was stronger than the inertia of people, systems and culture.

Another critical environmental change was government policy towards fostering venture firms. This stimulated many employees, especially those who had experience in R&D and management, to leave companies. The impacts of the post-2008 credit crunch also fit in here.

Strategic choice

A second explanation for changes is based on a strategic choice perspective. For some commentators increased labour costs and constraints on rights to hire and fire became increasingly burdensome to companies due to systemic rigidities and weak individual level motivation. It was argued that labour market numerical flexibility would improve competitiveness. Management was then presented with a golden opportunity to make a strategic choice to resolve these issues.

Institutional influences

Third, institutional theory and imitation can play a role. Three mechanisms of institutional change are:

- coercive isomorphism, to gain legitimacy;
- mimetic isomorphism, to avoid uncertainty; and
- normative isomorphism, stemming primarily from professionalisation (DiMaggio & Powell 1983).

It seems that mimetic isomorphism prevailed. This is understandable when there is no sense of direction or easy way out. This theoretical explanation was used to explain:

- downsizing (McKinley, Sanchez & Schick 1995);
- adoption of teams (Lee & Kim 1999);
- organisational legitimacy (Hyun 2001); and
- management transparency (Han & Bae 2001).

Similarity versus distinctiveness

These changes can also be related to the wider debates on the convergence of HRM practices.

Globalisation

A central proposition is that there is a global tendency for countries (and within them practices such as HRM) to become similar as copying and transfer (sometimes taken as 'best practices' linked to ideas of benchmarking) is encouraged. An implication is that there are 'universal truths' that can be applied everywhere.

The perceived universalising tendencies of globalisation can be located within earlier work (e.g. from Kerr, Dunlop, Harbison & Myers 1962 to Peters & Waterman 1982 and Womack, Jones & Roos 1990). Globalisation's impacts on HRM may come via the opening up of economies and their penetration by external forces and influences. Indicative of this was the post-1980s attention given to Japan and Japanese management practices. Attempts to imitate them included Malaysia's 'Look East' policy and the so-called 'Japanisation' of industries.

Best practices

There is, however, debate concerning:

- what 'best practices' are (Poon & Rowley 2008);
- the ways in which they affect organisations; and

- if there can be global transference (Bae & Rowley 2001).[1]

Assumptions that 'best practice' effects are not firm-specific, but rather universal and transferable (as via benchmarking) are only a start. Best practice only becomes a competitive advantage through institutionalisation (Kostova 1999). Also, for resource-based theorists (Barney & Wright 1998; Lado & Wilson 1994), 'unique' (i.e. rare, difficult to imitate and supported by the organisation) practices cannot be copied easily, hence they result in sustained competitive advantage. The paradox is that it is hard for 'best practices' to be imitated when embedded in the organisation. Such scepticism has echoes of earlier contingency-type arguments.

Contingency approaches

Contingency approaches explain diversity between (and even within) countries, even those grouped together as 'regions', such as Asia (see, *inter alia*, Turner & Auer 1996; Katz 1997; Rowley 1997).

Constraints on convergence

The impact of practices is dependent upon congruence with contingent variables and national context, such as institutions and culture. The term 'country institutional profile' (CIP) reflects this (Kostova 1999). The CIP is the set of:

- regulatory institutions (i.e. existing laws and rules);
- cognitive institutions (i.e. schemas, frames, inferential sets, etc.); and
- normative institutions (i.e. values and norms).

All of these factors can operate as constraints on convergence.

Therefore, differences could result not only from the more obvious variations (such as a country's stage of development) but also in operational environments and the spread, impact and way technology is configured and used. Neither are management authority and autonomy to introduce and use practices globally unilateral and unfettered. Furthermore, it is too easily forgotten that alternative solutions to common pressures and problems are possible, with no necessary single response to market competitiveness.

So, although new practices emerge, the particular forms and the extent of diffusion vary due to:

- differences in history and institutions; and
- the strategic choices of actors (Locke & Kochan 1995; Erickson & Kuruvilla 1998; Golden, Wallerstein & Lange 1997; Freeman & Katz 1995).

---

[1] For further discussion on this topic see Vo and Hannif chapter 8 in this book on the transfer of multinational practices in MNCs.

Thus, the manner in which changes are introduced, mediated and handled can lead to different outcomes, so that even convergence at the global level in terms of economic forces and technologies may result in divergence at other levels '… as these forces are mediated by different institutions with their own traditions and cultures' (Bamber & Lansbury 1998, p. 32). In short, varied national HRM systems remain as distinctive political, economic, institutional and cultural frameworks, and their features can restrict practice transference and thus convergence, in HRM.

Macro variables v. micro variables

A further issue is that convergence and contingency may operate at different levels (Becker & Gerhart 1996). Evidence for both growing similarity and distinctiveness may then result from different research foci. Thus, findings indicating convergence tended to concentrate on macro level variables (i.e. structure and technology), while studies targeting micro level variables (i.e. behaviour of people in organisations) found divergence (Child 1981; Rowley 1997). Also, we need to distinguish possible dimensions of HRM involving the level, alignment, and acceptance of HRM practices (see Bae & Rowley 2001; Rowley & Bae 2002).

Key issues for HRM

Several key issues for HRM in Asia, both practical and theoretical, emerge from this analysis.

Practical issues

At the practical level, there was a tendency for HR managers in Asia to lose their sense of direction post the 1997 crisis.

Focus on managing change

A 'change is good' mentality was increasingly promulgated. Subsequently, managers were too busy implementing new HR practices to give much thought or reflection beyond managing change.

Focus on organisational performance

Also, the linkage of HRM to organisational performance became more important. Consequently, companies paid much more attention to ideas such as the HR scorecard, auditing and the HR performance index.

Focus on professionalism

Furthermore, the HRM unit itself and HR professionals faced challenges. HR managers began to realise their new roles as strategic partners and internal consultants. For this, HR managers needed to increase professionalism. Mechanisms for this included professional organisations and HR-related education programs for HR managers. For example, the

Korean Society for HRM (KSHRM) and its in-house magazine *HR Professional* are involved in this area.

Paradoxes in HRM functions

Finally, HRM's individual functions, such as evaluation and compensation, on the one hand, and retention and outplacement, on the other hand, contain paradoxes. We note three paradoxes:

- emphasising short-term performance and long-term sustainability of the company at the same time;
- enhancing flexibility and retaining key talent simultaneously;
- executive evaluation and their reward systems.

Implications for theory

Best practice

Interest in 'best practice' generated debate on its efficacy beyond the boundaries of time and space. This is related to the transfer issue. Poon and Rowley (2008) note a number of problems with the notion of 'best practice' in relation to the meaning of practices and questions about consistency. Bae and Rowley (2001) argued that the transfer of 'best practices' occurred at multiple levels, suggesting transfer could be more successful at some levels than others. In short, the notion of 'best practice' may be superficially attractive, but there is still some way to go before any solid conclusions can be reached.

Multiple modes of employment

Nonetheless, one way to manage some paradoxes is to divide employees into distinct groups. For example, companies seek success through 'multiple architectures' (Tushman & O'Reilly 1997) or 'hypertext organisations' (Nonaka & Takeuchi 1995). Types of employment mode are also becoming multiple. One form of HR architecture was based on two dimensions: 'Value' and the 'Uniqueness' of human capital (Lepak & Snell 1999), a framework giving four employment modes:

- internal development' (high value and uniqueness);
- acquisition (high value and low uniqueness);
- contracting (low value and uniqueness); and
- alliance (low value and high uniqueness).

Adopting multiple employment modes within a single organisation, however, requires greater HR inputs, such as the juggling of roles by HR managers. Theorising this phenomenon is another task to be done.

Conclusion

Restructuring

Companies in Asia have made restructuring efforts. These included:

- adjustment in business (e.g. mergers and acquisitions, management buyout, spin-off or split-off, and outsourcing);
- financial (e.g. debt for equity swap, reducing inter-subsidiary loan guarantees, and enhancing transparency); and
- ownership and governance (e.g. reducing family control, adoption of independent external board members and separation and ownership and management) structures;
- restructuring efforts in employment through shifts in resourcing (e.g. downsizing, early retirement and contingent workers); and
- rewards (e.g. performance-based pay).

Institutional contexts

Institutional contexts in Asia (i.e. labour, product and venture capital markets) changed. With the increase of venture capital firms it became easier to raise funds for start-up enterprises. As the lifetime employment practice eroded, labour market numerical flexibility grew. In addition, owing to changed product markets, it was unnecessary for large corporations to internalise all business activities as multiple supplier sources were available. The development of these external labour, product, and venture capital markets promoted the formation of start-up, venture firms.

The war for talent

The changes in institutional contexts and organisation-wide structural adjustments pushed companies to greater flexibility. Firms deployed dual strategies for their core and the peripheral HR, pursuing numerical flexibility through contingent workers while paying more attention to core employees. There was also employee outflow to venture firms as governments encouraged new businesses by providing infrastructure and tax benefits. Companies experienced high turnover rates due to the consequent outflow of core employees. As a result, companies recognised that people really are important and realised that employee retention was important to competitive advantage. Thus, some corporations made a dash into the 'war for talent' against start-ups.

Directions for HR

In summary, what conclusions can be drawn about the direction of HRM? First, among several HRM areas, remuneration based on performance prevails more and is unlikely to move back towards traditional seniority-based systems. Another area is the growth of employment flexibility, but this is open to more argument as it is refers mainly to numerical, not functional, flexibility.

Second, some paradoxes also exist around these arguments. For example, companies adopt individually-focused performance-based remuneration while they emphasise knowledge sharing and cooperation. So questions concern whether or not companies can simultaneously face a talent war while they pursue numerical flexibility. Such paradoxes, if not impossible to resolve, require expert juggling from HR managers.

Third, companies are increasingly interested in the linkage between HRM and organisational performance. Several books have titles reflecting this — e.g. *The HR Scorecard* (Becker, Huselid & Ulrich 2001) and *The ROI of Human Capital* (Fitz-enz 2000). In this search some companies began to evaluate and audit HRM itself at several levels:

- HRM departments for their value-adding;
- business-level HRM units from corporate-level HRM units; and
- individual HRM practices for efficacy.

Fourth, following this line of argument, the transformation of the organisation itself along with new roles for HR managers, is required. However, such new roles as internal organisational consultants, change agents, strategic partners and employee champions, are unfamiliar to many Asian HR managers. To assist in this area, many companies started to develop educational programs for the development of HR managers.

Thus, uncomfortable uncertainties for management have been generated and noted. However, on a more positive note, these uncertainties could also generate new windows of opportunity for both HR managers and academics in the HRM field.

References

Bae, J 1997, 'Beyond Seniority-Based Systems: A Paradigm Shift in Korean HRM?, *Asia Pacific Business Review*, 3(4), pp. 82-110.

Bae, J & Rowley, C 2001, 'The Impact of Globalisation on HRM: The Case of South Korea', *Journal of World Business*, 36, 4, pp. 402-28

Bae, J & Rowley, C 2003, 'Changes and Continuities in South Korean HRM', *Asia Pacific Business Review*, 9 (4): 76-105.

Bamber, G & Lansbury, R 1998, 'An Introduction to International and Comparative Employment Relations', in G. Bamber and R. Lansbury (eds.) *International and Comparative Employment Relations*, London, Sage, pp. 1-33.

Barney, JB & Wright, PM 1998, 'On Becoming a Strategic Partner: The role of Human Resources in Gaining Competitive Advantage', *Human Resource Management*, 37(1), pp. 31-46.

Becker, B & Gerhart, B 1996, 'The Impact of Human Resource Management on Oganizational Performance: Progress and Prospects', *Academy of Management Journal*, 39(4), pp. 779-801.

Becker, BE, Huselid, MA & Ulrich, D 2001, *The HR Scorecard: Linking People, Strategy, and Performance*, Boston, MA., Harvard Business School Press.

Child, J 1981, 'Culture, Contingency and Capitalism in the Cross-National Study of Organisations', in L.L. Cummings and B.M. Staw (eds.) *Research in Organizational Behaviour*, Greenwich, CT., JAI Publishers.

DiMaggio, P & Powell, W 1983, 'The Iron Cage Revisited: Institutional Isomorphism and Collective Rationality in Organizational Field', *American Sociological Review*, 48, pp. 147-160.

Economist, The 1999, 'A Survey of the Koreas', July 10, pp. 1-16.

Economist, The 2000, 'Business in South Korea', April 1, pp. 67-70.

Erickson, CL & Kuruvilla, S 1998, 'Industrial Relations System Transformation', *Industrial and Labor Relations Review*, 52(1), pp. 3-21.

Fitz-enz, J 2000, *The ROI of Human Capital: Measuring the Economic Value of Employee Performance*, New York: AMACOM, American Management Association.

Freeman, R & Katz, L 1995, *Differences and Changes in Wage Structures*, Chicago, University of Chicago Press for NBER.

Golden, MA, Wallerstein, M, & Lange, P 1997, 'Unions, Employer Associations, and Wage-Setting Institutions in Northern and Central Europe, 1950-1992', *Industrial and Labor Relations Review*, 50(3), pp. 379-401.

Han, J & Bae, J 2001, 'The Determinants of the Level of Management Transparency in Korean Venture Firms', *Korean Management Review*, 30(4), pp. 1063-1092 (in Korean).

Hyun, S 2001, 'An Empirical Test of Institutional and Strategic Views on Organizational Legitimacy', *Korean Management Review*, 30(4), pp. 1291-1316 (in Korean).

Katz, H 1997, 'Introduction', in HC Katz (ed.) *Telecommunications: Restructuring Work and Employment Relations Worldwide*, Ithaca, NY., ILR Press.

Kerr, C, Dunlop, J, Harbison, EH & Myers, C 1962, *Industrialism and Industrial Man*, London, Heinemann.

Kim, D & Park, S 1997, 'Changing Patterns of Pay Systems in Japan and Korea: From Seniority to Performance', *International Journal of Employment Studies*, 5(2), pp. 117-134.

Kim, D, Bae, J & Lee, C 2000, 'Globalization and Labour rights: The Case of Korea', *Asia Pacific Business Review*, 6(3&4), pp. 133-153.

Kim, H & Bae, J 2003, Revitalizing big corporations through corporate venturing: The Korean experience, Working paper.

Kim, Linsu 1997, *Imitation To Innovation: The Dynamics of Korea's Technological Learning*, Boston, MA., Harvard Business School Press.

Korea Ministry of Labor 1999, *A Survey Report on Annual Pay Systems and Gain-Sharing Plans*, Korea Ministry of Labor (in Korean).

Kostova, T 1999, 'Transnational Transfer of Strategic Organizational Practices: A Contextual Perspective', *Academy of Management Review*, 24(2), pp. 308-324.

Krugman, P 1994, '*The Myth of Asia's Miracle*', Foreign Affairs, 73:62-78.

Lado, AA & Wilson, MC 1994, 'Human Resource Systems and Sustained Competitive Advantage: A Competency-Based Perspective', *Academy of Management Review*, 19, pp. 699-727.

Lepak, DP & Snell, SA 1999, 'The Human Resource Architecture: Toward a Theory of Human Capital Allocation and Development', *Academy of Management Review*, 24, pp. 31-48.

Locke, R & Kochan, T 1995, 'Conclusion: The Transformation of Industrial Relations? A Cross-National Review of the Evidence', in R Locke, T Kochan, & M Piore (eds.) *Employment Relations in a Changing World Economy*. Cambridge, MIT Press, pp. 359-384.

Lowe, KB, Milliman, J, De Cieri, H & Dowling, PJ 2002, 'International Compensation Practices: A Ten-Country Comparative Analysis', *Human Resource Management*, 41(1), pp. 45-66.

McKinley, W, Sanchez, C & Schick, AG 1995, 'Organizational Downsizing: Constraining, Cloning, Learning', *Academy of Management Executive*, 9(3), pp. 32-44.

Nonaka, I & Takeuchi, H 1995, *The Knowledge-Creating Company: How Japanese Companies Create the Dynamics of Innovation*, New York, Oxford University Press.

Oh, Ingyu 1999, *Mafioso, Big Business and the Financial Crisis: The State-Business Relations in South Korea and Japan*, Aldershot, Ashgate.

Park, J & Ahn, H 1999, *The Changes and Future Direction of Korean Employment Practices*, Seoul, The Korea Employers' Federation (in Korean).

Peters, T & Waterman, R 1982, *In Search of Excellence: Lessons from America's Best Run Companies*, London, Harper and Row.

Poon, I & Rowley, C 2008, 'HRM Best Practices and Transfer to the Asia Pacific Region', in C Wankel (ed.) *21st Century Management,* US, Sage, pp. 209-20.

Pucik, V & Lim, JC 2002, 'Transforming HRM in a Koran *Chaebol*: A Case Study of Samsumg', in C Rowley, TW Sohn & J Bae (eds.) *Managing Korean Businesses: Organization, Culture, Human Resources and Change*, London, Cass, pp. 137-160.

Rowley, C 1997, 'Conclusion: Reassessing HRM's Convergence', *Asia Pacific Business Review*, 3(4), pp. 197-210.

Rowley, C & Bae, J 1998 (eds.), *Korean Businesses: Internal and External Industrialization*, London, Cass.

Rowley, C & Bae, J 2002, 'Globalisation and Transformation of HRM in South Korea', *International Journal of Human Resource Management*, 13, 3, pp. 522-549.

Rowley, C & Bae, J 2003, 'Management and Culture in South Korea' in M Warner (ed.) *Management and Culture in Asia*, London, Curzon.

Turner, L & Auer, P 1996, 'A Diversity of New Work Organization: Human-Centred, Lean and In-Between' in FC Deyo (ed.) *Social Reconstructions of the World Automobile Industry*, London, Macmillan, pp. 233-257.

Tushman, ML & O'Reilly III, CA 1997, *Winning Through Innovation: A Practical Guide to Leading Organizational Change and Renewal*, Boston, MA., Harvard Business School Press.

Womack, J, Jones, D & Roos, D 1990, *The Machine that Changed the World*, NY., Rawson Associates.

Woo, J 2002, 'A Case on Recruitment Strategy and Selection Technique for Core Talents', in *Proceedings of the Annual Conference of the Korean Association of Personnel Administration*, Seoul, Korea (in Korean), pp. 151-163.

Yang, H & Rowley, C 2008, 'Performance Management in South Korea', in A Varma, P Budhwar & A DeNisi (eds) *Performance Management Systems: A Global Perspective*, London, Routledge, pp. 210-22.

Chapter 3

DEVELOPMENTS IN EMPLOYEE RELATIONS IN THE ASIA PACIFIC

Peter Waring

OBJECTIVES

By the completion of the chapter you should be able to:

1. describe developments in employment relations in the Asia Pacific since the turn of the millennium;

2. explain the role played by markets, unions and states in shaping employment relations outcomes;

3. describe developments in employment relations in detail in China, Japan and Singapore.

DEFINITIONS

Employment relations: The formal and informal rules which regulate the employment relationship and the social processes which create and enforce these rules.

Employment relations institutions: Rule-making bodies that create and enforce the rules of the employment relationship.

Unions: Continuous associations of employees that seek to advance the economic, social and sometimes political interests of their members.

States: The entire apparatus of formal roles and public institutions that exercise political authority over populations within a given territory (Bell & Head 1994, p. 3)

Introduction

The early part of the twenty-first century might well be described as belonging to the Asia–Pacific. The period from the turn of the millennium until 2007 was characterised by relatively strong global expansion but economic growth was especially strong in Asia as the two emerging titans, India and China began to fulfil their development promise and the rest of the region rebounded from the deep financial crisis of 1997.

Economic development in East Asia

East Asia in particular benefited substantially from strategic outsourcing by multinational companies and the creation of low cost value chains serving not only European and North American markets but also growing domestic markets in which rising incomes have fuelled an aspiring middle class. As manufacturing and low cost service provision shifted to these countries, the more developed Asian economies of Singapore, Hong Kong, South Korea and Japan have moved along the economic value chain to produce more elaborately transformed manufactured items, offer professional services and take positions as strategic investors in China, India and other lower cost locations in the region. The shift from low cost manufacturing to tertiary industries has not been without social and economic dislocation, but the abundant business opportunities and growth have somewhat ameliorated the adverse effects of economic restructuring in more advanced Asian countries.

Employment relations challenges

This period of unprecedented growth has been accompanied by some acute employment relations challenges. These include intense competition for skilled labour which has helped to drive wages growth for skilled professions and created stronger conditions for trade union activity where this is sanctioned by the state. Wages pressures have also been evident in industries employing unskilled labour although these have arguably not been as acute as for skilled professions. In spite of these prosperous market conditions, evidence of the exploitation of labour in Asian countries and the problem of the working poor persists. As the ILO (2006, p. 13) has pointed out, 'some 84 per cent of workers in South Asia, 58 per cent in South East Asia and 47 per cent in East Asia ... did not earn enough to lift themselves and their families above the $US2 a day poverty line'.

Employment relations institutions

The development of employment relations institutions has lagged market developments in Asia but in future these institutions will play important mediating roles. In China, for instance, a new labour law was introduced in 2008 seeking to limit the arbitrary and unjust use of managerial prerogative and also giving employees and unions the ability to enforce their rights at local employment arbitration courts. As the later discussion in this chapter suggests, these are modest improvements in protective labour law (whose force is frequently undermined by weak monitoring and compliance mechanisms) but nonetheless signal a desire from the state to re-regulate employment relations.

The global financial crisis

These and other regulatory developments came under increased pressure and scrutiny in the wake of the global financial crisis (GFC) which erupted in the second half of 2007. Beginning in the sub-prime debt markets of the United States, the financial contagion swept through financial markets as credit spreads grew, and banks and insurance companies failed or were 'bailed-out'. In 2008 and 2009, the GFC led to a precipitous decline in traded goods, with Asian economies especially exposed due to their significant reliance on export earnings. With the rapid de-leveraging of markets and predictions of double digit contraction of GDP in some especially vulnerable trade-dependent countries such as Singapore, the prospect for higher unemployment, exploitation and industrial disputation has grown.

Recent developments in employment relations in Asia

In this chapter, recent employment relations developments in Asia are examined. The chapter is organised into three main sections. The first section examines general employment relations developments in the period of largely unbroken economic expansion in the region from 2000 to 2007. This section examines developments for the main parties to employment relations including the state, unions and markets in the region. The second section examines developments in China, Japan and Singapore, chosen for closer analysis as they are extremely significant and interdependent trading economies in Asia and all three have introduced new labour laws and policies in recent years. Finally, the chapter concludes by commenting on the impact of the global financial crisis on the region's employment relations.

States, trade unions and markets in Asia

As Bray, Waring and Cooper (2009) assert, markets of various types significantly influence the context in which employment relations take place and affect and shape the strategic choices of employers, unions and the state.

Product markets

Product markets are perhaps the most tangible example of a market structure that shapes the interactions between the parties to the employment relationship. The type of product or service offered for sale (homogenous or heterogeneous), the number of market participants (both buyers and sellers), the extent of leverage suppliers enjoy in the market are all factors that not only shape the level of what Porter (1980) describes as 'industry rivalry' but also the decisions managers of firms make about the rules of the employment relationship and their interactions with trade unions and employees generally.

The labour market

The labour market also clearly has a strong bearing on the context in which employment relations is played out—the extent of labour market segmentation, the level of skills required in the production process as well as the relative scarcity of labour factors in the strategic choices of parties in employment relations.

The market for capital

More recently, researchers of employment relations have considered the way the market for capital and corporate control may impact on human resource management practices and drive employment and training and development decisions (see Jacoby 2004 for instance).

The importance of context in employment relations

The importance of context in employment relations is discussed because it is the argument of this chapter that contexts and markets have played an especially significant role in the development of employment relations in Asia. The rapid industrialisation of China over the previous two decades, and to a lesser extent India, perhaps only finds historical parallel with the great transformations that occurred during the industrial revolution of the 17th and 18th centuries in Britain with the shift from a largely agrarian based political economy to a burgeoning manufacturing economy.

While rapid industrialisation and economic development occurred in the Asian tiger economies of Singapore, Hong Kong, Taiwan and South Korea between the 1970s and 1990s, it is the immense scale and pace of development in China which is the story of the twenty-first century and which has heavily influenced the Chinese labour market. The rapid development of China's coastal cities and Beijing, for instance, has seen massive internal migration of largely unskilled factory workers while skilled labour remains in short supply.

Development of intraregional East Asian trade

A 2009 World Bank report observed that the eradication of trade barriers and the establishment of 'a dense array of regional production networks and supply chains' has driven extraordinary economic growth in the region and rapidly rising per capita incomes. The report further argues that 'economic congestion' in Japan, Singapore, Hong Kong and Taiwan has resulted in 'spill-over' effects in which intra-Asian foreign direct investment has found its way to lower income countries in the region such as China, Vietnam and Indonesia. The World Bank estimates that this intraregional East Asian trade approximates that of the European Union (World Bank

2009). The development of these regional markets has in turn been driven by external foreign direct investment and the rising purchasing power of consumers.

Employment relations and labour laws

Employment relations in the region are diverse and have been significantly influenced by these market developments as well as a prioritisation of economic development over employees' interests.

China, Vietnam, Malaysia, and Indonesia

In spite of there being a national labour law in place since 1994, there is a high degree of informality in employment relations in regional areas of China and in some parts of the rapidly industrialising coastal areas. Historically, compliance with labour law has also been extremely weak in other developing East Asian countries such as Vietnam, Malaysia, and Indonesia.

Japan and South Korea

In developed countries such as Japan and South Korea, labour law tends to be more protective of employee interests and compliance mechanisms are more robust. In Japan and South Korea, bargaining structures are formalised although, as in the West, there is an observable decline in collective bargaining coverage. The role of the state in employment relations throughout Asia has historically focused on attracting foreign direct investment. Thus, labour law in developing Asian states has tended to be either the 'light touch' variety or favoured employer prerogative.

Forces for and against protective labour law

Additionally, developing Asian countries such as Malaysia, India, China and others have established export processing zones (or Special Economic Zones) in which normal labour law is often suspended in favour of uninhibited managerial prerogative. There are, however, signs in some Asian countries that the state is prepared to strengthen protective labour law as a tool of economic development and to secure social harmony (see China and Japan analysis below for instance), especially in countries such as China where rapidly rising incomes and increased employment options have given birth to a generation of employees with fresh expectations about workplace rights and conditions.

Trade unions

Trade unions and the labour movement more generally are also quite diverse in Asia with varying levels of independence and legitimacy across the region. While labour law is typically weak in its support of free trade union activities such as collective bargaining, organising and industrial action, the developing strength of markets (prior to and post the global financial crisis) have strengthened the bargaining power of organised labour. In Japan, the electoral success of the Democratic Party of Japan is likely to strengthen the influence of the Rengo (Japanese Trade Union Congress) after many years of decline while in South Korea, the Korean Confederation of Trade Unions (KCTU) remains well organised and influential (ILO 2006).

Implications for human resource managers

The diversity of employment relations in the region in terms of labour regulation, bargaining structures, and trade union capabilities means that regional firms and multinational enterprises generally require human resource management employment relations expertise which is country specific but with high levels of regional coordination. Human resource managers typically require a strong sense of cultural sensitivity combined with a strong appreciation for the way in which markets are rapidly developing in Asia. As the next section indicates, human resource managers will also need to be increasingly cognisant of developments in labour law, as informal arrangements and unfettered managerial prerogative give way to regulation that is typically more protective of employee interests.

China

China's open-door policy

China's startling economic development began in 1978 with its 'Open-door Policy' leading to the reform of state-owned enterprises and the re-orientation of the Chinese economy to a model best described as a 'socialist market economy'. The private sector was encouraged to develop, and foreign direct investment flowed into China in ever increasing quantities. As a consequence, extreme poverty was reduced and real per capita gross domestic product rose tenfold between 1980 and 2002 (Josephs 2009, p. 376).

China's centrality to the global economy

Although first viewed by foreign investors as being a low cost location in which the world's manufacturers could take advantage of cheaper labour and other resources, by the 1990s China was increasingly viewed as a burgeoning market with rising purchasing power and aspirational consumers. Its centrality to the global economy was boosted further via its admission to the World Trade Organisation in 2001. Producing and selling in China therefore became a strategic imperative for the largest multinational enterprises and even in 2008, in the midst of the global financial crisis of 2007–2009, gross foreign domestic investment amounted to $108 billion (World Bank 2009).

The labour law of 2008

The rapid economic development of the Chinese economy has been matched by growing concerns over the treatment of labour by foreign and domestic companies in China. These concerns led to the introduction of a new and more protective labour law in January 2008. While China had implemented national labour law in 1994, it appeared only to be 'observed in the breach' as a consequence of local and regional governments prioritising economic development above that of workers' interests (Zhao 2009, p. 412). The new Chinese employment law (Employment Contract Law — Laodong hetong fa), however, represents a significant renewed effort on behalf of the central government to vouchsafe social harmony by addressing an increasing number of labour disputes (increasing at a rate of 27.3% annually according to Zhao 2009, p. 413) and growing public outrage and consciousness of the exploitation of labour[2].

Elements of the labour law

There are three main elements to China's new labour law. They include the *'Labour Contract Law'*, the *'Employment Protection Law'* and the *'Labour Mediation and Arbitration Law'*.

The Labour Contract Law

The *Labour Contract Law* (LCL) requires all employment contracts to be reduced to writing, thereby reducing the numerous informal employment arrangements that exist in China. It imposes heavy fines on employers who fail to comply. Additionally, employers are required to maintain a written employee handbook establishing the basic rules and policies of employment. If such a handbook is not maintained, the employer is prevented from terminating any employee's employment.

Interestingly, the new laws seek to place limits on managerial prerogative in determining work rules by requiring negotiations with labour unions, employees or their representatives prior to work rules being established. As Daubler and Wang (2009, p. 402) have noted, employees and unions can raise objections against unreasonable work rules but the law is unclear as to how disputes over work rules are to be resolved.

The Employment Protection Law

The new law also attempts to curtail the practice of providing only short fixed-term contracts to employees by demanding that only two fixed-term contracts can be provided to an employee (or ten years of service) before the employee's employment is considered continuing. As Daubler and Wang

---

[2] For instance Daubler and Wang (2009, p. 404) note that two weeks before the Act passed, the Chinese press revealed cases of exploitation at a brickworks in China where employees were kept in 'slave-like' conditions.

(2009) have observed, the importance of continuing employment lies in the additional protections it affords against arbitrary dismissal. Dismissal under the employment contract law is limited to a number of specified valid grounds for dismissal. The LCL also provides greater clarity over probationary periods, wage matters and non-compete agreements.

Dispute resolution

Complementing the new substantive rights afforded by the LCL is revised dispute resolution law which endeavours to provide workers with improved procedural rights in resolving claims against their employers. The new model for labour dispute resolution provides three channels for the resolution of disputes—mediation, arbitration and litigation. The new law emphasises mediation and arbitration as the preferred mechanisms of dispute resolution.

Interestingly, agreements produced as a result of mediation are enforceable at law in China. The new laws also emphasise expediting the resolution of disputes. Without the presence of an independent trade union movement with substantial collective bargaining powers, however, it is unlikely that the Chinese government will be successful in addressing exploitation along with building the domestic purchasing power.

Moreover, there remains the problem of weak enforcement. Some have argued that the new protective labour law will result in labour cost increases of between 10 and 20%. However, this is only likely to occur around the more dynamic growth areas of Shanghai, Guangzhou, Shenzhen and Beijing rather than the inland provinces where enforcement of the law is likely to be especially weak.

The law in practice

In an early test for the new labour law, a Chinese-owned telecommunications company called Huawei instituted an initiative that was believed to be an effort to circumvent the requirement that workers with either ten years of service or two consecutive fixed-term contracts be automatically granted continuing employment which carries with it protection against arbitrary dismissal. Huawei offered financial incentives for 7000 of its long-term workers to quit and be rehired on one- to three-year fixed-term contracts (Hong 2007). Labour rights advocates, the public, and the All China Federation of Trade Unions heavily criticised the move and Huawei was forced to abandon the initiative (Hong 2007).

While in some respects the employment contract law is progressive in its effort to provide greater protection for workers' interests and addresses a significant source of social unrest in China, its aims are modest compared with contemporary labour law in most parts of the developed world. As Josephs (2009, p. 392) has argued, '... even with the passage of the ECL, Chinese workers will be no better able to form independent unions or engage in meaningful collective bargaining over the terms and conditions of employment than they previously were'. Nonetheless, the new laws represent a significant rethinking of social and economic priorities by the central Chinese government and a renewed focus on protective labour regulation as an important tool of development.

Japan

In the early part of the twenty-first century years of anaemic economic growth in Japan ('the lost decade' of the 1990s) gave way to modest economic expansion. As Jacoby (2004) noted, after many years of being lectured to by the West about the need to change Japanese corporate governance (especially by the United States), Japan modified its system of life-time employment, seniority-based promotion and consensus decision-making. Japanese industry exported its way to recovery.

The global financial crisis of 2007–2009, however, stymied this modest growth — although the Japanese banking industry proved far more resilient than its US counterpart. Over the medium to longer term, the Japanese labour market was expected to be significantly influenced by the twin demographic problems of an ageing population and low birth rate. These problems were expected to impact upon the human resource planning of domestic and foreign firms.

Following the 1990s, Japanese employment relations were marked by three inter-related trends — a growth of precarious employment, a decline in union density and a declining coverage of collective bargaining agreements and a concomitant rise in individual contracts.

Decline in trade union density

Since the early 1990s, the Japanese labour movement has shown signs of weakness with the number of union members in decline and the annual spring labour offensive ('the Shunto') losing its traditional force. According to Nakamura (2009, p. 7) trade union density in Japan fell from 34.3% in 1975 to just 18.7% in 2005 with absolute trade union members falling by two million between 1994 and 2005. The declining rate of unionisation has been matched by a widening wage gap and increase in the number of non-regular employees such as those working on a part-time or contract basis. The Japanese seem either unwilling or unable to organise non-regular, peripheral workers which has compounded declining union density.

The Labour Contract Act *of Japan*

In 2008, against a background of worsening global economic conditions, Japan introduced new labour regulation. According to Yamakawa (2009), the *Labour Contract Act* of Japan was introduced as a result of the rise of individual employment contracts, reduced coverage of collective bargaining instruments and rising individual disputes.

The Act seeks to provide clearer rules on the basic rights and obligations to be incorporated within labour/employment contracts. For instance, the Act places limitations on the use of successive fixed-term labour contracts and provides minimum reasonable working conditions in employment contracts. The Act also provides for information to be provided to workers about the basic rules of their employment and prohibits employers making unilateral changes to labour contracts which result in employees being disadvantaged.

Influence of the Democratic Party of Japan (DPJ)

The historic Japanese national election on August 30, 2009 ended decades of Liberal Democratic Party rule in favour of the Democratic Party of Japan (DPJ). Led by new Prime Minister Yukio Hatoyama, it seems likely that the DJP will introduce more protective labour law in future.

The DPJ has historically been closer to the Japanese labour movement. On his first day in office, Prime Minister Hatoyama met with the Japanese Trade Union Confederation (Rengo) to call for strategies to improve employment and achieve a reduction in income disparities. Hatoyama has also pledged to raise the minimum wage and discourage temporary and precarious forms of employment (Pilling 2009; CNN 2009). Only time will tell if the DPJ is successful in reducing unemployment and achieving improvements to protective labour regulation.

Singapore

Employment relations in Singapore are overwhelmingly influenced by the strong relationship between the government (led by the People's Action Party since 1965) and the peak union body, the National Trade Union Congress (NTUC).

Declining trade union density

Although union membership is strongly promoted and encouraged by the government, trade union density in Singapore has been in decline over the last two decades. The NTUC and its affiliate unions have tended to emphasise a 'servicing' rather than an 'organising' model. The servicing model downplays industrial action and collective bargaining in favour of businesses offering discounted goods and services for union members.

Economic development priorities

Since the birth of the republic and its break from Malaysia, Singapore has pursued a highly successful development model. Within the space of three decades the model has resulted in rapid industrialisation and Singapore's elevation from third world to first world status.

Like Japan, Singapore's low birth rate (1.2 per cent) and rapidly ageing population pose distinct challenges to the country's continuous pursuit of rising living standards. Unlike Japan however, this challenge has partly been addressed by a relatively open immigration policy and extensive use of foreign guest labour in all sectors of the economy and especially construction.

The centrality of economic development priorities has tended to overshadow protective labour law—although Singapore has ratified twenty ILO conventions including the five core conventions (MOM 2009).

The Employment Act *1968*

The key labour law statute in Singapore is the *Employment Act* 1968 which regulates termination of employment, hours of work, rest days, annual leave and other basic conditions of employment. The Act, however, excludes managers and executives earning above S$2500 per month and 'workmen' earning above S$4500.

Supporting the Employment Act is the Ministry of Manpower's 'Advisory Services and Dispute Management' service which provides both employees and employers with advice on employment issues as well as a complaints and claim management service for alleged breaches of the Act. More serious disputes, which are uncommon in Singapore, are heard by the Industrial Arbitration Court; collective bargaining is regulated by the *Industrial Relations Act* 1960.

Developments in workplace regulation

While the labour market is subject to what could be described as 'light touch' regulation, the government has sought to improve occupational health and safety protection through the enactment of the *Workplace Safety and Health Act* 2006. Additionally, maternity leave benefits have been improved in line with the government's efforts to improve the birth rate such that female Singaporean citizens now enjoy four months paid maternity leave.

One important area of employment that remains conspicuously unregulated is that of employment discrimination. The Ministry of Manpower recognises employment discrimination as a significant challenge in Singapore and has instigated advertising campaigns to encourage employers to hire on the basis of merit only. Discrimination in employment is a persistent problem, however, and it may be that the Singapore Government will need to address this issue more firmly through a regulatory response.

Responses to the global financial crisis

As a small, open, and export-oriented economy, Singapore was initially hit extremely hard by the onset of the global financial crisis. Although the republic's banking industry was more robust than that of the United States, demand for its manufactured goods fell precipitously in 2008 and 2009, and the Singapore Government pessimistically forecast an annual decline in GDP of up to negative 9 per cent (AsiaOne 2009).

The government responded to the poor economic conditions by providing a job subsidy (Job Credit scheme—worth some $4.5 billion) which provided employers with a generous quarterly payment as a percentage of their payroll. It also introduced a new labour market program called SPUR (Skills Program for Upgrading and Resilience) which provides wage and course subsidies for employers who send their employees to approved training courses. The scheme was offered to employers on the basis that the recession offered an opportunity to upgrade the skill sets of their employees with the support of the government rather than to downsize their workforce.

Future prospects

By mid-2009, evidence was mounting that the worst of the global financial crisis was over and signs of recovery appeared ubiquitous throughout Asia. The Singaporean economy also quickly rebounded with GDP figures for the second quarter of 2009 showing that the economy surged by more than 20% on the back of higher pharmaceutical production (Foo 2009). These signs of recovery suggest that local and foreign 'pump-priming' may well have acted positively to restore both demand and confidence in the Singapore economy.

The consequences of recovery for employment relations among white-collar workers (perhaps with the exception of the banking sector) will undoubtedly be a tighter labour market (especially for highly skilled employees) and a resumption of the 'war for talent' between multinational companies whose regional head offices are often found in Singapore. For blue-collar workers, the future may be less rosy as multinational companies continue to relocate manufacturing operations to 'better cost locations' in the region.

Conclusion

The first decade of the twenty-first century has been characterised by rapid economic expansion in Asia followed by a sharp contraction as a consequence of the global contagion released by the United States mortgage industry between 2007 and 2009. Against this background, employment relations have been significantly influenced by the rise and fall of markets that are heavily dependent on intra-regional and external investment flows and trade.

Challenges of economic recovery

Although the global financial crisis of 2007–2009 led to higher unemployment throughout Asia and helped fuel industrial conflict over factory closures from Shenzhen to Seoul, the Keynesian pump-priming efforts of governments in the region (especially China) helped to restore more buoyant market conditions allowing growth to resume.

These stronger economic conditions, combined with relatively new and more protective labour regulation in a number of East Asian States are likely to pose fresh challenges for human resource managers and influence their strategic choices. Strategic deliberations over location decisions, union recognition, compensation and benefits, the use of fixed-term and contract labour, selection and promotion policies, and even development investments are likely to be significantly influenced by efforts of Asian states to renew labour regulation. Perhaps a new balance will be struck between economic development and the protection of employee interests.

Implications for human resource managers

In this context, the profile of human resource managers as strategic business advisors is likely to be raised further rather than diminish. The growth in protective labour law in rapidly developing Asian countries will strengthen compliance requirements and the importance of accurate, timely, and business-sensitive advice. In other words, increasing regulatory demands require not just technically sound advice but advice which is tempered by the pragmatic requirements of the business. Human resource managers rather than lawyers are especially well placed to provide such advice. Lawyers, while technically proficient, are often remote from the practicalities of the business.

The prospect of a return to resurgent labour markets in Asia suggests that a significant challenge for human resource managers will be to attract and retain key talent while containing the growth in labour costs. While these contrary pressures have always been present, they are likely to grow in significance as the pool of available labour contracts as a result of declining birth rates and an ageing population. More buoyant economic conditions, higher labour mobility, and the availability of only very weak restraints at law are likely to increase the prevalence of inter-firm poaching of executives. In this climate, human resource managers will need to use all their negotiation and creative thinking skills to develop practical strategies to cope with this central challenge.

Discussion questions

1. What is the likelihood that the new labour law in China will result in new human resource management strategies from multinational companies doing business there? If so, what changes do you think are likely?
2. How can labour law be used as a tool for economic development?
3. What future human resource management challenges are Japanese firms likely to face?
4. What future human resource management challenges are Singaporean firms likely to face?
5. What creative strategies could human resource managers use to successfully compete in the 'war for talent'?

References

AsiaOne Business 2009, *2009 Singapore GDP forecast maintained at -9.0 to -6.0 per cent*, date accessed 22/09/09, <http://www.asiaone.com/Business/News/Story/A1Story20090521-142839.html>.

Bray, M, Waring, P & Cooper, R 2009, *Employment Relations: Theory and Practice*, McGraw-Hill, Australia.

Employment Contract Act of the People's Republic of China.

CNN 2009, *Japan's new PM faces daunting in-tray*, date accessed 18/09/09, <http://edition.cnn.com/2009/WORLD/asiapcf/09/15/japan.prime.minister/>.

Daubler, W & Wang, Q 2008-2009, 'The New Chinese Employment Law', *Comparative Labor Law & Policy Journal*, vol. 30, No. 2, 395-408.

Foo, A 2009, 'Singapore GDP jumps 20.7%', *Straits Times*, 11 August.

Hong, C 2007, 'Thousands of Huawei staff 'quit'', *China Daily*.

International Labor Organisation 2006, 'Realising Decent Work in Asia', 14th Asian Regional Meeting, Busan Republic of Korea, August-September, 2006.

Jacoby, S 2004, *The Embedded Corporation: Corporate Governance and Employment Relations In Japan and the United States*, Princeton University Press, Princeton.

Josephs, H 2009, 'Measuring Progress Under China's Labor Law: Goals, Processes, Outcomes', *Comparative Labor Law and Policy Journal*, p. 373-394.

Meyer, R 2009, 'Once Feared, China Labor Law Eases Its Bite', Complianceweek.com, date accessed 16/09/09.

Ministry of Manpower 2009, *Workplace Relations and Standards*, date accessed 15/09/09, <www.mom.gov.sg>.

Nakamura, K 2007, 'Decline or Revival? Japanese Labor Unions', *Japan Labor Review*, vol. 4, No. 1 pp. 7-22.

Pilling, D 2009, 'A Wiser Japan casts its vote without illusions', *Financial Times*, September 2, 2009.

Porter, M 1980, *Competitive Strategy: Techniques for analyzing industries and competitors*, Macmillan, New York.

World Bank Office Beijing 2009, Quarterly Update, June, 2009.

World Bank 2009, *World Development Report: Reshaping Economic Geography*, date accessed 21/09/09, World Bank, <www.econ.worldbank.org>.

Yamakawa, R 2009, 'The Enactment of the Labor Contract Act: Its Significance and Future Issues', *Japan Labor Review*, vol 6, No.2, pp. 4-18.

Zhao, Y 2008-2009, 'China's New Labour Dispute Resolution Law: A Catalyst for the Establishment of Harmonious Labour Relationship?', *Comparative Labour Law and Policy Journal*, vol. 30, No. 2, pp. 409-430.

Chapter 4

MANAGING GLOBALISATION AND INTERNATIONAL HRM

Noelle Donnelly & Peter J Dowling

OBJECTIVES

By the completion of the chapter you should be able to:

1. understand the different perspectives on globalisation and the role that Multinational Enterprises (MNEs) play in the global economy;

2. describe aspects of the changing global context;

3. identify how globalisation impacts on the management of people across national borders;

4. appreciate the interrelationship between globalisation, MNEs and International Human Resource Management (IHRM); and

5. identify the key strategic IHRM challenges that organisations face as they manage global workforces.

DEFINITIONS

Multinational enterprises: MNEs are organisations with production, trading or service operations in more than one country.

Globalisation: Globalisation refers to the increasing economic, technological and cultural interdependence across national borders.

Regime shopping: Regime shopping is a process whereby MNEs compare different employment relations systems as part of their location decision-making processes.

Regime competition: Regime competition works from a belief that different countries compete for foreign direct investment (FDI). It is suggested that countries will promote a lowering of labour market conditions as part of their competitive strategy to attract FDI.

Talent management: Talent management refers to the strategies that organisations employ to identify, develop and promote potential within existing employees.

Talent pipeline: Talent pipeline is a strategy organisations employ to identify and engage with a pool of potential talent for future positions.

Anglo-Saxon capitalism: Typical of English-speaking economies, Anglo-Saxon capitalism is a liberal free-market model of capitalism characterised by deregulated labour and financial markets and low taxation. It is at the centre of the debate on 'varieties of capitalism'.

Globality: Globality is a term coined in 2008 by Sirkin, Hemerling and Bhattacharya to capture the rapid rise of developing economies and the reshaping of global competition. They developed the phrase 'competing with everyone from everywhere for everything' to describe the nature of future global competition.

Introduction

Organisations operate within an increasingly complex, changing and uncertain world economy (De Cieri & Dowling 2006; Dunning 2007). Globalisation is the process to which much of this change has been attributed (*The Economist* 17/7/2008).

Strategic International Human Resource Management

Mounting evidence suggests that international success depends on an organisation's ability to manage its human resources within the context of globalisation (Taylor, Beechler & Napier 1996; Adler & Gundersen 2008). Strategic international human resource management (SIHRM) aims to help us understand the strategic approaches MNEs adopt in mediating those dynamic global environments.

As a field of research, SIHRM concerns itself with examining the implications of globalisation on the policy and practice of HRM. It is this complex global context and its impact on the management of employees that distinguishes domestic from international HRM (Dowling, Festing & Eagle 2008). As others have noted, SIHRM only has meaning when placed within the context of changing economic and business conditions (Schuler, Budhwar & Florkowski 2002). It is on this changing global context that this chapter focuses.

The relationship of globalisation, MNEs and SIHRM

The chapter examines the impact of globalisation on the management of HRM within MNEs. Figure 4.1 presents the interrelationship of globalisation, MNEs and SIHRM in a changing global landscape. The aim of this chapter is to outline the relationship between these elements.

Figure 4.1 The role of strategic IHRM in managing globalisation need

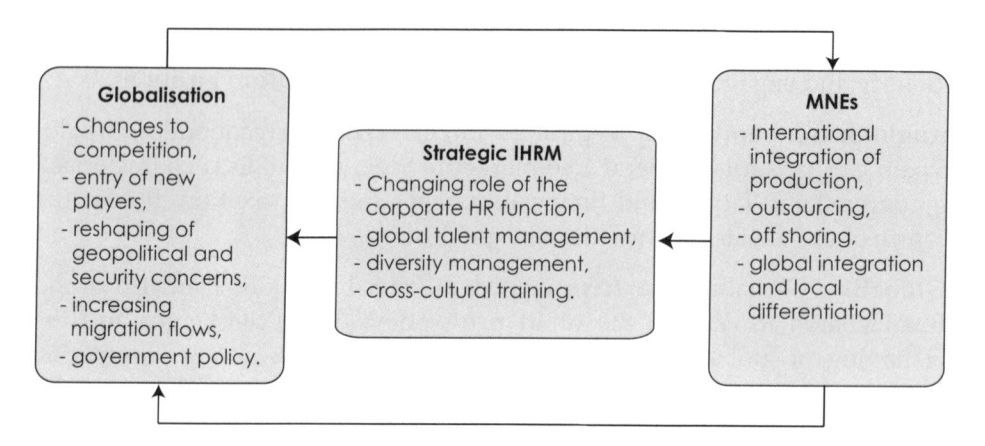

```
Globalisation                Strategic IHRM              MNEs
- Changes to                 - Changing role of the      - International
  competition,                 corporate HR function,      integration of
- entry of new               - global talent management,   production,
  players,                   - diversity management,     - outsourcing,
- reshaping of               - cross-cultural training.  - off shoring,
  geopolitical and                                       - global integration
  security concerns,                                       and local
- increasing                                               differentiation
  migration flows,
- government policy.
```

Chapter outline

The chapter begins by exploring the recent changes in the global landscape. This is followed by a discussion on the widely contested topic of globalisation. Section three demonstrates how globalisation encourages the development of MNEs and the critical role that MNEs play in shaping globalisation. Importantly, the chapter stresses that this relationship is not linear but interdependent—that MNEs are as much drivers of this process of globalisation as they are driven by it. The final section of the chapter examines how SIHRM can be seen as the mechanism through which this interrelationship is mediated. It focuses on the impact of globalisation on individual enterprises with particular emphasis on managing globalisation in Australia and New Zealand, and the role that the corporate HR function plays in managing competing pressures. It subsequently identifies the key SIHRM imperatives that contribute to a more strategically significant role for HRM in the global context, utilising:

- different focuses for the corporate HR function;
- global talent management; and
- diversity and cross-cultural management.

Case study

The chapter concludes with a short case study on milk contamination in the Chinese joint venture partner of a NZ MNE—a case that highlights a number of the SIHRM issues and challenges that MNEs may face.

The changing global landscape

The global landscape that MNEs operate in has changed significantly in recent years (Scullion, Collings & Gunningle 2007; UNCTAD 2009a).

Transformation to a global multipolar system

The international system that has dominated since the Second World War has been transformed into a global 'multipolar system' (National Intelligence Council 2008). A 'new global order' (*The Economist* 18/9/2008) has been created by:

- the recent global financial crisis and retrenchment of cross-border credit;
- the growing performance of such developing economies as Brazil, Russia, India, and China (generally referred to as the 'BRIC' economies);
- the reshaping of geopolitical structures; and
- the rise in global terrorism.

In response, attempts by nation states to reverse the shift towards economic deregulation have initiated

- a re-assessment of protectionist trade policies;
- the nationalisation of financial sectors; and
- a questioning of the relevance of the dominant Anglo-Saxon model of capitalism (Altman 2009).

Globality

The pace of globalisation over the last decade has been unprecedented. It has given rise to the term 'Globality' to describe the extension of global markets and the current nature of global competition.

Sirkin, Hemerling and Bhattacharya (2008) suggest that MNEs currently 'compete with everyone from everywhere for everything'. Contributing to this 'new era of competition' is the recent emergence and growth of large developing economies. Arguably, one of the major factors that have reshaped the nature of global trade and competition is the growth of large developing economies and, in particular, the entry of China and India to full participation in global markets (Mathews 2006).

China and India

The Chinese and Indian economies are estimated to have grown by over 700% and 250% respectively since 1980 (IMF 2004; Das 2006). As these economies have grown they have become host to significant levels of foreign direct investment (FDI). Described as the 'shopfloor of the world', these economies now compete on the basis of price, quality and skill (Steinfeld 2004). According to the US census bureau, 25 years ago Asia produced around one fifth of the world's output and had a population of over 54% of the world's population. Today that share stands at over one third of the world's output while the population figure remains the same (Stevens 2007). Ultimately, the entry of these new players has set a new transnational agenda.

Demand for goods, services and natural resources

A key consequence of the growth of emerging economies is the increasing demand for goods and services and natural resources. Economies like China have recently looked to the developing economies of the African continent to meet their appetite for energy and mineral resources. Trade between China and Africa is estimated to have grown from US$3 billion in 1995 to over US$32 billion in 2005 (Stevens 2007).

Sovereign Wealth Funds

A major feature of global FDI in recent years is the emergence of Sovereign Wealth Funds (SWFs) as direct investors in global markets. The size of these funds has grown significantly—from US$500 billion in 1990 to US$5 trillion (UNCTAD 2008).

This rise has attracted significant political attention and generated debate on the geopolitical nature of investment by these economies. Competition has largely centred on the demand for raw materials such as energy, mining and food. The recent involvement of Chinese SWFs in high profile mergers and acquisitions[3], coupled with their 'capital injections' into ailing financial institutions, has raised concerns about national security and the protection of natural resources (*The Washington Post* 3/8/2005; *The Economist* 28/5/2009).

---

[3] In 2005 the US Congress blocked an attempt by the 70% state-owned China National Offshore Oil Corporation (CNOOC) to acquire Unocal, an American rival, on the grounds that it threatened US national security and violated the rules of fair trade (*The Washington Post*, 13/8, 2005). In 2009, Chinalco, a Chinese state-controlled aluminium firm, made a bid to increase its stake in Rio Tinto, an Anglo-Australian mining giant. This produced a similar response of opposition within Australia (*The Economist*, 28/5/2009).

Global terrorism

A further threat to the national security of a country is the recent rise in global terrorism. As Kurth Cronin (2003, p. 30) notes,

> *'the current wave of international terrorism, characterised by unpredictable and unprecedented threats from nonstate actors, not only is a reaction to globalisation but is facilitated by it'.*

In managing this aspect of globalisation, she suggests that state responses should be flexible in exploring different avenues of globalisation.

What does globalisation mean?

Globalisation is a highly contested topic. Ever since McLuhan (1962) first mooted the ideal of a 'global village', the concept of globalisation has come to dominate much of Western social and economic discourse. Debates centre on its:

- definition;
- historical development; and
- policy implication.

Despite this pervasiveness, much of what is known of globalisation tends

> *'... to remain conceptually inexact, empirically thin, historically and culturally illiterate, normatively shallow and politically naïve'* (Scholte 2000, p. 1).

This section examines the contested nature of globalisation, identifies the dominant perspectives of globalisation and begins to prefigure the implications of globalisation for organisations.

Defining globalisation

There is little consensus regarding the precise nature of globalisation. Much of the confusion lies in the tendency to use the term 'internationalisation' interchangeably with 'globalisation' (De Cieri & Hutching 2008). As a process, globalisation can be seen to encompass:

- economic;
- social; and
- political aspects.

It is along these dimensions that globalisation has commonly been defined.

Globalisation of the economy

Definitions of globalisation tend to focus on recent economic developments, arguing that international trade leads to greater economic integration and mobility of people, products, and capital across borders. Playing a critical role in this process of economic integration are MNEs—regarded as key drivers of globalisation. More particularly, contributing to greater economic integration is the adoption of internationally integrated production systems by MNEs as they seek financial and synergistic efficiencies (Dunning 1991; Kogut 1998).

Globalisation of culture

Other definitions of globalisation point to greater homogeneity and standardisation of consumer tastes (Hofstede 1980). Such definitions argue that the spread of the internet and the media reduces cultural boundaries and promotes the diffusion of common values and ideas. Those who adopt a critical perspective of this form of globalisation argue that such developments lead to the promotion of western forms of capitalism rather than McLuhan's (1962) original notion of a global village.

Globalisation of politics

Lastly, globalisation is commonly defined along political lines that point to:

- the loss of national sovereignty;
- the reshaping of political structures; and
- the establishment of supranational institutions (such as the International Labour Office) that are designed to regulate the behaviour of MNEs on a global basis.

While definitions of globalisation can broadly be classified into one of the three dimensions outlined above, in simple terms globalisation is 'a process of increasing economic, technological and cultural interdependence that transcends national borders' (Eurofound 2008).

Perspectives on globalisation

Regardless of how globalisation is defined, as a process that shapes the global context, globalisation is generally viewed in either positive or negative terms.

The positive view of globalisation

Supporters of globalisation promote the idea that, as a process, globalisation leads to greater economic interconnectedness and prosperity. This is the stance adopted by the International Monetary Fund (IMF) and the World Bank. Advocates of this perspective argue that globalisation promotes greater efficiencies, primarily through:

- the outsourcing of support functions; and
- the relocation of production to low cost environments (Ohmae 1990).

With appropriate governance structures, globalisation is seen to contribute to a reduction in poverty in developing economies and, ultimately, leads to a redistribution of global wealth (Reich 1991; Stiglitz 2003; Bhagwati 2004).

The negative view of globalisation

Critics of globalisation regard the increase in economic integration as a threat to employment stability, national sovereignty and notions of 'decent work' (Hirst & Thompson 1996; Dicken 1998).

In a recent International Labour Office (ILO) report it was estimated that global unemployment increased from 29 million in 2007 to 59 million in 2009 (ILO 2009a). In response to the global job crisis, the ILO recently moved to promote 'global job pacts' between governments, employers, and employee representative groups. The pacts were designed to generate employment and protect workers from economic downturns (ILO 2009b).

Many who actively protest against globalisation do not question the original notion of a global village but rather rally against the notion of 'corporate globalisation'. At the core of the globalisation thesis is the belief that MNEs become 'stateless entities' as they shed their national identity and become globally oriented (Ohmae 1990).

In contrast, a body of research is emerging that questions the 'footlooseness' of MNEs. The research suggests that MNEs are largely 'embedded' within the institutional framework of their home countries. As Edwards and Ferner (2002, p. 96) have noted:

> *'The country in which the multinational originates exerts a distinctive effect on its management style. In short, the 'country-of-origin effect' or 'nationality effect' suggests that it is the institutional arrangements of their national business system that exerts a distinctive effect on the employment behaviour of MNEs (Ferner 1997a).*

For more on this topic see the chapter by Vo and Hannif regarding the transfer of HRM practices within multinationals.

The 'nothing new' view of globalisation

There is a further view that argues that the case for globalisation has been exaggerated. The 'nothing new' view of globalisation holds that 'the level of business interdependence is no greater now than in the nineteenth century' (Sparrow, Brewster & Harris 2004, p. 18).

Others suggest that globalisation is a myth, pointing out that:
- the assets and workforces of MNEs are largely domestic and/or regional;
- sources of capital are nationally focused;
- systems of corporate governance are distinctly national;

- senior management structures reflect home country nationality; and
- strategic processes like R&D and innovation are largely governed by national business systems (Ruigrok & van Tulder 1995; Rugman 2001; *The Economist* 2000).

The implications of globalisation

Despite the continuing debate regarding its merits, globalisation clearly creates greater options for MNEs in sourcing key factors of production and obtaining human inputs (Dunning 1991).

Geographical fragmentation of production chains

Greater international economic integration provides organisations with the opportunity to examine existing production chains and to fragment them geographically in order to minimise costs and gain greater access to markets and skills. The ability to benefit from comparative advantages has resulted in a shift of low-skill employment to overseas locations. In outlining the architecture of globalisation Kobrin (1997, p. 147) notes that:

> 'The dominant mode of organization of international economic transactions has changed significantly ... from the market (trade and portfolio investment) to hierarchy or the internationalization of production through MNEs'.

Regime shopping

The reconfiguration and coordination of production systems on a global basis has led to a number of concerns. In particular, the changing nature of global competition and capital mobility provides MNEs with the opportunity to compare overseas locations on the basis of labour costs and labour regulation—a process known as 'regime shopping' (Streeck 1992; Traxler & Woitech 2000).

Delocalisation

The ability of MNEs to explore cost differentials on a global basis has led to a concern that MNEs will shift production from high-wage to low-wage economies where employment is less regulated. Termed 'delocalisation', there is much debate that the relocation of production to low-wage economies will lead to a 'race to the bottom' and a reduction in employment standards.

Recent research suggests that while cases of delocalisation are often widely reported, they account for a very small proportion of employment loss (Eurofound 2008; Ferner 1997b). Despite the low incidence, the threat of MNEs shifting production to low-cost, less-regulated economies continues to be a policy concern for governments as global restructuring continues.

Regime competition

Managing globalisation at a national level places pressure on governments to remain globally competitive as they seek to protect and create high-quality jobs. The global competition for FDI investment is said to encourage the 'loosening up' of national employment regulatory frameworks as governments actively seek to attract overseas investment. In short, increased competition between countries for FDI encourages 'regime competition' whereby governments attempt to reduce the level of employment regulation as a means of attracting FDI.

Globalisation and multinational enterprises (MNEs)

Changing perceptions of MNEs

Attitudes towards multinationals have changed over time. During the 1970s, MNEs were denounced as large, imperial, monopolistic monsters, whereas in the 1980s they were regarded as clumsy conglomerates. By the 1990s they were seen to be sources of foreign capital, saviours of economic stagnation and importers of technology and knowledge (*The Economist* 1995). By early 2000, the status of MNEs had once again come under close scrutiny with high profile cases like Enron and Worldcom. A recent article by *The Economist* (2009), however, suggests that the 'balance of advantage' has once again shifted towards large MNEs, mostly driven by:

- a lack of venture capital for smaller start-ups;
- increased competition for resources;
- an awareness of the risks of subcontracting; and
- the ability of large MNEs to be both large and entrepreneurial.

Role of MNEs in the process of globalisation

Despite the changing attitudes towards MNEs, there is no disputing their importance and role in the process of globalisation. As Table 4.1 highlights, the number of MNEs have grown from an estimated 7,000 MNEs operating in 1970 to 82,000 MNEs by 2008, with direct control of close to 810,000 foreign affiliates (Franko 1976; UNCTAD 2009a).

Exports by foreign affiliates of MNEs account for a third of total world exports, while the number of people employed by MNEs is estimated to stand at 77 million (a 3.7% decline from the previous year) (UNCTAD 2009a). Growing in numbers and reach since the early 1990s, MNEs have overtaken international trade flows as the main source of international economic exchange (Marginson & Sisson 1994; Edwards, Armstrong, Marginson & Purcell 1996).

Not surprisingly, the pervasiveness of MNEs has been accompanied by a growth in the debate surrounding their role and importance in shaping the global economy. While there is little dispute about the dominant role MNEs play in the process of globalisation (Dunning 1993; Ferner & Hyman 1998), there is some debate as to the nature of that role. For some, the MNE represents 'the single most important force creating global shifts in economic activity' (Dicken 1998, p. 47). For others, MNEs are 'disseminators' of particular versions of capitalism, implying that MNEs may be proxies in the competition between the regulation and deregulation of employment models (Ferner 1994).

Table 4.1 The number and reach of MNEs (1970–2008)

Year	No. of parent corporations	No. of affiliates	Employment of foreign affiliates ('000s)
1970	7,000	n/a	n/a
1990	36,000	174,900	24,470
2000	63,312	821,818	45,587
2007	78,817	794,894	80,396
2008	82,053	807,363	77,386

Source: Franko 1976; UNCTAD, World Investment Reports, *various years*.

Managing globalisation in Australia and New Zealand

Increasing globalisation creates particular international employment challenges for small populated economies like Australia and New Zealand and their MNEs (Dowling & Boxall 1994). As Gyngell, Skilling and Thirlwell put it (2007, p. 3): while

> 'Globalisation is changing and reshaping the geography of the world economy in important ways; it hasn't in any way abolished geography. Indeed, the combination of geography and globalisation is likely to present both Canberra and Wellington with some significant international policy opportunities and challenges in coming years'.

Opportunities and risks

Opportunities and risks for Australian and New Zealand organisations alike have been created by:

- the rapid economic development of neighbouring Asian economies;
- the enlargement of trading areas;
- the emergence of regionalisation;

- the ability to exploit cost differentials through off-shoring; and
- the movement of talent from low to high wage economies (Stevens 2007).

The driving forces towards active and full engagement with global economic forces have been:

- the relative geographical isolation and small size of these economies;
- their shared historical trade ties with the United Kingdom; and
- abandonment of economic protectionism during the 1970s and 1980s.

The movement towards market-driven policies in each country, however, has had differing degrees of success (Castles, Curtin & Vowles 2006).

Geographical constraints and opportunities

There are few countries where geography is more of an issue than Australia and New Zealand.

The tyranny of distance v. the power of proximity

Much of the public discourse centres on overcoming 'the tyranny of distance' as relatively poor performance of Australia and New Zealand is often explained in terms of their distance from global centres of economic activity (Gyngell *et al.* 2007).

As research has noted, however, the shift of the centre of global activity to East Asia can be seen as a positive development for both countries. With the emergence of the Asia Pacific region, the 'tyranny of distance' is replaced with the 'power of proximity'. In other words, the emergence of developing Asian markets, along with recent developments in technology, are seen to provide Australian and New Zealand organisations with the opportunity to locate closer to their main markets and increase the speed with which they can meet market demands (Harcourt 2005; Gyngell *et al.* 2007).

Relative performance of MNEs in Australia and New Zealand

As Figure 4.2 demonstrates, the performance of both Australia and New Zealand in the last two decades has improved to differing degrees.

Much of Australia's recent performance is based on an increase in the demand for minerals, whereas improvements in the performance of New Zealand are largely attributed to the rise in demand for food products.

Performance of MNEs in New Zealand

While both economies are actively engaged in global markets, the relatively poor performance of New Zealand has generated significant discussion. The internationalisation model being pursued by New Zealand MNEs has been

> '... to establish a production presence closer to the end consumer or ... (to) contract this production out to other firms in these locations' (Skilling & Bowen 2007, p. 2).

In an attempt to overcome geographical isolation and improve the speed of products to consumer markets, NZ MNEs have steadily begun to offshore and outsource their operations. This 'flight of indigenous manufacturing' has led to concerns of a 'hollowing out' of indigenous manufacturing and has initiated debate on the future configurations and international management challenges for New Zealand organisations.

Economic interdependency of Australia and New Zealand

A deepening of the economic interdependency between these two economies has contributed to an increase in international migration flows between the two countries (Castles *et al.* 2006).

Australia, New Zealand's closest trading partner, currently 'exerts a significant gravitational pull' on New Zealand's human resources and assets. Reports suggest that since the late 1970s, a net average of 15,700 New Zealanders have left their home country for Australia on a permanent or long-term basis (Skilling 2007).

Competing to remain relevant is one of New Zealand's greatest challenges. In response, it has been recommended that the government focus on:

- tax reforms;
- the provision of incentives to increase the stock of domestic capital;
- improvements to the infrastructure and education system; and
- the active pursuit of FDI (Skilling 2007).

Gyngell *et al.* (2007) suggest investment in the infrastructure and capacity of the workforce is necessary to provide them with their strengths. In short, the greatest challenge that New Zealand faces is to identify the competitive advantages of managing internationally from this region.

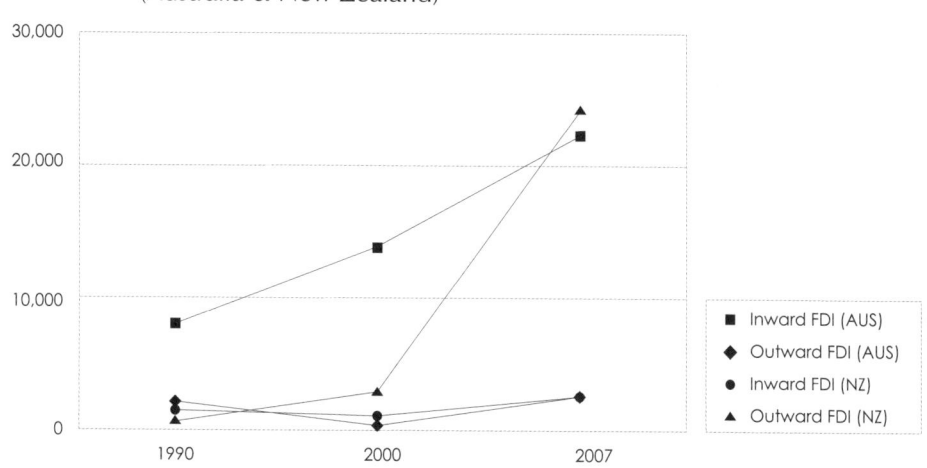

Figure 4.2 Foreign direct investment flows 1990–2007 (US$) (Australia & New Zealand)

[Chart showing Inward FDI (AUS), Outward FDI (AUS), Inward FDI (NZ), Outward FDI (NZ) from 1990 to 2007, with values ranging from 0 to 30,000]

Source: United Nations, Major FDI Indicators 2008.

Performance of MNEs in Australia

The Australian economy has fared better in global markets than New Zealand, its neighbouring economy. In the lead up to the global financial crisis, Australia benefited from rising demand for raw materials, while at the same time developing greater linkages with regional economies through trade negotiations—especially with Asian economies.

The upsurge in outward investment in the last two decades has largely been attributed to the policy reforms of the 1980s when the country shifted away from inward looking policies. Since those reforms, there has been a significant increase in the value of outward stock, indicating a growth in the activity of Australian MNEs.

As Merrett (2007) notes, while the total number of MNEs has not increased, it is the composition of this group of enterprises that has changed. While outward FDI has shifted to the US and UK, it was found that Australian MNEs located most of their affiliates in New Zealand and Asia—close to their home country.

Globalisation and the SIHRM challenges

In recent years the challenges that SIHRM traditionally focused on have expanded with the growth in global integration. The focus on expatriate management that traditionally lay at the 'coalface' of SIHRM has recently become overshadowed by such issues as:

- the strategic and structural configurations of MNEs;
- the changing role of the corporate HR function;

- global talent management; and
- diversity and cross-cultural management.

As a discipline, SIHRM is said to be characterised by three separate strands of research:

- cross-cultural management;
- comparative HRM; and
- strategic HRM in the multinational context (De Cieri & Dowling 2006).

Cross-cultural studies

Cross-cultural studies, which represent the earliest work in this field, examined the human behavioural issues that organisations face when managing across different cultures (Laurent 1986).

Comparative HRM research

In contrast, comparative HRM sought to analyse and assess the differences between HRM systems in various countries (Brewster & Hegewisch 1994; Boxall 2007).

Strategic HRM in the multinational context

The third, most recent strand of research adopts a more strategic macro focus. It examines the impact of globalisation on the way in which firms manage their employees and, in particular, the role of MNEs in shaping the process of globalisation (Ferner 1994).

These three strands are said to mirror organisational developments within MNEs themselves (De Cieri & Dowling 2006).

Strategic international human resource management

Recognition of the competitive nature of human resources and the need to 'achieve fit' with the strategic orientation of the organisation led to the emergence of the concept of strategic international human resource management. Schuler, Dowling and De Cieri (1993, p. 422) define this as:

> '… human resource management issues, functions and policies and practices that result from the strategic activities of multinational enterprises and that impact the international concerns and goals of those enterprises'.

The recent shift towards the strategic direction of MNEs and the impact of globalisation has given rise to a number of key human resource management challenges. These include:

- the role of the corporate HR function;
- global talent management; and

- diversity and cross-cultural management.

The changing role of the corporate HR function

Global integration v. local differentiation

One of the key issues that MNEs face in their drive to become globally oriented entities is managing the competing demands of global integration and local differentiation (Bartlett & Ghoshal 1989; Prahalad & Doz 1987). The dictum, 'think global, act local', coined by Levitt (1983), suggests that the increasing complexity and convergence of markets encourages MNEs to centralise the coordination and integration of operations, while at the same time seeking to remain locally responsive.

Resolving what is often referred to as the 'integration–differentiation dilemma' involves:

- the global organisational restructuring of MNEs (Mayer & Whittington 2002); and
- a reshaping of the role and function of the HR function at a corporate head office level (Marginson, Armstrong, Edwards & Purcell 1995, Ferner 1994).

The scope and content of the corporate HR function

Recognition that the management of human resources is a source of competitive advantage on a global basis has led to a growth in the scope and content of the corporate HR function (Kelly 2001; Scullion & Starkey 2000). As Kelly (2001, p. 541) notes, 'the changing multinational context presents opportunities for the personnel/HR function to proactively improve its status, power and influence'. According to Scullion and Starkey (2000) an increase in the status and influence of the corporate HR function took place from the mid 1990s as corporate HR functions became 'guardians of core competencies'. Their research, based on British MNEs, identified the core management competencies as including:

- the management of managers;
- succession planning;
- leadership development; and
- the development of a pool of international managers.

Strategy and structure v. domestic, institutional and political pressures

The global restructuring of MNEs has further highlighted the strategic nature of senior management as MNEs view this cohort of managers as critical to ensuring their future survival (Scullion & Starkey 2000). In this way the role of the corporate HR function is seen to be shaped by strategic and structural considerations. This stands in contrast to the view that the role of HR within MNEs is shaped by domestic, institutional and political pressures.

Research by Ferner and Varul (2000) found that German MNEs, given their highly regulated legislative environment and market, prescribed a more specialised role for HRM which was legalistic and administrative in orientation. As German MNEs expanded overseas they were found to adopt practices and structures originating in the UK and the US. Their research demonstrated that the manner in which German MNEs mediate globalisation reflects more of a political process (Ferner & Varul 2000).

Global talent management

> '... all large companies face globalization, as they either move into new global markets or face competition from them ... One of the main HR challenges that these companies will face in managing globalization is making sure that the right people are in place in the right locations and that there is effective and efficient cross-country and cross-cultural collaboration' (The Boston Consulting Group 2008, p. 6).

In recent years global talent management has become of critical strategic importance for MNEs—and an even more popular theme within the SIHRM literature. Discussions of the 'unique sources of competitive advantage' have shifted from the management of expatriation to the management of talent.

The war for talent

Global talent management is partially driven out of recognition that international success is dependent on managerial competencies and partially shaped by the global competition for talent (Collings, Scullion & Dowling 2009). The concept of talent management arose out of a McKinsey report in 1997 entitled *The War for Talent*. This report, whose ideas quickly rose to prominence, recommended that organisations focus on building a 'talent pool' in the drive for organisational performance. Since then, ensuring the ready supply of 'talented' employees has become a dominant focus for many MNEs.

Scope of global talent management

Notwithstanding its popularity, particularly amongst practitioners, global talent management lacks clarity with regard to its precise meaning and scope (Scullion, Collings & Caligiuri 2009). Lewis and Heckman (2006) identify three different ways in which talent management is viewed:

- first, as a 'euphemism' for managing people;
- second, as an effective planning process where the potential progression of employees through an organisation are mapped out; and

- third, as a mechanism for managing performance as organisations seek to differentiate the 'best and the brightest' from those who consistently perform at a poor level.

More recent research regards global talent management as focusing on the identification of a core group of employees—employees who are considered to be 'strategically important' to the future success of the MNE (Collings & Mellahi 2009). In keeping, Stahl, Bjorkman, Farndale, Morris, Paauwe and Stiles (2007) define global talent management (GTM) as an organisation's efforts to attract, select, develop and retain key talented employees on a global scale.

Attraction of talent a strategic priority

While the McKinsey report was set against a background of economic growth, others have since suggested that even within constricting labour markets, increased competition for human resources makes the attraction of talent a strategic priority (Warner 2000).

For MNEs from countries with large expatriate bases to draw from, 'reverse expatriation' is often the solution to this 'fight for talent', as MNEs seek to repopulate their corporate human resources by enticing their emigrants back to their homeland. Research within the Asia Pacific region found that MNEs are selective in their use of international assignments and seek to replace expatriate managers with local expertise (De Cieri 2003). Given the global competition for talent and an increase in the mobility of talent, global talent management will remain a strategic concern for MNEs operating with Asia Pacific.

Diversity and cross-cultural management

The growth, decline, ageing and diversification of workforces, together with increasing migration rates, provide organisations with their greatest global challenge thus far—the 'challenge of demography' (National Intelligence Council 2008).

International migration

International migration flows continue to increase as globalisation deepens (UNCTAD 2009b). In the last 50 years there has been a doubling of international migrants—from 75 million in 1960 to 191 million in 2005 (DESA 2009). The increase in mobility is driven by three forces:

- the pursuit of employment opportunities;
- humanitarian relief; and
- family reunification.

Globalisation, through its increased demand for the production of goods and services

'... has improved individuals' access to information, substantially increased the affordability of telecommunications and international transportation, and reduced physical and administrative barriers to the movement of people' (UNCTAD 2009b, p. 4).

Career management

The diversity of socio-economic, cultural and political contexts within the Asia Pacific region presents organisations with a number of key challenges (De Cieri 2003). New forms of international organisations and 'ways of working' have highlighted the need to manage career implications. As De Cieri (2003, p. 5) notes,

'Australian organisations face a particular challenge in increasing their international activities in this region, as Australian managers have been strongly criticised by Asian counterparts for lacking the cross-cultural skills and international managerial expertise suited to international work'.

Furthermore, there is a greater sense of job insecurity and a renewed focus on productivity within MNEs which have dampened down the labour mobility or 'job hopping' that dominated in some Asian labour markets during the 1990s (De Cieri 2003).

In effect, the changing demography of national and international workforces, coupled with a need to develop cross-cultural competencies, remain key challenges for MNEs operating within the Asia Pacific region.

Conclusion

This chapter addresses the employment challenges that MNEs face within a rapidly changing global context. 'Managing globalisation' from an Asia Pacific region perspective involves a number of key challenges:

- it requires greater understanding of the changing global economy and the employment implications it presents;
- it highlights the need to understand a diverse range of cultural and institutional frameworks that MNEs originate from and operate within; and
- it places pressure on MNEs to identify their key sources of competitive advantage—sources that have been shown empirically to reside in the management of human resources or the national business systems that MNEs and their HR practices originate from.

The chapter has shown how multinational enterprises are shaped by the global economy and the role they play in driving globalisation. It has demonstrated how SIHRM can be considered as a mediating mechanism through which MNEs position themselves to take advantage of globalisation. Managing SIHRM from small populated countries like

Australia and New Zealand highlights a number of distinct challenges for their organisations. Reports suggest that the key strategic IHRM challenges for Asia Pacific organisations will include:

- the management of demographics;
- the management of talent;
- the improvement of leadership development; and
- the management of change and cultural transformation (The Boston Consulting Group 2008).

Various reports (De Cieri 2003; Fish & Wood 1997) point out that Australian and New Zealand organisations are starting from a relatively low base with regard to cross-cultural management and international management expertise.

Case study: Fonterra and Sanlu

In September 2008 reports emerged that infants in China were dying as a result of contaminated baby milk. These reports revealed that melamine, a chemical normally utilised in the production of plastics and fertilisers, had been added to baby milk powder in an attempt to raise the protein count artificially. It was also suggested that the manufacturer, the Shijiazhuang Sanlu Group, had not ceased production when significant amounts of melamine were found in their products. Sanlu, the third largest dairy cooperative in China, entered into a joint venture with New Zealand's largest MNE, the Fonterra Cooperative Group, in 2006. The 43% stakeholding with Sanlu allowed Fonterra access to its largest growing market and secured them three managerial places on the seven-member joint venture board.

Investigations into the milk powder scandal revealed that the practice of adding melamine had begun as early as 2007. By March 2008 senior management at Sanlu had received complaints about its infant milk products from consumers who reported kidney problems after using the milk powder. It was not until August 2, however, that Sanlu's partner Fonterra learnt of the contamination. Fonterra subsequently requested from Sanlu a full and immediate recall of the formula milk and sought the intervention of local government officials. Neither approach resulted in the withdrawal of the product. At the same time, China was hosting the Olympic games which attracted a substantial amount of attention from the world media. In preparation for the Olympics, the media were issued with strict reporting rules set out by China's Central Propaganda Department which included that 'all food safety issues … [were] off limits' (Ching 2008).

Eventually, on August 14, Fonterra notified the New Zealand Embassy in Beijing of the unfolding scandal. On August 31, the New Zealand embassy sent reports of its findings to the New Zealand government, which informed the Beijing authorities of the issue. On September 11, seven months after they had received the first reports concerning their products, Sanlu ordered a full recall of their milk products. Further testing by the Chinese government revealed that 22 milk food firms failed safety testing due to melamine contamination.

Fonterra has been widely criticised for their poor quality control mechanisms and slow response in 'going public' with the issue. In their defence, the CEO of Fonterra, Andrew Ferrier, argued that from day one they 'had to make a call whether we could be more effective working with the Chinese government or taking matters into our own hands. The latter would have meant going 'outside the system', with no idea whether a proper recall would happen.'

The contamination of milk products led to the death of six infants and the infection of thousands of other infants. It also led to the arrest and prosecution of senior Sanlu management, the execution of two farmers found to have been responsible for the mixing of melamine in the milk, and the dismissal of the mayor of Shijiazhuang and four other city officials.

Fonterra have since written off their NZ$200 million investment in the Sanlu joint venture. Moreover, they have made major inroads in China through a NZ $8.4 million donation to the Soong Ching Ling Foundation for the creation of maternal and infant community hubs in rural China and the acquisition of a 3,000-cow dairy farm in northern Hebei province.

References

Ching, F 2008, 'Tainted food: China's history of using melamine', Hong Kong, *The National Business Review*, 20 September 2008.

Gardner, C, James, A 2008, 'Dairy head backs China reaction', *Waikato Times*, accessed 30 September 2008 at www.stuff.co.nz/.

Hembry, O 2008, 'Cost of disaster remains to be counted', *New Zealand Herald*, 22 September 2008, sourced on 23 September 2008.

NZ Herald 2008, Editorial: 'Fonterra poison milk scandal a disaster waiting to happen', accessed 21 September 2008 at www.nzherald.co.nz/

NZTE (New Zealand Trade Enterprise) 2006, December 12, 'Fonterra to set up dairy farm in China', accessed 22 September 2008 at www.nzte.govt.nz/.

Case study questions

1. What was the internationalisation strategy adopted by Fonterra as they entered the Chinese market?

2. What factors contributed to the seven month delay in recalling this product?

3. From a human resource management perspective, what could Fonterra have done to minimise the risk of the scenario described here?

References

Adler, NJ & Gundersen, A 2008, *International Dimensions of Organisational Behavior*, Case Western Reserve University, Thomson.

Altman, RC 2009, 'The Great Crash, 2008: A Geopolitical Setback for the West', *Foreign Affairs*, January/February, 2-14.

Bartlett, C & Ghoshal, S 1989, *Managing Across Borders: The Transnational Solution*, Harvard Business School Press, Boston.

Bhagwati, J 2004, *In Defense of Globalization*, Oxford University Press, Oxford.

Boxall, P 2007, 'Building the theory of Comparative HRM', *Human Resource Management Journal*, 5 (5): 5-17.

Brewster, C & Hegewisch, A (eds) 1994, *Policy and Practice in European Human Resource Management*, Routledge, London.

Castles, F, Curtin, J & Vowles, J 2006, Public policy in Australia and New Zealand: The new global context, *Australian Journal of Political Science*, 41 (2): 131-143.

Collings, D, Scullion, H & Dowling, P 2009, 'Global Staffing: A Review and Thematic Research Agenda', *International Journal of Human Resource Management*, 20 (6): 1253-1272.

Collings, D & Mellahi, K 2009, 'Strategic Talent Management: What is it and how does it matter?,' *Human Resource Management Review*, 19: 304-313.

Das, G 2006, 'The India Model', *Foreign Affairs*, July/August.

De Cieri, H & Dowling, PJ 2006, 'Strategic international human resource management in multinational enterprises: developments and directions', in G Stahl and I Bjorkman (eds), *Handbook of Research in International Resource Management*, Edward Elgar, Cheltenham.

De Cieri, H & Hutching, K 2008, 'The International Context of Human Resource Management ', in Macky, K (ed) *Managing Human Resources: Contemporary Perspectives in New Zealand*, McGraw-Hill, Sydney.

De Cieri, H. 2003, 'International Human Resource Management: Asia Pacific Challenges', Monash University, *Working Paper Series*, 7/03.

Dicken, P 1998, *'Global Shift: The Internationalization of Economic Activity'*, Paul Chapman, London.

Dowling PJ & Boxall PF 1994, Shifting the emphasis from natural resources to human resources: The challenge of the new competitive context in Australia and New Zealand. *Zeitschrift fur Personalforschung*, 8 (3): 302-316.)

Dowling, PJ, Festing, M & Engle, A 2008, *International Human Resource Management,* (5th edn), Cengage Thomson, London.

Dunning, J 1991, *Multinational Enterprises and the Global Economy*, Addison-Wesley, Wokingham.

Dunning, J 1993, *The Globalization of Business: The Challenge of the 1990s*, London, Routledge.

Dunning, J 2007, A new Zeitgeist for international business activity and scholarship, *European Journal of International Management*, 1 (4): 278-301.

Edwards, PK, Armstrong, P, Marginson, P & Purcell, J 1996, 'Towards the Transnational Company? The global structure and organisation of multinational firms' in R Crompton, D Gallie & K Purcell (eds), *Changing Forms of Employment*, London, Routledge.

Edwards, T & Ferner, A 2002, 'The renewed 'American Challenge': a review of employment practice in US multinationals', *Industrial Relations Journal*, 33(2), 94-111.

European Foundation for the Improvement of Living and Working Conditions (Eurofound) 2008, 'Around the World in 80 ways: The Truth about Delocalisation', http://www.eurofounf.europa.eu/resourcepacks/globalisation.htm.

Ferner, A & Hyman, R 1998, *Changing Industrial Relations in Europe*, (2nd edn), Oxford, Blackwell.

Ferner, A & Varul, M 2000, '"Vanguard" Subsidiaries and the Diffusion of New Practices', *British Journal of Industrial Relations*, 38 (1): 115-140.

Ferner, A 1994, 'Multinational Companies and Human Resource Management: An Overview of Research Issues', *Human Resource Management Journal*, 4(3): 79-102.

Ferner, A 1997a, 'Country of Origin Effects and HRM in Multinational Companies', *Human Resource Management Journal,* 7 (11): 19-37.

Ferner, A 1997b, 'Multinational, Relocation and Employment in Europe', paper for IESE Third International Conference, *Job Creation: The Role of Labour Market Institutions*, Barcelona, Spain.

Fish, A & Wood, J 1997, 'Cross-cultural Management Competencies in Australian Business Enterprises', *Asia Pacific Journal of Human Resources*, 35 (1).

Franko, L 1976, *The European Multinationals: A Renewed Challenge to American and British Big Business,* London, Harper Row.

Gyngell, A, Skilling, D & Thirlwell, M 2007, Australia and New Zealand in a Globalising World', *Lowry Institute Perspectives*, downloaded from www.lowryinstitute.org.

Harcourt, T 2005, 'The Tyranny of distance' or 'the Power of Proximity'? China, Asia and Australia's Export Future', Economist's Corner, *Australia Trade Commission*, Sydney.

Hirst, P & Thompson, G 1996, *Globalization in Question: The International Economy and the Possibilities of Governance*, Cambridge, Polity Press.

Hofstede, G 1980, *Culture's consequences: international differences in work-related values*. Beverly Hills, CA, Sage Publications.

International Labour Organisation (ILO) 2009a, *Global Employment Trends – Update*, ILO, Geneva.

International Labour Organisation (ILO) 2009b, *Recovering from the Crisis: A Global Jobs Pact*, ILO, Geneva.

International Monetary Fund (IMF) 2004, 'World Economic Outlook,' Washington D.C.

Kelly, J 2001, 'The role of the personnel/HR function in multinational companies', *Employee Relations*, 23 (6): 536-557.

Kobrin, SJ 1997, 'The Architecture of Globalization: State Sovereignty in a Networked Global Economy', in Dunning, J (ed) *Governments, globalization, and international business*, Oxford, Oxford University Press.

Kogut, B 1998, 'International Business: The New Bottom Line', *Foreign Policy*, 110, Spring, 152-165.

Kurth Cronin, A 2003, 'Behind the Curve: Globalization and International Terrorism', *International Security*, Winter, 27(3): 30-58.

Laurent, A 1986, 'The cross-cultural puzzle of international human resource management', *Human Resource Management*, 5: 581-608.

Levitt, T 1983, 'The Globalization of Markets', *Harvard Business Review*, May/June.

Lewis, RE & Heckman RJ 2006 'Talent Management: A Critical Review', *Human Resource Management Review*, 16: 139-154.

Marginson, P, Armstrong, P, Edwards, PK & Purcell, J 1995, 'Extending Beyond Borders: Multinational Companies and the International Management of Labour', *The International Journal of Human Resource Management*, 6(3): 702-19.

Marginson, P & Sisson, K 1994, 'The Structure of Transnational Capital in Europe: The Emerging Euro-Company and its Implications for Industrial Relations', in R Hyman & A Ferner (eds.), *New Frontiers in European Industrial Relations*, Oxford, Blackwell.

Mathews, J 2006, 'Dragon Multinationals: New Players in 21st Century Globalization', *Asia Pacific Journal of Management*, 23(1): 5-27.

Mayer, M & Whittington, R 2002, 'For boundedness in the study of comparative and international business: the case of the diversified multidivisional corporation', in Geppert, M, Matten, D & Williams, K (eds) *Challenges for European Management in a Global Context*, Palgrave Macmillan, Basingstoke.

McLuhan, M 1962, *The Gutenberg Galaxy: the making of typographic man*, Toronto, University of Toronto Press.

Merrett, D 2007, 'Australian Multinationals in Historical Perspective: Do you come from a land down under?' in Dick, H & Merrett, D (eds.) *The International Strategies of Small-country firms: The Australian Experience of Globalisation*, Edward Elgar Publishing, Cheltenham.

National Intelligence Council (NIC) 2008, *Global Trends 2025: A Transformed World*, Office of the Director of National Intelligence, USA.

Ohmae, K 1990, *The Borderless World: Power and Strategy in the Interlinked Economy*, New York, Harper.

Prahalad, C & Doz, Y 1987, *The Multinational Mission: Balancing Local Demands and Global Vision*, London, Collier Macmillan.

Reich, R 1991, *The Work of Nations: Preparing Ourselves for 21st Century Capitalism*, Vintage Books, New York.

Rugman, A 2001, 'The myth of global strategy', *International Marketing Review*, 18 (6): 583-588.

Ruigrok, W & Van Tulder, R 1995, *The Logic of International Restructuring*, London and New York, Routledge.

Scholte, JA 2000, *Globalization: A Critical Introduction*, Palgrave, Basingstoke.

Schuler, R, Budhwar, P & Florkowski, G 2002, International Human Resource Management: Review and Critique, *International Journal of Management Reviews*, 4 (1): 41-70.

Schuler, R 2000, 'The Internationalization of Human Resource Management', *Journal of International Management*, 6: 239-60.

Schuler, R, Dowling, PJ & De Cieri, H 1993, 'An Integrative Framework of Strategic International Human Resource Management', *International Journal of Human Resource Management*, 4 (4): 717-64.

Scullion, H & Starkey, K 2000, 'In Search of the Changing Role of the Corporate Human Resource Function in the International Firm', *International Journal of Human Resource Management*, 11:1061-81.

Scullion, H, Collings, D & Gunnigle, P 2007, 'International Human Resource Management in the 21st century: emerging themes and contemporary debates', *Human Resource Management Journal*, 17 (4): 309-319.

Sirkin, H, Hemerling, J & Bhattacharya, A 2008, *Globality: Competing with Everyone from Everywhere for Everything*, Grand Central Publishing.

Skilling, D 2007, 'Competing and cooperating: Growing New Zealand's economic relationships with Australia', *The New Zealand Institute Essay*, March.

Skilling, D & Bowen, D 2007, 'So far yet so close: Connecting New Zealand to the global economy', *The New Zealand Institute*, Discussion Paper 2007/1.

Sparrow, P, Brewster, C & Harris, H 2004, *Globalizing Human Resource Management*, Routledge, London.

Steinfeld, E 2004, 'China's Shallow Integration: Networked Production and the New Challenges for Late Industrialization', *World Development*, 32 (11): 1971-1987.

Stevens, W 2007, 'The Risks and Opportunities from Globalization', *New Zealand Department of Treasury*, Working Paper Series, 07/05.

Stiglitz, J 2003, *Globalization and Its Discontents*, WW Norton & Company, New York.

Streeck, W 1992, *Social Institutions and Economic Performance*, SAGE Publications.

Taylor, S, Beechler, S & Napier, N 1996 'Towards an Integrative Model of Strategic International Human Resource Management', *Academy of Management Review*, 21(4): 959-985.

The Boston Consulting Group 2008, 'Creating People Advantage: How to Address HR Challenges Worldwide Through 2015', in conjunction with the World Federation of Personnel Management Associations, Boston.

The Economist 1995, 'Survey of Multinationals', June 24.

The Economist 2000, 'The world's view of multinationals', January 27.

The Economist 2008, 'Globalisation's New Phase', September 18.

The Economist 2008, 'Globalisation', July 17.

The Economist 2009, 'Sino-Trojan horse', May 28.

The Washington Post 2005, 'Chinese drop bid to buy U.S. oil firm', August 3, 2005.

Traxler, F & Woitech, B 2000, 'Transnational Investment and National Labour Market Regimes: A Case of `Regime Shopping'?', *European Journal of Industrial Relations*, 6 (2): 141-159.

United Nations Centre for Trade and Development (UNCTAD) 2008, 'Transnational Corporations, and the Infrastructure Challenge', *World Investment Report*, United Nations.

United Nations Centre for Trade and Development (UNCTAD) 2009a, 'Transnational Corporations, Agricultural Production and Development', *World Investment Report*, United Nations.

United Nations Centre for Trade and Development (UNCTAD) 2009b, 'Contribution of migrants to development: trade, investment and development linkages' UNCTAD/DITC/TNCD/2009/2.

United Nations, Department of Economic and Social Affairs, (DESA) 2009, International Migration Report 2006: A Global Assessment, ESA/P/WP.209

Warner, M 2000, 'Globalization, labour markets and human resources in Asia-Pacific economies: an overview', *International Journal of Human Resource Management*, 13 (3): 384-98.

Chapter 5

SUSTAINABILITY IN STRATEGIC HUMAN RESOURCE MANAGEMENT

Robin Kramar & Grant Jones

OBJECTIVES

By the completion of the chapter you should be able to:

1. explain the way in which the concept of SHRM can be modified to take into account performance in the areas of economic, social and environmental outcomes;
2. explain the way SHRM contributes to these three outcomes; and
3. describe the capabilities required by individuals to further sustainable environmental, economic and social and human outcomes within organisations.

DEFINITIONS

Sustainability: Sustainability is often thought of as focusing on the three elements of Elkington's (1997) triple bottom line: economic outcomes, social impacts, and environmental impacts. The definition is limited, however, in that it focuses the attention of managers on their external impacts, without looking inwards to the internal dynamics that contribute to those impacts. For example, the HR focus tends to be limited to factors that make the organisation a good employer, factors which are then grouped under the social dimension.

Global responsibility: Global responsibility (Antal & Sobczak 2004; Perez 2003; Thevenet 2003) is a concept that recognises that the effects of decision making within an organisation go far beyond its walls. Organisations now have capacities that are potent enough to leverage the effects of internal decisions around the world.

This raises a second meaning of 'global'. Decision making is more global if it is more inclusive. This means that leaders recognise the wider range of stakeholders whose lives are affected by decision making and consider the implications for those stakeholders as they make their decisions. Anatal and Sobczak (2004) also point out that the concept of global responsibility surpasses its conceptual antecedent—'corporate social responsibility'— which tended to focus on the responsibilities of large, private sector entities. Global responsibility can also be exercised by small organisations, not-for-profit organisations and NGOs. This element is particularly salient in this chapter where we see the concept of global responsibility applied in our case study of PricewaterhouseCoopers, particularly with respect to that company's interactions with stakeholders across the three sectors.

Reflective practice: Reflective practice is a concept introduced by Donald Schon (1983, 1987). More recently it has been linked to the engagement of staff in thinking and acting in ways that enhance sustainability (Tilbury & Wortman 2004). Schon initially distinguished between 'reflection *on* action' and 'reflection *in* action'. Reflection *on* action is a kind of postmortem reflection after the action has been executed; reflection *in* action could be described as critical self reflection—it is a process of considering action while the individual is in the process of taking that action. The latter requires not only a cognitive ability to assess basic assumptions at the same time as those assumptions are driving actions, but has more recently been recognised as the capacity to deploy a highly developed affective competence enabling the actor to recognise the feelings that come into being during the action, take responsibility for those feelings and recognise their influence on judgement (Taylor 2007, p. 86).

Introduction

There are a number of advantages to be enjoyed by organisations that choose to adopt sustainability as an organisational theme and a corporate objective.

Sustainability is a theme with the potential to improve the corporate engagement of employees. An explicit objective to build sustainability presents the organisation as a good employer, and provided this presentation is genuine, attracts and retains people who want to be proud of the organisation for which they work.

Sustainability is universal in that it can operate at all levels of the organisation, from grand strategy to small group behaviour and local operations. The focus on organisational systems that is intrinsic to sustainability can help to build an awareness of the effects of action, which in turn encourages the growth of a broader sense of responsibility within the work force. Moreover, this sense of responsibility can compel action.

However, sustainability does not happen by itself. A sustainability-focused workforce is also a change-oriented workforce. To date, sustainability has largely been led by powerful champions within organisations but is likely to work best with more broadly based engagement throughout the organisation.

Sustainability is in sympathy with many of the positive values that drive an organisation's human resource philosophy — including empowerment, respect for a wide range of stakeholder interests, collaboration and reflective practice. Sustainability also sits well with the resource-based view of the firm, a view which focuses on the development of organisational capability.

Strategic Human Resource Management (SHRM) includes the development and use of the human capital necessary for the firm to give effect to strategy. Elements of human capital associated with sustainability include a focus on outcomes and longer-term visioning, organisational resilience, adaptability and a capacity for resource renewal rather than simple use and wastage.

A sustainable approach to SHRM provides mindful stewardship of all resources, but especially the human resource. It exploits the talents of people and renews their skill base and sense of vocation at the same time. In this sense the disciplines inherent in managing for sustainability support SHRM in delivering potency and economic viability for the organisation at the same time as nurturing social, environmental and human outcomes. In order to explore these themes in more detail this chapter examines:

- the way in which the concept of SHRM can be modified to take into account performance in the areas of economic, social and environmental outcomes;
- the contribution of SHRM to these outcomes; and
- the capabilities required by individuals to further sustainable environmental, economic and social and human outcomes.

Contemporary trends

Sustainable development

The concept of *sustainable development* is critical to understanding the relationship between strategic human resources and sustainability. Sustainable development has been defined by the Brundtland Commission of the United Nations (Brundtland 1987) as development that meets the needs of the present generation without compromising the ability of future generations to meet their own needs.

This definition highlights three aspects of sustainable development — reflected as outcomes in the economic, social and environmental areas.

Global managerial capacity

During the quarter of a century since the Brundtland Commission report, ecological degradation and climate change have accelerated, rapid economic development and environmental destruction in emerging economies (such as China, India and Brazil) have occurred and social and economic inequalities within and between countries have continued (Sneddon, Howarth & Norgaard 2006). The crisis has stimulated the development of more sophisticated forms of governance and there is evidence of *global* managerial capacity improving.

International consensus

The Kyoto Protocol marked a turning point in global attitudes and, in particular, a broadly based recognition that there are real and pressing limits to the capacity of the earth to absorb the current forms of economic growth. The Kyoto Protocol has given legitimacy to carbon trading, which has, in turn, made business more responsible for its carbon pollution.

The Montreal Protocol provides another example of a successful international consensus. Adherence to the protocol has reversed the growth in CFCs and reduced the size of the hole in the ozone layer.

Arguably, a globally coordinated fiscal response to the global financial crisis has averted economic catastrophe.

Intergenerational equity

In addition to this evident growth in institutional capacity for collaborative response, there has been a broadening in concern for and understanding of sustainability. The idea of intergenerational equity is now widely understood and there has been a change in the values that drive people in western economies. This change in values has coincided with a tendency for organisations to expand the realm of behaviours and outcomes for which they are willing to take responsibility. They have found their staff ready and willing to engage with this change.

Isolation of non-sustainable companies

Some global companies have shown leadership in progressively isolating non-sustainable companies by denying them custom and finance. For example, the world's largest miner, BHP Billiton, operates throughout the Asia Pacific region and routinely questions its suppliers on their practices with regard to workplace conditions and safety, human rights and environmental management before making procurement decisions. Seventy banks around the world (including Citibank, the Bank of America, Barclays, JP Morgan and BNP Paribus) have signed on to the Equator Principles which forbid the financing of any development that is non-sustainable. In the Asia Pacific, signatories include Westpac, ANZ, HSBC, China's Industrial Bank and Japan's Mizuho Corporate Bank and the Bank of Tokyo (Equator Principles Steering Committee 2009).

The GRI and the DJSI

Global companies are also developing management systems for sustainability. These systems build on and report against the triple bottom line. Since its conception in 1997, the Global Reporting Initiative (GRI) has grown to the point where it can boast 507 participating organisations in 55 countries. The GRI and an array of sustainability indexes operating in global share markets are channelling investment funds towards companies that meet minimum standards of sustainability. The Dow Jones Sustainability Index (DJSI) is exclusive in the sense that in any given year almost as many companies are expelled from the index for bad behaviour as those that join it. In 2009 the DJSI reported coverage of companies worth US$9.287 trillion worldwide and US$1.905 trillion across the Asia Pacific (Dow Jones a & b 2009).

Corporate social responsibility

These measurement systems facilitate assessments of the extent to which an organisation is producing outcomes which contribute to sustainable development. The term *corporate social responsibility* (CSR) has been used to reflect an organisation's achievement relating to areas concerning economic, environmental, and social and human factors. The SAS Institute has developed a complex footprint measurement tool that enables organisations to gather data on sustainability automatically by electronic transfer as it monitors its operations. The data not only presents a footprint but also enables statistical analysis of the effects of key investments on sustainability. The analysis includes the effects of categories of HR investment—such as training—on sustainability outcomes such as environmental fees, fines or power and water usage.

Problems of definition

It has been argued that there is no one commonly agreed definition of terms such as 'sustainability' or 'CSR', and therefore the concepts are of little use. It has been claimed the concept provides a limited basis for action (Henderson 2001, p. 21–22).

Against this, however, organisations could describe their own definitions for sustainability. The definition could then suit the organisation's particular circumstances, values and level of awareness (van Marrewijk 2003). All the definitions would reflect the principle that organisations need to balance their activities, would be accountable to a number of stakeholders (Freeman 1984), and reflect a view that businesses are responsible to the society in which they operate (van Merrewijk 2001).

Relationship between strategic HRM and sustainability

Academic theorists (such as Royal & O'Donnell 2005—see chapter in this book on HR metrics) have called for greater integration of human resource information into investment decision making. Watson Wyatt has developed the Human Capital Index to show a relationship between intelligent HR management and financial returns. Others have assembled case study based evidence that links HR more explicitly to sustainability (Dunphy, Griffiths & Benn 2003).

The questionnaire that organisations must use when applying for entry to the DJSI makes a crude assessment of HR practices and thereby gives some recognition of the role of HR in overall sustainability. Across both the literature and current practice, however, the exact nature of the relationship between strategic HRM and an organisation's sustainability, as measured by the triple bottom line, remains under-explored.

SHRM

Central to the process and activities of strategic human resource management (SHRM) is the notion that a pattern of planned policies and practices concerned with managing people can assist the organisation to further its strategy and achieve its goals. Essential components of this approach are the identification of aspects of business problems associated with the people doing the work and developing human resource (HR) practices to solve the problems.

HR practices and performance measurement

For many years HR practices have been identified as critical for the success of an organisation, particularly its financial success (Becker & Huselid 1999; Becker, Huselid, Pickus & Spratt 1997; Delery & Doty 1996). SHRM has also been identified as a source of sustained competitive advantage if particular conditions are met (Pfeffer 1998; Sparrow, Schuler & Jackson 1994).

Traditionally, business performance has been interpreted in a narrow way, emphasising financial and product/service outcomes and the interests of a limited number of stakeholders such as the owners and shareholders (Boxall 1998; Dowling & Schuler 1990). SHRM and the development of HR practices have therefore been shaped by an economic rationale (Walsh, Weber & Margolis 2003, p. 866), with the enterprise forming the primary unit for the development of HR policies and initiatives.

HR policies and national legislation

Although the enterprise is the focus for the development of HR policies, these policies will reflect national legislative requirements, such as health and safety requirements and environmental impact requirements. They will also reflect national or regional standards. For instance, in countries such as Germany, Switzerland, Sweden and Finland, organisations operate in a 'social market economy' and consequently they are concerned with the welfare of all the stakeholders of the organisation, not just the shareholders (Avery 2005, p. 14-15). HR policies in organisations in these countries favour teamwork, low turnover, expenditure on training and development and power sharing with trade unions and employees. They are therefore concerned with economic outcomes, but also social and environmental outcomes (Avery 2005, p. 32-33).

Dimensions of organisational performance

The SHRM framework can be modified to explicitly express organisational performance along a number of performance criteria, such as financial outcomes, social and community outcomes and environmental outcomes.

Social and human objectives

An organisation can choose from a variety of systems which measure organisational performance along a range of dimensions (Dahlsrud 2008). These systems can be used to demonstrate that the organisation and its people seek to balance the needs of a variety of stakeholders and that they are responsible to the society in which they operate (van Marrewijk 2001). The early model for SHRM developed by Beer, Spector, Lawrence, Mills and Walton (1984), known as the Harvard model, identified broader outcomes: individual well-being, societal wellbeing and organisational effectiveness.

Internal benefits

The achievement of these broader social and human objectives has been found to have a positive impact on an organisation's financial performance. The internal benefits include developing capabilities, efficiencies and culture, enhancement of employee morale, an ability to attract and retain employees and a subsequent reduction in costs resulting from turnover, lost productivity and recruitment (Albinger & Freeman 2000; Greening & Turban 2000; Petersen 2004).

External benefits

The internal benefits influence external benefits such as corporate reputation (Branco & Rodrigues 2006; Orlitzky, Schmidt & Rynes 2003). Research also demonstrates that the market rewards companies that are environmentally responsive (Schnietz & Epstein 2005; Wahba 2007). This suggests that the extension of the SHRM model to include a broader range of performance measures fulfils the objectives of satisfying a range of stakeholders (Friedman 1970) and improves shareholder or owner financial returns at the same time.

Economic outcomes

The modification of the SHRM framework to include broader goals can therefore be argued for in terms of the achievement of economic outcomes. The argument demonstrates the interrelationship between economic, social and environmental goals and indicates these goals are not independent of each other. Research has also revealed that there is a relationship between the implementation and maintenance of the environmental management system of an organisation, its human resource policies and the development of capabilities necessary for an organisation's sustainability (Benn & Dunphy 2004b; Daily & Huang 2001; Dunphy, Benveniste, Griffiths & Sutton 2000; Wilkinson, Hill & Gollan 2001) — to be discussed in the next section.

Interrelationship between SHRM and environmental sustainability

Specific human resource policies that create trust between employees, management, and the communities in which the organisation operates are required for the development and implementation of advanced environmental policies. It has been proposed (Benn & Dunphy 2004b; Dunphy *et al.* 2003) that progress towards environmental sustainability can be considered in terms of a number of stages. They found that progress from earlier stages to more advanced stages was facilitated by the following human resource processes.

- Building competence through raising awareness of human and environmental compliance requirements, OHS and EEO training, and identifying human rights requirements within the supply chain.
- Providing clear definition of the roles and responsibilities of every employee, including line and senior management, and implementing HRIS systems to track human resource performance.
- Including sustainability targets in performance evaluations, and establishing systems for employee empowerment.
- Developing informal and formal champions to foster employee commitment to sustainability, multi-skilled teams, and skill development — e.g. conflict resolution and problem solving.
- Growing a culture which encourages innovation, sharing learning and knowledge, diversity training, work–life balance programs, and flexible working arrangements.

- Including ethical concerns in staff performance measures, supporting participative decision making, and developing high level employee capabilities such as self confidence, process skills, proactive, collaborative leadership involving internal and external stakeholders, and visionary leadership.

Engagement of a variety of stakeholders

The approach to HRM adopted in many European countries reflects a view that organisational and social performance depends on the extent to which the HRM system effectively manages a variety of stakeholders. Rather than viewing SHRM as a process which tightly aligns internal and external factors to corporate strategy for the purpose of reaping financial rewards, in the more advanced stages proposed above, an organisation explicitly adopts this broader stakeholder view. Human resource activities and processes support the engagement of a variety of stakeholders, including employees and communities in the development of the desired culture.

Stakeholder relationships

The management of a range of internal and external stakeholders is at the heart of environmental management (Freeman 1984, p. 46; Savage, Timothy, Whitehead & Blair 1991, p. 61). Central to stakeholder management are relationships between the stakeholders and the flow of communication between them. These stakeholder relationships represent a 'complex interplay of shifting, ambiguous and contested relationships' (Gao & Zhang 2006, p. 725).

Buysse and Verbeke (2002) state that in order to manage stakeholders the important stakeholders need to be identified and the most important ones selected. Then investment and reallocation of resources in a number of areas, including technology, the strategic planning process, routine-based management systems, processes and employee skills and capabilities will need to be made.

Building relationships with stakeholders

Finally, a long-term vision that broadens the relationship between the stakeholders and leaders in environmental management could work with regulators to develop environmental rules. The Accountability Standard 1000 (AA1000) specifies that stakeholder engagement involves organisations building relationships with stakeholders through processes such as dialogue, involvement in defining the terms of engagement, providing sufficient information and time to make informed decisions and conditions that enable stakeholders to present their views (Gao & Zhang 2006, p. 726).

Culture change

Culture change is at the heart of the creation of an organisation which is seeking to be sustainable in economic, social, human and environmental terms.

Facilitating culture change

Culture change can be facilitated by the HRM processes that engage people who do the work, define the activities to be performed, reward and compensate people, influence the way people are involved in the workplace, foster learning and particular knowledge creation and transfer, and provide feedback on performance and involvement in the workplace. According to the features of SHRM discussed previously, these HR processes are interrelated and need to provide consistent messages about the sort of behaviour required in the organisation (Schuler 1992).

Values statements

However, these processes are not value free. Choices about the development and implementation of HR policies reflect values which are either explicitly stated in documents such as codes of conduct or policy statements, or implicitly embedded in decisions. A stated policy on the values which should be reflected in employee behaviour in the workplace provides an explicit guide to employees. Such a statement captures the desired obligations to others within the organisation when engaging with external stakeholders and beyond. When the natural environment is considered as part of an organisation's moral responsibility it has the potential to change the choices managers and employees make.

Westpac's code of conduct

At Westpac (an Australian bank) sustainability is regarded as an overarching management approach requiring understanding the true value-drivers of the business, the need to operate according to ethical standards and to take a broad view of risk and opportunity (Westpac 2007a; Westpac 2007b).

The financial institution's dedication to sustainability is reflected in its detailed document 'Our Principles' which specifies how members of Westpac should behave with regard to governance and ethics, employee practices, customer practices, care for the environment, community involvement and supply chain management. It states that 'Woven throughout everything we do are our values of teamwork, integrity and achievement'.

Westpac states that profitability and improved performance outcomes will be achieved through quality people supported by performance management processes, employee commitment and behaviours that reflect the Westpac values. Trust between a variety of stakeholders is at the heart of Westpac success. The Code of Conduct outlines seven principles which build the trust. These principles are:

- acting with honesty and integrity;
- respecting the law and acting accordingly;
- respecting confidentiality and not misusing information;
- valuing and maintaining professionalism;
- working as a team;
- managing conflicts of interest responsibly; and
- being a good corporate citizen (Westpac 2007a).

Explicit principles and codes of conduct such as Westpac's 'Our Principles' specify the way in which people should work together, the way they should be managed, the promotion of equal opportunity, diversity, training, learning and development, work–life balance, occupational health and safety, job restructuring, protecting employee entitlements, fair remuneration, respectful and dignified working conditions and freedom of association (Westpac 2007b).

Role of leaders and managers

The statement of desired values makes explicit the behaviours expected and is an essential first step in the building of the desired culture. However, this formal statement is not enough to further the development of these behaviours. Leaders and managers are required to role model required behaviour (Thomas, Schermerhorn & Dienhart 2004), publicly commit to espoused values, provide the necessary resources to train employees in behaviour that reflects those values, and talk to employees about the values (Gagne, Gavin & Tully 2005).

Formal assessments of corporate culture, identification of the desired culture and actions taken to reduce the gap between the two cultures can assist in providing a further means of enabling employees to internalise desired organisational values.

SHRM and the development of skills towards furthering sustainability and stakeholder management

The successful implementation of the human resource processes discussed above requires certain ways of thinking, communicating and operating in the workplace.

Relationships between individuals

Individuals require a view of the world which reflects an understanding of the inter-relationships between individuals, groups, organisations and the environment (Heron 1999, p. 312-313).

They also need to have:

- high levels of self knowledge;
- respect for individual differences;
- an ability to innovate, learn, and to share with others; and
- an ability to work in teams.

Relationships between individuals are therefore essential for understanding issues and dynamics in organisations, society and the planet (Taylor 2007, p. 21). The provision of information and knowledge about the consequences of their actions on the wider society and on the environment can assist in the development of this broader understanding and the process of collaborative learning.

The political nature of society and management

Decisions about the treatment of humans and the environment typically reflect the systems of power and privilege embedded in social and economic institutions (Steingard 2005, p. 231). Consequently individuals need to recognise the political nature of society and management.

Understanding values and assumptions

Progress towards sustainability is a normative, values-based, and overtly political process which appears to clash with a supposedly neutral, value-free story of management (Alvesson & Willmott 1996). Individuals and leaders therefore need to develop techniques to understand the nature of the values and assumptions embedded in existing frameworks and understandings. They need to explore social, political, economic, cultural, technological and environmental forces that foster or impede sustainability These techniques include:

- critical thinking and reflection;
- affective competence;
- collaborative learning;
- participation in partnerships and decision making;
- visioning and imagining, and
- systemic thinking.

Critical thinking

Critical thinking and reflection facilitate uncovering taken-for-granted assumptions. It requires abilities to uncover the real meaning of information and messages, to formulate a response to the information or message and not to take information at face value.

Affective competence

These abilities enable confronting and challenging what is taken as 'truth' and what is regarded as 'logical'. In order to do this, individuals need to be attuned to their feelings (*affective competence*) and be aware how these influence their interpretation and response to an issue. It requires individuals to take responsibility for and accept a range of emotions. This is more than emotional intelligence—rather individuals 'have intelligent ways of managing their feeling life' which assists with the process of change required for environmental sustainability (Taylor 2007, p. 86).

Collaborative learning

Working and learning for environmental sustainability occurs when individuals participate in decision making, in partnerships and with a range of stakeholders. All of these collaborative activities require interpersonal skills such as the ability for immediacy of response, attentiveness to others, capacity for self management, openness to new experiences and openness to others (Taylor 2007, p. 112-3).

Participation in partnerships and decision making

Participation in decision making can take a variety of forms. It can involve individuals merely being informed of a decision or involve active participation in the processes which lead to the outcome.

Participation requires individuals to be aware of the different power relations between the groups. The skills required for effective participation in decision making include:

- building knowledge through dialogue about the issues and problems;
- confidence to share knowledge and negotiate with others;
- persuasion skills;
- conflict management skills;
- an ability to think through problems; and
- patience. Patience is essential (Tilbury & Wortman 2004, p. 54–56).

Visioning and imagining

Before a process of change towards an environmentally sustainable world can occur, such a world needs to be imagined. Individuals need to imagine or vision what such a world would look like. They need to explore what the characteristics of their preferred future or futures would be and examine how realistic this is.

Change to this future could require a re-evaluation of lifestyle, values and priorities (Tilbury & Wortman 2004, ix). The envisioning or imaginative process can enhance and integrate any learning that the individual has achieved (Taylor 2007, p. 82-3). It can also be driven by imagining what sort of world they don't want in the future.

A good example is the Tata Iron and Steel Company (Tata Steel), India's oldest, largest, yet most environmentally aware steel plant. The founder of Tata Steel, J. N. Tata had a clear vision of the environmental and social context in which the steel plant would operate. He envisioned a city with wide streets, many trees, gardens and shade. Tata Steel is located in Jamshedpur, which is now a 'model for the harmonious co-existence of industry and environment' (Sarhkar 2005, p. 194). In India, Tata Steel takes the lead in maintaining the parks and places of interest.

Systemic thinking

Systemic thinking involves synthesising information and building a whole picture to foster an understanding of the interconnections, relationships and dynamic processes. When this is done it 'helps (individuals) see how the effects of even a simple action can have effects on social, economic or environmental conditions beyond the original intention across time and geographic space' (Tilbury & Wortman 2004, p. 89).

Systemic thinking requires individuals to be inquisitive, questioning and empathic, and to accept feedback. Rather than focusing on a single, linear cause and effect, systemic thinking requires individuals to look for multiple influences and interactions, question their assumptions, seek out deeper issues that might be influencing the issue, and at the same time look to the big picture.

Living systems

An extension of this systems view is the notion that there is a strong level of interdependence between all the elements of the system at a number of levels. Living systems develop new patterns of organising that cannot be predicted from past experience. Systems are therefore 'self organising'. They are a reflection not only of the elements of the system, but also of ourselves (Senge, Scharmer, Jaworski & Flowers 2005, p. 201).

A community of leaders

Unilever Foods Asia (UFA) is seeking to develop a 'community of leaders' and a company mission that is infused with strong personal values.

Learning journeys

UFA uses learning journeys through different parts of Asia to enable its high performing staff to understand themselves and other people, and at the same time create a 'collective consciousness'.

It encourages people to learn about their motives, ambitions and themselves through traditional instruments such as personality tests, 360 degree feedback and coaching, and through storytelling about their life histories and the lessons they have learnt while on these journeys. The sharing of stories builds a sense of commonality and consensus. Using the process of 'dialogue', individuals are able to confront 'difficult issues' that would normally be avoided. There is also time for reflection and time to observe how the collective is operating.

One such journey was a trip through India involving 17 'study groups' living in different communities, such as the Dalai Lama's monastery in Dharmashala, Mother Teresa's hospital, and cloth spinning communities. The participants worked through a study guide using their five senses and a sixth one, intuition, to identify how these communities functioned (Mirvis & Gunning 2005).

Skills development

In order for an organisation to enhance its social, human and environmental outcomes, as well as its financial results, employees will require the above skills and personal attributes. This has implications for the criteria used in recruitment and selection, performance management, development of training, development and learning opportunities and reward and recognition initiatives. It has implications for role and job structures which should ideally facilitate the development and application of skills such as critical reflection, systems thinking and participation.

Ethical leadership

A critical aspect of SHRM is the attention to developing and appointing leaders who 'understand themselves', have a commitment to working collaboratively, and who see the decision-making process as a way of enhancing more than just their own interests and business outcomes (Mitroff & Denton 1999; Sinclair 2006; Steingard 2005, p. 235). This form of leadership has been labelled by Resick, Hanges, Dickson and Mitchelson (2006) as ethical leadership.

Six attributes characterise ethical leadership:

- character and integrity,
- ethical awareness,
- community and people orientation,
- motivating,
- encouraging,
- empowering and managing ethical accountability (Resick *et al.* 2006, p. 346).

Analysis of the data of the GLOBE study which involved 17,000 middle managers in 931 organisations in 62 societies explored ethical leadership in terms of four attributes:

- character and integrity;
- altruism;
- collective motivation; and
- encouragement.

The analysis found all four attributes were supported to differing degrees in all cultures.

Character/integrity was supported most strongly in the Nordic European countries, while South East Asian societies endorsed the altruism attribute most strongly. Latin American and Anglo societies supported collective motivation more than other societies, in particular Middle Eastern societies. Ethical leadership in Middle East countries would most likely involve behaviour that models and respects Islamic values (Resick *et al.* 2006).

Case study

SHRM and sustainability in the Asia Pacific region

PricewaterhouseCoopers' approach to leadership development for its most senior leaders embodies many of the principles that link SHRM to sustainability.

Although the program operates globally, its management is increasingly regionalised, with the Asia Pacific program (the 'Eastern Cluster' in PWC terms) being coordinated from the Melbourne office. Within the program employees who have recently achieved the status of 'partners', or are about to become partners, engage with local communities in developing countries to apply PWC expertise to development projects. The actions are typically designed to address problems of poverty, disease, environmental degradation and violence. For example, in Laos, a PWC team helped a local company set up electric power generation from renewable resources for communities that were isolated from the national grid. Another PWC team then went back to Laos to boost the company's business planning capacity so that it could expand the project to 40 isolated villages.

While the program appears to be philanthropic in nature it draws heavily on the resource-based view of the firm and is primarily concerned with building capacity both in the community and within the leadership of PWC.

For PWC, the program has been a significant and longer-term investment. Since 2002, 120 senior staff and partners have been taken off line, most of them for three months. The opportunity cost in billable hours for a three-month period is about AUD$2 million per staff member. However, the resource-based view is primarily concerned with the increased capacity that such an investment generates. As such, the experience is designed to be transformational for the individual in the short term and for the company culture in the medium term.

The program is carefully designed to increase self awareness and to concentrate critical self reflection. The management of the program includes a careful selection process followed by an induction phase where the successful candidates are introduced to the underlying themes of diversity, sustainability and leadership. The teams are then sent into the field, where they negotiate the project with other stakeholders and implement the action. Once the PWC teams have finished the field assignment there is a period of guided reflection in order to help make tacit learning explicit.

PWC has assessed program participants as developing a more mindful approach to leadership, a stronger sense of vocation, and a desire to leave a legacy.

As the program has evolved, PWC has continuously reflected on the meaning and purpose of the program. Its explicit goals have emerged as generating a more globally responsible style of leadership. For PWC global responsibility means an understanding of the consequences of action throughout the global system and a more inclusive sense of responsibility that takes into account a wider array of interests and needs.

A sense of responsibility is a matter of personal volition, so deep emersion in a challenging and foreign experience is critical and formative. The program uses diversity to sharpen the challenge to embedded assumptions. Each PWC team is made up of three or four leaders each from a different culture. In the field, leaders must negotiate reality with stakeholders from vastly different cultures. Pless and Maak (2008, p. 65) document one such experience:

> *'I had a similar "evolving perspective" during my experience – our work was to conduct a micro-business case study of rural villages to provide data and guidance in determining which villages should receive electricity when a hydro power system was constructed. We had initially thought that bringing electricity would of course be good for these villages and would allow them to be happier and more developed. After some time observing the simple life that they lived without electricity and without being connected to the outside world we began to feel that perhaps providing electricity and connectivity would not be that good an idea since it would likely change and perhaps corrupt the wonderfully simple life that people enjoyed.'*

The capacity of leaders to consider not only the *how* of implementation but the value base behind implementation and the effects on stakeholders with different world views is one of the outcomes that PWC is seeking from this HR investment.

Such dramatic common experience has built a global community of leadership within PWC, which it frames as an 'alumni'. Alumni is a term that symbolically communicates the learning objective of the program. Alumnus is a continuous, individual status. While the alumnus stays with the organisation, the status of alumnus supports the ongoing professional identity of the individual as one who has adopted a more global sense of responsibility. PWC runs regular networking events to strengthen ties between members of the alumni. Through this process the leadership principles and values assimilated though the experience become more durable.

Transformative experiences, however, tend to have unpredictable consequences. Some alumni have so thoroughly reassessed their assumptions that they no longer want the high profile, fast-paced life of the PWC partner or the rewards that it offers, and turnover has increased as a result of the program.

A common element of self awareness of those that stay with PWC is a sense that they are stewards of the company's moral legitimacy in the world. They are better equipped to provide ethical leadership because the projects force them into situations which challenge and clarify accepted ethical principles.

For example, many of the projects put them into contact with confronting issues such as child labour, incest, and other exploitative relationships. They need to distinguish between what is universally wrong, what is culturally relative, and the means by which people can attempt to give legitimacy to practice.

Between 2005 and 2009 a series of teams has worked with Hagar International in Cambodia, an organisation creating social enterprises that generate income for women and children who have been victims of abuse, violence and/or trafficking. PWC teams have been working with Hagar on its strategic direction. Their aim is to help victims find rehabilitation by providing supportive economic empowerment.

Working in partnership with a number of groups also develops networking capability. A PWC team worked with an organisation called Gram Vikas, based in the Indian region of Orissa. Gram Vikas works for sustainable rural development. The pilot PWC team worked with Gram Vikas to develop a capacity for strategic

> networking. Later PWC teams have helped Gram Vikas extend its networks further by engaging with organisations in other regions. Gram Vikas' networks now reach hundreds of thousands of people.
>
> These longer-term relationships also build communities of practice. Because the means for improvement is collaborative learning, the program not only builds the human capital of PWC, but also that of the NGOs and the community representatives that engage in the process. Important leadership skills gained by participants include increased self knowledge and affective competence, the capacity to share and work in teams, a more effective innovation process, an ability to build relationships, more participative decision making and a respect for individual differences. PWC has found that these capacities persist in the work place and give form to a more collaborative learning culture within the company.
>
> PWC is a powerful company and its executives are powerful people. The cultural shift aims to match this power with a sense of responsibility. Because the program is focused on development and gives status to indigenous knowledge, leaders learn to formulate visions which have a broader horizon and are composed of multiple elements. The communities themselves tend to develop a more positive, futuristic orientation and consequently optimism grows.
>
> The task-focused, KPI-driven nature of the PWC executive is tempered by a longer-term perspective and patience. As a rite of passage to partnership within the company, participation in the program influences the participants to attribute status to the values that underpin the program. Even the most sophisticated players need time, complete emersion in alternative realities, and guided reflection to internalise the new values.

Conclusion

There is strong reason to believe that Strategic Human Resource Management has a role to play in any organisation's efforts to become more sustainable. To become a 'sustaining organisation' (i.e. in Dunphy et al.'s (2003) terms), the organisation must add to the life of those with whom it interacts and must operate in ways which renew its internal resources including its people.

The actual connections between investment in human resource management and sustainability need to be elucidated in order for SHRM to fulfil this promise and receive the recognition that it merits. A better appreciation of these links will provide additional reason for organisations to commit resources to building their core strength.

Examined through a sustainability lens there are a number of HR practices that combine to build a sense of responsibility across organisations that wish to achieve higher levels of sustainability. These include:

- managing for diversity;
- networking;
- relationship building;
- group learning processes such as action research;
- affective competence;
- participative decision making; and
- stakeholder engagement.

The outcome that can be expected is thinking that is visionary, futures oriented and systems focused. The cultures that emerge include a sense of responsibility which is more global, a performance ethic which is broader, and an execution capacity which copes more easily with complexity and challenge.

Discussion questions

1. Is sustainability something that needs to be driven by powerful elites within organisations or does it have the characteristics of a social movement that drives leadership?

2. How do we know when we are part of an organisation which is sustaining of its human resources and environment?

3. What terms can be used to discuss an organisation's sustainability that will both meet its interests and potentially avoid the prejudices of sceptics?

4. How might an organisation maintain a focus on the long-term issues of sustainability in the face of short-term crisis?

References

Albinger, HS & Freeman, SJ 2000 'Corporate Social Performance and Attractiveness as an Employer to Different Job Seeking Populations' *Journal of Business Ethics*, vol. 28, no. 3, December.

Alvesson, M & Wilmott, H 1996, *Making Sense of Management: a critical introduction*, Sage, London.

Antal, A & Sobczak, A 2004 'Beyond CSR: organisational learning for global responsibility' *Journal of General Management*, vol. 32, no. 2, pp. 77-98.

Avery, G 2005, *Leadership for Sustainable Futures*, Edward Elgar, Cheltenham, UK.

Bachaus, KB, Stone, BA & Heiner, K 2002 'Exploring the relationship between corporate social performance and employer effectiveness', *Business and Society*, vol. 41, no. 3.

Becker, BE & Huselid, MA 1999, 'Overview: strategic human resource management in five leading firms', *Human Resource Management*, vol. 38, no. 4.

Becker, BE, Huselid, MA, Pickus, PS & Spratt, MF 1997, 'HR as a source of shareholder value: Research and recommendations', *Human Resource Management*, vol. 36, no. 1.

Beer, M, Spector, B, Lawrence, P, Mills, D & Walton, R *1985, Human Resources Management: A General Managers Perspective*, Free Press, New York.

Benn, S & Dunphy, D 2004 'Case Study in Corporate Sustainability Fuji Xerox Eco Manufacturing Centre Sydney, Australia', Special issue, Corporate Sustainability and Innovation: Governance, Development, Strategy and Method, *International Journal for Innovation Research Policy Analysis and Best Practice*, ed., A Griffiths, vol. 6, no. 2.

Boxall, P 1998, 'Achieving competitive advantage through human resource strategy: towards a theory of industry dynamics', *Human Resource Management Review*, vol. 8, no. 3.

Branco, MC & Rodrigues, LL 2006, 'Corporate Social Responsibility and Resource-Based Perspectives', *Journal of Business Ethics*, vol. 69, no. 2, December.

Bruntland, G (ed) 1987, *Report of the World Commission on Environment and Development: Our Common Future*, Oxford University Press, Oxford.

Buysse, K & Verbeke, A 2002, 'Proactive Environmental Strategies: A Stakeholder Management Perspective', *Strategic Management Journal*, 24.

Dahlsrud, A 2006, 'How Corporate Social Responsibility is Defined: an Analysis of 37 Definitions', *Corporate Social Responsibility and Environmental Management.*

Daily, B & Huang, S 2001 'Achieving sustainability through attention to human resource factors in environmental management', *International Journal of Operations and Production Management*, vol. 21, no. 2.

Delery, JE & Doty, H 1996, 'Modes of theorizing in strategic human resource management: Tests of universalistic, contingency and configurational performance predictions', *Academy of Management Journal*, vol. 39, no. 4.

Dow Jones (a), *Dow Jones Sustainability World Index Factsheet*, October 2009, accessed 20 November 2009, <http://www.sustainability-index.com/djsi_pdf/publications/Factsheets/SAM_IndexesMonthly_DJSIWorld.pdf>.

Dow Jones (b), *Dow Jones Sustainability Asia Pacific Index Factsheet*, October 2009, accessed 20 November 2009, <http://www.sustainability-index.com/djsi_pdf/publications/Factsheets/SAM_IndexesMonthly_DJSIAP.pdf>.

Dowling, P & Schuler, R 1990, 'Human Resource Management', in Blanpain, R (ed) *Comparative Labour Law and Industrial Relations in Industrialised Market Economies*, vol. 2, Klumer Law and Taxation Publishers, Boston.

Dunphy, D, Benveniste, J, Griffiths, A & Sutton, P 2000 (eds), *Sustainability: Corporate Challenges of the 21st Century*, Allen and Unwin.

Dunphy, D, Griffiths, A & Benn, S 2003, *Organizational Change for Corporate Sustainability*, Routledge, London.

Elkington, J 1997, *Cannibals with Forks: The Triple Bottom Line of 21st Century Business*, USA, New Society Publishers.

Equator Principles Steering Committee 2009, http://www.equator-principles.Com, accessed 5 March 2010.

Freeman, RE 1984, *Strategic management: A stakeholder approach*, Prentice-Hall, Englewood Cliffs, NJ.

Freidman, M 1970, 'The social responsibility of business is to increase profits, *New York Times Magazine*, September 13, p. 32.

Gagne, M, Gavin, JH & Tully, GJ 2005, 'Assessing the Cost and Benefits of Ethics: Exploring a Framework', *Business and Society Review*, 110, 2.

Gao, SS & Zhang, JJ 2006, 'Stakeholder engagement, social auditing and corporate sustainability', *Business Process Management Journal*, vol. 12, no. 6.

Greening, DW & Turban, DB 2000, 'Corporate Social Performance As Competitive Advantage in Attracting Workforce', *Business & Society*, vol. 39, no. 3.

Henderson, D 2001, *Misguided Virtue: False Notions of Corporate Social Responsibility*, New Zealand Business Roundtable, Wellington, New Zealand.

Heron, J 1999, *The Complete Facilitators Handbook,* Kogan Page, London.

Mirvis, P & Gunning, L 2005, 'Creating a Community of Leaders', *Organizational Dynamics*, vol. 35, no. 1.

Mitroff, II & Denton, EA 1999, 'A study of spirituality in the workplace', *Sloan Management Review*, 40, 83-92.

Orlitzky, M, Schmidt, FL & Rynes, SL 2003, 'Corporate Social Financial Performance: A Meta-Analysis', *Organizational Studies*, vol. 24, no. 3.

Perez, R 2003, 'About 'Global Responsibility' in Management', *Corporate Governance,* vol. 3, 3:78-89.

Peterson, DK 2004, 'The Relationship between Perceptions of Corporate Citizenship and Organizational Commitment', *Business & Society*, vol. 43, no. 3.

Pfeffer, J 1998, *The Human Equation*, Harvard Business School Cambridge, MA.

Pless, N & Maak, T 2009, 'Responsible Leaders as Agents of World Benefit: learnings from 'Project Ulysses'', *Journal of Business Ethics,* vol. 85, pp. 59-71.

Resick, CJ, Hanges, PJ, Dicksonand, MW, Mitchelson, JK 2006, 'A Cross Cultural Examination of the Endorsement of Ethical Leadership', *Journal of Business Ethics*, vol. 63.

Royal, C & O'Donnell, L 2005, 'Embedding Human Capital analysis in the investment process: A human resources challenge', *Asia Pacific Journal of Human Resources*, vol 43: 1, pp. 117-136.

Sarhkar, R 2005, 'Environmental Initiatives at Tata Steel: Greenwashing or Reality?', in Hooker, J, Kolk, A & Marsden, P (eds), *Perspectives on International Corporate Responsibility*, Carnegie Borsch Institute, Philosophy Documentation Centre, Virginia.

Savage, GT, Timothy, N, Whitehead, C & Blair, JD 1991, 'Strategies for assessing and managing organisation stakeholders', *Academy of Management Executive*, vol. 5, no. 2.

Schnietz, KE & Epstein, MJ 2005, 'Exploring the financial value of a reputation for corporate social responsibility', *Corporate Reputation Review*, vol 7, no 4, January, pp. 327-345(19).

Schon, D 1983, *The Reflective Practitioner Basic Books*, New York.

Schon, D 1987, *Educating the Reflective Practitioner*, Jossey-Bass, San Francisco.

Schuler, R 1992, 'Strategic Human Resource Management: Linking the People with the strategic needs of the business', *Organizational Dynamics*, Summer.

Senge, P, Scharmer, CO, Jaworski, J & Flowers, S 2005, *Presence: Exploring profound change in people, organizations and society*, Nicholas Brealey Publishing, London.

Sinclair, A 2006, *Leadership for the disillusioned*, Allen and Unwin, Crows Nest.

Snedden, C, Howarth, R, & Norgaard, N 2006, 'Sustainable Development in a Post Bruntland World', *Ecological Economics*, 57 (2): 253 – 268.

Sparrow, P, Schuler, RS & Jackson, SE 1994, 'Convergence or divergence: human resource practices and policies for competitive advantage worldwide', *International Journal of Human Resource Management*, vol. 5, no. 2, May.

Steingard, DS 2005, 'Spiritual-Informed Management Theory: Towards Profound Possibilities for Inquiries and Transformation', *Journal of Management Inquiry*, vol. 14, no. 3.

Taylor, B 2007, *Learning for Tomorrow: Whole Person Learning*, Oasis Press, West Yorkshire.

Thevenet, M 2003, 'Global Responsibility and Individual Exemplarity', *Corporate Governance,* 3(3):114-125.

Thomas, T, Schermerhorn, JR & Dienhart, JW 2004, 'Strategic Leadership of Ethical Behaviour in Business', *Academy of Management Executive*, May.

Tilbury, D & Wortman, D 2004, *Engaging people in sustainability*, IUCN, Gland Switzerland and Cambridge, UK.

Van Marrewijk, M 2001, *The Concept and Definition of Corporate Responsibility*, Triple P Performance Centre, Amsterdam.

Van Marrewijk, M 2003, 'Concepts and Definitions of CSR and Corporate Sustainability: Between Agency and Communion', *Journal of Business Ethics*, 44.

Wahba, H 2007, 'Does the market value corporate environmental responsibility? An empirical examination', *Corporate Social Responsibility and Environmental Management*.

Walsh, JP, Weber, K & Margolis, JD 2003, 'Social Issues and Management: Our Lost Cause', *Journal of Management*, 29, 6.

Westpac 2007a, *ESG Report Our Principles for doing business*, <http://www.westpac.com.au/internet/publish.nsf/content/WICRST=Our+Principles>.

Westpac 2007b, *Stakeholder Impact Report*, accessed 26 August 2008, <http://www.westpac.com.au/internet/publish.nsf/content/WISCRSR=2007+Stakeholder+IMpact+Report>.

Wilkinson, A, Hill, M & Gollan, P 2001, 'The sustainability debate', *International Journal of Operations & Production Management*, vol. 21.

Chapter 6

THE BUSINESS CASE FOR HUMAN CAPITAL METRICS

Loretta O'Donnell & Carol Royal

OBJECTIVES

By the completion of the chapter you should be able to:

1. clarify the *what, how* and *why* of HR metrics, as we need to understand *what it is we are measuring*;

2. explain why human capital of listed companies is becoming increasingly strategic to CEOs, boards and investors;

3. use a range of human capital models (superficial aspects of human capital can be measured using traditional accounting and quantitative data);

4. appreciate the importance of human capital in determining the future financial sustainability of listed firms, and its relevance for the human resource management profession;

5. recognise that human capital patterns in organisations are a valuable lead indicator of future financial performance;

6. apply Bassi and McMurrer's (2007) attributes of measurement systems to human capital metrics; and

7. identify the importance of the value created by human capital (rather than the costs of managing and accounting for human capital) which presents the most compelling argument for systematic human capital analysis by investors.

Chapter 6 – The Business Case for Human Capital Metrics

DEFINITIONS

Human capital: Human capital refers to the sustainability of people management systems which are likely to have an impact on the share price of a firm.

Sustainability: 'Sustainable' human resource management systems are those which are internally consistent with a firm's strategy and with the broader context in which the firm is operating (Royal & O'Donnell 2005a, p. 3).

Human capital v. social capital: The term 'human capital' is used here to define the practices used in organisations which work towards the long-term sustainability of organisations. It is distinguishable from the more commonly used term 'social capital' which is defined by Dunphy *et al.* (2000, p. 6) as human sustainability, which implies building human capability and skills for sustainable high level organisational performance, and for community and societal well being.

Human capital v. employee engagement: While the literature concerning the concept of 'employee engagement' is increasingly compelling, it is an incomplete proxy for human capital *per se*. Human capital is broader than employee engagement, and incorporates management systems of recruitment, retention, training, performance management and knowledge management.

Intangible assets: Human capital is a subset of the concept of intangible assets. The International Accounting Standards (IAS) Board defines intangibles as an identifiable non-monetary asset without physical substance, held for use in the production and supply of goods or services, for rental to others or for administrative purposes. One International Accounting Standard (Number 38) prescribes that an intangible asset is a resource controlled by an enterprise as a result of past events, from which future economic benefits are expected to flow to the enterprise (Pitkanen 2006).

Human capital metrics: Human capital metrics can be seen broadly as a component of a firm's risk management, which is an essential component of management particularly since the GFC corporate collapses.

Risk management: Risk management is defined by Standards Australia (1999, p. iii) as follows:

> *'To be most effective, risk management should become part of the organisation's culture. It should be integrated into the organisation's philosophy, practices and business plans rather than be viewed or practiced as a separate program. When this is achieved, risk management becomes the business of everyone in the organisation.'*

It is this underlying principle which informs this chapter's approach to human capital metrics.

Introduction

In recent years, the human resources profession has been challenged to adopt the language of accounting in order to argue the business case for various initiatives. While much of this trend can help create more evidence-based decision making, we take Ulrich's (1999) view that the HR profession may have fallen into the trap of measuring what it *can* measure rather than what it *should* measure.

Temporal limitations of accounting figures

De Geus (1997) found that long-lived companies recognise the temporal limitations of accounting figures; that profitability was only a 'symptom' of corporate health, and delivering shareholder return on investment has nothing to do with longevity. Collins and Porras (2002) similarly argued that shareholder wealth/profit maximisation is not the driving force or main objective of visionary companies.

Need for human capital indicators

Measurement of a wide range of variables using sophisticated quantitative models failed to forewarn investors and other stakeholders during the global financial crisis (GFC) of 2007–9 (Salmon 2009; Triana 2009; Hubbard 2009; Tett 2009).

While there is always a strong case for robust quantitative measurement, quantitative models alone are not sufficient as a means of articulating and communicating human capital value. Even world-renowned economists now reflect that the financial performance of firms requires a much deeper, more robust understanding of human behaviour than economists previously admitted (Akerlof & Shiller 2009). This admission points to the need for strong, fundamental human capital indicators. Firms such as Google recognise this and use human capital indicators as a key strategic component of the business cycle (Lawrence 2009; Lowe 2009; Girard 2009).

Economic value of intangible assets

This chapter takes what may be considered to be a relatively unusual perspective. Because it is clear that human capital has an impact on future financial performance, it analyses human capital metrics from the perspective of financial markets and the investment community (Bassi & McMurrer 2007; Watson Wyatt 2002).

Particularly in knowledge intensive firms, there is a gap between the book value and the market value of the firm, and that gap tends to consist of different views of intangible assets (Boedker 2005). One subset of intangible assets is human capital (HC). Human capital can be analysed systematically for both managers and employees and provide investors in the financial markets with more transparent ways to make investment decisions.

Employee engagement scores and the value of the firm

An important shift in human capital analysis occurred in 2006 when the Australian investment bank, Macquarie Equities, valued retail banks ANZ and NAB differently as a direct result of their different employee engagement scores (Plakalo 2006). A Macquarie Bank research report found employee engagement scores correlated with better financial performance, including revenue, profit and shareholder returns. The data suggested that companies with an engagement score of 60% or higher had an average five-year shareholder return of more than 20%. Companies with an engagement level below 40% tended to have negative shareholder returns of 10% over the same period (James 2005).

At Insurance Australia Group (IAG), an Australian listed insurance company, engagement scores are the most 'cherished' indicators. KPIs are set at the individual and team level on these scores (Mostyn 2006).

Employee engagement scores were analysed by Harter, Schmidt and Killham (2003), who found some evidence for their validity. In practice, employee engagement surveys are increasingly used as a specific resource, and potentially as a proxy for all forms of human capital analysis (Hatch 2005; James 2005; Jones 2005). This is a mistake, however, as engagement scores by themselves do not reflect the key systems by which people are managed and do not indicate aspects of change management which can be significant to future financial performance. Other models, such as Bassi and McMurrer (2007) and Royal and O'Donnell (2008) are more systems-based and do address some of these concerns.

Pressures for changing the nature of the human capital metrics debate

One of the outcomes of the GFC was a focus on the urgency of creating clearer communication between boards and all stakeholders, including investors.

A series of corporate collapses (for example, the Lehman investment bank in the US and corporate governance issues at James Hardie in Australia) gave rise to a questioning of what boards know, when they know it, and when they are likely to communicate what they know. While boards are increasingly clear on their obligations to disclose price-sensitive information under a regime of continuous disclosure, there are no guidelines on how the information is related to analysing and communicating the value of human capital as a fundamental driver of future firm value.

United Nations Principles for Responsible Investment

At a broad level, however, there are international pressures for increasing the transparency of the investment process. The United Nations Principles for Responsible Investment (UNPRI 2009) are a symbol of the ongoing momentum for change in attitudes to investment. The UNPRI had around $US14 trillion invested under principles of environmental, social, and governance best practice. Socially responsible investment, however, can only be optimised when human capital metrics and other measures of intangible value are as robust as possible.

A survey of Australian superannuation funds noted that all respondents were aware of the UNPRI and that 75% of respondents had either signed the principles or were intending to do so in the next 12 months (Australian Council of Super Investors ESG Survey 2007, p. 5.1). Clearly, these principles are going to have an impact on the Australian and global investment and business community for some time.

The need for clearer lead indicators of financial performance

There are pressures on the finance industry to move beyond the trend to commoditisation in their products and services, and these pressures have generated a need for the analysis of superior intangibles (Bassi & McMurrer 2007; Ackerloff & Shiller 2009). High profile corporate collapses, such as the Lehman investment bank in late 2008, mean that firms need to provide clearer lead indicators of financial performance.

Most traditional human capital metrics and models (such as employee engagement surveys, staff turnover and retention figures, and recruitment success rates), however, cannot be systematically adopted by analysts and fund managers without breaching regulatory boundaries, since those metrics rely on an in-depth understanding of an organisation which can only be gained by access to privileged and confidential company data.

The Australian Stock Exchange works on the principle of transparency, so share price sensitive information of any kind, including human capital information, needs to be communicated promptly to the Exchange by listed companies. Thus, new approaches to human capital metrics will increasingly be needed to comply with investment information needs.

Valuation of intangible assets

Researchers such as Wiig (2004) and Marr (2005) have established the case for both observers and participants in organisations to possess highly sophisticated interpretations of intangibles within organisations. Yet it is ironic that the knowledge required for securities analysts to make investment decisions has traditionally been based on mathematical modelling.

Non-financial factors in investment decisions

In a study of over two hundred active portfolio managers, Bassi, Lev, Low, McMurrer, and Sissfield (2001) found that non-financial insights make up a large proportion of investment decisions. Therefore human capital experts within firms, primarily the HR profession, need to distinguish and report on the capability of the management team to execute strategy. Hence the imperative to understand the 'information on the human capital function that helps them assess rate of return on investment in human resources and predict future performance' (Bassi *et al.* 2001, p. 368) is a critical factor for success for themselves as individual professionals, and for the credibility of the industry as a whole.

Microsoft and Google have valuations based overwhelmingly on intangible assets, including human capital, intellectual property, and ongoing ability to innovate. Investors in these firms need to understand the drivers of value in these knowledge intensive organisations, as traditional investment models based on tangible assets are not sufficiently detailed from the perspective of investment decisions.

Three views on human capital measurement principles

Human capital metrics have traditionally applied quantitative principles from accounting and finance to the human resources function.

Quantitative analysis

It is not surprising that investors generally use a quantitative approach to the analysis of human capital. In a case analysis of investment banking in Australia, over 90% of financial analysts studied had degrees in quantitative disciplines such as econometrics, actuarial studies, economics, engineering, and accounting (Royal & Althauser 2002). In addition, the professional socialisation of financial analysts, via professional associations such as Stockbrokers Australia, has continuous professional development based primarily on quantitative research methods.

Typically, investment analysts develop mastery learning in quantitative analysis. Within investment banking they find that their quantitative skills are rewarded, creating a bidirectional influence on behaviour, personal cognitive factors and environmental factors (similar to DiMaggio and Powell's (1983) concept of the role of professionalization in creating and embedding norms).

Similarly, Scott (2001, p. 57) notes the importance of cultural cognitive processes. These are 'taken-for-granted' notions that pervade the institutional environment so that 'other types of behaviour are inconceivable'. In other words, the analysts contribute to a self-sustaining system which rewards high quality quantitative analysis, often at the expense of high quality qualitative analysis.

Qualitative measures

Given the economic shifts resulting from the GFC, however, there are new opportunities for the HRM profession to create new models of human capital value which are more qualitative, more descriptive, more cognitively complex and better able to predict organisational change and, therefore, provide more reliable lead indicators of future financial performance. Bassi and McMurrer (2007) list their views on the attributes of a human capital measurement system stating that they should be:

- credible;
- descriptive;
- predictive;
- detailed;
- actionable; and
- cost-effective.

The accounting perspective

Alternatively, from an accounting perspective, Mayo (2001) suggests that human capital measures should be 'roughly right' rather than 'precisely wrong', simple to understand, clearly defined and able to be interpreted in the same way. Furthermore, he argues that the process of measurement should:

- have integrity;
- be consistent and reliable;
- have no inherent biases;
- not be based on one person's judgement;
- make sense in the context of other measures;
- focus on what is important and comprise key outputs or be linked to them;
- have the right level of detail for action to be taken;
- be used for tracking change and incorporate data that are useful, provide the right level of detail, show clear ownership by an individual or team, have the right frequency, and provide useful trends and comparisons.

Business measurement theory

Pike and Roos (2004) provide a pure mathematical perspective and suggest that five conditions for business measurements are derived from measurement theory:

- completeness (the attributes must completely describe the company);
- distinctness (which eliminates double counting);
- independence (this concerns the relationship between entities so that aggregation to overarching measures can be undertaken safely);
- agreeability (mapping from an empirical to numeric system); and
- commensurability (measurements must be observed using a ration scale and be normalized onto a common scale).

Need for both quantitative and qualitative measures

Researchers, however, have found that a purely mathematical approach to the analysis of human capital is counterproductive. Pike and Roos (2004), for instance, examined a range of business measurement systems, including direct intellectual capital methods, market capitalization methods, return on asset methods and scorecard methods, and concluded that none of the approaches achieved all five of their measurement conditions.

Other non-mathematical perspectives of human capital value creation are compelling. For instance, Pike and Roos critique the Balanced Scorecard (BSC) approach of Kaplan and Norton (1996) and note:

> '...the BSC does not seek to base itself on the nature of the firm but, instead, takes a strategic focus which at once compromises completeness since the BSC addresses what ought to be at the expense of what actually is. The selection of metrics raises further problems as the most common method of selecting metrics is not a structured and considered process but ... a pragmatic approach resulting from brainstorming. As many metrics as required are developed and care is taken to ensure that they include leading measures, lagging measures and within them a core set which may be benchmarked. There seems to be little attempt to align with measurement theory' (p. 253).

That said, Kaplan and Norton may not have perceived the mathematical measures applied by Pike and Roos to be of significant value. The BSC is widely used by practitioners who have used brainstorming sessions to clarify and articulate appropriate measures to be incorporated into it.

The process of brainstorming itself may have more value than some of the metrics it includes, for example, through gaining employee 'buy in' as part of the consultative process. Pike and Roos cite Rigby (2001), who estimates that more than half of the largest 1,000 global companies use the BSC. This point highlights the value of incorporating both qualitative and quantitative measures of the value of intangible value creation within firms.

International perspectives on the context for human capital metrics

From a global perspective, particularly since the onset of the GFC, it has become increasingly clear that metrics of all kinds are needed to help senior executives

- analyse and predict future financial performance;
- minimise all forms of risk; and
- consider the needs of a broad range of stakeholders, including investors.

While boards are being tasked to consider stakeholders other than shareholders in their decision making, known in the UK as 'enlightened shareholder value' (Ramsay 2005), clearer methods of assessing risk and predicting future value have become essential in the environment in which, some suggest, the crisis was actually caused by seductive but incomplete financial models (Triana 2009, p. xvii).

Need for non-financial measures

In contrast, the head of a $1.5 billion Australian superannuation fund told the authors:

> 'We want to know about human capital, and about managers' backgrounds and experience, because our business is backing management teams' (August 2009).

British accounting academic Mayo (2001) found that non-financial measures can have equal or greater value than monetary/financial measures can. He also found that intangible assets are the 'powerhouse' of value—people drive value. The intrinsic worth of our people comprises the human capital available to the firm. At the same time, that worth is a value-creating asset. All intellectual assets are maintained and grown by people, and without them will wither away. This amounts to employees loaning their personal 'human capital' to the organisation in terms of their individual capability and commitment, personal knowledge and experience.

Irrelevance of traditional HR metrics

Valuation of human capital is a fundamentally different approach from traditional measures of HR which, often by default, measure accomplishment by how busy the HR department has been (Cascio 1991). For instance, some HR teams focus on data such as:

- how many people they have recruited/interviewed;
- how many hours of training they have provided;
- how many grievance procedures they have handled; or
- the average time taken to fill a position.

Not surprisingly there is criticism in the literature of the irrelevance of these traditional HR metrics because such measures are not correlated with important organisation-wide outcomes such as growth, profitability or even customer service (Brown 1999). They are 'flat' measures with no depth; their significance depends on the context that they are viewed in. They may also measure inputs, such as training days, rather than outputs, such as value-added initiatives.

Need for systems to analyse how human capital creates value

These simplistic measures operate at Bloom's (1956) least complex levels of analysis, whereas the needs of contemporary organisations require a system of analysing how human capital creates value, and lead indicators of future financial performance.

The audience of human capital metrics is not merely internal stakeholders. Particularly since the GFC, the audience now includes the investment community, which is increasingly cognisant of the value of human capital in the creation of firm value (Ackerloff & Shiller 2009; Tett 2009).

Failure of traditional approaches to human capital analysis

Traditional approaches to human capital analysis have traditionally fallen into five categories (Mayo 2001, p. 55).

- Attempts to value people as assets (by applying accounting valuation principles to people).
- Creating an index of 'good' HR practices and relating these to business results.
- Statistics about the composition of the workforce and measures of the productivity and output of people.
- Measuring the efficiency of HR functions/processes and the return on investment (ROI) in people initiatives/programs.
- Integrating people-related measures in a performance management framework.

None of these traditional approaches (some of which are illustrated below), however, seek to analyse the fundamental drivers of human capital in ways which can be readily understood by investors.

Human capital data is hard to compare across industry sectors and across individual companies. It is important, therefore, that human capital metrics move away from a focus on simple, easily accessible data to a focus on the management systems which underpin firm performance. Investors need to be able to assess whether a firm can deliver on its stated strategy, and to understand whether management systems are internally consistent with that strategy.

Unlike the more traditional models, a range of contemporary approaches to human capital analysis described below are more focused on fundamental *systems* which create value and provide insights to external stakeholders on potential future firm value.

Traditional approaches to human capital metrics

Traditional approaches to human capital metrics include (Mayo 2001):

- Watson Wyatt's Human Capital Index;
- The European Business Excellence Model;
- Malcolm Baldrige Criteria for Performance Excellence;
- William Mercer's Human Capital Wheel;
- Measuring ROI of Human Capital;
- The Balanced Scorecard;
- The Skandia Navigator;
- The HR Scorecard;
- The Intangible Assets Monitor;
- The Human Capital Monitor; and
- The Intellectual Capital Index.

Watson Wyatt's Human Capital Index

This index is based on a 2001 survey of over 400 Canadian and U.S. companies. The index uses 30 HR practices grouped into five categories. Watson Wyatt found a strong correlation between HR practices and increases in shareholder value over a five-year period.

European Business Excellence Model

This model balances 'enablers' against 'results'. It comprises audit questions resulting in a set of scores placed against an ideal, in the areas of leadership, people, and 'people results. All these elements are found to be significant for business excellence.

Malcolm Baldrige Criteria for Performance Excellence

This process uses 1000 points allocated over seven categories of performance excellence — namely:

- leadership;
- strategic planning;
- measurement, analysis and knowledge management;
- customer and market focus;
- human resource focus;
- process management; and
- business results.

The HR focus category includes:

- work systems;
- employee training and development; and
- employee wellbeing/satisfaction.

These need to be internally consistent to help drive the organisation towards business excellence.

William Mercer's Human Capital Wheel

This model incorporates a wheel divided into six segments:

- people;
- structure;
- processes;
- decision making;
- information flow; and
- reward.

There are concrete measures for each. Changes that have happened in each sector over the past three to five years are plotted on the wheel and are then related to measures of performance and quality.

Measuring ROI of Human Capital

This model compares the ROI of human capital on three levels:

- enterprise;
- process/function; and
- human capital.

It notes appropriate measurement concerns and provides relevant statistical ratios. At the enterprise level, for example, one measure of the ROI on human capital is training and development costs as a percentage of payroll costs. See Figure 6.1.

Figure 6.1 Jac Fitz-Enz's model of Return on Investment on Human Capital

Levels	Concerns	Examples/Ratios	
1. Enterprise level	Measuring the ROI on human capital at the level of enterprise. Using the 'total cost of people remuneration' as denominator, not per headcount	· Total employee costs per FTE · Remuneration per FTE · % of specified types of employee · Employee costs: contingent worker costs	· Training and development costs as a % of payroll costs · Training days per FTE · Attrition rate · Hiring rate

Strategic HRM: Contemporary Issues in the Asia Pacific Region

Levels	Concerns	Examples/Ratios	
2. Process/ function level	Measuring the human contribution to increasing structural capital	· Service · Quality · Productivity	
3. Human capital itself	Measuring the effectiveness of human resources functions	· Costs (per unit of activity) · Time (elapsed per activity) · Quantity (numbers handled)	· Error rates (% of 'right 1st time) · Reaction (levels of satisfaction)

Source: Mayo, p. 47–58.

The Balanced Scorecard

Kaplan and Norton (1996) created a model to balance four 'perspectives' that are the backbone of the scorecard:

- financial;
- customer;
- internal business process; and
- learning and growth.

The model distinguishes between lead and lag measures, and emphasises the need for both kinds of measures. See Figure 6.2.

Figure 6.2 Balanced Scorecard Model

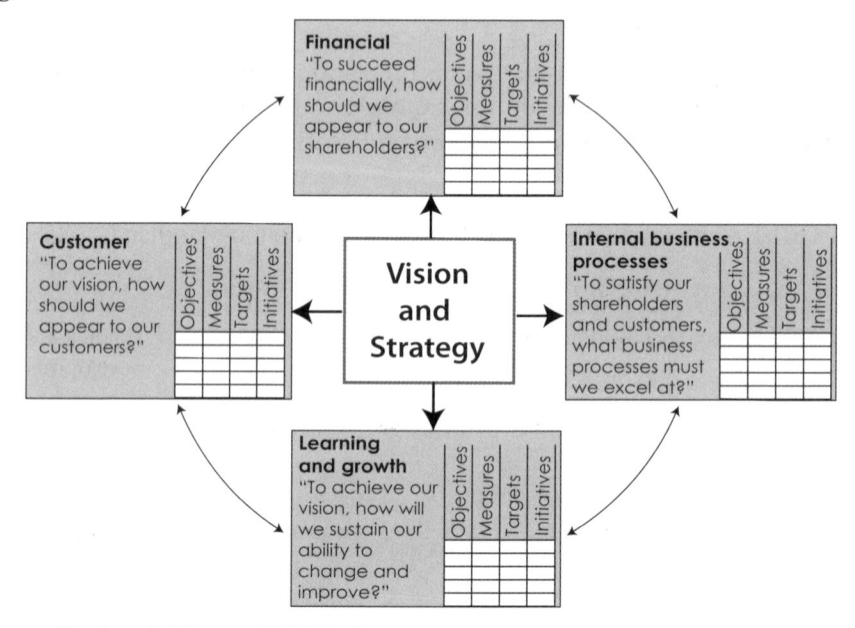

Source: Kaplan & Norton 1996, p. 9.

The Skandia Navigator

The Skandia Navigator is an adaptation of the Balanced Scorecard. Creator Leif Edvinsson (1997) placed 'people' in the centre, as the driver of the four outcomes. He lists a number of possible measures for each area. The model is based on a set of assumptions about market value being made up of a range of tangible and intangible elements, as per Figure 6.3, Components of Market Value.

Figure 6.3 Components of Market Value

```
                        Market value
                       /            \
              Financial capital   Intellectual capital
                                  /            \
                          Human capital    Structural capital
                                           /            \
                                    Customer      Organisational
                                    capital          capital
                                                   /         \
                                            Innovation     Process
                                             capital       capital
                                            /        \
                                    Intellectual   Intangible
                                     property       assets
```

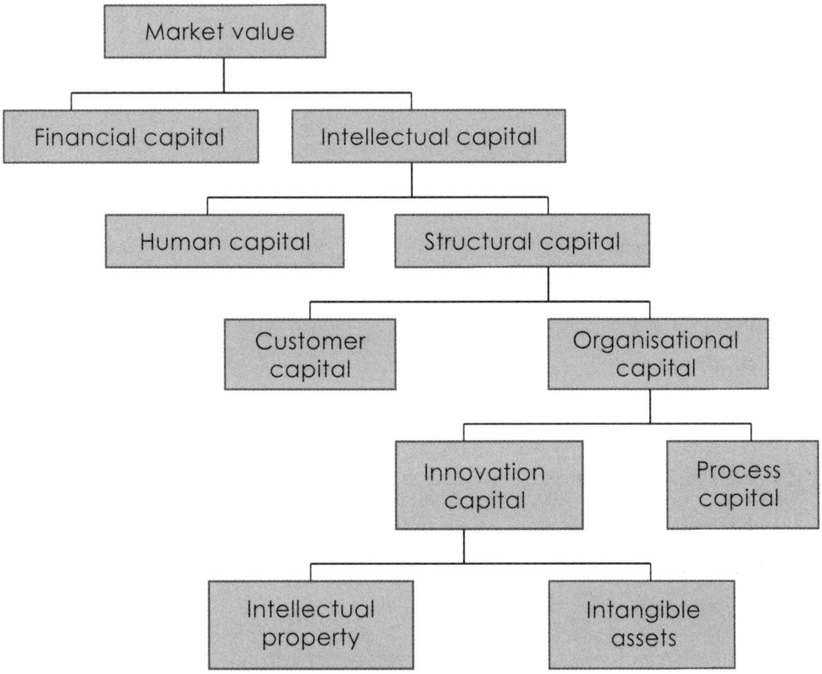

Source: Adapted from Edvinsson 1997.

The HR Scorecard

The HR Scorecard model by Becker *et al.* (2001)) has four components designed to balance the two human resource imperatives of cost control and value creation (see Figure 6.4):

- HR deliverables (% of employees who have requisite competencies, % of turnover of staff, employee behaviour);
- high-performance work systems (competency model as a basis for activity — e.g. design and implement a valid competency model to every element in HR and provide regular performance appraisals);
- HR system alignment (% of selection based on competency model, appropriate retention policies, uniform strategic emphasis tending to align HR elements, HR element index above 80%); and
- HR efficiency measures (cost per hire, lead or lag indicators).

Figure 6.4 The Balanced Scorecard

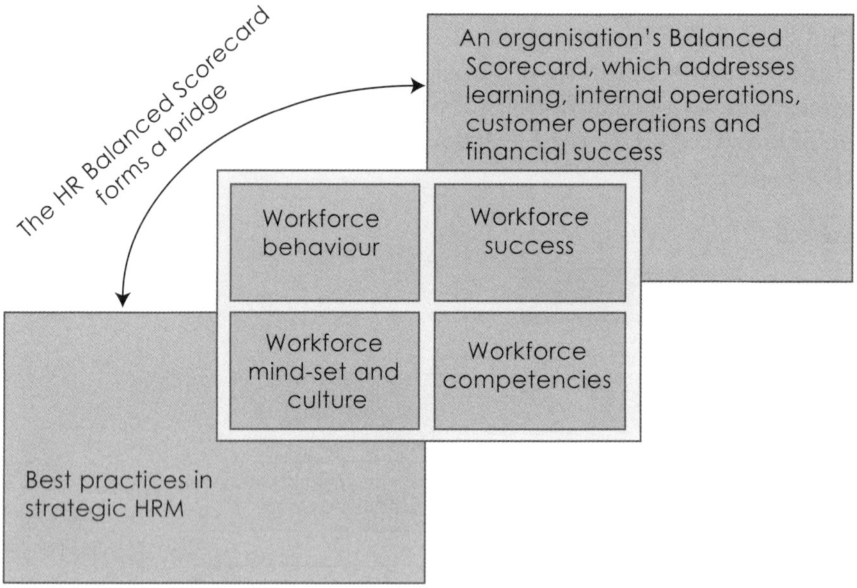

The HR Balanced Scorecard forms a bridge

An organisation's Balanced Scorecard, which addresses learning, internal operations, customer operations and financial success

- Workforce behaviour
- Workforce success
- Workforce mind-set and culture
- Workforce competencies

Best practices in strategic HRM

Source: Becker *et al.* 2001.

The Intangible Assets Monitor

Sveiby (1997) took the three standard components of intellectual capital:

- external structure;
- internal structure; and
- competence

and chose measures for each under three indicators:

- growth/renewal;
- efficiency; and
- stability.

He also developed a 'leverage effect' formula which illustrates the positive ripple effects of strong intangible value within firms.

The Human Capital Monitor

Mayo (2001) offers his own approach, which he calls the Human Capital Monitor (Figure 6.5). Using an adaptation of traditional accounting principles, the monitor is designed to link the intrinsic worth of the human capital available with the working environment. See Figure 6.5.

The Human Capital Monitor focuses on three key areas:

- people as assets;
- people motivation and commitment; and
- people contribution to added value.

Figure 6.5 Human Capital Monitor

People as assets	+	People motivation and commitment	=	People contribution to added value
*Human asset worth = employment costs x IAM/1000 * IAM: capability, potential, contribution, values alignment * Maximising HC: acquisition, retention, growth		The work environment that drives success *Leadership, practical support, the workgroup, learning and development, rewards and recognition*		The value added to each stakeholder *Financial/ Non financial* *Current/Future*

Source: Mayo 2001.

Intellectual Capital Index

Stacey (2001) noted that intellectual capital analysis can be divided into two main categories, defined as human capital and invisible assets, or 'non-thinking' capital. These can readily be analysed, using apparently valid quantitative methods. For instance, human capital can be divided into three main areas:

- competence (e.g. average duration of employment, hours of training per employee, IT literacy);
- attitude (e.g. a leadership index, a motivation index); and
- intellectual agility (e.g. savings from employee suggestions, company diversification index).

The second area of social capital, as distinct from human capital, is often seen as invisible assets and processes, 'non-thinking' capital, such as:

- relationships (e.g. customer retention, length of supplier relationship);
- internal efficiency (e.g. revenues from patents, processes completed without error); and
- renewal and development (percentage of business from new products, new patents filed, training costs per hour per employee).

These types of measures can be combined into a weighted intellectual capital index, which, on the surface, has meaning and rigour. For instance, knowledge in an organisation is more than numbers of hours in training sessions, or number of patents held, even though these are often mistaken for intellectual property. They are mistaken for knowledge itself but knowledge genuinely exists only when it is used in the context of communication between people.

Table 6.1 Summary of ten traditional approaches to human capital metrics

Model	Author(s)	Date	Comments
1. Human Capital Index	Watson Wyatt Worldwide	2001	Indicates human capital systems are a lead indicator of future financial performance.
2. European Business Excellence Model	European Foundation for Quality Management (EFQM)	2009 updated	Compares real human capital situation with ideal benchmarks.
3. Malcolm Baldrige Criteria for Performance Excellence	Baldridge National Quality Program, National Institute of Standards and Technology, MD	2009 updated	Is used for both corporates and not-for-profit organisations to compare standards of quality of management.
4. William Mercer's Human Capital Wheel	William Mercer	1997	Tailored to individual organisations.
5. Return on Investment in Human Capital	Jac Fitz-Enz	2000	Focus on total remuneration rather than headcount as key unit of analysis.
6. Balanced Scorecard	R.S. Kaplan and D.P. Norton	1996	Double loop feedback process to focus attention of management on a small number of critical issues. Widely used across a variety of industry sectors.

Model	Author(s)	Date	Comments
7. Skandia Navigator	Leif Edvinsson	1997	Influential model, developed for one firm, drawing on Kaplan and Norton's ideas. This model is applied globally.
8. HR Scorecard	Brian Becker, Mark Huselid, Dave Ulrich	2001	The HR Scorecard forms a bridge between strategic HRM practices and Balanced Scorecard practices.
9. Human Capital Monitor	Andrew Mayo	2001	Works on the fundamental assumption that human capital is a key strategic asset in organisations. Applies accounting principles to human capital systems.
10. Intellectual Capital Index	R.D. Stacey	2001	Acknowledges that measures of human capital, such as patents, are useful only if they indicate dynamic processes between people in organisations.

Limitations of traditional approaches to human capital metrics

The frameworks outlined in Table 6.1 are helpful but limited. Limitations include:

- the measurement of what they *can* measure rather than what they *should* measure;
- a lack of focus on underlying systems;
- targeting the information needs of internal senior executives rather than the information needs of external stakeholders, such as investors;
- failure to target the need for investors to have lead indicators of future changes in financial performance; and
- failure to incorporate aspects of change management.

In contrast, the three frameworks listed below have been developed to incorporate an investment perspective, while drawing on management systems as a primary unit of analysis.

Systems-based approaches to human capital metrics

Systems based approaches to human capital analysis analyse management systems as the drivers of human capital value creation. Such systems-based approaches include:

- Four Tools for Human Capital Analysis (Royal & O'Donnell 2008);
- the Human Capital Scorecard (Bassi & McMurrer 2007); and
- the Leadership and Management Systems Matrix (O'Donnell & Royal 2009).

Each will now be discussed in turn.

Four tools for human capital analysis

Based on field research in the finance industry, Royal and O'Donnell (2008) derive four tools for human capital analysis. These tools are based on an analysis of management systems, allowing for some comparability across industry sectors and firms while also incorporating aspects of change management.

Tool 1: Mapping human capital using drivers of the value of human capital

Human capital analysts can create a 'human capital map' illustrating the drivers of sustainable people management systems and the importance of various interrelated features that recur throughout a company's history.

Tool 2: Analysing human capital systems using the Human Capital Wheel

After the creating of the human capital map, a further round of detailed research can be conducted using the Human Capital Wheel (Royal & O'Donnell 2008), see Figure 6.6, which incorporates comparisons of critical systems such as corporate governance, recruitment, rewards, leadership, remuneration, career planning and performance management to assess whether these systems are both internally consistent and consistent with an organisation's strategy.

Tool 3: Rating the organisation's human capital using a star rating system

The next step in the human capital analysis process is a five-star rating system, which can be revisited on a regular basis (Royal & O'Donnell 2004). For example, a one-star rated company would have the following characteristics:

- the organisation is not aware of or is operating outside the formal or informal guidelines for industry best practice for its own industry sector;
- HR systems of recruitment, training, career planning and performance management are unsophisticated relative to the pressures of the industry sector and are, in the long term, likely to be unsustainable.

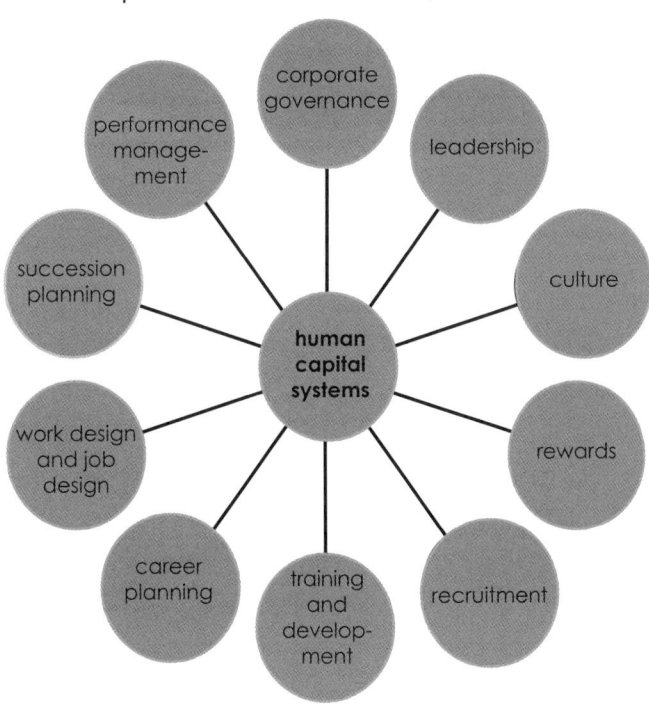

Figure 6.6 Human Capital Wheel

Source: Royal & O'Donnell 2008.

Tool 4: Change Management Matrix

The change leadership style of leadership teams can be plotted on the Dunphy and Stace Change Matrix (2001). This matrix compares the style of change leadership to the scale and urgency of change. As the matrix in Figure 6.7 illustrates, in Stage 1 of the life cycle of an example firm, the pioneer entrepreneur demonstrated a highly collaborative and collegiate form of change leadership.

In contrast, in Stage 2 of the life cycle of this firm, the second CEO is likely to demonstrate a more directive style of change leadership. Stace and Dunphy observe that it is unlikely that firms can stay in the dramatic corporate transformation cell for more than a few years. It is likely, therefore, that in the third stage of the life cycle of this organisation, the next leadership style is likely to revert to a mid-range level as the organisation moves beyond its pioneer phase into a professional bureaucracy or an adhocracy (Mintzberg 1979).

Finally, the second part of this fourth tool considers the strengths, weaknesses, opportunities and threats (SWOT) for understanding an organisation's human capital.

The four tools model enhances the ability of internal and external stakeholders to assess the human capital systems of a listed organisation as one key variable affecting future firm performance.

Figure 6.7 Change leadership analysis – Company XYZ

Style/Scale and urgency of change	Fine tuning at the individual level	Incremental adjustment at the work unit level	Modular transformation at the business unit level	Corporate transformation at the organisational level
collaborative			Stage 1: Pioneer entrepreneur - highly collegiate	
consultative				
directive				Stage 2: Replacement CEO, successful commercial turnaround executive - highly directive
coercive				

Source: Adapted from Stace & Dunphy 2001.

The Human Capital Scorecard

The second systems-based model is the Human Capital Scorecard (see Figure 6.8). Bassi, Lev, Low, McMurrer and Sissfield (2001) found that 35% of investment decisions by professional portfolio managers and traders are based on non-financial information. This means that the training for investment managers lacks the theoretical underpinning to assist them in the non-quantitative aspects of investment decision making.

Later work by Bassi and McMurrer (2007) highlighted that, because of accounting principles which have traditionally focused on tangible rather than intangible assets, human capital is often undervalued within firms. As a result, they found that there is a broad-scale under-investment in people. In other words, firms must invest in human capital despite the pressures of financial markets rather than because of those pressures. They conclude that, while the market penalises organisations for doing 'the right thing' in the short term, it rewards them for it in the long run. This creates a tension between what investors should be measuring and what they typically do measure when analysing companies for investment purposes.

Figure 6.8 Human Capital Scorecard

Financial and non-financial business results				
Leadership practices	Employee engagement	Knowledge accessibility	Workforce optimisation	Learning capacity
1. Communication 2. Inclusiveness 3. Supervisory skills 4. Executive skills 5. Systems	1. Job design 2. Commitment to employees 3. Time 4. Systems	1. Availability 2. Collaboration & teamwork 3. Information sharing 4. Systems	1. Processes 2. Conditions 3. Accountability 4. Hiring decisions 5. Systems	1. Innovation 2. Training 3. Development 4. Value & support 5. Systems

Source: Adapted from Bassi & McMurrer 2007.

Leadership and Management Systems Matrix

The third systems model is the Leadership and Management Systems Matrix (adapted from O'Donnell & Royal 2009). It is a synthesis of a range of approaches highlighting key aspects of leadership styles as firms mature over time. It links those leadership styles with change management themes and with management systems. For instance, in the entrepreneurial stage of an organisation's life cycle, the change management theme is systematic trial and error and the management systems are based on innovation across all products, services and processes.

As the firm matures, however, it may move through a range of leadership styles, including transactional and systems-based. If a strategic realignment is appropriate, it may require a change-agent basis for leadership. Each of these primary leadership styles has relevant change management themes and management systems.

The final style in the matrix is visionary leadership, which can work either to sustain ongoing change or, alternatively, be a force for organisational decline. Following Collins's (2009) stages in organisational decline, these leadership styles are not necessarily sequential and firms can incorporate a range of these different styles in different sequences over time.

Table 6.2 Leadership and Management Systems Matrix

	Leadership style	Change management theme	Management systems
Stage 1	Primary leadership style: Entrepreneurial leadership	Systematic trial and error	Innovation of products, services and processes—all management systems
Stage 2	Transactional leadership	Steady growth	Stability of management systems
Stage 3	Systems based leadership	Divisionalisation—accelerated complex growth, organically or mergers and acquisitions	Reproduction of systems, rapid execution, clarity of core and non core systems
Stage 4	Change agent basis for leadership	Realignment of overall business to new conditions	Openess to change, flexibility, transformational change
Stage 5	Visionary leadership for new strategies	Organisational sustained success or organisational decline	Embedded systems to sustain success—alternatively, no embedded systems implies fragmentation, stagnation and failure

Source: Adapted from O'Donnell & Royal 2009.

The brief case study below illustrates how one organisation, Westpac, analyses and communicates some of these aspects of human capital for internal use and for investors.

Case study

Westpac's approach to communicating human capital

In early 2006, Westpac senior executives briefed financial markets analysts on Westpac's approach to measuring intangibles. In April 2006, Dr David Morgan, then CEO, stated that analysts should consider intangibles such as:

- culture;
- values and links to the community;
- how a firm works to help the environment; and
- issues like customer service

when measuring the worth of a company.

This commitment to broader forms of sustainability, including social sustainability, provides a potential model for other firms to follow.

Westpac has been recognised by the Dow Jones Sustainability Index as a leader in the global banking sector from 2002–2009, including sector leadership from 2002–2006 inclusive. As part of this broad approach to sustainability, Westpac prioritises the process of communicating the creation of intangible value:

> *'There's no doubt the smart analysts are working out the importance of things like employee engagement and voluntary turnover measures as good forward indicators of likely performance. There's no doubt those things are absolutely drivers of financial performance' (Westpac Investor Relations executive, Noel Purcell, quoted by Kitney & Buffini 2006).*

In its April 2006 disclosures to the ASX, the firm also revealed that it saved AUS$50 million a year in employee turnover by introducing flexible leave polices and saved A$2.5 million in lost injury time.

While human capital and broader aspects of social sustainability are part of Westpac's agenda for sustainable growth, previous CEO, Dr David Morgan, has observed it is often very difficult to measure the true worth of such principles.

> *'Because outperformance in the area goes to the heart of our competitive advantage, we will continue to work on better understanding the value linkages between the non-financial performance drivers and the financial outcomes' (Morgan 2006, in ASX market disclosure).*

Even though the measurement process may be complex, Westpac's experience would suggest that there is potentially a profitable outcome of the journey to systematically analyse the drivers of intangible value.

Summary

This chapter demonstrates the importance of gathering firm data on HR metrics. It also poses a challenge for HR professionals to create appropriate human capital metrics providing valid and useful information for both internal use and, increasingly, for use by the broader investment community.

It is clear that while a range of human capital metrics can be derived from research, there are no clear agreements as yet on measurement principles and no standards equivalent to accounting standards. It is timely, therefore, to consider more qualitatively based approaches to human capital metrics highlighting fundamental principles driving value. Purely financial metrics based on traditional accounting principles have not served investors well, as shown during the collapse of Lehman Brothers investment bank in late 2008.

The HR profession needs to create and use a range of human capital metrics having the attributes noted by Bassi and McMurrer (2007). They should be:

- credible;
- descriptive;
- predictive;
- detailed;
- actionable; and
- cost-effective.

Additionally, human capital metrics need to be rigorous and simple. Most importantly, however, they need to be used by financial markets and investors.

As the research suggests, these metrics are more likely to be based on qualitative, systems-based data (rather than pure accounting data) in order to provide more insight on human capital as a driver of intangible value. It may seem like a complex and expensive task but, given the research on human capital systems and financial performance, it is in the interests of the firm, its employees and its investors if qualitative human capital metrics can be used extensively, effectively and efficiently.

Discussion questions

1. Do you agree with the view of Ulrich (1999) that the HR profession has fallen into the trap of measuring what it can measure, rather than what it should measure? In your opinion, what should the HR profession be measuring?

2. The Human Resources profession has, in recent years, applied models from Accounting and Finance to create business cases for a range of initiatives. Has the time now come for the Accounting and Finance professions to understand and apply the more qualitative language of Human Capital?

3. Identifying the importance of the value created by human capital, rather than the costs of managing and accounting for human capital, presents the most compelling argument for systematic human capital analysis. Do you agree with this statement? Why/why not?

References

Akerlof, GA & Shiller RJ 2009, *Animal Spirits: How Human Psychology Drives the Economy, and why it Matters for Global Capitalism*, Princeton University Press, Princeton, New Jersey.

Anon 2006, 'Reporting Intellectual Capital to Augment Research, Development and Innovation in SMEs Report to the Commission of the High Level Expert Group on RICARDIS', European Commission, Directorate General for Research, ISBN 92-79-02149-4.

Australian Council of Super Investors, Inc 2007, *The ESG Survey Report*, April 2007, Australian Council of Superannuation Investors Inc, Melbourne, VIC. http://www.acsi.org.au/documents/ESG%20Survey%20Report%20.pdf, accessed 10 May 2007.

Barney, J 1991, 'Firm Resources and Sustained Competitive Advantage', *Journal of Management*, vol. 17; no. 1 (1991), 99-120.

Bassi, L & McMurrer, D 2007, 'Maximising Your Returns on People', *Harvard Business Review*, March.

Bassi, LJ, Lev, B, Low, J, McMurrer, DP, & Sissfield, GA 2001, 'Measuring Corporate Investments in Human Capital', in MM Blair & TA Kochan (eds), *The New Relationship: Human Capital in the American Corporation*, Brookings Institute, New York, pp. 334-382.

Becker, BE, Huselid, MA & Ulrich D 2001, *The HR Scorecard: Linking People, Strategy and Performance*, Harvard Business School Press, Boston.

Bloom, BS ed., 1956, *Taxonomy of Educational Objectives: Handbook 1: Cognitive Domain*, Longman, New York.

Boedker, C 2005, 'Australian Guiding Principles on Extended Performance Management: A Guide to Better Managing, Measuring and Reporting Knowledge Intensive Organisational Resources', *GAP Congress on Knowledge Capital*, Melbourne, November 3-4, 2005, Society for Knowledge Economics.

Brown, D & Armstrong, M 1999, *Paying for Contribution: Real Performance Related Strategies*, Kogan Page, London.

Cascio, WF 1991, *Applied psychology in personnel management*, 4th edn, Prentice-Hall International, Englewood Cliffs, NJ.

Cohan, WD 2009, *House of Cards: How Wall Street's Gamblers Broke Capitalism*, Allen Lane/Penguin, New York.

Collins, J 2009, 'How the mighty fall…and why some companies never give in', Jim Collins, May 19 2009.

Collins, J & Porras J, 2002, *Built To Last: Successful Habits of Visionary Companies*, Harper Collins, New York.

Creelman, D 2006, *Reporting on Human Capital: What the Fortune 100 tells Wall Street About Human Capital Management*, http://www.corporater.com/forums/human-capital-report-review.aspx, accessed February 6 2007.

De Geus, A 1997, 'The Living Company, and correspondence', *Harvard Business Review*, March-April, pp. 51-9, 182, 187 and 190.

Di Maggio, PJ & Powell, WW 1983, 'The iron cage revisited: Institutional isomorphism and collective rationality in organizational fields', *American Sociological Review*, 48, 2 (147-160).

Dunphy, D, Benveniste, J, Griffiths, A & Sutton P (eds), *Sustainability: The Corporate Challenge of the 21st Century*, Allen and Unwin, Sydney.

Edvinsson, L & Malone, MS 1997, *Intellectual Capital: Realizing Your Company's True Value by Finding Its Hidden Brainpower*, Harper Collins, New York.

Girard, B 2009, *The Google Way: How One Company is Revolutionising Management as we Know It*, No Starch Press, San Francisco.

Harter, JK, Schmidt FL & Killham, EA, 2003, *Employee Engagement, Satisfaction and Business-Unit-Level Outcomes: A Meta-Analysis*, The Gallup Organisation, Omaha, July, 2003.

Hatch, B 2005, 'Investors ignore human factor', *Australian Financial Review*, 19 April, 2005.

Hubbard, DW 2009, *The Failure of Risk Management: Why It's Broken and How to Fix It*, John Wiley & Sons, New Jersey.

James, D 2005, 'The cultural advantage', *Business Review Weekly*, 20 October, 2005.

Jones, D 2005, 'Money: Besides being lonely at the top, it can be disengaging as well', *USA Today*, 21 June 2005.

Kaplan RS & Norton DP 2006, *Alignment: Using the Balanced Scorecard to Create Synergies*, Boston, Harvard Business School Press.

Kaplan, RS & Norton DP 1996, *The Balanced Scorecard*, Harvard Business School Press, Boston.

Lawrence, A 2009, 'Google Inc: Figuring Out How to Deal with Chine', in E Raufflet & AJ Mills (eds), *The Dark Side: Critical Cases in Business*, Greenleaf Publishing, Sheffield.

Lepak, DP & Snell, SA 1999, 'The human resource architecture: Toward a theory of human capital development and allocation', *Academy of Management Review*, 24 (1), 31-48.

Lev, B 2002, *Intangibles: Management Measurement and Reporting*, Brookings Institution, Washington, DC.

Lowe, J 2009, *Google Speaks: Secrets of the World's Greatest Billionaire Entrepreneurs Sergey Brin and Larry Page*, John Wiley & Sons, New Jersey.

Marr, B, ed. 2005, *Perspectives on intellectual capital: Multidisciplinary insights into management, measurement and reporting*, Elsevier Butterworth Heinemann, Oxford.

Mayo, A 2001, 'Measuring Human Capital', Chapter 3 in *The Human Value of the Enterprise*, Nicholas Brearley Publishing, London, pp. 40-70.

Mintzberg, H 1979, *The Structuring of Organizations*. Prentice Hall, Englewood Cliffs, New Jersey.

Morgan, D 2006, 'Its not all profits: Westpac boss, quoted in Business Section', *Sydney Morning Herald*, April 12th, 2006.

Mostyn, S 2006, Presentation to Human Resources Magazine Breakfast, 4th May 2005, Sydney, Group Executive, Culture & Reputation at Insurance Australia Group (IAG).

O'Donnell, L & Royal, C 2009, *Leadership Matrix, in Cognitive Complexity in Board Market Dialogue*, GCCM presentation, AGSM, UNSW, Sydney, April.

O'Reilly, CA & Pfeffer, J 2000, *Hidden Value: How Great Companies Achieve Extraordinary Results with Ordinary People*, Boston, Harvard Business School Press.

Pike, S & Roos, G 2004, 'Mathematics and Modern Business Management', *Journal of Intellectual Capital*, 5(2), 243-256.

Pitkanen, A 2006, 'The importance of intellectual capital for organizational performance', PhD Research proposal, Turku School of Economics and Business Administration, Department of Economics and Finance, University of Finland http://www.lut.fi/kati/tutoriaali/materiaalit/Seminaaripaperi%20_Lappeenranta_%20Antti%20Pitkanen.pdf, accessed 18 July 2006.

Plakalo, T 2006, 'Untangling intangibles', Special Report in *MIS Magazine*, Wednesday, February 01, 2006 http://www.misweb.com/magarticle.asp?doc_id=25428&rgid=2&listed_months=0, accessed 20 July 2006.

Purcell, N 2006, *Westpac's Approach to Managing Intangible Value*, ASX Market Briefing, April 2006.

Ramsay, I 2005, 'Pushing the Limit for Directors', *Australian Financial Review*, 5 April, p. 68.

Rigby, DK 2001, 'Management Tools and Techniques: A Survey', *California Management Review*, Vol. 43, No. 2.

Roos, G, Burgman, R, Pike, S & Fernstrum, L 2005, *Intellectual Capital in Practice*, Elsevier, USA.

Royal, C & Althauser, 2002, 'Working in the Turbulence of Mergers and Acquisitions: The Shape of Careers and Labour Markets in Three Divisions of an International Investment Bank', *Working Paper Series: School of Industrial Relations and Organisational Behaviour, University of New South Wales*, 143.

Royal, C & O'Donnell, L 2005, Embedding Human Capital Analysis in the Investment Process – A Human Resources Challenge, *Asia Pacific Journal of Human Resources.* 43(1), 117-136.

Royal C & O'Donnell, L 2008, 'Emerging Human Capital Analytics for Investment Processes', *Journal of Intellectual Capital,* Volume 9, No. 3, 2008.

Salmon, F 2009, 'Recipe for Disaster: The Formula that Killed Wall Street', *Wired*, 23rd February http://www.wired.com/techbiz/it/magazine/17-03/wp_quant? currentPage=all, accessed 30 March 2009.

Scott, WR 2001, *Institutions and Organisations*, Thousand Oaks, Sage.

Stace, D & Dunphy, D 2001, *Beyond the Boundaries: Leading and Recreating the Successful Enterprise, (2nd edition),* McGraw Hill, Roseville.

Stacey, RD 2001, *Complex Responsive Processes in Organizations: Learning and Knowledge Creation,* Routledge, London.

Sveiby, K-E 1997, *The New Organizational Wealth - Managing & Measuring Intangible Assets*, Berrett-Koehler, San Francisco.

Tett. G 2009, *Fool's Gold: How Unrestrained Greed Corrupted a Dream, Shattered Global Markets and Unleashed a Catastrophe*, Little and Brown, London.

Triana, P 2009, *Lecturing Birds on Flying: Can Mathematical Theories Destroy the Financial Markets?,* John Wiley & Sons, New Jersey.

Ulrich, D, Smallwood, N & Creelman, D 2006, Preface, pp. 5-6, *Reporting on Human Capital: What the Fortune 100 tells Wall Street About Human Capital Management*, http://www.rbl.net/beta/reportingHC.php.

Ulrich, D 1999, 'Measuring Human Resources: an Overview of Practice and a Prescription for Results', Chapter 24 RS Schuler & SE Jackson, *Strategic Human Resource Management*, Blackwell Business, Oxford, pp. 462-482.

United Nations website, *United Nations Principles for Responsible Investing*, http://www.unpri.org/principles/, accessed 29th October 2006.

Watson Wyatt 2002, Human Capital Index European Survey Report, Watson Wyatt.

Whitaker, D & Wilson L 2007, 'Human Capital Measurement: From Insight to Action', *Organization Development Journal,* Fall, 25(3), 59-64.

Wiig, 2004, *People Focused Knowledge Management: How Effective Decision Making Leads to Corporate Success*, Oxford, Elsevier Butterworth-Heinemann.

Chapter 7

HUMAN RESOURCE OUTSOURCING AND SHARED SERVICES: AN ASIAN PACIFIC PERSPECTIVE

Ajay K Jain & Debi S Saini

OBJECTIVES

This chapter seeks to examine the nature and extent of HR outsourcing practices in the Asia Pacific region in general and India in particular. By the completion of the chapter you should be able to:

1. define the terms outsourcing, HR outsourcing, offshoring and shared services;
2. identify the place of HR outsourcing in the changing business context;
3. outline the different HR activities that can be outsourced;
4. identify the factors that contribute to a firm's decision to outsource;
5. discuss HR shared services as an alternative to HR outsourcing;
6. identify trends in HR outsourcing across regions;
7. identify the nuances of outsourcing dynamics as confronted by an Indian prepress company to facilitate application issues in classroom learning;
8. discuss the key goals of HR outsourcing and the challenges that HR outsourcing faces in India.

Definitions

Outsourcing: The term here refers to assigning one or more business processes to an external service provider who takes over the responsibility of owning and managing these processes and delivering the envisaged service as per the terms of the agreement. Outsourcing thus enables an organisation to shift its responsibility for certain operations and/or processes to another entity.

HR outsourcing: In common with other aspects of the outsourcing business, HR outsourcing places 'responsibility for various elements of the HR function with a third-party provider' (Turnbull 2002, p.11).

Offshoring: The term is sometimes related to outsourcing but is often incorrectly used interchangeably with it. Offshoring can be defined as the process of outsourcing business activities or services to a third party overseas and/or an employer moving its business activities or services to another country directly or indirectly. In other words, offshoring may not always involve the services of an external provider.

HR shared services: HR shared services is a system of providing well-defined services for internal customers that consist of more than one unit. According to Oates (1998), although shared service centres remain within the organisation concerned, they have a high degree of independence that allows them to act in a manner similar to an external outsourcing provider.

HR outsourcing in the changing business context

As the global economy is caught in fierce competition in the post-globalisation era, HR professionals are expected to search for more effective rearrangement of HR systems and processes.

ROI of HR interventions

Senior executives who are able to recognise the economic value expected by customers are likely to demand more from the HR function in terms of aligning employee behaviours, attitudes and skills to the business needs. They will also expect each process to be examined critically so as to facilitate the realisation of organisational goals. HR is under tremendous pressure to measure the return on investment (ROI) on HR interventions. In this context, human resource outsourcing (HRO) has emerged as one of the key areas of interests for providing potential business benefits to organisations.

HRO on the increase

As noted earlier, HRO is used by organisations to obtain HR services of a third party or to take care of its complete HR function. Companies may outsource a few or all of their HR related activities to one or more service providers in their own countries or to providers located in offshore destinations. For example, it is evident that many global organisations have been outsourcing to establishments based in India, China, the Philippines and other developing countries. Research evidence indicates that HR outsourcing has substantially increased over the last decade (e.g. Woodall, Gourlay & Short 2000).

Categories of HR service providers

In this sense, the HR outsourcing service provider firms or HR outsourcing companies can be divided into four categories depending on the services they offer:

- PEOs (professional employer organisation);
- BPOs (business process organisation);
- ASPs (application service providers); or
- e-services.

The PEOs assume full responsibility for a company's HR function whereas BPOs, ASPs, and e-services provide web-based HR solutions such as:

- database maintenance;
- HR data warehousing;
- maintaining records;
- developing and maintaining HR software and similar.

The outsourcing of HR activities can range from routine administrative HR activities to the entire package, including the design of HR systems that are likely to have a fundamental impact on organisational culture and performance (Klaas, McClendon & Gainey 2001).

To outsource or not: A strategic decision

The resource-based view (RBV) of the firm argues that organisations obtain sustained competitive advantage by implementing strategies that exploit their internal strengths. They achieve this through

- responding to environmental opportunities;
- neutralising external threats; and
- avoiding internal weaknesses (Barney 1991).

Hence, RBV theory indicates that outsourcing can be productive to the development of core competencies within organisations.

Advantages and pitfalls of HRO

HRO allows companies greater flexibility and increased productivity by using temporary subcontractors to cover fluctuating demands for labour (Cooke 2006). Though HRO is generally lauded for its advantages to the business, scholars warn against the pitfalls of mindless outsourcing. Handing over unnecessarily complex or badly understood systems to an external provider can limit potential benefits from outsourcing.

Continuity of skill supply

Arguably, one of the most serious issues with HR outsourcing is maintaining the continuity of skill supply and the retention of in-house knowledge and expertise (Cooke, Shen & McBride 2005). Organisations may outsource the delivery of key skills so as to avoid the need to train their own staff. For example, many companies do not have experts to train their staff in special skills their staffs are expected to possess. They outsource this function to others—e.g. training in leadership building or coaching.

Creating a business case for HR outsourcing

When considering HR outsourcing, an organisation needs to ask at the outset why it needs to change the way the HR function currently operates. Specifically, what aspects of the existing HR systems are not satisfactory and/or would benefit from improvements?

By probing these responses HR can then focus on the type and scale of changes that may be required. These will help decide whether HR outsourcing might be an appropriate response. Creating a business case for HR outsourcing is an important step in establishing its legitimacy. There are a number of potential benefits and challenges in HR outsourcing. The literature suggests the following key factors as the main reasons that organisations choose to outsource:

Core v. periphery activities

Some scholars use the concept of 'core' and 'periphery' activities to explain the outsourcing of a firm's functions (Atkinson 1984; Pollert 1987; Torrington & McKay 1986). This line of thinking argues that the outsourcing of non-core HR activities allows the HR department to focus on its core strategic HR activities which are critical for realising business strategy.

Transaction cost economic model (Williamson 1985)

The decision to produce or outsource HR should rest upon the relative costs of production and transaction.

Lack of in-house expertise

Firms are seen to outsource so as to gain from the rising comparative advantage of highly specialised service providers who may have expertise in the concerned areas.

To perform one-time tasks

This includes issues such as integration in the case of mergers and acquisitions (M&A). Another reason why companies may consider HR outsourcing is to perform a one-time activity — e.g. change management.

To overcome cultural differences

Greater resort to outsourcing may be undertaken when the organisation's culture is significantly different from the local culture. Companies also tend to outsource their HR processes, especially recruitment, so as to overcome problems arising from cultural differences.

Cost efficiency

Downsizing and tougher competition put HR under increasing pressure to demonstrate value both in terms of efficiency and effectiveness (Roberts 2001; Cooke, Shen & McBride 2005). Outsourcing some of their activities allows companies to cut direct and indirect costs.

HR outsourcing saves costs on recruiting, overtime working, training and development. It saves costs involved in higher incidence of absenteeism and also reduces administrative and backup costs. Scholars have observed that HR outsourcing decisions are taken often in response to demand for reducing costs for HR services (Greer, Youngblood & Gray 1999).

HR activities that can be outsourced

As observed by Cooke, Shen and McBride (2005), HR outsourcing activities can be categorised into core and non-core activities.

Core and non-core HR activities

Core HR activities include activities related to top-level strategy and HR policies; non-core HR activities include specialist activities such as recruitment and routine personnel administration (Finn 1999). According to Ulrich (1998), all non-transformational activities are part of the core HR function whereas transactional activities are part of non-core HR function.

The specific processes included within any outsourcing HRO arrangement vary from organisation to organisation. Some organisations outsource virtually all of their HR processes whereas others select specific components such as payroll or resourcing (Morgan 2006). The most common areas outsourced are:

- payroll;
- training; and
- resourcing of temporary positions (Kersley, Alpin & Forth 2005).

So far, very few organisations have outsourced their entire HR function.

Outsourcing in large and small organisations

In large organisations, outsourcing is most commonly applied to the operational elements of delivering HR activities whilst control over HR strategy and decision making is retained by the firm. A number of large, well-publicised, mainly global organisations have outsourced large parts of their HR operational activities for periods ranging between five and ten years. These include BT, Boots the Chemist, Procter & Gamble, and Unilever.

Small organisations often do the reverse, effectively outsourcing their strategy (to HR consultants and other professional advisers) while keeping the delivery of HR processes internal.

Alternatives to HR outsourcing

HR Shared Services

An HR shared services model is a new concept which has recently become very popular with organisations that have multiple locations. Some organisations are also using shared services to combine processes common across the organisation into one shared services division.

Back-office processes

The Shared Services Centre (SSC) has emerged as a major alternative to HR outsourcing. SSC enables the operation of certain back-office functions to work in a more competitive and business-like way, creating an internal client–vendor relationship.

Some functions that are common across the organisation are standardised and processed at a single location for the whole organisation as back-office processes. The aim is not only to save cost but also to improve quality and responsiveness.

Call-centre technologies and approaches to work organisation

The adoption of HR shared services is a result of increasingly sophisticated call-centre technologies and call-centre approaches to work organisation (Fernie & Metcalf 1998; Korczynski 2002). Driven by recent advances in sophisticated IT systems and ever increasing competitive pressures, many well-known organisations have set up their own HR shared services centres. These organisations include Barclays, Motorola, Compass Group, Bank of Ireland, Cable & Wireless, Zurich Financial Services, Shell, Compaq, Deutsche Bank, Allied Signal Inc., Ontario Government of Canada, and the ABB Group (Cooke 2006).

In order to maintain best practices, monitor delivery, be more sensitive to customer needs, and generally reposition HR as more strategic and less encumbered by administrative tasks, organisations opting for shared services often keep a small HR team at the corporate level to focus on high-level strategy, governance, and policy (Reilly 2000).

Main tasks of shared services centres

HR shared services mostly focus on issues such as:

- administrative tasks;
- relocation services;
- recruitment administration;
- training support; and
- the maintenance of personnel data.

The main task of a shared services centre is to supply information and advice on HR policy and practice to operational managers and employees via a call centre and/or intranet (Reilly 2000). An emerging trend with some large firms, such as Accenture, is the taking over of the entire HR function of their client firms, to deliver a complete outsource of HR services.

Advantage of the shared services model

The main advantage of the shared services model lies in the change of activities and roles of different departments. For example, a former context process of a department (e.g. invoice processing) becomes a core process of the SSC.

The concentration of homogenous tasks in an SSC brings economies of scale and a significant decrease in costs—the primary reason for the creation of SSCs. According to Chartered Institute of Personnel and Development (CPID) of the United Kingdom (UK), it is due to this reason that more organisations are opting to set up SSCs than choose outsourcing.

Employee self-service (ESS) and manager self-service (MSS) systems

Increasingly some organisations are looking to put in place comprehensive HR information systems that also enable non-HR employees and managers to undertake many HR-related activities. They do so themselves via a portal or intranet, without the need for any external intervention. For example,

- in an ESS system, individuals may be able to update their own personal details when their particulars alter, and
- in an MSS system, managers could review absence records for all their staff.

This is one example of how HR can harness technology to deliver services.

Buying-in consultancy services

Another way of using outside expertise in a business process is buying a consultancy service. The services of external consultants might be used to advise on specific HR issues or on the implementation of HR processes.

Typically, consultants do not then manage or deliver these services once implemented; this work is eventually taken on by the internal HR team. For example, an organisation may outsource installation and maintenance of the balanced score card and the HR score system in the organisation.

Trends in HR outsourcing

In recent years, firms have outsourced an expanding variety of activities in an attempt to:

- improve service and product quality;
- reduce production cycle time;
- lower costs;
- increase their focus on core competencies; and, in general,
- enhance organisational effectiveness.

This view of the use of outsourcing has found enthusiastic proponents among both scholars and practitioners (Quinn 1992; Hirschhorn & Gilmore 1992).

Growth in HR outsourcing

The growth of HR outsourcing, however, has not followed the anticipated speed predicted by some commentators. Nor has the scope of outsourcing been as radical as some may assume. For example, only 3% of organisations surveyed in 2005 by the Shared Services and Business Process Outsourcing Association (SBPOA) reported that they outsourced the entire HR function (Pickard 2006).

It is reported that the diversity of the HR function makes it difficult for firms to outsource their HR function as a whole to a single service provider to gain economies of scale. Instead, they tend to outsource single processes to different service providers to take advantage of their unique strengths. Single-process outsourcing is therefore believed to be the main growth area (Pickard 2006).

Differences between countries

Although many western countries have adopted HR outsourcing there are differences in the level of HR outsourcing in different parts of world. For example, instances of HR outsourcing in Europe are less evident than reported in the US. These differences are said to be due to differences in:

- the size of the businesses;
- the degree of sophistication of the HR function;
- the extent of development of the HR outsourcing market;

- cultural norms; and
- other institutional factors in specific countries and regions (Sparrow 2008).

Predicted growth

Despite the current recessionary period, surveys and studies conducted by professional consultancy firms predict continuing growth of the HRO industry (albeit at a slower rate) as a global trend.

According to a survey conducted by the Everest Research Institute in 2008, the HRO industry would grow 5% in 2009 when its annualised contract value would reach $3.2 billion (Everest Research Institute 2008). Another survey report shows that outsourcing to India, China, Southern and Eastern Europe and South Africa is expected to grow exponentially over the next ten years according to the current clientele. Investors and management are anticipating 30+% annual revenue leaps. There would, however, be pressure on suppliers for cost cutting. As a result most of the suppliers would see reduced margins and smaller contract value.

Growth in single process outsourcing

According to Anthony Bruce, Director of HR services at Price Waterhouse Coopers (PWC), the European market would not see much multi-process HR outsourcing. 'The big surge', he says, 'is in single process outsourcing'. The trend would be for companies to buy small amounts of HR administration and supporting technology across multiple processes, to gain access to a supplier's superior technology capability (Pickard 2006).

Differences between Europe and North America for multi-process HRO

North American-headquartered buyers traditionally dominated the global multi-process HRO market, with over 70 per cent of the deals through the end of 2007 signed in this region. In comparison, the European HRO market saw limited activity from a deal origination perspective. While European organisations have traditionally been more conservative than their North American counterparts in embracing outsourcing, various legislative and demographic considerations that impact on HRO have also contributed towards a lower adoption level in the European region.

Europe's share in the global HRO market

However, in the last two years, Europe saw increased activity from a deal-origination perspective. This led to an increase in Europe's share in the global HRO market in the post-2005 period. In terms of the number of deals it has grown from 20% to 30%. Some of the factors influencing the growth of HRO in Europe have been:

- suppliers becoming more receptive to the unique challenges present in Europe, making HRO a viable strategy for buyers to drive efficiency and generate cost savings;
- increased adoption of HRO by the public sector in the UK;
- increased acceptance of global sourcing; and
- entrance of new suppliers.

There are also some key differences in the way the European HRO market is evolving in terms of its path to HRO adoption compared to North America. These include technology considerations, HR process inclusion, and the usage of global sourcing.

The North American market for HRO

North America is considered to be the main market of HRO. A survey by the HR Outsourcing Association reports North America to be the largest buyer of HRO services. The most commonly outsourced activities, either partially or totally, include:

- outplacement services;
- employee assistance programs;
- defined contribution plans; and
- defined benefit (pension) plans.

It has been found that by 2008 US organisations also plan to outsource:

- leave management;
- learning and development;
- payroll;
- recruiting;
- health and welfare; and
- global mobility (Sparrow 2008).

Latin America

Latin America is leveraging its competitive advantage in certain high-growth areas of offshore outsourcing and continues to be an attractive labour arbitrage alternative for US clients.

Brazil, in particular, has vast potential due to its large population, the innovative creativity of its engineers, and government programs supporting the outsourcing industry. Other countries such as Chile and Uruguay have capitalised on their time zone advantages and back-office proficiencies by adding government incentives to attract outsourcing work.

According to the growing US clientele base, one major obstacle to becoming an offshore giant for these countries is the language difference. Although South American universities are graduating larger numbers of extremely qualified engineers, analysts and business managers, few are fluent in English and this is bound to limit their employment in the outsourcing industry.

HR outsourcing in Asia Pacific region

The leading HR consultancy firm, Hewitt Associates, recently provided details on HR outsourcing in the Asia Pacific market. A June 2002 on-line survey by the firm on 'Outsourcing in the Asia Pacific', threw up some interesting highlights. The survey, responded to by over 424 company representatives around the Asia Pacific region, revealed the following issues related to outsourcing and HR outsourcing:

- 50.04% of participants cited the concentration on core competencies to be the key reason for outsourcing;
- 29.9% of participants said they had considered outsourcing as a means by which to control costs;
- an average of 5.7% companies across the various geographical locations placed a great emphasis on confidentiality;
- payroll processing and training and development were the most important functions, accounting for 20.3% and 18.9% respectively of all participants across the region; and
- benefits administration ranked third, accounting for 15.6 per cent of the participants.

India was home to marginally the greatest percentage of companies that had not yet considered outsourcing HR functions—amounting to 26.2% of participants. Some 19.9% of the participants in India also claimed there was a lack of suitable vendors.

According to 53.3% of the participants, their biggest apprehension about outsourcing was the quality of the outsourcing vendor. Security was the second biggest concern.

India as an HR outsourcing destination

In the pre-liberalisation era India had a closed economy and highly monopolistic market conditions. In the post-1990s, India has started to follow the path of the open market, substantially liberalising and globalising its economy.

A suitable destination for outsourcing

Being the largest democracy and having one of the largest English-speaking work forces in the world, India has become one of the most attractive countries for business transactions. Additionally, India has a large, young work force with good educational backgrounds, making it one of the most suitable destinations for outsourcing.

Major services and strengths

The major services provided by the outsourcing industry in India and their potential markets are in:

- customer care;
- content development (such as animation);
- finance;
- HR services;
- payment services; and
- administration.

India's National Association of Software and Services Companies (NASSCOM) has an exclusive website on outsourcing industry <www.bpo.nasscom.org> highlighting India's value proposition, key issues, and challenges. A SWOT (strengths, weaknesses, opportunities and growth) analysis of the Indian outsourcing industry is shown in Table 7.1.

Table 7.1 SWOT analysis of the Indian outsourcing industry

Strengths	Weaknesses
1. English proficiency	1. Positioning and brand management
2. Government support	2. Industry is still at low end in value chain
3. Cost advantage	3. Infrastructure deficiency
4. Growing influence of Indian Diaspora abroad	4. Cultural differences
5. Process quality focus	5. Sales and marketing
6. Skilled workforce	6. Leverage expertise for higher value education
7. Reasonable technical innovations	7. Business process experience
8. Reverse brain drain	8. Very long distance from US
9. Existing long-term relationship	9. Legal system not quite efficient
Opportunities	**Threats**
1. Creation of global brands	1. Internal competition for resources
2. BPO and call centre offerings	2. Over promising / under delivering
3. Expansion of existing relationships	3. Regional geopolitical uncertainty
4. Chinese domestic and export markets	4. Rising labour costs
	5. Competition from other countries
	6. (Sometimes) blinding nationalism
5. Leveraging of relationships in the west to access Asia Pacific and Middle East markets	7. Government blocking reforms/deals
	8. Corruption/piracy/lack of trust
6. Indian domestic market growth	9. Political and religious instability

Growth of HRO in India

Many medium- and large-sized organisations are using the services of external consultants to take care of their HR functions.

Recruitment process outsourcing

Outsourcing the recruitment process (RPO) in the organised sector is growing at 40% and many organisations are outsourcing their recruitment processes right from entry-level jobs.

Varadrajan (2008) reports that Asim Handa, country head of Futurestep (an outsourced recruiting subsidiary of Korn/Ferry International, a premier global provider of talent management solutions), estimates the present value of the RPO industry in India at about $2.5 billion. Companies such as Futurestep are providing customised solutions to suit clients' requirements across all sectors.

Complete HR delivery

There is a marked interest in outsourcing to improve on services such as payroll and benefits, as well as complete HR delivery. The trend towards outsourcing all HR functions is starting to take hold, particularly for companies that have been operating in other parts of the Asia Pacific region and are starting up operations in India. Companies are looking towards outsourcing the complete range of HR delivery and designing products concerning policies, compensation, structure, and recruitment.

By opting for HR outsourcing, Indian companies are not only making their own HR function global class, but also creating a significant opportunity for service providers in the domestic space. India is being seen as a huge market for HR services. Currently, the organised sector of HR servicing is catering to only about 2% of the total market.

Potential for global growth

For HR outsourcing services providers operating out of India, these statistics reflect a major advantage. Not only do they have a wide playing field in the global arena for these services, they also have a high-potential domestic market to turn to, which will fuel their future growth.

HR outsourcing is one area where the Indian and global outsourcing industry is predicted to see tremendous growth. As a matter of fact, HRO is projected as the fastest growing segment over the next three years. This projection can be further substantiated by the fact that large-scale HR offshoring has already taken place. Some of the giant names such as Fidelity, Exult and Hewitt are expected to set up their workshops in India for their HR operations.

Factors operating against the growth of HRO in India

Cost and confidentiality

HRO has failed to show the predicted growth in India in line with global trends. Many offshore companies are reluctant to outsource to India. The major reasons for this reluctance are cost and concern about confidentiality of sensitive internal information (Frost & Sullivan 2005).

Sentiment against offshoring

Another reason for HRO not really picking up is increasing sentiment against offshoring. Against the backdrop of economic downturn and rising unemployment, more and more countries are legislating to restrict the outflow of jobs. Organisations are also deterred from outsourcing due to the threat of losing control over their financial data while some cast doubts over the quality and ethics of the outsourcing vendors in India.

Cultural and psychological mindsets

Cultural and psychological mindsets also prevent the growth of HR outsourcing in India. Many offshore companies are of the opinion that an HR outsourcing agency will not be able to tackle critical issues such as employee incentive programs and the resolution of work-related problems.

New models of industry-specific solutions

New models of industry-specific solutions and functional improvements by niche HRO firms are transforming the delivery of HR services for both new and established clients. Over the past five years, HRO giants Convergys, Hewitt, Gevity and Mercer had risen quickly to the top ranks of the top 50 vendors, just to fall completely off as HRO satisfaction scrutiny escalated by Q2 2008 (Brown & Wilson Report 2008).

Ready availability of HR skills

As has been argued by Cooke (2008), Indian firms seem to be of the view that it is more effective to manage their HR processes in-house due to cost factors and potential risks in confidentiality, quality, security breaches, ethics, and control. Moreover, due to the easy and competitive availability of skills, it would be difficult for the Indian firms to justify the outsourcing of HR processes. The most common HR processes outsourced in India include:

- training;
- payroll processing;
- surveys;
- resume management services;
- online performance management solutions;

- benefits administration;
- travel and expense management;
- compensation consulting;
- benchmark studies; and
- statutory compliance (Sparrow 2008).

Types of HR services outsourced to India

HR outsourcing can be mainly grouped into two categories—namely:

- transaction and administration outsourcing services; and
- consultancy outsourcing services.

HR transaction outsourcing services include monthly HR activities such as payroll processing. HR consultancy services are some of the other services that can be outsourced to India. Though organisations outsource transaction management and HR consultancy services to India, many organisations still take care of strategic and policy functions within their organisation.

Repetitive outsourcing HR services to India can benefit client organisations from the skills, expertise, latest technology and professional services that India offers in the field of HR. India is one of the largest countries in terms of English-speaking population and cheapest in terms of labour cost, giving it competitive advantage as an outsourcing destination.

Case study

Dynamics of HR outsourcing at ABC Ltd, India

ABC Ltd, a prepress company, was started by Mr Thomas, an RIT (Rochester Institute of Technology) graduate of the 1998-batch. He had five years' work experience in the graphics software industry in US and Europe.

Prepress is an innovative technology that involves producing publications using all digital workflows and computer-to-plate (CTP) methods. The trend started in the printing industry in 1996.

Thomas started ABC as a software company from a garage in 2003. He hails from a family that owns one of India's largest and most renowned prepress houses. In 2004–05, ABC gained funding from a venture capitalist introduced by Mr Roger, ex-head of marketing of one of the world's largest prepress houses.

Each of them has an equal stake in the company. They started providing prepress services to Europe and United States along with the usual provision of software services. They were using the experienced workforce from the Thomas family owned company in these services. Thomas manages the operations and Roger brings in the business. ABC established itself as a separate entity with an attractive 200 seat office in Bangalore, the IT hub of India. The office is expandable to 1000 seats. By the end of 2005 the revenue of the company rose to a million dollars.

Towards the end of 2005 ABC was awarded a big contract from the world's largest news group—so they added another 40+ employees to their existing workforce. The software project manager played a pivotal role by using his contacts in the industry to get 40 designers on board in the space of a month.

The assistant manager for quality, the only printing technology graduate in the company, was elevated as the manager for training. He had visited the client site for the transition. The business flourished and by the end of financial year 2006 they had 100+ employees with a support staff of six (three account executives, two administrative executives and one front-office executive). HR in the company was being managed by the software project manager and the senior accounts executive.

Owing to the growing need of the main business, the software department was outsourced at the beginning of 2006. The software project manager was appointed the company's first HR manager. With the services of the front office and the accounts executive he managed the whole HR function.

The role of client servicing manager was assigned to the client servicing executive who was instrumental in the whole transitioning process, client pitches, and commissioning. The production manager, an arts graduate with 10+ years experience in the printing press, was elevated to the position of production manager.

The first employee appraisals were carried out in October 2006. The HR manager issued letters to all employees suggesting that they should cooperate as such a process takes more than a month. The appraisals were based on productivity scores and 180 degree appraisal. Most of the staff came in at the A and B categories of performance and received a percentage raise.

Case study questions

1. Which of the four HR options (employee self-service (ESS), manager self-service (MSS), HR outsourcing, and shared services) should ABC Ltd aim for? Discuss.

2. Discuss the scope of the service opted—for example what should be the ideal mix/ composition—i.e. which vertical to be managed which way and why?

Conclusion

More and more organisations at the global level are promoting flexibility in order to remain cost-effective. The strategies include the outsourcing of many non-core operations, including HR transactional activities.

Benefits of HRO

HR outsourcing has proved to be beneficial to organisations in terms of:

- enhancing professionalism;
- reducing cost;
- meeting urgent demands;
- managing employee relations;
- focusing on core competence (e.g., Barney 1991);
- shifting the burden of risk and uncertainty associated with business (Williamson 1985); and
- getting a competitive tender (Domberger 1998).

Care is required when services are outsourced to an outside agency. When things go wrong, the responsibility may be diffused by both the parties. The vendor concerned should be made responsible and accountable for issues related to HR services like:

- delivery;
- quality;
- continuity;
- safety; and
- security.

Cost-cutting v. transactional activities

In the Asia Pacific region, the most significant factor contributing to HR outsourcing is not cost-cutting. Rather, it is the opportunity to focus the involvement of HR in strategic activities by minimising its involvement in transactional activities.

Cost-cutting, however, is also a significant factor—it is the second most important reason for companies to outsource HR. Across the region, payroll processing and training and development are the most important HR functions being outsourced. Organisations in India are also making increasing use of HR outsourcing for the above-mentioned reasons. Recruitment process outsourcing (RPO) in the organised sector is growing at a significant pace; this includes recruitment processes right from the entry-level jobs.

Growth of HRO in India

HR outsourcing to Indian companies is growing into a major opportunity for both global and Indian players. India has intrinsic advantages in the outsourcing industry. These include:

- low labour and other costs;
- a ready pool of English-speaking manpower; and
- its geographic positioning.

These factors have contributed to the country emerging as a viable destination for HR outsourcing companies to set up their businesses.

The HR outsourcing business opportunity is large and India is likely to garner a still larger piece of this pie in the future, as organisations seek to gain a competitive edge. But overall, given the size of its English-speaking population and the growth of the information technology industry, the growth of HR outsourcing in India is much below expectations.

The slow growth is not quite in consonance with global trends. There is scope for Indian companies to provide HR outsourcing services beyond their present involvement in payroll services and training/survey requirements, but Indian vendors will have to allay the fears of offshore companies about the confidentiality of sensitive internal information.

The HR profession in India, however, is growing at a fast pace. Overseas HR servicing companies are beginning to see the Indian market as a viable investment destination where they can set up their operations to cater to the needs of the international market.

Acknowledgement

The authors are thankful to Ajith Paninchukunnath, Madhu Smita, and Bhanu Sharma at Management Development Institute, Gurgaon for their help in the literature survey on human resource outsourcing (HRO).

References

Atkinson, J 1984, 'Manpower strategies for flexible organizations', *Personnel Management*, pp. 28-31

Barney, J 1991, 'Firm resources and sustained competitive advantage', *Journal of Management*, Vol. 17 No.1, pp. 99-120.

Brown & Wilson Report 2008, '2008 Black Book of Outsourcing—State of the Industry Report', http://www.theblackbookofoutsourcing.com/docs/2008%20State%20of%20Outsourcing%20Industry%20Report.pdf, accessed on 31 March 2009.

Chartered Institute of Personnel and Development 2005, *HR Outsourcing: The Key Decisions: Executive Briefing*, CIPD, London, http://www.cipd.co.uk/surveys.

Chartered Institute of Personnel and Development 2006, *Offshoring and the Role of HR: Survey Report*, London: CIPD, London, http://www.cipd.co.uk/surveys.

Cooke, FL 2008, 'HR Outsourcing in China and India: Practices and Pitfalls for Western MNCs' http://www.ssonetwork.com/topic_detail.aspx?id=3184&ekfrm=50, accessed on 30 June 2009.

Cooke, FL 2006, 'Modelling an HR shared services centre: experience of an MNC in the UK', *Human Resource Management*, 45, 2, pp. 211-27.

Cooke, FL, Shen, J & McBride, A 2005, 'Outsourcing HR as a competitive strategy? A literature review and an assessment of implications', *Human Resource Management*, Vol. 44 No. 4, pp. 413-32.

Domberger, S 1998, *The contracting organization: A strategic guide to outsourcing*, Oxford, UK, Oxford University Press.

Everest Research Institute 2008, '2009 Market Predictions—FAO, Global Sourcing, HRO, ITO, PO, and Supplier Intelligence', http://itonews.eu/files/f1225730191.pdf, accessed on 16 October 2009.

Fernie, S & Metcalf, D 1998, '(Not) hanging on the telephone: Payment systems in the new sweatshops', Discussion Paper No. 390, *Centre for Economic Performance*, London School of Economics.

Finn, W 1999, 'The ins and outs of human resources', *Director*, 53, 66–67.

Frost & Sullivan 2005, Shared Services and Outsourcing (SSO) Hub Potential Analysis, http://www.mscmalaysia.my/codenavia/portals/msc/images/pdf/ awards_accolades/frost_sullivan_sso.pdf, accessed on 23 September 2009.

Greer, C, Youngblood, S & Gray, D 1999, 'Human resource management outsourcing: the make or buy decision', *The Academy of Management Executive*, 13, 3, pp. 85-96.

Hewitt Associates 2004, 'Time to focus', *Hewitt Quarterly Asia Pacific*, 3, 2, Internet source: http://was4.hewitt.com/hewitt/ap/resource/rptspubs/hewittquart/HQ_10/time_to_focus.html, accessed on 12 March 2006.

Hewitt Associates 2007, China Opens the Door to HR Outsourcing. http://www.hewittassociates.com/Intl/AP/enCN/KnowledgeCenter/ArticlesReports/hr_outsourcing.aspx, accessed on 22nd October 2007.

Hirschhorn, L & Gilmore, T 1992, The new boundaries of the boundaryless company, *Harvard Business Review*, May-June, 104-115.

Kersley, B, Alpin, C & Forth, J 2005, *Inside the workplace: first findings from the 2004 Workplace Employment Relations Survey (WERS 2004)*, London, Economic and Social Research Council.

Klaas, B, McClendon, J & Gainey, T 2001, 'Outsourcing HR: the Impact of organizational characteristics', *Human Resource Management*, 40, 2, pp. 125-38.

Korczynski, M 2002, *Human resource management in service work*, Basingstoke, UK, Palgrave.

Morgan, D 2006, *Relocation, outsourcing and the interim market: the latest facts* [online], *Human Resourcefulness*, January, available at http://www.digbymorgan newsletter .co.uk/ story3_HR_11_05.html.

National Economic Development Office 1986, 'Changing working patterns: How companies achieve flexibility to meet new needs', London.

Oates, D 1998, *Outsourcing and the Virtual Organization: the Incredible Shrinking Company*, London, Century Business

Pickard, J 2006, 'Multiple choice', *The Guide to HR Outsourcing*, Chartered Institute of Personnel and Development, February, pp. 7-11.

Pollert, A 1987, 'The 'flexible firm': A model in search of reality (or a policy in search of a practice)?', Warwick Papers in Industrial Relations, No. 19. Coventry, UK, University of Warwick, Industrial Relations Research Unit.

Quinn, JB 1992, *Intelligent Enterprise*, New York, Free Press.

Reilly, P 2000, 'HR shared service and the realignment of HR', IES Report, p. 368.

Roberts, Z 2001, 'Outsourcing and e-HR will expand', *People Management*, p. 10.

Shared Services and Business Process Outsourcing Association 2005, http://www.ephorie.de/pdfs/Kris_SBPOA.pdf.

Sparrow, P 2008, 'HR Offshoring and outsourcing: Research issues for IHRM', *Handbook of International HR Research: Integrating People, Process and Context* Oxford, Blackwell.

Torrington, D & Mackay, L 1986, 'Will consultants take over the personnel function?', *Personnel Management*, pp. 34–37.

Turnbull, J 2002, 'Inside Outsourcing', *People Management*, pp. 10-11.

Ulrich, D 1998, 'A new mandate for Human Resources', *Harvard Business Review*, Jan/Feb 98, Vol. 76, Issue 1.

Varadrajan, S 2008, 'HR Outsourcing gaining Steam' http://www.futurestep.com/pdf/HRoutsourcingGainingSteam.pdf accessed on 22 October 2009.

Williamson, OE 1985, The *Economic Institutions of Capitalism*, New York, Free Press.

Woodall, J, Gourlay, S & Short, D 2000, 'Trends in outsourcing HRD in the UK: The implications for strategic HRD', Working paper.

Web sites

http://www.noa.co.uk/

http://www.hewittassociates.com/

http://www.cipd.co.uk/surveys

http://www.ephorie.de/pdfs/Kris_SBPOA.pdf

http://www.jeitosa.com/resources/karen_beaman/HROinAsiaPacific.pdf

http://www.emeraldinsight.com/Insight/

Chapter 8

THE TRANSFER OF HRM POLICIES AND PRACTICES IN MULTINATIONAL COMPANIES

Anne Vo & Zeenobiyah Hannif

OBJECTIVES

This chapter addresses the transfer of human resource management (HRM) policies and practices of multinational companies (MNCs) across borders in the context of globalisation, with an emphasis on the transfer of HRM practices from developed to developing countries. The chapter specifically explores how and to what extent the

- macro level (the home and host countries);
- meso level (the industry);
- micro level (the firm); and
- HRM-specific level

influence subsidiary HRM behaviour.

By the completion of the chapter you should be able to:

1. identify the key forces influencing the shape and implementation of MNCs' HRM practices at their subsidiaries;
2. describe the ways MNCs transfer their HRM practices; and
3. identify the possible constraints and opportunities posed by host countries with regard to the transfer of MNCs.

DEFINITIONS

Globalisation: Globalisation is a phenomenon 'driven by many factors, of which technology, the related mobility of people, goods and ideas, and a liberal trading environment are perhaps the most obvious' (McKenna 2000, p. 75). It emphasises a 'freeing up of labour and capital flows' (Floyd 2001, p. 109) at the global scale to achieve a competitive advantage through 'efficiency and low cost labour' (Floyd 2001, p. 111). Globalisation is marked by:

- trade liberalisation;
- international economics integration;
- the formation of regional economic communities such as North America, Europe and the Asia Pacific;
- cultural homogeneity; and
- political universalism.

Transfer of HRM policies and practices: The transfer of HRM policies and practices between organisational units is 'a process that covers several stages starting from identifying the knowledge to the actual process of transferring the knowledge to its final utilization by the receiving unit' (Minbaeva, Pedersen, Bjorkman, Fey & Park 2003, p. 587). The transfer process can occur not only from the headquarters to the subsidiary and from one subsidiary to another, but also from the subsidiary to headquarters (through a reverse diffusion process).

Organisational units: In the context of MNCs, organisational units are the headquarters and/or other subsidiaries in the corporation.

Receiving unit: The receiving unit is the focal subsidiary.

Global perspectives

The recent trends to:

- regional integration;
- removal of trade barriers;
- deregulation and opening of closed national markets to international competition;
- the rise of Asian countries; and
- the integration of Central and Eastern Europe and China into the world economy,

have inevitably led to a more globalised world, in which an increasing number of companies widen their horizon of activities beyond their countries' borders.

Growth of transnational corporations

According to the United Nations, there were only about 30,000 MNCs in 1990, while in 2005 there were 77,000 parent companies with over 770,000 foreign subsidiaries (United Nations 2006, p. xviii). These foreign subsidiaries generated an estimated $4.5 trillion in value added, employed about 62 million workers, and exported goods and services valued at more than $4 trillion (United Nations 2006, p. xviii). As Dicken (2003, p. 197) puts it 'more than any other single institution, the transnational corporation ... has come to be regarded as the primary shaper of the contemporary global economy'.

Behaviour patterns of MNEs

The important role of MNCs and their expansion to national and world economies has led to continuous research interest in MNCs and their behaviour patterns. There are two opposing views with regard to the existence of an homogenous model of firms' behaviours—namely:

- the globalisation thesis; and
- the culturalist perspective.

The globalisation thesis

The globalisation thesis argues that a truly global economy has emerged (or is in the process of emerging) in which national economies and national economic management models are losing their distinctiveness (Edwards & Rees 2006).

Pluralistic industrialism

The globalisation thesis dates to the 1960s when Kerr, Dunlop, Harbison and Myers (1960) argued that the logic of industrialisation tends to drive pre-modern societies towards a form of 'pluralistic industrialism'. Although the different strategies of ruling elites and cultural heritages may remain sources of the continuing diversity in those societies, the 'iron hand of technology' is the main driving force of the convergence of social institutions including industrial relations across different countries (Kerr *et al.* 1960, pp. 259–63).

The contemporary globalisation/convergence theory is in the tradition of 'pluralistic industrialism'. The renewal and persistence of the theory draws today, not only on technological determinism but also on conceptions of the impact of the intensifying of economic, political, social and cultural relations across borders.

A globalised economy

The globalisation thesis provoked some interesting speculation about a 'globalised economy' in which distinct national economies are subsumed into region-states which are effective ports of entry to the global economy (Levitt 1983; Reich 1990). Ohmae (1996, p. 11) claims that

'... in terms of real flows of economic activity, nation states have already lost their role as meaningful units of participation in the global economy of today's borderless world.'

In the field of HRM, globalisation has become the force of change. The globalisation thesis suggests that under the intensifying pressure of global competition, companies will:

- follow the same set of 'best practices';
- adopt a convergent model of organisation; and
- become more homogenous in their behaviour to the detriment of national management models.

Denationalisation of MNCs

Bartlett and Goshal (1989) argue that firms have increasingly adopted common responses in order to respond to the demands of the international competitive environment and that a new organisational model is emerging—namely, the transnational firm. The authors further argue that there is 'one best way' which firms should follow if they wish to be successful in the global economy. Similarly, Ohmae believes that MNCs are being transformed into transnational companies, which represent footloose capital, without specific nationality but with a strong corporate identity.

'Country of origin does not matter. Location of headquarters does not matter. The products for which you are responsible and the company you serve have become denationalised.' Ohmae (1990, p. 94)

Criticism of the globalisation thesis

The globalisation thesis has been heavily criticised for being overly enthusiastic, the strongest criticism being that globalists make their claims without supporting data.

Hirst and Thompson (1999) argue that the trend to globalisation has been overstated as a process. They point out that the world economy is far from being genuinely 'global', and for the time being remains a 'worldwide international economic system'. The global economy, they argue, is still characterised fundamentally by exchanges between relatively distinct national economies. Many outcomes (such as the competitive performance of firms and sectors) are substantially determined by processes occurring at the national level. They argue that most MNCs are not transnationals, considering that the major proportion of their income, employment, strategic decisions, composition of corporate board and share ownership are rooted in the parent country (see also Doremus, Keller, Pauly & Reich 1998).

Moreover, Guillén (2001) argues that globalisation increases inequality across countries, especially between developed and developing countries. Even though developing economies have become increasingly internationalised and integrated into the global system, they are, like those in East Asia, in a weaker position in the 'global commodity chains' compared to MNCs, in the sense that the latter play the central role in:

- controlling the production system in 'producer-driven chains' or
- setting up decentralised production networks in exporting countries in 'buyer-driven chains' (Gereffi 1996).

Therefore, globalisation accentuates uneven development between different countries. It increases the dependency of 'peripheral' developing countries on investment from 'central' economies.

Comparative perspectives

Research literature has long developed different frameworks to analyse and examine the relationship between social settings and the behaviours of economic organisations. There are several frameworks from comparative perspectives, including:

- the industrialism or contingency perspective;
- the capitalism perspective;
- the cultural perspective; and
- the institutional perspective.

So far, however, the most significant contributions to the debates seem to have come from the cultural and comparative institutionalism approaches.

The culturalist perspective

The culturalist perspective explains organisational structure and practice as a collective enactment of beliefs and values concerning shared cognitive structures. Although it does not deny the material constraints or benefits of organising, it explains organisational patterns as driven by shared ideas and understandings.

Dimensions of cultural difference

This approach has found theoretical underpinning in the work of notable authors such as Hofstede (1980), Laurent (1986), Trompenaars and Hampden-Turner (1998) and House, Hanges, Javidan, Dorfman and Gupta (2004). Hofstede (1980), for example, postulates that the dominant value patterns of managers and employees vary on four dimensions of cultures — namely:

- power distance;
- uncertainty avoidance;
- individualism versus collectivism; and
- masculinity versus femininity.

He later added a fifth dimension (Hofstede 1997), opposing a long-term orientation in life to a short-term orientation.

He argues that power distance is related to preferences regarding the distribution of authority, and that uncertainty avoidance is related to the importance of rules and procedures—both of which might have important implications for the preference of certain types of entry modes (Hofstede 2001).

Problems with the cultural approach

Applying a cultural approach in the study of a society's structure, however, especially in a comparative perspective, can be insufficient and problematic.

Firstly, the cultural approach tends to simplify national cultures into straightforward numbers and indexes, and constructs cross-culture comparative analysis on the basis of exaggerated cultural stereotypes.

Secondly, a cultural perspective sees national cultures as characterised by stability and slow change (Hofstede 1997). In his investigation into the transferability of the flat British hierarchical structure into Chinese society (perceived to place a traditionally high value on hierarchy) Gamble (2001) successfully argues that cultures should be considered 'not as a static monolith but a shifting and changeable repertoire with diverse strands'.

Thirdly, the cultural approach is not a sharp enough tool to explain organisational choices and behaviours. Research adopting a cultural approach has to point out, with a reasonable degree of precision, which elements of national culture are seen to influence aspects of business organisation. Harzing (2003) claims that a large number of studies do not take this step.

The institutional perspective

The institutional perspective sees business organisations as socially constituted, thus reflecting national distinctiveness in institutional settings.

Dominant institutions are integrated and their features mutually reinforcing. National institutional arrangements, therefore, are strong and robust. They demonstrate significant inertia in the face of any pressure for change (Hollingsworth 1997).

The effects of variation in the institutional context on the behaviour of companies are prominent, as a 'firm will gravitate towards the mode of coordination for which there is institutional support' (Hall & Soskice 2001, p. 9). A systematic analysis of main national institutions and the interactions between these institutional arrangements and the activities of business organisations has been conceptualised in terms of:

- societal logic (Maurice, Sellier & Silvestre 1986);
- social systems of production (Hollingsworth & Boyer 1997);

- industrial orders (Herrigel 1996);
- national industrial order (Lane 1992); or
- national business systems (Whitley 2000).

There are some disparities among authors on what the dominant social institutions are. A sub-system considered as a significant part of a business system by some authors might be excluded from other authors' lists. Lane's (1992) framework for example, consists of:

- the state;
- the financial system;
- the system of education and training; and to a lesser extent
- the network of business associations and the system of industrial relations.

Country perspectives

In the process of HRM transfer, there are two (or in some cases, more than two) business systems involved, either as a home base or a host base for the MNCs' operation. The transfer process is dependent on the institutional and cultural difference between the two systems and the distinctive characteristics of home and host countries.

The country of origin perspective

From the country of origin perspective, the variables are:

- the institutional and cultural characteristics;
- the distinctiveness of national HRM models; and
- the dominance effect of the home system.

There is some evidence that the home country exerts a distinctive influence on the way labour is managed in MNCs (Harzing & Sorge 2003; Harzing & Noorderhaven 2006).

Corporate identity

Ferner (2000) argues that the parent company is embedded in an institutional environment located in the home country. To varying degrees, the particular features of the home country become an ingrained part of each MNC's corporate identity. They shape its international orientation in the design of the HRM systems to be used in its overseas subsidiaries. Thus, 'ethnocentricity' and 'polycentrism' have been seen as traits that are characteristic of multinationals of different national origins. Japanese and American companies, for example, tend to be more ethnocentric than their European counterparts, other things such as sector of operation being equal (Ferner 1994, p. 88).

The dominance effect

The 'dominance effect' (Elger & Smith 1994) or inferiority of a business system determines the transfer of the HRM system from one business system to another. Elger and Smith (1994) argue that the dominance of a home system, largely in economic terms, is itself one mechanism of diffusion. Dominant states are more able to exercise or invite dissemination and adoption of their version of capitalism in other national systems.

> *'Firms from strongly integrated and successful economies may carry over national character to subsidiaries when locating abroad, and transfer home country practices rather than adopt the practices encountered in the host country' (Smith & Meiksins 1995, p. 262).*

The host country perspective

From the host country perspective, the variables consist of:

- the nature of the host business system;
- its cultural characteristics; and
- its relative power in the relation with MNCs.

Open v. closed environment of host country

The superiority/inferiority of the host system determines its relative openness or receptiveness to dominant 'best practice' (Whitley 1992). In a permissive/open host country environment which imposes fewer constraints on firms, the introduction of country-of-origin practices is easier (Whitley 1992). In contrast, MNCs may be prevented from transferring country-of-origin practices into a constraining/closed host country environment which is highly regulated and distinctive (Whitley 1992). The subsidiaries can utilise their resources (expertise about local environment and market, specialist knowledge, culture, etc.) to block diffusion (Edwards, Ferner & Sisson 1993).

Internal strength and economic power

Different national contexts provide frameworks which allow MNCs greater or lesser flexibility for external management policies (Ferner & Hyman 1992). A combination of internal strength and economic power determines a host country's relative 'power' position towards MNCs.

A host country's internal strength can be seen in:

- the coherence and integration of the national business system and sub-systems;
- predictability and enforceability of regulations; and
- quality of socio-economic infrastructure.

Its economic position can be measured by a series of indices, such as:

- the level of GDP;
- GNI per capita;
- size of domestic market; and
- dependence on an external source of capital to promote industrialisation (Vo 2004).

Developing countries

Vo (2004) argues that developing countries are 'low power' host countries to the operation of MNCs. A low power context has a high level of permissiveness and imposes minimal constraints on the transfer of production and/or managerial technology by MNCs if they do wish to transfer.

A variety of factors, however, suggest the existence of a more complex situation for MNC operations in developing countries. These factors include:

- change in terms of economic growth (e.g. China and Vietnam);
- shift in political arrangements (e.g. Russia and the Eastern Bloc);
- the acceptance of and demand for host country values; and
- the clash between traditional and new social and cultural values.

They require MNCs to employ a very high level of flexibility (and in some cases compromise) when forming and implementing their managerial strategies.

Sector perspectives

'Firms compete in industries, not nations' (Porter 1990, p. 619). Several studies point out the relevance of the role of industry in the analysis of MNCs' operations—including their HRM strategy (e.g. Colling & Clark 2002).

Porter (1990) argues that industries vary along a continuum from multidomestic to global in their international competition. In global industries, a firm's competitive position in one country affects and is affected by competition in other countries, whereas in multidomestic industries, competition in each country is independent of competition in other countries.

Multidomestic industries

Foreign subsidiaries of MNCs in multidomestic industries are relatively independent of the headquarters. They rely primarily on inputs from the local environment and are driven by local competition with different firms, including local ones.

As they are usually more dependent on local resources, foreign subsidiaries in multidomestic industries have a relatively greater need to gain local legitimacy. It is likely, therefore, that they will adopt more of the features of the host country's firms and be more responsive to the host country and the local situation (Bartlett & Ghoshal 1989). As far as HRM is concerned, the role of HRM in a multidomestic industry is likely to be more domestic and locally responsive, and less international in orientation (Schuler, Dowling & De Cieri 1993).

Industries considered as traditionally multidomestic are:

- retailing;
- commercial banking;
- insurance;
- distribution;
- consumer food products; and
- branded packaged products and related industries.

Global industries

On the other hand, foreign subsidiaries in global industries show a higher degree of interdependence with the headquarters and other subsidiaries of the MNC. Their production is an integrated and rationalised process to produce standardised products in a cost-effective way (Bartlett & Ghoshal 1989).

Due to the need for integration and coordination, foreign subsidiaries in a global industry receive a high level of support from headquarters in terms of technology as well as managerial know-how. These subsidiaries are less dependent on the local environment and so are under less pressure to conform to local norms (Rosenzweig & Singh 1991).

As far as HRM is concerned, the transmission of country-of-origin influence is more marked in MNCs operating in more global industries compared with multidomestic ones (Ferner 1997). A number of industries (such as automobiles, chemicals, consumer electronics, and semiconductor industries) have developed into global industries since the 1970s.

Organisational perspectives

A parent company might have a functional focus on one (or more than one) HRM aspect which they wish to transfer to a subsidiary. Thus a firm's resources may be focused on these functions to the detriment of other functions. As a consequence, viewing multinationals in terms of an overall orientation obscures the internal differentiation of management practices within an MNC. Instead, an MNC is viewed as a nexus of differentiated practices (Rosenzweig & Nohria 1994). Its HRM system is comprised of a range of HR functions, and each of these HR functions is influenced by different forces (Kostova & Roth 2002).

Parent company v. host country

In the same subsidiary, some management practices might closely follow the parent company practices, while others may more closely resemble those of the host country.

Schmitt and Sadowski (2003) consider the costs and benefits to US and British MNCs of centralising or decentralising different industry relations (IR) and HRM issues of subsidiaries in Germany. They found that the strongest centralisation aspects related to training and that there was moderate centralisation in relation to variable pay and employee ownership arrangements. With respect to IR, due to legitimacy considerations, there was clear evidence of a nearly complete dominance of host country effects.

Forces affecting transfer of HRM practices

The most cited organisational factors to affect the transfer of HRM practices include:

- business strategy,
- administrative heritage; and
- the nature of the subsidiary (such as its function, age, size and ownership type).

Business strategy

Beechler and Yang (1994) argue that business strategy is a fundamental source of human resource contingencies and that strategy shapes the strategic HRM practices of the firm.

Administrative heritage

Each firm has a body of administrative heritage that invisibly but strongly shapes 'how things are done' (Bartlett & Ghoshal 1989).

Nature of the subsidiary

Yuen and Kee (1993) believe that there is a tendency for HRM practices to become more standardised and formalised with time. The bigger the company, they argue, the more likely it will be to develop a formal HRM function and the less it will depend on the external labour market. Furthermore, subsidiaries which are established through greenfield investments are more likely to adhere to the operations of their foreign parents than brownfield ones (Tayeb 1998).

To summarise, the evidence presented here indicates that the profile of HRM policies and practices in an MNC subsidiary is shaped by the interplay of parallel or opposing forces for internal consistency or isomorphism with the local environment (Figure 8.1). These forces include:

- the home country;
- the host country; and
- industrial and organisational effects.

Low power host countries

Furthermore, the transfer of HRM practices is dependent on a host country's relative 'power' position towards MNCs. Developing countries present the case of 'low power' host countries to the operation of MNCs. Such environments, on the one hand, facilitate the penetration of novel forms of economic organisation. On the other hand, they suggest a complex situation for MNC operations and require from them a very high level of flexibility (and in some cases compromise) when forming and implementing transferred managerial practices.

Dynamics of influence

A force of influence is not fixed; on the contrary, it is changeable. When one force of influence changes, the relative weight of the different forces in their interaction changes; the existing nature of HRM may be altered or replaced by a new configuration.

Ferner, Almond, Clark, Colling, Edwards, Holden and Muller-Carmen (2004) argue that the pattern of oscillation between centralisation and subsidiary autonomy reflects external facts in the environment (such as increasing market competition and technological change) and internal negotiation of individuals and groups with their own specific interests within the company.

Subsidiary autonomy is earned on the basis of:

- its importance to the global company;
- its distinctive capabilities or resources (such as new skills, competences, knowledge of the local system); and
- its exploitation of ambiguities and tensions between different headquarters' policies (see also Birkinshaw's (1996) study on subsidiary mandates' gain, development and loss).

Chapter 8 – The Transfer of HRM Policies and Practices in Multinational Companies

Figure 8.1 The interaction of different forces in the shaping and implementation of MNC subsidiaries' IR/HRM policies and practices

Home business system
- The business system characteristics
- Distinctiveness of IR/HRM practices
- The dominance effect

Global forces

Host business system
- The business system characteristics
- Regulated/ unregulated
- The relative power in relation to MNCs

MNCs
- IR/HRM competences
- HQS international orientation
- Competitive strategy

Industry
- Industry characteristics
- Host country's industrial development strategy

Partner in joint venture (JV)
- Share proportion
- Leadership in JV
- Staff in JV

Subsidiary
- Business strategy
- Size
- Age
- Ownership type
- Etc.

- Recruitment & selection
- Training & development
- Reward system & performance management
- Industrial relations
- Etc.

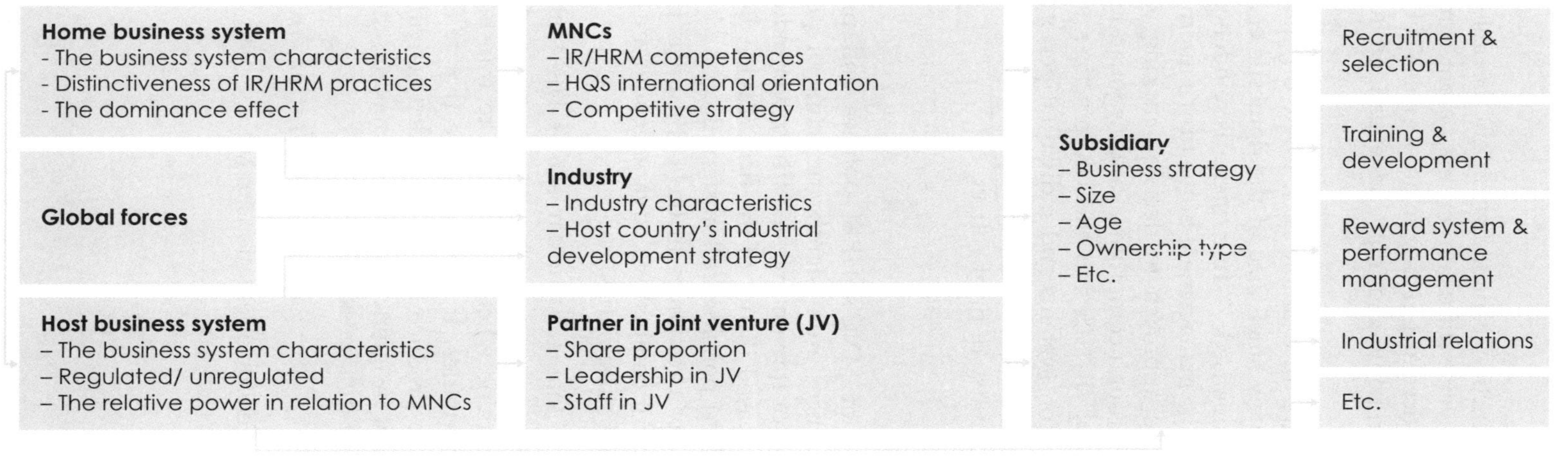

Source: Created by the author for this chapter.

Reverse diffusion

Subsidiaries which possess distinctive capabilities might be able to go against the trend by imposing 'reverse diffusion' on the parent companies (Edwards 1998). In this case, practices originating in an overseas subsidiary are imported by the parent company and may be expanded to other subsidiaries.

Edwards and Rees (2006) provide an example of a MNC originating in Sweden where, due to the relatively small size of the domestic economy, companies are highly internationalised. While there is evidence of a distinctively Swedish element to the management of the firm's international workforce (such as a democratic approach to decision making and the tradition of seeking agreement through compromise and negotiation) there is also evidence that firms adopt the US and the UK practices such as 'flexible' or 'variable' compensation systems and individual performance-related pay schemes (Edwards & Rees 2006). Thus the process of 'reserve diffusion' gradually erodes the country-of-origin effect.

The transfer process

Most literature on the transfer of MNC's HRM policies and practices assume that superior HRM practices are a significant actual or potential source of competitive advantage for foreign invested firms over indigenous firms. Drawing on the resource-based theory of the firm, Taylor, Beechler and Napier (1996) argue that HRM policies are transferred only when it is believed that the parent company's resources in the HRM areas provide MNCs with an important source of competitive advantage and are critical to the successful operation of their subsidiaries.

Even if it can be demonstrated that a particular set of HRM practices contributes significantly to superior performance in home country operations, a MNC has to determine whether it wishes to transfer these practices to their overseas subsidiaries. If MNCs decide that it is more profitable to leave subsidiaries to produce low-value added activities and view HRM strategies as relatively insignificant to profit maximisation, the transfer of home practices becomes unnecessary.

Generic orientations in MNCs

Taylor *et al.* (1996) identify three generic orientations in MNCs:

- adaptive;
- exportive; and
- integrative.

The adaptive approach

An adaptive approach is one in which MNCs seek low internal consistency with the rest of the firm and high external consistency with the local environment where the subsidiary is located. This approach emphasises the decentralisation of HR systems and the adoption of local practices to suit local conditions. An adaptive approach leaves the design of the subsidiary's HRM system to the subsidiary.

The exportive approach

An exportive approach is one in which MNCs seek high internal consistency and low external consistency. This approach emphasises a centralised HRM system in which the subsidiary's system is highly integrated with that of the parent company. An exportive approach places the design of the subsidiary's HRM system in the hands of the parent company.

The integrative approach

An integrative approach is one in which MNCs seek high internal consistency and moderate external consistency. This approach focuses on combining the characteristics of the parent company's HRM system with those of its overseas subsidiaries to create the optimum HR solution and then diffusing it worldwide. An integrative approach represents shared responsibility between the parent company and the subsidiary for decision making in the design of the subsidiary's HRM system.

Transfer mechanisms

An international HRM approach is realised at MNCs' subsidiaries through complex transfer mechanisms. Liu (2004) categorises these mechanisms into direct and indirect ones.

Direct mechanisms

Direct mechanisms refer to a formal set of HRM policies, rules, programs, and procedures set by the parent company that the subsidiaries must follow. Ferner and Edwards (1995) argue that this issuing of HRM guidelines and rules by the parent company is based on authority relations between the parent company and subsidiaries, particularly when they are backed up by formal systems of management control with reward and penalty systems.

Indirect mechanisms

Indirect mechanisms rely on building a common organisational culture and implementing control through the international transfer of managers (Liu 2004).

Organisational culture comprises cultural values and corporate values and philosophy (Liu 2004). Meanwhile, 'expatriate managers have a considerable role as interpreters and implementers of HR and business strategy' (Harris & Holden 2001, p. 85). Japanese companies for example, are well known to rely heavily on a large number of personnel dispatched from the parent company to cultivate a distinctive set of organisational features in their overseas subsidiaries (Vo 2009).

Case study: The transfer of the reward system of performance management from Japanese MNCs to Vietnamese subsidiaries

Vietnam presents an excellent case for the analysis of HRM transfer in the context of a developing country.

In 1986 the Vietnamese government introduced a comprehensive reform program, known as *Doi Moi*, to liberalise the economy from a socialist, centrally planned economic system to a more market-oriented one.

Although the results of the economic reforms were very encouraging, Vietnam remains a very poor country. In 2007, Vietnam's Gross National Income per capita was $US690, thus classified by the World Bank as a low-income economy (World Bank 2008). In the middle of a radical transformation process, the formation and implementation of new legislation (including regulations governing the status and operations of foreign firms) remain a major source of uncertainty. The sub-systems (the state, the financial system, the system of education and training, the network of business associations, and the system of IR/HRM) are constantly under pressure with regard to changes and innovations.

Meanwhile, foreign direct investment constitutes an essential part of the Vietnamese economy. Vietnam has been highly conscious of the need to keep foreign investment law attractive to hold foreign investors' interest. Gillespie (1990, p. 417) notes that there are 'very few mandatory regulations that purport to govern or restrict the internal management' of the foreign invested firm.

Vietnam's weak position in the world economy, the under-developed nature of the main components of the national business system and its dependence on external sources of capital to promote industrialisation make Vietnam a low power host country in the operation of MNCs' subsidiaries. MNCs have considerable flexibility in the design and implementation of their HRM systems.

Japan, in the role of home country, has a very strong presence in the Vietnamese economy. Over the period 1998–2007, Japan was continuously ranked the largest investor in Vietnam. Japanese MNCs have a distinctive and ingrained way of managing their labour forces, rooted in differences in their institutional systems. The Japanese wage system is characterised by a seniority-based wage structure (*nenko*) which regulates pay rises according to age and length of service in the organisation (Littler 1982). The 'dominance effect' of the Japanese economy and their MNCs facilitates the transfer of their home practices to their Vietnamese subsidiaries.

In this example, the companies studied are coded JP Auto1 and JP Auto2. The findings presented constitute part of a study conducted in the period from 2002 to 2008 of Japanese MNCs operating in the automotive industry in Vietnam.

The research finds that the Japanese firms have transferred their *nenko* system to their Vietnamese subsidiaries with some adaptations. There are three determinants in the basic salary in the Japanese firms. The first determinant, the personal salary, is determined by each employee's qualifications, experience, skills and the result of their performance appraisal. The second determinant, the job salary, is determined by job grade (based on job complexity and position responsibilities). The third determinant is the age-linked salary. JP Auto1 and JP Auto2 use the so-called 'life module' in defining the level of salary they pay to their employees.

The Vietnamese life module is the result of research conducted in Vietnam by compensation and benefit specialists from the Japanese headquarters with the support of the Vietnamese staff at the subsidiaries. The life module estimates the cost of living of an average employee from the age of 18 to 60. The salary of the employee is meant to increase in pace with their promotion in the firms (from team member to team leader to supervisor, etc.) and their personal needs (from being single to being married, having children, paying for children's tuition fees, buying a house in the early or mid-40s, etc.). The age-linked salary rises more sharply in the younger ages and then is held constant after the age of 50 until retirement.

Thus, in the form of age-linked payment, the *nenko* system manifests itself in the remuneration system of big Japanese firms in Vietnam. However, the companies studied did not attempt to implement a fully-fledged Japanese style seniority-based wage system.

First of all, the HRM manager of JP Auto1 and JP Auto2 claimed that greater weight is given to individual merit in determining wages and

> promotions, due to the much greater influence of the external labour market in Vietnam compared with Japan.
>
> Secondly, due to the limited number of qualified professionals and upper levels in the Vietnamese labour market, in order to attract candidates for their vacancies, the starting salary paid by these Japanese subsidiaries is relatively higher than would be expected by firms adhering strictly to the *nenko* principle (compared to their headquarters).
>
> The case studies offer a good example of how MNCs, using formal transfer mechanisms, have successfully transferred their HRM practices overseas and the flexibility and adaptation they need to adopt in order to embrace the process.

Conclusion

This chapter has provided an overview of the transfer of HRM policies and practices of MNCs.

The role of nationality in the global market

The chapter has reviewed two opposing positions with regard to the role of nationality in today's global market. One position argues that globalisation has become the force of change and that under the forces of globalisation, economic organisations are following the same rules of capitalism, leading to a process of homogenisation in their behaviour. Conversely, the other argues that nationality is enduring and strongly affects economic organisations' behaviour at home and abroad. Contrasting though they seem to be, such theories complement each other. They contribute to an understanding of the structural commonalities and specificities between societies and firms and the interrelation and positions of national business systems in the global economy.

Perspectives on HRM transfer

We have explored how and to what extent

- the macro level (the home and host countries);
- the meso level (the industry);
- the micro level (the firm); and
- the HRM specific level

influence subsidiary HRM behaviour.

We have also examined the power relation between host countries and MNCs. Three generic orientations in MNC transfer are said to shape the level of HR centralisation or localisation:

- adaptive;
- exportive; and
- integrative.

Mechanisms of transfer

The mechanism of transfer, either direct or indirect, determines the way that HR practices are transmitted overseas. A subsidiary's HRM function is composed of related yet differentiated areas, within which there are a range of HRM practices. Each HRM practice is the result of interaction among various forces of influence and their relative weight in relation to other forces.

Furthermore, it is argued in this chapter that the degree of central control and subsidiary autonomy is not determined in a mechanical way by headquarters, but emerges from a process of negotiation between headquarters and subsidiary. It is, therefore, essential that the transfer of HRM practices within subsidiaries be attached to the notion of 'dynamism' and 'openness to change'.

References

Bartlett, CA & Ghoshal, S 1989, *Managing across borders the transnational solution*, Great Britain, Mackays of Chatham PLC, Chatham, Kent.

Beechler, S & Yang, JZ 1994 'The transfer of Japanese-style management to American subsidiaries: contingencies, constraints, and competencies', *Journal of International Business Studies*, Vol. 25, No. 3, pp 467-492.

Birkinshaw, J 1996, 'How multinational subsidiary mandates are gained and lost', *Journal of International Business Studies*, Third Quarter, pp. 467-495.

Colling, T & Clark, I 2002, 'Looking for 'Americanness': home- country, sector and firm effects on employment systems in an engineering services company', *European Journal of Industrial Relations*, Vol. 8, No. 3, pp. 301-324.

Dicken, P 2003, *Global shift: Reshaping the global economic map in the 21st century*, 4th edn, London, Sage.

Doremus, PN, Keller, WW, Pauly, LW & Reich S 1998, *The myth of the global corporation*, Princeton, Princeton University Press.

Edwards, T 1998, 'Multinationals, labour management and the process of diffusion', *International Journal of Human Resource Management*, Vol. 9, No. 4, pp. 696-709.

Edwards, T & Rees, C 2006, 'The transfer of human resource practices in multinational companies', in Edwards, T & Rees, C (eds), *International human resource management globalisation, national systems and multinational companies*, Prentice Hall, pp. 91-110.

Edwards, P, Ferner, A & Sisson, K 1993, *People and the process of management in the multinational company: A review and some illustrations*, Warwick Papers in Industrial Relations, Coventry, IRRU.

Elger, T & Smith, C 1994, 'Global Japanization? Convergence and competition in the organisation of the labour process', in Elger, T & Smith, C (eds) *Global Japanization? The transformation of the labour process*, London, Routledge.

Ferner, A 2000, *The embeddedness of US multinational companies in the US business system: implications for HR/IR*, Occasional Papers No. 61, Leicester, De Montfort University Business School.

Ferner, A 1994, 'Multinational companies and human resource management: An overview of research issues', *Human Resource Management Journal*, Vol. 4, No. 3, pp. 79-102.

Ferner, A 1997, 'Country of origin effects and HRM in multinational companies', *Human Resource Management Journal*, Vol. 7, No. 1, pp. 19-37.

Ferner, A & Edwards, P 1995, 'Power and the diffusion of organizational change within multinational enterprises', *European Journal of Industrial Relations,* Vol. 1, No. 2, pp. 229-257.

Ferner, A & Hyman, R 1992, 'Introduction: industrial relations in the New Europe', in Hyman, R & Ferner, A (eds.) *Industrial relations in the New Europe*, Oxford, Blackwell, xvi-xxxvii.

Ferner, A, Almond, P, Clark, I, Colling, T, Edwards, T, Holden, L & Muller-Camen, M 2004, 'The dynamics of central control and subsidiary autonomy in the management of human resources: case study evidence from US MNCs in the UK', *Organization Studies*, Vol. 25, No. 3, pp. 363-391.

Floyd, D 2001, 'Globalisation or Europeanisation of business activity? Exploring the critical issues', *European Business Review*, Vol. 13 No. 2, pp. 109-13.

Gamble, J 2001 *Transferring business practices from the United Kingdom to China: the limits and potential for convergence*, Paper presented to 'Multinational companies and human resource management: Between globalisation and national business systems' Conference, De Montfort University Graduate School of Business, Leicester.

Gereffi, G 1996 'Commodity chains and regional divisions of labor in East Asia', *Journal of Asian Business*, Vol. 12, pp. 75-112.

Gillespie, J 1990, 'Foreign investment in S.R. Vietnam revisited', *International Business Lawyer*, Vol. 18, October, pp. 416-424.

Guillén, M 2001, 'Is globalization civilizing, destructive or feeble? A critique of five key debates in the social science literature', *Annual Review of Sociology*, Vol. 27, pp. 235-260.

Hall, P & Soskice, D 2001, *An introduction to varieties of capitalism*, in Hall, P & Soskice, D (eds) *Varieties of capitalism: The institutional foundations of comparative advantage*, Oxford, Oxford University Press.

Harris, H & Holden, L 2001, 'Between autonomy and control: expatriate managers and strategic IHRM in SMEs', *Thunderbird International Business Review*, Vol. 43 No. 1, pp. 77-101.

Harzing, AW 2003, 'The role of culture in entry mode studies: from negligence to myopia?', *Advances in International Management*, Vol. 15, pp. 75-127.

Hazing, AW & Noorderhaven, NG 2007, 'Knowledge flows in MNCs: An empirical test and extension of Gupta & Govindarajan's typology of subsidiary roles', *International Business Review*, Vol. 15, No. 3

Hazing, AW & Sorge, AM 2003, 'The relative impact of country-of-origin and universal contingencies on internationalization strategies and corporate control in multinational enterprises: World-wide and European perspectives', *Organisation Studies*, Vol. 24, No. 2, pp. 187-214.

Herrigel, G 1996, *Industrial constructions: the sources of German industrial power*, New York, Cambridge University Press.

Hirst, P & Thompson, G 1999, *Globalization in question*, 2nd edn, Polity Press.

Hofstede, G 1980, *Culture's consequences: international differences in work-related values*, London, SAGE.

Hofstede, G 1997, *Cultures and organizations: software of the mind*, 2nd edition, London, McGraw-Hill.

Hofstede, G 2001, *Culture's consequences: Comparing values, behaviors, institutions, and organizations across nations*, London, SAGE.

Hollingsworth, RJ & Boyer, R 1997, 'Coordination of economic actors and social systems of production', in Hollingsworth, RJ & Boyer, R (eds) *Contemporary capitalism the embeddedness of institutions*, USA, Cambridge University Press.

Hollingsworth, JR 1997, 'The institutional embeddedness of American capitalism', in Crouch, C & Streeck, W (eds) *Political Economy of Modern Capitalism*, London, Sage.

House, RJ, Hanges, PJ, Javidan, M, Dorfman, PW & Gupta, V 2004, *Culture, leadership, and organisations, the global study of 62 societies*, Thousand Oaks, Sage.

Kerr, C, Dunlop, JT, Harbison, FH & Myers, CA 1960, *Industrialism and Industrial man*, London, Heinemann.

Kostova, T & Roth, K 2002, 'Adoption of an organisational practice by subsidiaries of multinational corporations: institutional and relational effects', *Academy of Management Journal*, Vol. 45, No. 1, pp. 215-233.

Lane, C 1992, 'European business systems: Britain and Germany compared', in Whitley, R (ed.) *European business systems firms and markets in their national contexts*, SAGE publications.

Laurent, A 1986, 'The cross-cultural puzzle of international human resource management', *Human Resource Management*, Vol. 25, No. 1, pp. 91-102.

Levitt, T 1983, 'The globalisation of markets', *Harvard Business Review*, Vol. 61, No. 3, pp. 92-102.

Littler, C 1982, *The development of the labour process in capitalist societies*, London, Heinemann.

Liu, W 2004, 'The cross-national transfer of HRM practices in MNCs: An integrative research model', *International Journal of Manpower*, Vol. 25, No. 6, pp. 500-517.

McKenna, B 2000, 'Labour responses to globalization: the Australian experience', *Asia Pacific Business Review*, Vol. 7 No. 1, pp. 71-104.

Maurice, M, Sellier, F & Silvestre, JJ 1986, *The social foundations of industrial power*, Cambridge, Mass., MIT Press.

Minbaeva, D, Pedersen, T, Bjorkman, I, Fey, CF, Park, HJ 2003, 'MNC knowledge transfer, subsidiary absorptive capacity, and HRM', *Journal of International Business Studies*, Vol. 34, pp. 586-99.

Ohmae, K 1990, *The borderless word*, London, HarperCollins.

Ohmae, K 1996, *End of the nation state: the rise of regional economies*, London, HarperCollins.

Porter, M 1990, *The competitive advantage of nations*, London/Basingstoke, MacMillan.

Reich, R 1990, *Who is us?*, Harvard Business Review, Vol. 62, No. 1, pp. 53-65.

Rosenzweig, J & Nohria, N 1994, 'Influences on human resource management practices in multinational corporations', *Journal of International Business Studies*, Second quarter, pp. 229-251.

Rosenzweig, PM & Singh, JV 1991, 'Organizational environments and the multinational enterprise', *Academy of Management Review*, Vol. 16, No. 2, pp. 340-361.

Schmitt, M & Sadowski, D 2003, 'A rationalistic cost-minimization approach to the international transfer of HRM/IR practices: Anglo-Saxon multinationals in the Federal Republic of Germany', *International Journal of Human Resource Management*, Vol. 14, No. 3, pp. 409-430.

Schuler, RS, Dowling, PJ & De Cieri, H 1993, 'An integrative framework of strategic international human resource management', *The International Journal of Human Resource Management*, Vol. 4, No. 4, pp. 717-764.

Smith, C & Meiksins, P 1995, 'System, society and dominance effects in cross-national organisational analysis', *Work, Employment & Society*, Vol. 9, No. 2, pp. 241-267.

Tayeb, M 1998, 'Transfer of HRM practices across cultures: an American company in Scotland', *The International Journal of Human Resource Management*, Vol. 9, No. 2, pp. 332-358.

Taylor, S, Beechler, S, Napier, N 1996, 'Toward an integrative model of strategic international human resource management', *Academy of Management Review*, Vol. 21, No. 4, pp. 959-985.

Trompenaars, A & Hampden-Turner, C 1998, *Riding the waves of culture: understanding cultural diversity in global business*, McGraw-Hill.

United Nations 2006, *World Investment Report 2006*, 25 February 2009, <http://www.unctad.org/en/docs/wir2006_en.pdf>.

Vo, A 2004, *The interaction of home and host country effects in a low power host environment: The case of industrial relations and human resource management in US and Japanese multinational subsidiaries in Vietnam*, Unpublished PhD thesis, UK, De Montfort University.

Vo, A 2009, 'Career Development for Host Country Nationals: A Case of American and Japanese Multinational Companies in Vietnam', *The International Journal of Human Resource Management*.

Yuen, EC & Kee, HT 1993, 'Headquarters, host-culture and organisational influences on HRM policies and practices', *Management International Review*, Vol. 33, No. 4, pp. 361-383.

Whitley, R 1992, 'Societies, firms and markets: The social structuring of business systems', in Whitley, R (ed) *European business systems firms and markets in their national contexts*, SAGE publications.

Whitley, R 2000, *Divergent capitalisms the social structuring and change of business systems*, Oxford University Press.

World Bank 2008, *World development indicators database*, World Bank, 3 April 2008, <http://siteresources.worldbank.org/DATASTATISTICS/Resources/GNIPC.pdf>.

Part II: Inner Context—Organisational Culture, Structure, Politics/Leadership, Task-Technology, Business Outputs

Chapter 9

WORK–LIFE MANAGEMENT

Anne Bardoel & Kerry Grigg

OBJECTIVES

By the completion of the chapter you should be able to:

1. identify the major demographic and socio-cultural changes taking place at a global and local level that have altered the traditionally established dynamics of work, family and personal life;

2. define the terms work–family and work–life;

3. identify the issues regarding the public policy and legal context of work–life policies and practices in Australia;

4. identify and analyse workplace initiatives aimed at helping individuals manage work, family, and life roles;

5. analyse the business case for work–life initiatives in organisations and the role of HR professionals in implementing work–life policies and practices.

DEFINITIONS

Work-family balance: Refers to how you manage your family responsibilities towards children, ageing parents, a disabled family member, or a partner/spouse.

Work-life balance: A more holistic term that includes your ability to balance your overall life, including your responsibilities to yourself, your community, and your many priorities, which may or may not have to do with family.

Work-life initiatives: Those strategies, policies, programs and practices initiated and maintained in workplaces to address work-family conflict, quality of work and life, and need for flexibility.

Introduction

Work–life initiatives

Although there is no uniformly accepted definition of work–life initiatives, three primary categorisations are generally applied when examining work–life initiatives in organisations:

- pre-recruitment;
- dependent care, family leave, and
- flexible scheduling (Arthur & Cook 2003).

Work–life initiatives are defined as those strategies, policies, programs and practices initiated and maintained in workplaces to address:

- work–family conflict;
- quality of work and life; and
- need for flexibility.

Work–life issues in the Asia Pacific

The Asia Pacific region is an interesting context in which to examine work–life issues because it includes western and Asian nations, as well as developing and developed economies.

The work–life issues differ depending on the country and economic environment. However, global work/life needs assessments conducted by leading work/life consultants Shapiro and Noble (2001) identified three consistent themes of what employees from around the world identify as being important barriers to reconciling their work and personal lives. The three issues identified included:

- a lack of flexible work policies and practices;
- the availability and affordability of dependent care; and
- the negative impact of work over-load and long working hours.

These three factors form the basis for understanding how organisations operating in different countries in the Asia Pacific region respond. Hence the strategic challenge for HR professionals is to ensure the significant changes in work patterns and in family structures that have occurred in Australia and other parts of the Asia Pacific region over the last thirty years are matched by changes in organisational culture and practice.

Research in the work–life concept

The work–life concept was first identified and developed in the USA and in developed economies (Hein 2005). Over recent years a considerable growth in the research and interest in the work–life concept has been witnessed in the United States (Drago & Hyatt 2003) and Australia (Bardoel, De Cieri & Santos 2008; Skinner, Pocock & Williams 2008).

Collectivist cultures v. individualistic cultures

Despite the proliferation of management research in Asia in recent years there has been little research on managing work–life needs for employees in an Asian context (Bruton & Lau 2008). Some micro-level research conducted from an Asian perspective has examined differences in the experience of work–family conflict (e.g. Choi 2008; Lu, Gilmour, Kao & Huang 2006) but the organisational perspective has been mostly overlooked to date.

Lu, Gilmour, Kao and Huang's (2006) cross-cultural study of work–family demands for British and Taiwanese employees found that people from collectivist societies saw work as a means of supporting the family rather than a means of enhancing self. Thus, even when work demands are high, the demands are less likely to generate work–family conflict. People from individualistic cultures (e.g. Australia), however, tend to perceive work and family demands as competing for limited personal resources such as time and energy and are thus more likely to experience work–family conflict.

Links between work–life and nationality

A significant body of work from the work–life field has now demonstrated the link between nationality (including cultural, social, economic and technological influences) and the experience of work–life issues for employees living in those countries (e.g. Joplin, Shaffer, Francesco & Lau 2003; Lyness & Kropf 2005; Poelmans, Spector, Cooper, Allen, O'Driscoll & Sanchez 2003).

Given the heterogeneous nature of the countries making up the Asia Pacific region, the work–life issues facing employees in Australia will be different, for example, from those faced by their counterparts in Korea. This diversity makes a broad-brush discussion of work–life issues within the region a complex endeavour and one that is beyond the scope of this chapter. Instead the following section provides a very brief overview of the salient work–life issues facing Australian organisations.

Scope of the chapter

In this chapter we:

- introduce the work–life concept;
- discuss the trends unfolding at a global and local level that are driving the increased interest and concern for work–life issues by individuals, organisations and governments;
- overview the role of public policy in work–life issues;
- discuss why and how organisations are striving to meet the work–life needs of their employees better;
- provide examples of how companies in Australia and the Asia Pacific region address work–family conflict and work–life issues.

This last section includes:

- coverage of the 'business case' for work–life organisational support;
- the different work–life perspectives organisations can apply;
- the antecedent factors critical to the successful implementation of work–life initiatives in organisations, including the availability of work–life policies and a strategic approach to work–life across the organisation; and
- a discussion of the emerging challenges for researchers and practitioners related to work–life management in Asia Pacific.

Defining work–life issues

Work–life research is interdisciplinary, spanning the boundaries of disciplines such as:

- sociology,
- psychology;
- organisational behaviour;
- human development;
- labour economics;
- industrial relations;
- management;
- demography and
- women's studies (Drago & Kashian 2003).

Work–life research

Early studies

Theorising on the sphere of work and family can be traced to studies as early as 1949. These studies addressed conflicts arising from gender roles in families (MacDermid 2004). The 1970s and 1980s, however, can be viewed as the substantial developmental phase in the work–family arena (Gonyea & Googins 1992):

- Kanter's (1977) critical review of the dynamic intersections of work and family systems in contemporary American society broke new ground in the understanding of links between work and family (Barling & Sorensen 1997; Rayman & Bookman 1999);
- other seminal works (e.g. Pleck 1977; Rapoport & Rapoport 1969) contribute to the notion that the interaction between work and family leads to both positive and negative consequences; and
- the term 'work–family' came to focus only on negative consequences—for example, work–family conflict (Greenhaus & Beutell 1985).

The whole person—interacting spheres of work, family and life

Work–life researchers have long recognised that people come to work in organisations not just as individuals, but also as members of private systems, such as families (Kanter 1977). These systems are themselves influenced by the policies and practices of the organisations. It is important to consider the connections, intersections, and transactions between workplaces and families in order to be able to identify the reciprocal, micro-level dynamics between these spheres. Figure 9.1 presents a summary of the major factors that comprise the spheres of an individual's work, family and life and how these different domains overlap.

Figure 9.1 The whole person – work, family and life

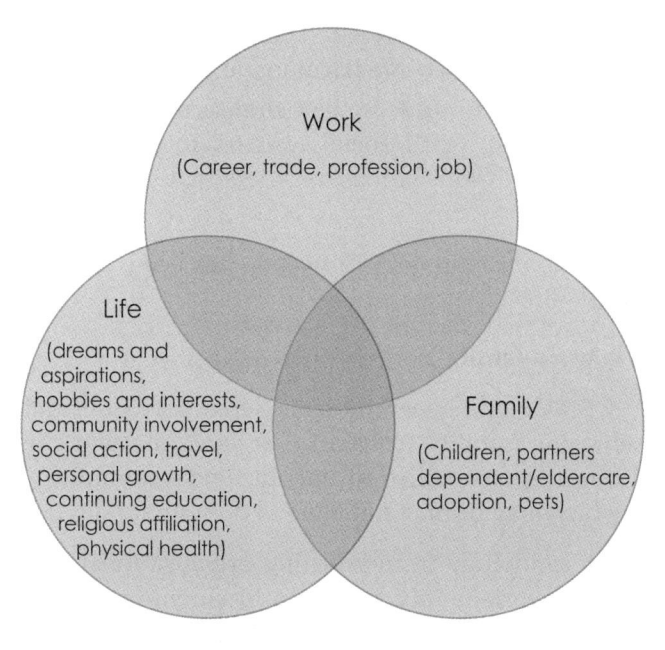

Role-related expectations and responsibilities

Grzywacz and Carlson's (2007) approach to conceptualising work–family balance focuses on the accomplishment of role-related expectations that are negotiated and shared between an individual's role-related responsibilities at work and with their family. An understanding of role-related responsibilities can also be extended to include not only family responsibilities but also include responsibilities to oneself, one's community, and the many priorities that may or may not have to do with family (Bardoel 2006).

Balancing work and personal life

A number of terms have been used to conceptualise the area of balancing work and personal life. They all imply a connection between the two-paired terms of work and family or work and life. Examples include:

- work–family nexus;
- balancing work and family;
- juggling work and family; and
- balancing work and lifestyle (Thorne 1999).

Emphasis on integration and harmony

Other leading work–life researchers and practitioners reject the notion of 'balance' and argue that life is a dynamic journey that cannot possibly accommodate a static or ideal state. They argue that the journey is about moving through the course life offers (Caproni 1997; Galinsky 2001; Spinks 2003).

- Spinks (2003) and Polach (2003) favour terms such as work–life integration or work–life harmony to reflect this different emphasis.
- Barnett (1999) argued that the term 'work–family' should be replaced with 'work/social systems' to reflect that employees have needs and responsibilities to others that go beyond their immediate families.

The most common terminology, however, has been 'work–family' and more recently 'work–life'.

Work–life v. work–family

The term 'work–life' is generally considered a broader, more holistic term that includes one's ability to balance or integrate work into one's overall life, including responsibilities to oneself, one's community, and the many priorities, which may or may not have to do with family (Lewis 2003).

The shift in terminology from labelling organisational initiatives as work–life rather than work–family reflects a broadening of quality-of-life issues and career issues for both men and women. It also reflects a need for HR practitioners to shift from the simple provision of programs to viewing work–life issues more systemically—to include them in work process redesign and cultural change processes. In this chapter, in response to this shift in terminology, we will use the more expansive work–life term.

Inconsistencies in terminology aside, work–life issues have become an important consideration for HR practitioners in the Asia Pacific region due to demographic, socio-cultural, and business trends taking place at both a global and local level.

Global trends

A number of major global demographic changes have impacted on the way men, women and families connect to the workplace. Collectively, these globally occurring transformations in labour, industry and urbanisation make it important for HR professionals to understand the experiences of work–family conflict faced by working men and women in different countries in widely varying contexts (Hein 2005). This understanding is increasingly important as organisations find themselves operating in a globalised world with multicultural workforces.

Work–family conflict

A number of linking mechanisms have been proposed to explain the nature of the relationship between work and family roles (Edwards & Rothbard 2000). One of the most prominent is conflict (or interference) (Greenhaus & Singh 2003). Work–family conflict refers to simultaneous, mutually incompatible demands of work and family. Meeting the demands of one role makes it difficult to meet the demands of the other (Greenhaus & Singh 2003).

Historical and current trends

Hein (2005) identifies a number of historical and current trends that have resulted in work–family conflict since the second half of the twentieth century in both developed and developing countries.

Urbanisation

The first factor is the separation of home and the workplace—caused by the decline in agricultural labour and the marked urbanisation of societies (Hein 2005; Heymann, Earle & Hanchate 2004). The United Nations has predicted that by the year 2030, 60% of the world's population—including 56% of the developing world's population—will live in urban areas.

Urbanisation plays a key role in the changes that are occurring in work and family life.

- When individuals migrate to urban areas they often move away from the support provided by extended families.
- Families living in urban areas often need to have a large number of adults in the paid workforce in order to subsist.
- Work environments in urban areas are often designed in ways that make it impossible for children and other dependants to accompany adults to work.

Women in the workforce

The second factor that contributes to work–family conflict is the entry of an increasing number of women into the industrial and post-industrial labour forces. From 1960 to 2000 the percentage of the labour force made up of women increased markedly in many regions. For example, from:

- 27% to 43 % in Australia;
- 31 % to 41 % in Western Europe;
- 17% to 25% in the Middle East; and
- 21% to 35% in South America (International Labour Organization 1999; World Bank Group 2000).

China has seen a modest growth from an existing high level of 49% in 1980 to 56% in 1996. In the same period, other south-east Asian countries have also seen increases in women participating in the labour market—from:

- 27% to 37% in Indonesia;
- 26% to 30% in Malaysia; and
- 33% to 40 % in Singapore (International Labour Organization 1999).

The 'traditional' family roles (stay-at-home mother, breadwinner father) are being replaced by workplace structures, roles, and resources based on the dual-earner model. A review of early childhood care undertaken in Cambodia, Indonesia, Laos, Malaysia, Philippines, Thailand, and Vietnam by Kamerman (2002) concluded that women in these countries are increasingly unavailable to provide care at home for young children and consequently the need for non-parental care is likely to increase.

Dependent care

The third factor that has contributed to working men and women experiencing work–family conflict is the declining availability of family assistance to support care of dependents (Hein 2005).

The impact of urbanisation, the increased participation of women in the labour force, and both internal and external migration has meant that the traditional family support for family care and domestic tasks is not always available.

Heymann (2006) makes the point that there is a mistaken belief that in developing countries, working parents can appeal to traditional family solidarity and find a grandparent to help. As part of the Project on Global Working Families, Heymann analysed survey data from 55,000 families in 180 countries around the world. She found that extended families were not always available because:

- grandparents themselves may need to work,
- members of the extended family may be in need of care themselves; or
- they may live too far away to be able to offer help on a regular basis.

Aged care

Another factor that has contributed to increased levels of work–family conflict has been the increasing care needs of the elderly. Based on the Indonesian Family Life Survey 2000, an analysis of elderly care-giving on the labour supply of co-resident household members found that care-giving for elderly household members had a significantly adverse impact on labour supply, particularly for a household's female members (Magnani & Rammahan 2007).

Other pressures

Other significant factors that have led to working adults around the world experiencing work–family conflict have been:

- increasing pressures of work;
- long work hours; and
- increased travel times.

These factors have put enormous pressure on working families (Hein 2005; Heymann, Earle & Hanchate 2004).

Reconciling work, family and personal needs is not just an issue for industrialised and developed nations. Increasingly, working adults in developing countries are struggling to reconcile work and family responsibilities. These global changes present enormous challenges for the HR professional in assisting employees with managing work–life issues in organisations.

The Australian perspective

The changes taking place in Australia's demographic profile will have a substantial impact on the labour market. It is likely to stimulate interest in and concern for work–life balance into the future.

Forces driving the work–life agenda

Women in the workforce

Women's increased participation in paid work in Australia, especially women with caring responsibilities, and the corresponding rise of the dual-earner household is one of the main drivers for the emergence of work–life considerations (Bardoel, De Cieri & Santos 2008; Skinner, Pocock & Williams 2008).

Furthermore, due to the ageing population and the trends to delayed and reduced fertility, women are having fewer babies later in life than their mothers did in the 1950s, 60s and 70s (Lattimore & Pobke 2008). This has evolved into what is becoming known as the 'sandwich' generation where women have care responsibilities both for dependent children and ageing parents (Duxbury & Higgins 2008).

Generational values

In addition to the dramatic changes to the demographic profile of Australia, generational values are also changing. Researchers in the field suggest young people today emphasise and value achievement of work–life more than their predecessors did (Smola & Sutton 2002; Sturges & Guest 2004, p. 5). Furthermore, the stereotypical 'Gen Y' employee considers lifestyle to be their 'anchor', as opposed to the anchors of career and strong work ethic with its emphasis on 'face time' identified by older employees (McDonald & Hite 2008).

Working hours

Another force driving the work–life agenda is the changing nature of work in affluent societies, including Australia, and the impact it has on quality of life. While some countries have been reducing working hours to better accommodate a balanced approach to work and life, Australia (along with the US, Canada, Iceland and New Zealand) have been moving in the opposite direction (Pocock 2005). By international standards, Australian employees work some of the longest full-time working hours among OECD countries (van Wanrooy, Jakubauskas, Buchanan, Wilson & Scalmer 2008).

Work–life initiatives

Furthermore, the ongoing interest in work–life balance in Australian society (as evidenced by media interest and the plethora of work–life award programs available to organisations—e.g. the Australian Government's

Department of Education, Employment and Workplace Relations National Work–life Balance Awards program) has placed increased pressure on organisations to respond to the changing work–life needs of their employee stakeholders (Pocock 2003).

These dramatic changes have been reflected in the steps Australian companies are taking in providing work–life initiatives. A comparison of work and family entitlements reported in the 2006 and 2008 Victorian Workplace Industrial Relations Surveys (Table 9.1) shows there has been a notable increase in the provision of leave for work and family matters across the majority of Victorian workplaces between 2006 and 2008 (Workforce Victoria 2009a). The survey reported that almost half of all workplaces had a formalised work and family policy—a considerable increase from 2006 where only 29.5% had such a policy. In terms of work and family entitlements, 31.1% of workplaces in 2008 provided paid maternity leave for the majority of their non-managerial staff compared to 25.8% in 2006 (Workforce Victoria 2009a).

Table 9.1 Work and family provision and entitlements 2006 and 2008 Percentage change entitlement[4]

Entitlement	2008	2006	Percentage change
Work and family policy	49.7	29.5	68.5
Family or carer's leave	70.8	63.3	11.8
Maternity leave	31.1	25.8	20.5
Use paid annual leave	86.4	81.1	6.5
Unpaid family leave	85.5	77.6	10.2
Long service leave	58.1	na	na
Flex-time	65.3	43.2	51.2

Source: Adapted from the Victorian Industrial Relations/Workplace Surveys, 2006, 2008)

---

[4] Workforce Victoria 2009a.

Public policy and the legal context

Australian employers face a range of legal obligations to employees who are parents or carers.

Discrimination on the basis of parental or carer responsibilities

Under both state and federal equal opportunity legislation, it is against the law for employers to discriminate against job applicants and employees (including contract workers, those working on a commission basis and partners in a firm) with parental or carer responsibilities.

Parental leave

Employees who have completed at least 12 months continuous service with an employer have a basic minimum entitlement to up to 52 weeks unpaid parental leave under the *Workplace Relations Act* 1996 (Cwth). This may include casual employees in specific circumstances. Parental leave includes:

- maternity leave;
- paternity leave; and
- adoption leave.

When returning to paid work from parental leave, employees are entitled to return to the position they held immediately prior to taking leave or a promoted or transferred position to which they agreed during their leave. If the position no longer exists, and the employee is qualified and able to return to work in another comparable position, the employee is entitled to return to that position or, if there is more than one position, the one nearest in status and remuneration (Workforce Victoria 2009b).

Requests for changes in working arrangements

More recently, the right of employees to request flexibility formed an integral part of the National Employment Standards introduced in 2010. According to section 65(1) of the *Fair Work Act*, permanent or long-term casual employees with children either under school age or under 18 with a disability have the right to request a 'change in working arrangements' to enable them to provide care for their children.

On 1 September 2008 the State of Victoria introduced changes to the *Equal Opportunity Act* 1995 (Vic). The changes provide that employers must not unreasonably refuse to accommodate the parental and carer responsibilities of a person offered employment or to adapt an employee's working arrangements (including contract workers, those working on a commission basis, and partners in a firm) (Victorian Equal Opportunity & Human Rights Commission 2008).

Similar legislative arrangements can be found in other states and territories across Australia. Combined with federal legislation, these legislative arrangements impose on organisations the responsibility at least to consider the family care responsibilities of their employees.

While legislative requirements are designed to compel employers to consider the family and caring responsibilities of its employees, it is the well reported positive outcomes for both individual employees and employers that form the basis of the 'business case' argument in support of work-life initiatives.

The business case for work-life initiatives

Work-life policies and practices have been linked to a range of benefits for both the employee and organisation.

Human capital as a competitive advantage

The business case argument is built on the premise that the cited benefits of work-life policies and practices — e.g.

- enhanced employee trust;
- job satisfaction;
- commitment; and
- performance

are considered critical to the organisational performance of the firm (Wright, Dunford & Snell 2001). This view underlies the SHRM approach to business strategy. The strategy is based on the belief that resources such as human capital can become a competitive advantage when the resource is difficult to imitate (Kossek & Friede 2006). In other words, a healthy, satisfied, committed, and high performing workforce will create a sustainable competitive advantage for organisations.

Work-life programs provide benefits at both the employee and organisational levels. These benefits can be built into a convincing business case and strategic lever for the introduction of work-life programs across a spectrum of industry sectors (Harrington & Ladge 2009).

Employee benefits

The direct benefits for employees working in organisations with a strong commitment to work-life include:

- enhanced work-life balance (Hayman 2009);
- enhanced employee health and well-being (Grzywacz, Carlson & Shulkin 2008); and
- job satisfaction (Forsyth & Polzer-Debruyne 2007; Muse *et al.* 2008).

Other reported benefits that flow through to the organisation include:

- improved employee commitment (Allen 2001; Muse 2008; Richman, Civian, Shannon, Hill & Brennan 2008);
- greater employee trust towards the organisation (Scholarios & Marks 2004);
- improved staff morale (McCampbell 1996);
- improved employee performance and organisational citizenship behaviour (Lambert 2000; Muse *et al*. 2008); and
- a reduction in employee turnover intentions (Batt & Valcour 2003; Forsyth & Polzer-Debruyne 2007).

Organisation benefits

At the organisational level of analysis, work–life policies and practices have been linked to:

- improved organisational performance (Perry-Smith & Blum 2000);
- increased organisational productivity (Konrad & Mangel 2000);
- improved share market performance (Cascio & Young 2005), and
- an enhanced ability to attract and retain a high quality workforce (Kossek & Lambert 2005; Thompson & Aspinwall 2009).

These factors are, in turn, often linked to the acknowledgement that the organisation is a 'good' corporate citizen and/or 'employer of choice' that cares about its employees (Harrington *et al*. 2009).

While acknowledging the reported organisational benefits of work–life strategies it is important to recognise that researchers in the field have suggested the effectiveness of work–life programs is not unequivocal (Sutton & Noe 2005). While the evidence supporting the business case for organisational work–life support is convincing, some studies have failed to demonstrate a link between work–life programs and benefits (e.g. Bailey & Kurland 2002; Comfort, Johnson & Wallace 2003).

A strategic approach to work–life implementation issues

Responsibility for work–life initiatives are located in many different areas within human resource departments. The location depends on the organisation's perspective on work–life and the primary focus of its efforts.

Seven work–life perspectives

Harrington *et al*. (2009) identify seven work–life perspectives that influence an organisation's approach to developing work–life initiatives:

- diversity/inclusion;
- talent management;

- culture change;
- health and wellness;
- employee relations;
- total rewards; and
- corporate citizenship.

Using Harrington *et al.*'s framework of work–life perspectives, the following discussion gives examples of how these approaches have been applied in organisations. It also highlights how staff who are responsible for work–life initiatives may report to different departments within the human resource function.

Diversity/inclusion

A diversity perspective will see an emphasis on creating an inclusive workplace expanding the development opportunities for women and different minority groups. It will develop work–life policies and programs designed to respond to a variety of employee needs, family situations, and cultural contexts.

Talent management

One of the most commonly identified reasons for organisational interest in developing work–life initiatives relates to the talent management agenda (i.e. developing and retaining the best talent), a key concern of SHRM. The talent perspective emphasises the contribution of work–life to an organisation being regarded as an employer of choice. It is particularly pertinent in industries with skill shortages where competition for top talent is also strong.

Culture change

The culture change perspective focuses on creating an organisational culture that supports employees in the integration of their work and personal lives. An example would be initiatives designed to create a flexible work environment where work is measured on outcomes rather than face time.

The Australian Council for Educational Research (ACER) was a recent recipient of the Victorian Government's Fair and Flexible Employer recognition program. In its approach to developing work–life initiatives the ACER combines elements of the diversity, talent, and cultural perspectives. The ACER relies on attracting and retaining highly specialist staff from a national and international pool of candidates; it employs a range of people from different age groups, cultural backgrounds and nationalities. It has created flexible policies and practices that cater for as many people as possible. These include:

- different types of flexible leave;

- religious and ceremonial leave; and
- company contributions to staff superannuation when a staff member is on parental leave (Workforce Victoria 2009c).

Health and wellness

Another approach identified by Harrington *et al*. (2009) is that which seeks to improve employees' overall health and wellness. This approach is often associated with employee assistance programs (EAP), health promotion activities, or medical programs (e.g. fitness centres, stress reduction programs, and onsite medical services).

An example of the health and wellness approach is the Singapore-based Land Transport Authority's (LTA) work–life strategy. The strategy is based on a holistic framework that emphasises taking care of the heart, body and mind. In this regard, it has placed a special focus on the retention of mature workers, whom LTA values for their experience, knowledge and skills set. LTA has seen a decrease both in stress reported by staff and in the percentage of staff with high cholesterol. The latter fell from 16% in 2006 to 13% in 2007 (Ministry of Manpower Singapore 2009).

Employee relations

The emphasis in the employee relations approach to work–life initiatives is on creating and sustaining a positive work environment by providing programs to recognise and reward employees' contributions to the organisation and helping employees to resolve personal and work-related challenges. This approach is likely to include measures related to the integration of work and life—such as:

- employee recognition programs;
- employee assistance programs;
- job relations counselling;
- conflict resolution and avoidance;
- policy interpretation; and
- grievance processing for employees.

Total rewards

The total rewards perspective sees work–life initiatives as non-monetary components of the total rewards package and a major contributor to employee attraction and retention.

Corporate citizenship

The corporate citizenship approach places work–life initiatives within the organisation's citizen and corporate responsibility efforts. The focus of work–life programs is to provide employees with time to give back to their communities. For example, Mars (the global producer of pet products and snack foods) has recently launched the 'Mars Ambassador Program'. The program allows employees to seek out personal growth opportunities by volunteering in undeveloped and developing communities around the world (Mars 2009).

Summary

There are many and varied perspectives on work–life, but all demonstrate the need for HR practitioners to:

- view the employee as a whole person; and
- develop work–life initiatives that take into account the needs of all types of employees, at all levels in the organisation, and at all stages of their careers (Harrington *et al.* 2009).

The preceding section also highlights the fact that work–life programs in a large organisation with a proactive approach to work–life may actually be the responsibility of a wide range of HR practitioners. For example:

- the well-being adviser/manager will drive the work–life programs in organisations applying an employee health and well-being focus;
- the diversity adviser/manager will drive work–life programs geared at creating an inclusive and equitable work environment for all;
- in smaller organisations the HR function may be performed by a single person or even the owner-operator in very small organisations; that person may have responsibility for multiple roles depending on the work–life approach taken by the organisation.

HR policies and strategic implementation issues

Despite differing views on the value of work–life programs and a range of different work–life perspectives available to the organisation, there is widespread agreement that for organisations to deliver on the widely reported business-case benefits of work–life programs, HR practitioners must consider both HR policies and strategic implementation issues.

Human resource policies

As summarised by Kossek (2005) the domain of employer support for work–life issues includes:

- formal human resource policies to support employees' ability to integrate their work and non-work roles (e.g. job-share arrangements, part-time work, flexitime);
- job design and terms and conditions of employment such as pay and work hours; and
- the informal occupational and organisational culture and norms.

Strategic human resource management

Organisations, however, must look beyond operational HRM policy considerations. Merely creating a set of work–life policies available to employees is not enough. Incorporating work–life initiatives into the strategic HR plan of the organisation and fostering an organisational culture that encourages and supports the use of available policies is critical if both employees and employers are to enjoy the benefits afforded by work–life strategies (Bardoel 2003; McDonald, Brown & Bradley 2005; Thompson, Beauvais & Lyness 1999).

Other factors considered critical to delivering the benefits of work–life programs include:

- supervisor/line manager support (Duxbury & Higgins 2008; Hammer, Kossek, Yragui, Bodner & Hanson 2009; Muse 2008); and
- a supportive work-group social context (Bernard & Phillips 2007; Blair-Loy & Wharton 2002).

So regardless of the work–life perspective being applied, the potential 'business case' gains will only be realised if:

- HR practitioners develop and communicate relevant work–life policies and programs;
- supervisors are trained and supported to implement the policies; and
- the broader work–life organisational culture encourages employees to actually use the available policies and programs.

Conclusion

We began this chapter with a discussion of the work–life concept, arguing that the significant demographic, social and cultural changes taking place on a global scale have placed work–life issues firmly on the agenda for individuals, organisations and governments alike.

Over recent years the much hyped 'talent wars' breathed new life into the focus on work–life issues as a major strategic HRM activity. Companies embraced organisational support for work–life as a key tool for talent management.

Now in the shadow of the global financial crisis we are seeing trends that will have ongoing implications for managing work–life issues in organisations in the Asia Pacific region. These include:

- work becoming more unstable;
- increases in the number of 'working poor'; and

- increased demands for flexibility from employers that are not necessarily employee oriented (e.g. casualisation of labour or the reduction of work hours at the behest of employers).

If the cited benefits of work–life initiatives are to be realised, HR professionals must:

- reconcile these competing challenges;
- ensure work–life initiatives are underpinned by senior executive 'buy-in' and support at the upper levels of the organisation;
- reinforce work–life initiatives with the required suite of work–life policies; and
- secure cultural and supervisor support across the organisation.

Further research into the implementation of work–life initiatives in organisations in other Asian Pacific countries will help establish the relevance of the strategies and initiatives employed by organisations in developed countries such as Australia.

Case study

The making and keeping of work–life organisational promises in a local government setting

The local government sector provides an illuminating example of the work–life issues organisations face within the context of challenging workforce planning issues.

Of particular concern for the local government sector are the rapidly ageing workforce and the challenges it faces in recruiting young graduates—particularly in engineering and town planning—given some of the negative stereotypes associated with a career in local government (Jacobs & Harvey-Beavis 2006).

As a result, the sector is aware of the potential for work–life balance programs as a tool for attracting, retaining, and engaging talent. To varying degrees, organisations in the sector actively promote their work–life balance programs both to potential recruits and existing employees (Municipal Association of Victoria 2005).

The organisation in this case study is located in metropolitan Melbourne, Australia. Given its inner city location, the organisation is culturally diverse and, due to the requirements to deliver a diverse range of services, it is complex. The Council employs, among others, accountants, gardeners, swimming instructors, librarians, mechanics, engineers, early-childhood nurses, garbage collectors, information technology professionals and parking inspectors.

The 1994 council amalgamations in Victoria have resulted in a complex employee relations and payroll system with employees at the Council employed on a range of different awards, agreements, and access to WLB policies. Adding to the complexity is the multi-site nature of local government organisations, with 'Town Hall' acting as the headquarters, and a range of other satellite sites (including community and health centres, library, recreation and sports facilities, works centres) located within the Council's geographical boundary. This multi-site, diverse organisation presents significant challenges for the organisation to develop, communicate and implement a successful work-life balance program.

The council in this case study is typical of many local government organisations: it has a wide range of work-life policies available to employees but employee awareness of and access to the actual policies is not universal. To explore employee perceptions of how the organisation communicates and implements its work-life balance policies and programs the researcher conducted eleven focus groups (n=95) at various locations with a cross-section of employees. Two hundred and four employees were surveyed, representing a response rate of 24.8%.

Results of the survey

The majority of employees surveyed (almost 70%) indicated the organisation had made some sort of implied or explicit promise or commitment to provide work-life balance policies/programs. In terms of the extent to which employees perceived the Council had met its promise or commitment to provide work-life balance policies/programs almost 90% of respondents felt that those promises had been met, at least to some extent.

The 9% (n=11) of respondents that felt the organisation had exceeded their WLB promises or commitments were a very happy group of employees. Of those 11 respondents, nine felt that a written or verbal promise had been made by the organisation to assist them with their work-life issues. These employees had high expectations and when they were exceeded the consequent attitudes and behaviours were very positive.

Ten of the 11 respondents felt the Council's approach to work-life had a 'definite positive impact' on employee performance, commitment, trust in the organisation, motivation, well-being and overall relationship with their employer. Furthermore, the role of the supervisor and immediate workmates in supporting the individual was reinforced in this subgroup. All respondents 'agreed' or 'strongly agreed' that within their work team their supervisor/team leader and workmates were supportive of their work–life balance requirements. Interestingly, they had a relatively low organisational tenure (2.7 years) when compared to the broader sample.

At the other end of the scale, 10% (n=13) of respondents reported the organisation had not met its promise or commitment to provide work–life balance policies/programs. The results from this small sample suggest that making promises (either implied or explicit) and then failing to keep them in the eyes of the individual employee can lead to a range of negative attitudes and behaviours. This subgroup of respondents had an average organisational tenure of 12 years. Approximately 85% of this subgroup felt the organisation's management of its work–life promises and commitments had either a 'negative effect' or 'no effect' on their sense of employee performance, commitment, trust in the organisation, motivation and overall relationship with the organisation.

Conclusions

While the exploratory case study is based on a very small data set from a single organisation it does highlight the need for care to be taken when communicating WLB policies and programs and the importance of careful implementation of such programs. The analysis and discussion of the extreme ends of the 'work–life balance promises and commitments' spectrum identifies both the very positive work attitudes and behaviours that can result from explicitly making and keeping WLB promises and commitments, and the corresponding negative attitudes and behaviours when employees perceive promises to have been broken.

Discussion questions

1. Drawing on your understanding of the implementation issues and challenges discussed in the chapter, can you think of at least three possible explanations for the perception of the group of disenchanted employees that the organisation had failed to deliver on its work–life promises?

2. How can two groups of employees at one single organisation report such different degrees of satisfaction with the organisation's approach to work–life issues?

3. Assuming the organisation is taking a strategic talent management approach to work–life issues, what is your assessment of the Council's performance? Clearly justify your answer.

References

Allen, TD 2001, 'Family-supportive work environments: The role of organizational perceptions', *Journal of Vocational Behavior*, 58, 414-435.

Arthur, M & Cook, A 2003, 'The relationships between work–family human resource practices and firm profitability: A multitheoretical perspective', *Research in Personnel and Human Resources Management*, 22, 219-252.

Bailey, DE & Kurland, NB 2002, 'A review of telework research: findings, new directions, and lessons for the study of modern work', *Journal of Organizational Behavior*, 23(4), 383-400.

Bardoel, EA 2003, 'The provision of formal and informal work–family practices: the relative importance of institutional and resource dependent explanations versus managerial explanations', *Women in Management Review*, 18(1/2), 7-19.

Bardoel, EA 2006, 'Work–life and HRD', in P Holland, & H De Cieri (eds.), *Contemporary Issues in Human Resource Development: An Australian Perspective*, Pearson Education, Sydney, 237-259.

Bardoel, EA, De Cieri, H, & Santos, C 2008, 'A review of work--life research in Australia and New Zealand', *Asia Pacific Journal of Human Resources*, 46(3), 316-333.

Barling, J & Sorensen, D 1997, 'Work and family: In search of a relevant research agenda', in *Creating tomorrow's organizations*, CL Cooper & SE Jackson (eds), 157-169, New York, John Wiley and Sons.

Barnett, RC 1999, 'A new work–life model for the twenty-first century', *ANNALS of the American Academy of Political and Social Science*, 562(562), 143-158.

Batt, R & Valcour, PM 2003, 'Human Resources Practices as Predictors of Work–family Outcomes and Employee Turnover', *Industrial Relations*, 42(2), 189-220.

Bernard, M & Phillips, JE 2007, 'Working carers of older adults. Community', *Work & Family*, 10(2), 139-160.

Blair-Loy, M & Wharton, AS 2002, 'Employees' use of work–family policies and the workplace social context', *Social Forces*, 80(3), 813-845.

Bruton, GD & Lau, C-M 2008, 'Asian management research: Status today and future outlook', *Journal of Management Studies*, 45(3), 636-659.

Caproni, PJ 1997, 'Work/life balance: You can't get there from here', *Journal of Applied Behavioral Science*, 33(1), 46-56.

Cascio, W & Young, C 2005, 'Work–family balance: Does the market reward firms that respect it?', n D Halpern & S Murphy (Eds.), *Work–family balance to work–family interaction: Changing the metaphor,* pp. 49-63, New Jersey, USA, Lawrence Erlbaum Associates.

Choi, J 2008, 'Work and family demands and life stress among Chinese employees: The mediating effect of work–family conflict', *The International Journal of Human Resource Management,* 19(5), 878 - 895.

Comfort, D, Johnson, K & Wallace, D 2003, 'Part-time work and family-friendly practices in Canadian workplaces', *Human Resources Development Canada,* 6, 1-78.

Drago, R & Hyatt, D 2003, 'Symposium: The effect of work–family policies on employees and employers', *Industrial Relations,* 42(2), 139-144.

Drago, R & Kashian, R 2003, 'Mapping the terrain of work/family journals', *The Journal of Family Issues,* 24(4): 488-512.

Duxbury, L & Higgins, C 2008, *Work–life balance in Australia in the new millennium: rhetoric versus reality,* Beaton Consulting, Melbourne, Australia.

Edwards, JR & Rothbard, NP 2000, 'Mechanisms linking work and family: clarifying the relationship between work and family constructs', *The Academy of Management Review,* 25(1), 179-199.

Forsyth, S & Polzer-Debruyne, A 2007, 'The organisational pay-offs for perceived work–life balance support.', *Asia Pacific Journal of Human Resources,* 45(1), 113-123.

Galinsky, E 2001, 'Toward a new view of work and family life', in R Hertz & NL Marshall (Eds), *Working families: The transformation of the American home.* Berkeley, CA., University of California Press.

Gonyea, JG & Googins, BK 1992, 'Linking the worlds of work and family: Beyond the productivity trap', *Human Resource Management,* 31(2), 209-226.

Greenhaus, JH, & Beutell, NJ 1985, 'Sources of conflict between work and family roles', *Academy of Management Review,* 10(1), 76-88.

Greenhaus, J & Singh, R 2003, 'Work–family linkages', in M Pitt-Catsouphes, EE Kossek, & P Raskin (eds), *Sloan work–family encyclopedia,* Chestnut Hill, MA., Sloan Work and Family Research Network, retrieved 3 April 2006, http://wfnetwork.bc.edu/encyclopedia_template.php?id=263.

Grzywacz, JG & Carlson, DS 2007, 'Conceptualizing Work–family Balance: Implications for Practice and Research', *Advances in Developing Human Resources,* 9(4), 455-471.

Grzywacz, JG, Carlson, DS, & Shulkin, S 2008, 'Schedule flexibility and stress: Linking formal flexible arrangements and perceived flexibility to employee health', *Community, Work & Family,* 11(2), 199 - 214.

Hammer, L, Kossek, E, Yragui, N, Bodner, T & Hanson, G 2009, 'Development and validation of a multidimensional measure of family supportive supervisor behaviors (FSSB)', *Journal of Management,* 35(4), 837-857.

Harrington, B & Ladge, JJ 2009, 'Present Dynamics and Future Directions for Organizations', *Organizational Dynamics,* 38 (2), 148–157.

Hayman, JR 2009, 'Flexible work arrangements: exploring the linkages between perceived usability of flexible work schedules and work/life balance', *Community, Work & Family*, 12(3), 327 - 338.

Hein, C 2005, *Reconciling work and family responsibilities: Practical ideas from global experience,* Geneva, Switzerland, International Labor Organization.

Heymann, J, Earle, A & Hanchate, A 2004, 'Bringing a global perspective to community, work and family', *Community, Work & Family*, 7(2), 247-272.

Heymann, J 2006, *Forgotten families: ending the growing crisis confronting children and working parents in the global economy*, New York, Oxford University Press.

International Labor Organization 1999, *Key indicators of the labor market*, Geneva, Switzerland, ILO.

Jacobs, E & Harvey-Beavis, O 2006, *Workforce planning in local government,* Melbourne, Municipal Association of Victoria.

Joplin, JRW, Shaffer, MA, Francesco, AM, & Lau, T 2003, 'The Macro-Environment and Work–family Conflict: Development of a Cross Cultural Comparative Framework', *International Journal of Cross Cultural Management*, 3(3), 305-328.

Kamerman, S 2002, *Early childhood care and education and other family policies and programs in South-East Asia*, Paris, Unesco.

Kanter, RM 1977, *Work and family in the United States: A critical review and agenda for research and policy*, New York, Russell Sage Foundation.

Konrad, A & Mangel, R 2000, 'The impact of work–life programs on firm productivity', *Strategic Management Journal,* 21, 1225-1237.

Kossek, EE & Lambert, SJ 2005, 'Work–family Scholarship: Voice and Context', in EE Kossek & SJ Lambert (Eds.), *Work and Life Integration: Organizational, Cultural, and Individual Perspectives,* pp. 3-17, New Jersey, Lawrence Erlbaum Associates, Inc.

Kossek, EE & Friede, A 2006, 'The Business Case: Managerial Perspectives on Work and the Family', in M Pitt-Catsouphes, EE Kossek & S Sweet (Eds.), *The work and family handbook: Multi-disciplinary perspectives and approaches,* pp. 611-626, New Jersey, USA, Lawrence Erlbaum Associates, Inc.

Lambert, SJ 2000, 'Added benefits: The link between work–life benefits and organizational citizenship behavior', *Academy of Management Journal*, 43(5), 801-815.

Lattimore, R & Pobke, C 2008, *Recent Trends in Australian Fertility*, Productivity Commission, Canberra, Australia.

Lewis, S 2003, 'Flexible working arrangements: Implementation, outcomes and management', in CL Cooper & IT Robertson (Eds) *International Review of Industrial and Organizational Psychology,* Vol. 18, Chichester, New York, John Wiley and Sons, Ltd.

Lu, L, Gilmour, R, Kao, S.-F & Huang, M-T 2006, 'A cross-cultural study of work/family demands, work/family conflict and wellbeing: the Taiwanese vs British', *Career Development International*, 11(1), 9-27.

Lyness, K., S & Kropf, MB 2005, 'The relationships of national gender equality and organizational support with work–family balance: A study of European managers', *Human Relations*, 58(1), 33.

Magnani, E & Rammahan, A 2007, 'The effect of elderly care-giving on female labour supply in Indonesia', 5th International Research Conference on Social Security, Warsaw.

Municipal Association of Victoria 2005, 'Quality Part-Time Work in Local Government: Assisting with work and family balance', Melbourne, Victoria, Australia.

MacDermid, SM 2004, '(Re)considering conflict between work and family', in EE Kossek & S Lambert (Eds), *Work and life integration in organizations: New directions for theory and practice*, 19-40, Mahwah, NJ, Erlbaum.

Mars 2009, *Mars Ambassador Program*, http://www.mars.com/global/Commitments/ Mars+Ambassador+Program.htm, accessed 17 September 2009.

McCampbell, AS 1996, 'Benefits achieved through alternative work schedules', *Human Resource Planning*, 19(3), 31-37.

McDonald, P, Brown, K, & Bradley, L 2005, 'Explanations of the provision-utilisation gap in work–life policy', *Women in Management Review*, 20(1), 37-55.

McDonald, KS & Hite, LM 2008, 'The Next Generation of Career Success: Implications for HRD', *Advances in Developing Human Resources*, 10(1), 86-103.

Ministry of Manpower Singapore 2009, *Work–life Excellence Award 2008 Winners*, retrieved 13 September 2008, from http://www.mom.gov.sg/publish/momportal/en/communities/workplace_standards/work-life_harmony/Work-life_Excellence_Award.html#AC.

Muse, L 2008, 'Work family conflict, performance and turnover intent: What kind of support helps?', paper presented at the 2008 Academy of Management Meeting, Anaheim, U.S.

Muse, L, Harris, SG, Giles, WF, & Feild, HS 2008, 'Work–life benefits and positive organizational behavior: is there a connection?', *Journal of Organizational Behavior*, 29(2), 171-192.

Perry-Smith, J, & Blum, T 2000, 'Work–family human resource bundles and perceived organizational performance', *Academy of Management Journal*, 43 1107-1117.

Pleck, JH 1977, 'The work–family role system, *Social Problems,* 24: 417-427.

Pocock, B 2003, *The work/life collision*, Sydney, The Federation Press.

Pocock, B 2005, 'Work–life 'balance' in Australia: Limited progress, dim prospects', *Asia Pacific Journal of Human Resources*, 43(2), 198-209.

Poelmans, S, Spector, PE, Cooper, CL, Allen, TD, O'Driscoll, M, & Sanchez, JI 2003, 'A Cross-National Comparative Study of Work/Family Demands and Resources', *International Journal of Cross Cultural Management*, 3(3), 275-288.

Polach, J 2003, 'HRD's role in work–life integration issues: Moving the workforce to a change in mindset', *Human Resource Development International* 6(1), 57-68.

Rapoport, R & Rapoport, RN 1969, 'The dual-career family: A variant pattern and social change', *Human Relations*, 22, 3-30.

Rayman, PM & Bookman, A 1999, 'Creating a research and public policy agenda for work, family, and community', *The Annals of the American Academy of Political and Social Science*, 562, 191-211.

Richman, AL, Civian, JT, Shannon, LL, Jeffrey Hill, E & Brennan, RT 2008, 'The relationship of perceived flexibility, supportive work–life policies, and use of formal flexible arrangements and occasional flexibility to employee engagement and expected retention'. *Community, Work & Family*, 11(2), 183 - 197.

Scholarios, D & Marks, A 2004, 'Work–life balance and the software worker', *Human Resource Management Journal*, 14(2), 54-74.

Shapiro, A & Noble, K 2001, 'A work/life lens helps bring a global workforce into focus', *Its about time*, 2 (Spring), 1-2.

Skinner, N, Pocock, B & Williams, P 2008, 'Work–life issues in Australia: What do we know?', paper presented at the Conference of the Association of Industrial Relations Academics of Australia and New Zealand (AIRAANZ), Melbourne, Australia.

Smola, KW & Sutton, CD 2002, 'Generational Differences: Revisiting Generational Work Values for the New Millennium', *Journal of Organizational Behavior*, 23(4), 363.

Spinks, N 2003a, *Work–life and Well-Being Action Strategy Framework*, www.worklifeharmony.ca, Work–life Harmony Enterprsies.

Sturges, J & Guest, D 2004, 'Working to live or living to work? Work/life balance early in the career', *Human Resource Management Journal*, 14(4), 5-20.

Sutton, KL & Noe, RA 2005, 'Family-Friendly Programs and Work–life Integration: More Myth Than Magic?', in EE Kossek & SJ Lambert (Eds.), *Work and Life Integration: Organizational, Cultural, and Individual Perspectives*, pp. 151-169, New Jersey, Lawrence Erlbaum Associates, Inc.

Thompson, CA, Beauvais, LL & Lyness, KS 1999, 'When work–family benefits are not enough: The influence of work–family culture on benefit utilization, organizational attachment, and work- family conflict', *Journal of Vocational Behavior*, 54(3), 392-415.

Thompson, LF & Aspinwall, KR 2009, T'he recruitment value of work/life benefits', *Personnel Review*, 38(2), 195-210.

Thorne, B 1999, 'Pick-up time at Oakdale Elementary School: Work and family from the vantage points of children', Vol. Working Paper # 2, San Francisco, UC Berkeley Center for Working Families.

van Wanrooy, B, Jakubauskas, M, Buchanan, J, Wilson, S & Scalmer, S 2008, *Australia at Work - Working lives: Statistics and stories*, Workplace Research Centre, The University of Sydney.

Victorian Workplace Industrial Relations Survey 2006, http://www.business.vic.gov.au/busvicwr/_assets/main/lib60047/irv-pay-equity-women-in%20work.pdf, accessed 16/2/10.

Victorian Equal Opportunity & Human Rights Commission 2008, *Building eQuality in the workplace: Family Responsibilities - Guidelines for Employers and Employees*, Victorian Equal Opportunity & Human Rights Commission, Melbourne.

Workforce Victoria 2009a, Work and Family Entitlements – Comparison between the 2006 and 2008 Victorian Workplace Industrial Relations Surveys (VWIRS), *Research Note prepared for the Working Families Council of Victoria*, Workforce Victoria.

Workforce Victoria 2009b, *Employers - Legal Obligations*, Victorian Government's Work and Family Balance online resource, www.ways2work.business.vic.gov.au, accessed September 13, 2009.

Workforce Victoria 2009c, *Case study: The Australian Council for Educational Research*, Victorian Government's Work and Family Balance online resource, www.ways2work.business.vic.gov.au, accessed September 13, 2009.

World Bank Group 2000, *World Development Indicators 2000*, Washington, DC, World Bank.

Wright, PM, Dunford, BB & Snell, SA 2001, 'Human resources and the resource based view of the firm', *Journal of Management*, 27(6), 701.

Chapter 10

MANAGING TALENT: EXPLORING HR STRATEGIES IN A DYNAMIC ENVIRONMENT

Peter Holland & Rob Hecker

OBJECTIVES

By the completion of the chapter you should be able to:

1. define the concept of talent;
2. discuss the changing dynamics of the workplace in the 21st century facilitating an increased emphasis on talent management;
3. consider strategies for dealing with the potential 'war for talent';
4. draw from research issues that have been identified in the area of talent management.

DEFINITIONS

Talent: The sum of a person's knowledge, skills, ability and experience as well as their ability to learn and grow.

Talent management: The ability to attract, retain and utilise the human resource talent available to the organisation.

Chapter 10 – Managing Talent: Exploring HR Strategies in a Dynamic Environment

Introduction

> **Talent trove**
>
> The recent skills shortage has been swept away but recession has, in some cases, been replaced with fearful humility as many employees are grateful just to hold on to their jobs. In such conditions, why should employers care about creating a great workplace?
>
> It's easy to forget that a productive and motivated workforce is a company's greatest asset when the business is fighting for its survival. But it was excessive short-term thinking that got the economy into this current mess. Long-term success depends on planning for what is around the corner as well as what is happening right now.
>
> The accounting firm Deloitte is among the top multinationals on the *BRW Great Places to Work* list. The accounting firm's chief executive in Australia, Giam Swiegers, is clear about the value of being an employer of choice in bad times as well as good. 'There is no doubt in my mind the economy will turn, maybe sooner than many expect, and when that happens, when we go back to the skills shortage, you will be remembered for what you did in these times,' he says.
>
> *Source:* Adapted from McColl 2009.

The first decade of the 21st century has seen what can best be described as a rollercoaster of labour market fluctuations from deepening talent shortages to a global financial crisis (GFC) threatening the largest shedding of labour since the great depression of the 1930s.

In this context it could be argued that the management of talent is too difficult as there are so many variables to deal with. However we would argue (in line with Deloitte's approach) that this point in time creates an ideal opportunity or 'litmus test' of an organisation's real attitude to talent management when their bottom line is under pressure.

This chapter draws on the resource-based view of the firm (RBV, Barney, 1991) as the theoretical perspective underpinning the argument for developing talent management strategies in a dynamic environment. We argue that in an environment characterised by increasing volatility, organisations need to design employment systems that prioritise human resource attraction, retention, and development as key elements in retaining a competitive advantage in and post the global financial crisis.

The chapter will also explore the practical aspect of talent management in the 'new' workplace from both the employee's and employer's perspectives. The chapter will also look at contemporary research on the management of talent.

Defining talent

In attempting to quantify the concept of talent, Michaels, Handfield-Jones and Axelrod (2001, p. xii), have argued that in its broadest sense:

> 'Talent is the sum of the person's abilities – his or her intrinsic gifts, skills, knowledge, experience, intelligence, judgement, attitude, character and drive. It also includes his or her ability to learn and grow.'

In a human resource management context, this can be seen as the knowledge, skill and ability an organisation would want to attract and retain. The ability to learn and grow is the developmental potential of that talent.

For a variety of reasons, talent management has grown increasingly important in advanced market economies over the last two decades.

Declining birth rates

Over the latter half of the 20th century, population trends across OECD countries reveal almost static populations and declining birth rates (OECD 2004). The past few decades have seen birth rates in most OECD countries falling sharply to just 1.6 children per woman, well below the average of 2.1 children per woman needed to maintain current population levels.

Less than 30 years ago, the overwhelming majority of OECD governments considered their country's birth rate as 'satisfactory', while today most OECD countries consider it 'too low' (OECD 2007). This has generated growing concern regarding the long-term labour market, with the first wave of baby-boomers reaching retirement.

Shortfalls in skilled labour

Under current employment and retirement strategies, more people will be leaving the workforce than will be actually joining it over the next few years (Critchley 2004). A global study by the Boston Consulting Group in 2003 estimated a shortfall in skilled labour worldwide of the order of 60 million by 2020. It posited the following labour shortages:

- USA 17 million;
- Japan 9 million;
- China 10 million;
- Russia 6 million;
- Germany 3 million;
- France 3 million;
- Spain 3 million;
- UK 2 million; and
- Australia 500,000.

These scenarios, however, have been challenged. Cappelli (2003, 2005) and Critchley (2004) for example, acknowledge the changing demographics but argue that the critical flaw in the scenarios suggested above is that they assume employment strategies and relationships will not adapt accordingly.

Continuing need for talent management

Whichever scenarios develop, and whilst these projections pre-date the global financial crisis, it is clear that the need for attracting, retaining and developing highly skilled workers is likely to remain a pressing issue for many organisations as economies move to a knowledge and service base and the influx of the next generation of workers declines.

Findings from PricewaterhouseCoopers' (2009, p. 30) 12th Annual Survey of CEOs (1,124 CEOs from more than 50 countries) show that

> '... ninety-seven percent of CEOs believe that the access to and retention of key talent is critical or important to sustaining growth over the long term'.

Therefore the need for talent management is likely to remain strong for the near future.

Managing talent—a theoretical perspective

Within the resource-based view of the firm there are three types of resources that act as sources of competitive advantage:

- physical capital;
- organisational capital; and
- human capital (Barney & Wright 1998).

Increasing levels of technological sophistication and the immediate transfer of information, however, have diminished the competitive advantage that was once available through physical and organisational capital.

Critical nature of human capital

Products are now more readily copied and processes replicated. Differentiation is increasingly focused on the human resources that generate new ideas (knowledge) or with those who deliver the product (service). There is increasing recognition, therefore, of the potential of the last of the three resources, human capital, to make a substantial and lasting impact on sustainable competitive advantage (Barney & Wright 1998; Wright, Gardner, Moynihan & Allen 2005).

This is supported by Cappelli and Crocker-Hefter (1996) and Coff (1997), who argue that it is the human resources that are at the core of a firm's unique strategic advantage. The Australian federal government's recent Review of the National Innovation System (2008) also identified human resources as being critical to national development.

Ensuring sustained competitiveness

The RBV (Barney 1991; Penrose 1959) provides a framework within which to analyse appropriate organisational approaches to the long-term development of human resources (Boxall 1996; Sherman 2007). In recent years, the attraction, retention and development of employees has become an increasingly significant aspect of building organisational capabilities to ensure sustained competitiveness (Holland, Hecker & Steen, 2002).

Attraction and retention of employees

It has been argued that those organisations that invest resources in employee attraction and retention turn a potential problem into an opportunity thus gaining industry leadership (Boxall & Steenveld 1999), (*see* opening vignette: Talent trove.) The RBV perspective focuses on how organisations build unique 'bundles' of resources that generate sustained competitive advantage (Boxall & Purcell 2008). Inimitability is potentially increased as groups of skilled workers form unique dynamics that are difficult to replicate and can be leveraged in the organisation's favour (Barney 1991).

Long-term organisational renewal

In line with the RBV perspective, the approach developed by Hamel and Prahalad (1993) and Leonard (1992, 1998) argues that long-term investment in core competencies provides sustained advantage over time as contemporary competencies become baseline capabilities. Both Hamel and Prahalad (1993) and Leonard (1992) highlight that in response to a shift to a knowledge-based economy, attraction, retention and, increasingly, the development of human resources are the key to the long-term renewal of the organisation.

These points are supported by Boxall and Purcell (2008, p. 175) who argue that firms need to attract and nurture people who have the competencies and ability that will make the organisation productive. An inability to do this will doom the organisation to failure or, at the very least, stunt its growth.

Skilled employees

Given the above, there should be observable evidence of human resource policies and practices focusing on attracting, retaining and developing employees. As Coff (1997) argues, the strategic management of human resources throws out particular challenges to organisations that base their advantages on these 'free' and highly mobile resources. Such resources focus on employability rather than employment and do not seek the traditional employer–employee relationship and psychological contract. This has created major changes in the balance of power with regard to highly skilled employees (Losey 2005; Salt 2004; Tsui & Wu 2005).

Organisations need to refocus their employment systems, practices, and organisational structures in order to capture this unique resource.

Managing talent—a practical perspective

In a response to the changing talent landscape at the turn of the century, McKinsey & Co. embarked in 1998 on a study entitled *The War for Talent*. The study involved 77 companies and almost 6,000 managers and executives in the USA. The strategic overview report identified that the principal corporate resource over the next 20 years would be human resource talent. Through the demographic changes identified, human resource talent would become more difficult to find and more costly to contest (Michaels, Handfield-Jones & Axelrod 2001).

Recommendations of the McKinsey report

The research recommendations included a fundamental change in how organisations design their human resource management practices, including finding more imaginative ways to attract and retain talent. In addition, the report highlighted the changing psychological contract within the employment relationship, noting that employees will increasingly look for employability rather than employment, and will want to change jobs often.

The McKinsey report also identified that 75 per cent of organisations in their survey either did not have enough talent or were chronically short of talent. These trends indicate that those organisations that are prepared to focus on attracting and developing talent will be in a stronger position to retain key human resources as the so-called 'war for talent' intensifies. It is also clear that the way organisations seek to retain these highly skilled resources will also have to change. This places the human resource management and development function at the centre of policy development and systems to achieve these outcomes.

Flexible work options

Whilst the McKinsey study was undertaken in a time of economic boom, the central values are still the same for core competitive advantage. These values are being seen in the current strategies of many organisations dealing with the GFC. Qantas, for example, has explored flexible work options to mitigate job losses. These options include:

- job-sharing;
- part time work; and
- the use of annual and long-service leave (Schneiders 2009).

KPMG (UK) is considering the idea of a four-day week or lengthy sabbaticals for staff, something that has already occurred in the Australian advertising industry (Toomey 2009). This approach has also been adopted by several organisations in the Australian Timber industry (Myer 2009).

Strategies to avoid retrenching workers

To avoid retrenching workers, GM Holden Ltd (whose parent is General Motors Corp) switched from a two-shift operation to one shift (Roberts 2009). Leading Sydney restaurateur, Peter Doyle, implemented a similar approach, arguing that:

> 'We try not to cut staff because you lose good people. We are very mindful that the better the staff you have, the better business you've got, so what we do is ask staff to take fewer hours in the week' (cited in Myer 2009).

This paradigm shift reflects the increasing understanding of the resource-based view. Organisations are becoming more thoughtful about job-cutting, actively restructuring instead of just slashing the workforce (The Economist 2009).

A less well known but growing strategy is that of secondments to community organisations. Whilst this may involve reduced income it maintains a role for the employee and provides a creative experience for the employee. As Myer (2009, p. 8) notes:

> 'Organisations such as Indigenous Enterprise Partnerships have been placing secondees into indigenous organisations in Cape York and Central Victoria. Westpac, Boston Consulting Group, KPMG, Gilbert and Tobin and the ANZ, among others, have been active in their support for seconding staff.'

Problems created by redundancies

Whilst these examples do not negate the need for downsizing, it is worth noting that a recent Drake International survey (2009) found that in the first six months after downsizing:

- 45% of employers employed new permanent or contract workers into the same roles that had been made redundant;
- 46% of directly affected staff were less likely to recommend their employer to a colleague as a place to work; and
- 41% of remaining staff said their respect for their employer had diminished.

The last two of these indicate potential problems in attraction and retention of staff in the future. Clearly, the savings associated with redundancy may be reduced both in the short and longer term (Vas 2009).

New workplace—new perspectives

In this new work environment, workers who own the means of production–knowledge will have the ability to move these valued skills around the external labour market. The management of these key resources therefore assumes greater significance.

Knowledge workers

As Newell, Roertson, Scarbrough and Swan (2002) note, knowledge workers need to be provided with excellent working opportunities which Michaels Handfield-Jones and Axelrod (2001) describe as exciting, challenging and having significant development potential. Newell *et al.* (2002) also argued that it is not possible to develop competitive advantage without consideration of the people that form the core of a firm's knowledge base. As such, the management of human resources poses particular challenges to an organisation.

Motivating essential employees

The key to developing human resource strategies that attract, retain and develop essential employees is to understand what motivates them. As Barnes (1999) points out, such workers

- think differently,
- have different needs; and
- tend to behave differently

from what has been considered as being traditional employee expectations.

Typically, such workers are self-focused and less interested in conventional benefits of employment like job security and working conditions (Rousseau 1995). This is supported by Storey and Quintas (2001) who argue that the core issue for organisations to identify is 'employability'. Key employees expect that an organisation will play a part in securing employment and enhancing employees' knowledge, skills and ability so that they remain in demand not only within the organisation but also the wider employment market. As a recent Deloitte research study identifies:

> 'A growing number of successful companies, such as Microsoft, Southwest Airlines, and SAS ... Rather than starting with recruiters they first look inside to match employee experience and aspirations to the company's evolving strategic needs ... their historically low turnover rates let them spend much less time battling churn – and far more time outmanoeuvring the competition' (Wall & Aijala 2008, p. 6).

Job-hopping

Whilst the concept of job-hopping may become the norm, encouraging this approach may paradoxically be a factor in reducing turnover and making the organisation an 'employer of choice'. As Wall and Aijala (2008, p. 9) point out, it is not unusual for people to try different roles before they find the match that best suits them. They note that:

> 'Organisations that help valued people redeploy typically win their commitment. If a mutually satisfactory solution can be struck, then they win it immediately. If an arrangement can't be struck, then they may win it in the future – even if valued employees choose to leave. Successful talent management includes strategies to stay engaged with alumni. Individuals granted latitude by their employers to explore new territory often make their way back with renewed vigour and insight.'

The move to a contingent workforce

These fundamental changes to the nature of the employment relationship will further accelerate the move from human resources strategies associated with the traditional psychological contract (Hecker & Grimmer 2007).

These workers increasingly manage their own careers. They seek out 'employers of choice' who will provide them with the opportunity to upgrade their skills. Employers need to be aware that these 'new' workers direct their own training and development needs and accept greater role ambiguity and responsibility (e.g. developing skills in a particular area such as project management) in order to broaden their level of employability (Arnold 1996; Scholarious, Lockyer & Johnson 2003; Turnley & Feldman 2000).

Cappelli (in Powell 2007, p. 41) suggests that:

> '... many companies do not wish to invest in their people because they fear the investment will be lost when people leave – and so, of course, people leave because there hasn't been any investment in them'.

In effect, the new core workforce will be a contingent workforce, looking to the organisation to provide the relevant skills and rewards to allow them to develop their skills and then move on (and perhaps return as well). This places human resources at the centre of organisational policies.

The structural changes driving the 'war for talent' are as inexorable as they are widespread across many advanced market economies. As Michaels, Handfield-Jones and Axelrod (2001) argue, these changes are creating a new business reality. The old and new realities of work are listed in Table 10.1.

Table 10.1 The old and new realities of work

The old reality	The new reality
People need companies	Companies need people
Machines, capital and geography are the competitive advantage	Talented people are the competitive advantage
Better talent makes some difference	Better talent makes a huge difference
Jobs are scarce	Talented people are scarce

The old reality	The new reality
Employees are loyal and jobs are secure	People are mobile and their commitment is short term
People accept the standard package they are offered	People demand much more

Source: Michaels, Handfield-Jones & Axelrod 2001, *The War for Talent,* Harvard Business School Press, Cambridge MA., p. 6.

New managers — new perspectives

One often overlooked aspect of this 'new' talent management environment is the role and development of management.

Need for high-calibre managerial talent

As Davenport and Prusak (1998) have noted, the most dramatic improvements in knowledge management capability will be human and managerial. The need for high-calibre managerial talent is increasing to meet the challenge of globalisation and deregulation underpinned by rapid and complex change.

As noted in the examples of Qantas and KPMG, the development of fluid organisations and informal and intuitive patterns of work need a management base that has the skill to:

- acquire;
- transform; and
- exploit knowledge and patterns of work

which seek new ways to attract, retain and develop these human resources. Management must have the leadership skills to harness new practices and shed old habits such as a culture of hierarchy and power (Hibbard & Carrillo 1998) while empowering continual change (Scarbrough & Swan 2003).

Strategies to regenerate the knowledge base

Research by Macdonald (1986) on headhunting practices for key employees in the US found that organisations which developed a culture where employees were encouraged to see their organisation as a supportive platform for advancing elsewhere (and for returning when opportunities became available) were likely to facilitate the growth of knowledge stocks within the firm.

Australian research by Holland *et al.* (2002) on a medium sized ICT firm supports this. Human resource policies and practices were identified as the key platform in developing an environment that attracted employees in a very competitive market. The practices included:

- employee mobility;
- training;
- development; and
- career management.

'Consultancies and other knowledge-intensive organisations ... might see a turnover level around 15–18% as desirable ... this allows a reasonable number of career opportunities and a continuous influx of fresh talent' (Scarbrough, Swan & Preston 1999, p. 10).

As Kamoche and Mueller (1998) have argued, the reputation of an organisation, underpinned by sophisticated employment policies, may make the organisation an attractive place to work. In contemporary language, it will be an employer of choice that can attract high quality knowledge workers.

Training and development the top benefit

In a survey of its own incoming graduates and CEOs (more than 4,000 from 44 countries) PricewaterhouseCoopers (2009) found that both graduates and CEOs understood that training and development, particularly through mentoring, was the top benefit most respondents wanted.

Training and development is particularly important in the period following recruitment and selection when the worker is no longer a 'new' employee. For an employee to be properly integrated may require an onboarding program beginning at the interview stage and lasting up to six months (McCain & Isbell 2009). Rollag (2007) argues the most successful programs last one to two years.

Embracing a new mindset

It is the management of human resource strategies that enable the organisation to develop and regenerate its knowledge base (Storey & Quintas 2001). Management skills are central to understanding the critical issues raised by these new patterns of work (Sparrow 1998). As Michaels *et al.* (2001) argue, in some cases management needs to embrace a completely new mindset as Tables 10.2, 10.3 and 10.4 illustrate.

Chapter 10 – Managing Talent: Exploring HR Strategies in a Dynamic Environment

Table 10.2: The changing dynamic of human resource management

The old way	The new way
HR is responsible for people management	All managers, starting with the CEO, are accountable for strengthening their talent pool
We provide good pay and benefits	We shape our company, our jobs, even our strategy to appeal to talented people
Recruiting is like purchasing	Recruiting is like marketing
We think development happens in training	We fuel development primarily through stretch jobs, coaching and mentoring
We treat everyone the same and like to think that everyone is equally capable	We affirm all our people but invest differently in our A, B and C players

Source: Michaels, Handfield-Jones & Axelrod 2001, p. 16.

Table 10.3: New patterns of work

Old mindset about people management	New talent mindset
A vague notion that 'people are our most important asset'	A deep conviction that better talent leads to better corporate performance
HR is responsible for people management	All managers are accountable for strengthening their talent pool
We have a two-day succession planning exercise once a year	Talent management is a central part of how we run the company
I work with people I inherit	I take bold actions to build the talent pool I need

Source: Michaels, Handfield-Jones & Axelrod 2001, p. 22.

Table 4: Changing perspectives on attraction and retention

Old recruiting strategies	New recruiting strategies
Grow your own talent	Pump talent in at all levels
Recruit for vacant positions	Hunt for talent all the time
Go to a few traditional sources	Tap many diverse pools of talent
Advertise to job hunters	Find ways to reach passive candidates
Specify a compensation range and stay within it	Break the compensation rules to get the candidates you want
Recruiting is about screening	Recruiting is about selling as well as screening
Hire as needed with no overall plan	Develop a recruiting strategy for each type of talent

Source: Michaels, Handfield-Jones & Axelrod 2001, p. 70.

Managing talent—a research perspective

Talent management in Australia

A recent OECD report claims that:

> 'Australia is in an enviable position. Unemployment is low, and labour force participation is high. Yet, labour market outcomes still lag behind the leading OECD countries. There is much scope for improving incentives to work' (2008, p. 63).

Sheehan, Holland and DeCieri's 2006 Australia-wide survey of human resource managers through members of the Australian Human Resource Institute (AHRI) analyses how policies and practices link to talent management. An overview analysis of the research reveals some contradictions in the focus of organisations.

Contradictions in organisational focus

In describing their roles as HR managers (see Table 10.5) the Australian managers identified strategic HRM as their primary emphasis, with training and development clearly second. This reflects a shift in strategic focus in the need to attract and, more importantly, retain talent.

Table 10.5 Primary emphasis of the HR position

Role function	n = 1372 %
A broad range of human resource issues	45
HRM strategic development	21
Training & development	11
Recruitment & selection	7
Employee relations	7
Remuneration / performance management	3
Occupational health and safety	2
Industrial relations	2
Human resource information systems	1
Wage / salary administration	1

Source: Holland, Sheehan, & DeCieri 2007, 'Attracting and Retaining Talent: Exploring Human Resource Development Trends in Australia', *Human Resources. Development International*, 10(3): 247-261.

Chapter 10 – Managing Talent: Exploring HR Strategies in a Dynamic Environment

However, further analysis of the major emerging issue in HRM in both the previous five years and in the next five years (Table 10.6) indicates that becoming an 'employer of choice' was not a 'front-of-mind issue', being in seventh place in the former and sixth in the latter. What was significant was training and development. Participation and teamwork issues were in the bottom quartile for both tables. Considering the nature of the labour market, this appears a significant paradox, particularly with regard to the findings in Table 10.5.

This research also showed that over the previous two years training and development has been the most outsourced HR function at 48.2 per cent, almost 15 per cent more than recruitment and selection at 33.5 per cent. Considering these are key aspects of attraction and retention, this overview analysis suggests that Australian organisations are not responding to the changing labour market as might be expected and are maintaining the hegemony of traditional aversion to investment in human capital.

Table 10.6 Emerging areas of importance in the HRM field

HRM issues	Last 5 years n = 1372* %	Next 5 years n = 1372* %
Connecting performance management systems to organisational strategy	84	89
Strategic integration of HRM policies	83	89
Change management	80	81
Management of employee relations	75	72
Measuring the contribution of HRM to company performance	75	86
Managing flexible work patterns	65	84
Becoming an employer of choice	60	76
Devolution of HRM responsibilities to the line	57	60
Performance based remuneration	55	66
Worker participation and team work	51	59
Defining productivity outcomes of training & development	47	65
Quality Issues	38	49

*Respondents could select more than one response.

Source: Holland, Sheehan & De Cieri 2007.

Employment v. employability

An analysis of attraction and retention polices indicated mixed results in respect of the organisation discerning what potential employees look at in terms of whether the organisation is offering employment or employability. Organisations may therefore not be paying enough attention in terms of resource allocation to these areas. This is also supported by research conducted by Butler and Waldrop (2001), Kinnear and Sutherland (2000) Horwitz, Heng and Quazi (2003) who identify that bundles of retention practices such as

- work design;
- challenging work; and
- autonomy

help retain high-skilled employees, and also act as effective attraction practices.

The Asia Pacific Talent Index

Despite the rhetoric, it appears that organisations in Australia are still coming to terms with the importance of investing in retention and development strategies as a source of competitive advantage and may not have a long-term view of the consequences.

The Asia-Pacific Talent Index (Heidrick & Struggles 2008) is an attempt to quantify and map potential hot spots for human capital and recruiting talent, now and in five years time across the Asia Pacific region. Currently Australia heads the index, ranking first in five categories:

- quality of compulsory education;
- quality of universities and business schools;
- quality of the environment to nurture talent; and
- proclivity to attracting talent.

By 2012, however, the Index predicts that:

- Australia will rank second behind Singapore;
- Australia will rank first only in the quality of the environment to nurture talent;
- New Zealand will take over first rank in terms of the quality of compulsory education;
- Japan (with China in second place) will rank first in the quality of their universities and business schools; and
- Singapore will lead in proclivity to attracting talent.

Although individual firms have little influence on a country's standing in the index, a falling rank is indicative that a country may fail to fully realise and manage its human talent. This will make it more difficult for individual firms to 'understand the supply and demand of the critical workforce segments' (Wall & Aijala 2008, p. 12) necessary to maintain competitiveness in an increasingly globalised market.

Conclusion

It has become increasingly evident that the war for talent is heating up, irrespective of the global financial crisis. As a result, organisations will need to better understand the supply and demand of critical human resources. As Ralph Norris, CEO of the Commonwealth Bank of Australia has stated:

'Clearly, we're going to see a situation where the war for talent is only going to increase in intensity ... As a result, we're doing a lot of thinking at the moment about how we handle workforce flexibility and the different requirements of the various generations that comprise our staff' (cited in PricewaterhouseCoopers 2009, p. 33).

The war for talent occurs across all industry sectors as the following case study of a major Australian firm demonstrates.

Case study: TempInc

TempInc is the leading supplier of labour hire work (also known as 'on-hire', 'temp' or 'agency' work) in Australia. Its labour hire staff can be:

- employees who are then on-hired to a client firm (but are not employees of that firm); or
- self-employed contractors for whom TempInc finds clients and handles administrative and financial affairs.

Initially providing supplementary trades, TempInc developed a white-collar sector providing customer contact services, healthcare and general office placement staff. During 2008, more than 70,000 labour hire workers chose to work for TempInc in a diverse range of industries in Australia and New Zealand and to a smaller extent in developing markets overseas. Sales revenues have more than doubled in the last five years to almost A$2 billion in 2007/08.

Growth in agency work over the last two decades has outstripped the growth in direct employment, with the majority of Australia's top 500 companies using contract labour. TempInc offers up to 25% salary loading to 'talented' workers, although attracting these workers is a major problem for the whole labour hire industry.

TempInc argues that to attract and keep talented workers, the work needs not only to be about opportunity and variety but also about:

- quality training;
- development; and
- career progression.

This is probably best demonstrated in its provision of human resource development opportunities as a means of increasing the skills base of labour hire employees. The variety of jobs with different client firms is also an important learning feature of work. It is seen by TempInc as a training and development opportunity and is interpreted this way by labour hire workers who value the new experiences.

TempInc's aim is to become an employer of choice by giving employees and potential employees 'a sense of belonging but not a sense of being owned' — by providing a range of benefits and doing all the things a normal employer would do. TempInc treats both its temporary and permanent staff as if they are committed to the organisation. It allows TempInc to demonstrate that although an assignment is limited or short-term it will not lead to disinterest or second-rate treatment on the part of the agency. This has led to significantly lower employee turnover than the industry average.

Becoming an employer of choice in the labour hire industry raises the issue of talented staff being poached by client organisations. TempInc, however, claims to be able to compete with any permanent employer. This is supported by the fact that they do not see themselves as a provider of peripheral workers but rather as working within a partnership to manage these key employees. TempInc sees its competitive advantage as working in areas where it has acknowledged expertise corresponding with areas of labour shortage. Since labour hire workers may be subject to conflicting policies and procedures on clients' sites, in many cases there is a TempInc supervisor on site who looks after the TempInc employee under every circumstance, even if a client supervisor is present.

As we continue to embrace a knowledge- and service-based economy, and our neighbours in the Asia Pacific region compete with us as advanced market economies, the war for talent will be both national and international. As the case study demonstrates, the ability to attract, retain and develop talent may be the only real competitive advantage that a firm possesses. With the changing employment relationship it is not sufficient simply to develop human resource policies and practices to attract talent and become an employer of choice. We would argue that it is equally essential to develop management and leadership skills to manage this talent.

Case study questions

1. Discuss how changes in the structure and composition of the Australian workforce have provided opportunities for TempInc to develop its business model of labour hire.
2. What strategies has TempInc developed to attract and retain talent in its workforce?
3. What HRM issues will become critical to enable TempInc to retain its ability to attract talented workers in the future?

References

Arnold, J 1996, 'The Psychological Contract: A Concept in Need of Closer Scrutiny?', *European Journal of Work and Organizational Psychology,* 5 (4), 511-520.

Barnes, D 1999, *Perspectives on Total Rewards: Recruitment and Retention,* Towers Perrin.

Barney, J 1991, 'Firm resources and sustained competitive advantage', *Journal of Management,* 17: 99-120.

Barney, JB & Wright, PM 1998, 'On becoming a strategic partner: the role of human resources in gaining competitive advantage', *Human Resource Management'* 37 (1): 31-46.

Boxall, P 1996, 'The Strategic HRM debate and the resource-based view of the firm' *Human Resource Management Journal,* 6(3): 59-75.

Boxall, P & Steenveld, J 1999, 'Human Resource Strategy and Competitive Advantage: A Longitudinal Study of Engineering Consultancies', *Journal of Management Studies,* 36(4): 443-463.

Boxall, P & Purcell, J 2008, *Strategy and Human Resource Management (2nd edn),* Basingstoke, Palgrave Macmillan.

Butler, Y & Waldrop, J 2001, 'Job Sculpting: The Art of Retaining Your Best People', *Harvard Business Review,* 179-203.

Cappelli, P 2003, 'Will there really be a labor shortage', *Organizational Dynamics,* 3:15-24.

Cappelli, P 2005, 'Will There Really be a Labor Shortage', in M Losey, S Meisinger & D Ulrich, *The Future of Human Resource Management,* 5-14.

Cappelli, P & Crocker-Hefter, A 1996, 'Distinctive Human Resources are a Firm's Core Competitive Advantage', *Organizational Dynamics,* Winter: 7-23.

Coff, R 1997, 'Human Assests and Management Dilemmas: Coping with Hazards on the Road to Resource-Based Theory', *Academy of Management Review,* 22: 374-402.

Critchley, R 2004, *Doing Nothing is Not an Option: Facing the Imminent Labor Crisis*, Australia, Thomson, South Western.

Davenport, TH & Prusak, L 1998, *Working Knowledge: How Organizations Manage What They Know*, Boston, Harvard Business School Press.

Drake International 2009, *Downsizing research report*, viewed 25 June 2009, www.drakeintl.com.au.

Hamel, G & Prahalad, C 1993, 'Strategy as Stretch and Leverage', Boston, MA., *Harvard Business Review*, 71(2): 75-84..

Hecker, R & Grimmer, M 2007, 'The Evolving Psychological Contract', in P Holland & H De Cieri, *Contemporary Issue in Human Resource Development*, pp. 183-210.

Heidrick & Struggles International Inc. 2008, *Mapping Asia-Pacific Talent 2007–2012: Insights and Data*, Economist Intelligence Unit Ltd., London.

Hibbard, J & Carillo, KM 1998, 'Knowledge revolution: Getting employees to share what they know is no longer a technology challenge it's a corporate culture challenge', *Information Week*, 663.

Holland, P, Hecker, R & Steen, J 2002, 'Human resource strategies and organisational structures for managing gold-collar workers', *Journal of European Industrial Training*, 26: 72-80.

Holland PJ, Sheehan, C & DeCieri, H 2007, 'Attracting and Retaining Talent: Exploring Human Resource Development Trends in Australia', *Human Resources Development International*, 10(3): 247-261.

Horwitz, F Heng CT & Quazi HA 2003, 'Finders, Keepers? Attracting, Motivating and Retaining Knowledge Workers', *Human Resource Management Journal*, 13(4): 23-44

Kamoche, K & Mueller, F 1998, 'Human resource management and the appropriation-learning perspective', *Human Relations*, 51: 1033-1061.

Kinnear, L & Sutherland, M 2000, 'Determinants of Organisational Commitment Amongst Knowledge Workers', *South African Journal of Business Management*, 32(2): 106-111

Leonard, D 1992, 'Core Capabilities and Core Rigidities', *Strategic Management Journal*, 13: 111-125.

Leonard, D 1998, *Wellsprings of Knowledge: Building and Sustaining the Sources of Innovation*, Boston, MA., Harvard Business School Press.

Losey, M 2005, 'Anticipating Change: Will there be a labour shortage Will There Really be a Labor Shortage', in M Losey, S Meisinger & D Ulrich, *The Future of Human Resource Management*, pp. 23-37.

Macdonald, S 1986, 'Headhunting in high technology', *Technovation*, 4: 233–245.

McCain, K & Isbell, M 2009, 'Workforce strategies to improve your organizations bottom line', *American Water Works Association Journal*, 101(8): 32-39.

McColl, G 2009, 'Talent trove', *Business Review Weekly*, April 30, p. 28.

Michaels, E, Handfield-Jones, H & Axelrod, E 2001, *The War for Talent*, Harvard Business School Press, Cambridge MA.

Myer, R 2009, 'Don't Press the Panic Button', *The Melbourne Age*, April 17, p. 8, Melbourne, Fairfax Publications.

Newell, S Robertson, M Scarbrough, H & Swan, J 2002, *Managing Knowledge Work*, Hampshire, Palgrave.

OECD 2004, Labour Force Statistics (For non-OECD countries), OECD, Paris.

OECD 2007, 'Can policies boost birth rates?', *OECD Policy Brief*, November OECD, Paris.

OECD 2008, 'Australia', *OECD Economic Surveys*, 18/8, OECD, Paris.

Penrose, E 1959, *The Theory of Growth of the Firm*, Blackwell, Oxford.

Powell, S 2007, 'Spotlight on Peter Cappelli', *Human Resource Management International Digest*, 15(1): 40-43.

PricewaterhouseCoopers, 2009, '12th Annual Global CEO Survey-Future proof Plans', viewed 27 July 2009, www.pwc.com/ceosurvey.

Review of the National Innovation System, 2008, *Venturous Australia: Building strength in innovation*, Department of Innovation, Industry, Science and Research, viewed 2 July 2009, www.innovation.gov.au/innovationreview/pages/home.aspx.

Roberts, P 2009, 'Profit factories', *Business Review Weekly*, 37 (27): 20-26.

Rollag, K 2007, 'Defining the Term 'New' in New Employee Research', *Journal of Occupational and Organizational Psychology*, 80: 63-75

Rousseau, DM 1995, *Psychological Contracts in Organizations: Understanding written and unwritten agreements*, Sage Publications, London.

Salt, B 2004, *The Big Shift*, 2nd edn, Hardie Grant Books, South Yarra, Australia.

Scarbrough, H & Swan, J 2003, 'Discourses of knowledge management and the learning organization: Their production and consumption', in M Easterby-Smith, & M Lyles (eds.), *Handbook of Organizational Learning and Knowledge Management*, Blackwell, Oxford.

Scarbrough, H, Swan, J & Preston, J 1999, *Knowledge Management: A Review of the Literature*, Institute of Personnel and Development, London.

Schneiders, B 2009, 'Qantas pledges to minimise job cuts', *The Melbourne Age*, April 21, p. 8, Fairfax Publications, Melbourne.

Scholarios, D, Lockyer, C & Johnson, H 2003, 'Anticipatory socialisation: The effect of recruitment and selection experiences on career expectations', *Career Development International*, 8(4); 182 – 197.

Sheehan, C, Holland, P & De Cieri, H 2006, 'Current developments in HRM in Australian organisations', *Asia Pacific Journal of Human Resources*, August 1, 2006; 44(2): 132 – 152.

Sherman, WS 2007, 'Improving Organizations by Coaching Individual Development Using the Resource-based Business Strategy', *S.A.M. Advanced Management Journal*, 72(4): 40-47.

Sparrow, P 1998, 'New Organisational Forms, Processes, Jobs and Psychological Contracts: Resolving the HRM Issues', in P Sparrow & M Marchington (eds), *Human Resource Management: The New Agenda*, Financial Times/Pitmans, London, pp. 117-141.

Storey, J & Quintas, P 2001, 'Knowledge management and HRM' in J Storey (ed.), *Human Resource Management: A Critical Text*, Thomson Learning, London.

The Economist 2009, 'Help not wanted', 13 August.

Toomey, S 2009, 'Companies Move to Cut Hours, Not Staff, in Tough Times', *The Australian,* April 21, p. 1, News Limited Publications, Sydney.

Tsui, AS & Wu JB 2005, 'The New Employment Relationship versus the Mutual Investment Approach: Implications for Human Resource Management', in M Losey, S Meisinger & D Ulrich, *The Future of Human Resource Management,* Wiley & Son, Virginia, pp. 44-54.

Turnley, WH & Feldman, DC 2000, 'Re-examining the effects of psychological contract violation: unmet expectations and job dissatisfaction as mediators', *Journal of Organizational Behaviour,* 21(1): 25-42.

Vas T 2009, 'Maximising your ROI with effective redeployment strategies', 3rd *Australasian Talent Conference,* viewed 20 July 2009, www.atcevent.com.au.

Wall , J & Aijala, A 2008, *It's 2008: Do You Know Where Your Talent Is?,* Deloitte.

Wright, PM, Gardner, TM, Moynihan, LM & Allen, MR 2005, 'The relationship between HR practices and firm performance: Examining causal order', *Personnel Psychology,* 58, 409-446.

Chapter 11

AN AGEING WORKFORCE: HRM CHALLENGES

Jennifer Waterhouse & John Burgess

OBJECTIVES

This chapter discusses the impact on HRM of an ageing workforce. It outlines the dimensions of an ageing workforce in Australia and Japan. By the completion of the chapter you should be able to:

1. identify the challenges that emerge from an ageing workforce in terms of HRM;
2. describe some of the national and organisational responses to an ageing workforce.

DEFINITIONS

Ageing workforce: A changing demographic composition of the workforce where the average workforce age is increasing. An ageing workforce reflects an underlying ageing of a general population.

Aged Dependency Ratio: Ratio of the population 65 years and over as a percentage of the population aged 20–64 years.

Introduction

This chapter explores the policy and human resource implications of an ageing workforce. Population ageing has significant policy implications in a number of areas. They include:

- adjustment for the changing patterns for supply and demand of social services (such as child care, elderly and dementia care);
- immigration policy; and
- labour policy.

Labour policy

The major concern of labour policy has largely been to address the effects of ageing on the national dependency ratio. This is arguably the major labour policy concern for all OECD member nations (OECD 2006).

The trend to an ageing workforce

Ageing general populations mean that workplaces are already naturally ageing; however, with labour market policies aimed at specifically retaining workers in the workforce longer, the trend to an ageing workforce will arguably continue and accelerate. To overcome the economic and social effects of an increasing old-age dependency ratio it has become a policy direction for many nations to seek ways of retaining older workers (generally considered as workers over the age of 45 or 50, depending on source) in the workplace longer.

A counter-argument to this perceived trend is that, as in the past, when unemployment rates increase the first workers targeted for layoffs are older workers. Thus, harsher economic times associated with the 2008/09 global economic slowdown may forestall an ageing workforce but aggravate economic and social issues associated with increased old-age dependency ratios. Furthermore, the employment of older workers has been problematic and has in some cases met with considerable resistance from employers, employees and society generally.

Retention of older workers

The International Labour Organization continues to consider it imperative to retain older workers in the workforce. In its report to the G8 High Level Meeting on Employment in May 2003, it noted that considerable combined effort of key actors and partners was needed to address ageing population and workforce issues by means of:

- private companies through their human resource practices;
- governments through effective anti-discrimination laws;

- social partners (both employee associations/unions and employer associations) through their deliberations and agreements; and
- the support of society as a whole (ILO 2003).

In addition, the OECD (2006) notes additional roles for government in implementing pro-active employment policies including financial incentives to both employees and employers and training to support and encourage older people to remain in the workforce. Additionally, governments are encouraged to initiate policies that act as a disincentive for early retirement.

Growing diversity of the workplace

Regardless of future trends, it remains the case that for the first time in the history of work, four generations of employees are now concurrently employed. This alone suggests an important diversity issue for workplaces to address through their HRM practices. At the very least it will force employers to consider the architecture of workplaces (in terms of facilities and ergonomics) and the organisation of work (especially hours and shifts) for a diverse demographic profile of employees.

Scope of the chapter

This chapter broadly considers the role of the various actors in the employment of an ageing workforce. We will

- outline the global perspectives of an ageing workforce by exploring the dimensions of the ageing workforces of Australia and Japan;
- explore policy initiatives;
- consider the current implications of an ageing workforce for workplaces and more specifically for human resource management (HRM); and
- examine implications for workplaces and HRM based on recent and possible future policy responses.

Population and workforce ageing

At present, all OECD nations are experiencing population ageing. The OECD therefore identifies population ageing as one of the most important and immediate challenges for all member countries (OECD 2006).

Demographic differences

There are differences, however, between OECD nations in terms both of their current age demographics and the rate at which their populations are ageing. Nations therefore face different challenges in addressing their ageing populations and associated ageing workforces.

Nations with an existing older population with longer life expectancy and a significantly shrinking birth rate face a more significant ageing challenge than others. Particularly identified in this regard are Italy and Japan, both of which have relatively old populations.

Older-worker participation rates

One way to reduce the old-age dependency ratio is to increase the workforce participation rate of older persons nearing or passing 'normal' retirement age. If governments can encourage older workers to work longer, they may be able to reduce, or at least slow, future increases in the old-age dependency ratio.

Governments of nations which already have high labour market participation rates among older workers are more restricted in utilising this policy response. Therefore older-worker participation rates, in concert with old-age dependency ratios, are important indicators of the type of ageing challenge faced by national economies. This combination for OECD nations is outlined in Table 11.1.

Table 11.1 Projected dependency ratios among OECD economies

Participation rates of 50–64 year olds, 2004	Projected change in the old-age dependency ratio, 2000–2050		
	Moderate	**Large**	**Very large**
High	Denmark, Iceland, Sweden, Switzerland, USA	Canada, New Zealand	Japan
Average	Netherlands, UK	Australia, Finland, France, Germany, Mexico, Ireland	Czech Republic, Korea, Portugal
Low	Belgium, Luxembourg, Turkey	Austria, Hungary	Greece, Italy, Poland, Slovakia, Spain

Source: OECD 2006.

Workforce diversity

The challenges of an ageing population and older workforces are a complex demographic issue and are associated with other types of workforce diversity. The ageing workforce is gendered as well as educationally splintered and, for some countries, racially differentiated.

Workforce participation and gender

The increased participation rate of women over several decades suggests that in the future there will be a larger increase in the participation of older women in the workforce than older men. In some OECD countries the gendered participation gap among older workers is significant and needs to be addressed if labour supply is to be more fully mobilised (OECD 2006).

Workforce participation and education

Higher levels of workforce participation are experienced among those of higher educational attainment, with the result that certain industries, such as education, have a higher average workforce age than others.

Racial differences and workforce participation

In nations such as New Zealand, general population ageing is being experienced more among the Caucasian populations than the Maori indigenous population. Changes to the cultural mix of workplaces can therefore be predicted in the future (Statistics New Zealand 2004).

Global perspectives

As a result of the trends outlined above, all OECD governments are facing the implications of general population ageing in terms of:

- increasing social security and health costs;
- growing dependency ratios; and
- having a sufficient supply of labour.

The last two of these concerns have significant implications for the future composition of the workforce based on the policy initiatives of governments. Both the old-age dependency ratio and the sufficiency of the labour force are increasingly being addressed in many countries through general social and employment policies seeking to alleviate some of the social and economic costs associated with an ageing population.

In regard to the employment of older workers, the ILO views the role of governments as two-fold:

- as makers of policies aimed at defending the human rights of older workers especially through anti-discrimination legislation; and
- implementing active labour market policies including 'job counselling, labour market training, subsidised employment, self-employment promotion measures and mobility promotion measures. (ILO 2003, p. 9).

Age discrimination

The ILO (2003) suggests that while nearly all countries have legislation banning discrimination on the basis of gender, race, and religion, few have enacted laws banning discrimination on the basis of age.

Outcomes of this uneven legislative response have been that many countries retain mandatory retirement ages and that some organisations actively and legally engage in discriminating on the basis of age in their recruitment, selection, employment, training and retrenchment practices. Where laws covering discrimination based on age exist, they are highly varied in their content and coverage, with implications for the extent to which they address the ILO's objective of defending the rights of older workers.

Table 11.2 Patterns of ageing in selected economies (population share aged 65+ %)

Country	1950	2000	2050
Japan	4.9	17.2	36.5
Italy	8.3	18.1	34.1
Australia	8.1	12.3	24.9
New Zealand	9.0	11.8	22.9
China	4.5	6.8	22.9
Malaysia	5.1	4.1	15.7
Korea	3.2	7.1	30.5
USA	8.3	12.3	20.0
United Kingdom	10.7	15.9	23.3

Source: Productivity Commission 2005, 17.

Supply and demand

Both demand and supply sides of the labour market are critical to the employment of older workers (OECD 2002). In regard to the supply of older workers, the OECD (2002) predicts that in response to ageing populations, governments will alter policies so that incentives for early retirement will be reduced or eliminated.

In this section we consider the current situations facing Australia and Japan and suggest that this 'disincentive' approach has been a very popular policy direction but one that is largely passive in that it fails to address the human capital needs of older workers to attain or remain in employment.

Nor do such passive approaches provide incentives for employers to employ older workers. These passive policy initiatives represent only one part of the three-pronged response the OECD (2006) considers necessary to address an ageing population, namely:

- remove work disincentives and provide choice in work-retirement decisions;
- change employer attitudes and employment practices; and
- improve the employability of older workers (OECD 2006).

Table 11.1 identifies Australia and Japan as being located in different age dependency categories in that they face a different combination of current workforce participation rates for persons aged 50 to 64 and projected old-age dependency ratios 2000–2050. Below we consider in greater depth the current demographics of these nations, their existing policies, and recent policy responses to these different challenges.

Japan

On current projections it is estimated that by 2050 within the OECD Japan will be second only to Spain with the highest percentage of people over the age of 65. Japan already has a comparatively high percentage of persons over the age of 65 and this, combined with its higher than average ageing population rate, means that Japan potentially faces a larger social and economic challenge in regard to ageing than most nations.

In terms of their workforce, Japan has a very large projected old-age dependency ratio. Significant in the case of Japan, however, is that Japan already has high workforce participation rates among older workers.

Tienen

Japan's statistics, however, disguise a significantly untapped workforce in its population over the age of 60. A significant feature of the older labour market in Japan is that most workers would prefer to work longer but are often forced out of the workforce by a widespread cultural and organisational practice where work contracts cease at a specific age — known as *tienen* (a chronological age at which work contracts expire) (Oka 2008). As a result there are potential policy options for Japan to tap into this older labour market; however custom and practice need to be overcome in order to achieve this.

Implementing job security post-tienen

Legislation implemented in 2004 seeks to encourage employers to raise the tienen age, implement policies to improve the retention of workers past age 60 or abolish the tienen rule altogether. The changes to *Tienen* are set to occur in stages over six years and align with phased increases in the age for access to the pension system.

Up until 2007, successive governments have sought to implement positive employment policies aimed at encouraging older workers to work and employers to employ older workers. The aim of these policies is to encourage employers to offer job security for all job applicants post-tienen i.e., all workers wishing to work past obligatory retirement are to be offered positions by their current employers. The success of this approach has, in most cases, been disappointing with case examples demonstrating that even municipal councils were unwilling to offer positions to all applicants. Further, the salary, bonus and pension benefits made available to those offered positions post-tienen were generally well below those of other permanent employees (Oka 2008).

Age discrimination

An issue for the employment of older workers in Japan is the prevalence of age discrimination combined with comparatively weak regulations in regard to age discrimination (Oka 2008). In 2007, the *Employment Measure Act* 1966 (EMA) was amended to include Article 10 — Japan's first anti-age discrimination legislation in regard to hiring practices.

An earlier amendment of the EMA in 2001 had included a section on age discrimination, but had provided for ten allowable matters that permitted age discrimination on the basis of three main exclusions:

- the inherent requirements of the job including where businesses seek to mirror their clientele's demography for business purposes;
- to comply with statutes; and
- to maintain typical Japanese employment practices including such practices as the exclusive recruitment of new graduates.

Significantly, even where employers were not able to argue an allowable matter there were no legal rights for injured parties to claim for remedies of any kind.

The 2007 amendments

Neither do the 2007 amendments provide remedies. They refer only to hiring, and oblige employers to provide equality of opportunity in their hiring practices. Where there is failure to do so, the courts can order consolation money be paid for non-economic damages but cannot award employment (Sakuraba 2009).

A combination of minimal compensation and the continuation of protection for some Japanese traditional employment practices has led to a view that the legislation is not aimed at the protection of human rights. Rather, the amendments form an employment policy aimed at achieving specific and narrow policy objectives. The regulations, therefore, 'take on a patchwork aspect' (Sakuraba 2009, p. 69)

Australia

In the twentieth century Australian life expectancy increased by 20 years and average income per capita increased five-fold. The result has been a change in how Australians view their work–life balance with a key feature being an expectation of a much longer retirement.

Table 11.1 identifies Australia as having average participation rates of persons aged between 50 and 64 and a large projected change in the old-age dependency ratio as most baby boomers near or pass the (recently revised) pensionable age of 65.

In 2003, 17% of Australia's population was over the age of 60 compared with 16% in 1998. In its 2005 report, the Productivity Commission estimated dependence ratios based on two possible scenarios—see Table 11.3.

- *Scenario P1* By 2050-51 the total fertility rate rises to 2.05, life expectancy increases only to 83 and 86 years for males and females respectively and net migration level increases to 140,000 per year (which will give the least aged population structure).

- *Scenario P2* By 2050-51 The total fertility rate falls to 1.65, life expectancy increases to 92.2 and 95 years for males and females respectively and the net migration level drops to 90 000 per year. Among the range of plausible scenarios, this produces the most aged population structure.

Table 11.3 Measures of ageing under different scenarios %

	2044–45		2100–01	
	P1	P2	P1	P2
Share aged over 65	21.4	28.9	22.7	35.2
Share aged over 85	3.9	7.8	4.7	13.6
Share aged under 15	18.4	13.4	18.2	12.2
Aged dependency ratio	35.5	50.1	38.4	67.1

Source: Productivity Commission 2005, p. 44.

Even under the favourable P1 scenario there are projected increases in the age dependency ratio and in the proportion of the population aged over 65 years.

The HREOC enquiry into age discrimination in Australia

In 2000 the Human Rights and Equal Opportunity Commission (HREOC) completed its major enquiry into age discrimination in Australia. The Commission published its findings in its report 'Age Matters'. The report concluded that the federal legislation was now weaker than all individual state legislation in protecting human rights in the matter of age discrimination.

Its recommendations were therefore broad in their scope and included a review of all federal legislation with a view to eliminating age-discriminatory clauses. It recommended the federal government undertake pro-active labour market campaigns to encourage the employment of older workers. Its pinnacle recommendation was the enactment of specific legislation in the form of an age discrimination act—a recommendation acted on by the federal government in the *Age Discrimination Act* 2004 (ADA).

The *Age Discrimination Act* 2004

The ADA does not delineate an age range. Rather, it outlaws discrimination based on age generally. Its policy scope is comprehensive in that it extends beyond the area of employment and work to other key aspects of public life—including access to goods, services and facilities, public places and transport and education.

The ADA covers both direct and indirect discrimination. Complaints regarding violations of the Act can be referred to HREOC for conciliation. Outcomes through conciliation may include:

- an apology;
- reinstatement to a job;
- compensation for lost wages;
- changes to an organisational policy; or
- developing and promoting anti-discrimination policies (HREOC).

Unresolved or unsatisfactorily resolved complaints may be referred to the Federal Magistrates Court or Federal Court of Australia for hearing.

The *Fair Work Act* 2009

The ADA acts in concert with the *Fair Work Act* 2009 (FWA) which prevents employers taking adverse action against an employee on the basis of age (and other characteristics). The FWA, however, permits discriminatory treatment on the basis of age in regard to employment if the reason is the inherent requirements of the particular position held by the employee. These exceptions in FWA are in keeping with the previous *Workplace Relations Act* 1996 that also permitted age discrimination on the basis of inherent job requirements. The legislation places an onus on the employer to evidence inherent requirements.

The 'National Ageing Strategy' and the 'Intergenerational Report'

In March 2002 the former coalition government implemented the 'National Ageing Strategy' which was quickly followed and largely overtaken by the 'Intergenerational Report'.

Neither the strategy document nor the Intergenerational Report committed the government to any specific programs. They did not address fiscal policy challenges or discuss the extra revenue that would be required to address the increased costs of an ageing population. Instead, they emphasised user-pay schemes through personal savings, largely encouraged through personal and employer-sponsored superannuation funds.

The pension eligibility age

Acting in concert with the policy direction of the private funding of retirement has been an increase in the pension eligibility age—firstly by incrementally increasing the pension age for women to 65 (an initiative of the former coalition government), and secondly by increasing the eligible pension age for all Australians to age 67 (an initiative of the federal government in its 2009 budget).

Tax incentives

Workers were also encouraged to remain in the workforce longer by the introduction of tax incentives such as the Mature Age Worker Tax Offset scheme. The scheme effectively enabled workers over the age of 55 earning less than $58,000 to reduce their tax, in some cases to zero.

The national policy agenda

The national policy agenda has therefore largely focused on promoting increased saving for retirement and extending retirement ages. Other potential areas for addressing the consequences of workforce ageing such as flexible employment arrangements, immigration, and removing barriers to workforce participation have been largely neglected (Burgess & Strachan 2005).

Summary

This overview of Japan and Australia highlights differences in the magnitude of the ageing workforce issue, but also identifies significantly different policy approaches to addressing the social and economic implications of an ageing workforce.

An ageing workforce—an issue of human rights or economics?

Most obvious is the extent to which the ageing workforce is considered a human rights issue or as an economic issue.

Australia has implemented anti-discrimination legislation that incorporates age discrimination. This legislation is, however, distilled by a consideration of business interests through various exclusions. Japan on the other hand, has a cultural background of respect for older people, yet this does not equate to older workers being protected through anti-discrimination legislation. Legislation in Japan has therefore tended to support both cultural and business practices that respect the older worker without codifying protective measures.

A focus on economic goals

The most remarkable feature has been the limited use of pro-active policies to foster the employment and retention of older workers. Most policy has been aimed at reducing incentives for early retirement, rather than providing positive initiatives such as monetary reward and training programs for both workers and employers. This suggests that the focus is on economic goals rather than a true valuing of the skills and abilities of older workers with ramifications for the way in which older workers are viewed and treated in the workforce. These current 'patchwork' and passive policy responses suggest that governments are not yet prepared to fully address the issue of ageing workforces nor do they actively discourage business practice that has, in the past, used early retirement as a preferred means for reducing workforces in an economic recession.

Industry issues and organisational responses: Australia

Just as there are national variances regarding population ageing, different industries also face greater or lesser challenges with regard to ageing workforces. This section provides a brief overview of the ageing workforce challenges faced by the public sector in Australia before proceeding to an examination of some organisational responses in the area of banking and finance.

The public sector

The OECD's report on the public sector (2007) notes that, for many countries, public service workforces are already older and/or ageing faster than the general workforce.

Public service workforces globally tend also to be less age diverse, with the largest concentrations of workers in the 50–54 and 55–59 age brackets, depending on the retirement age of the country concerned.

Early retirement

This concentration of workers in older age brackets is of serious concern for the sector in Australia where the retirement age for public servants is usually younger than for the workforce generally. The prevalence of earlier retirement is due mainly to

- better superannuation entitlements,
- early retirement incentives and/or
- cultural practice where the retirement age is 60 but where practice and financial incentives result in an average retirement age in the public sector of 57 (OECD 2007).

Increase in average age of public servants

The average age of the public service in Australia is increasing by one year every three years. The sector therefore faces significant challenges in managing its ageing workforce. It must replace its retirement-depleted workforce with younger workers or adopt methods to deliver public services with fewer public servants. Throughout the late twentieth century these methods included:

- restructuring;
- contracting out;
- partnerships;
- internet delivery; and
- privatisation.

Such managerial practices have arguably escalated the problem of an ageing workforce.

Consequences of an ageing public service workforce

All public service departments do not face the same demographic challenges in terms of ageing. However, many departments are already very lean with high levels of staff nearing 'normal' retirement age. These characteristics exacerbate the impact of tacit and organisational knowledge loss as key staff members retire. Associated with the ageing of the public sector workforce are issues of funding retirements where many public superannuation funds are not fully funded to meet future retirement obligations.

Policy directions

The West Australian government has circulated discussion papers on the consequences for the public service, business and society in general of an ageing workforce (Ministry of the Premier and Cabinet 1999). These reports put forward a number of proposals including the following:

- Given that many departments are already operating on depleted staff numbers, departments need to identify staff nearing retirement age, implement strategies to retain those with key organisational knowledge;
- Provide flexible transition retirement options;
- Implement succession management plans for the transferral of tacit organisational knowledge;
- Proactively address age discrimination and stereotyping in the workforce;
- More extensive training, particularly competence based, be offered to older workers to assist retention and productivity;

- Assist workers with balancing elder care responsibilities and work through the provision of information services, education and training for managers to understand the issues associated with elder care, provision of flexible work arrangements, government provision of elder care centres and greater provision of family leave.

Recognising organisational commitment to engaging an older workforce

In Australia there has been a lack of pro-active policies aimed at either improving the employability of mature workers and or encouraging employers through financial schemes to employ them (Encel 2008). Any encouragement for employers has principally occurred through the Mature Age Employer Champion Award, now the Employment and Inclusion of Mature Age Workers Award. These awards recognise employers with a proven record of implementing age-positive human resource policies. Industry has also championed awards recognising organisational commitment to engaging an older workforce. For example, HR Leadership awards organised by HR Leader Magazine have recognised a category of 'Best Mature Age Workforce Implementation'.

Managing diversity—the business case argument

Until the turn of the twenty-first century, age had not been an obvious item on the diversity agenda. Since then, the ageing workforce has emerged as an important arena for the political promotion of the ideologies of the approach. Such promotion has been most evident in the business case argument, which espouses the benefits of matching the age demography of an organisation's customer base with its labour force (Riach 2009).

The banking and finance industry

In Australia, the banking and finance industry has responded strongly to the business case argument for employing older workers. Westpac, for example, developed a campaign to hire 900 mature-age workers over a three-year period. One of the principle reasons put forward was that a more mature workforce would better reflect and thus respond to Westpac's client base (Westpac Banking Corporation, n.d.).

Going one step further, Westpac's campaign also recognised the multi-faceted nature of an age-diverse workforce. Aspects recognised included stereotypical descriptions of younger and older workers and the particular issues facing older women often due to interrupted careers. The need to address such stereotypes has seen the emergence of the term 'age management' which refers to the explicit age profile of a workforce as well as the overall management of an ageing workforce (Walker 1999).

Business case arguments are also reflected in the responses of other banks in Australia. The Commonwealth Bank, for example, has commenced in-depth research into workforce trends. One of the findings was that employees were responsive to delaying retirement provided flexible work arrangements were available. As a result, the bank has been proactive in the provision of part-time work, career breaks, job-share arrangements and flexible start and finish times (DEEWR, n.d.).

A summary of better practice projects in relation to the various HR aspects of managing an ageing workforce within the Australian Banking Industry are outlined in Table 11.4.

Table 11.4 Better practice projects for an ageing workforce

Project summary	Challenges	Opportunities	Evaluation
Recruitment: Better practice example			
Company: Westpac Banking Corporation (Australia) **Sector:** Banking and Finance **Size:** Approx. 27,000 **Project:** Better Balance	**Ageing:** Workforce ageing **Attraction:** Seeking to attract available pool of labour (45+ group) **Customer:** Align staff and customer profiles	Explored approaches to increasing the recruitment of older workers to their call centres. Information sessions, pre-employment training and support were offered in partnership with Hudson, Westpac's volume recruiter.	Candidate expectations needed to be managed to ensure that there was a balance between 'preference' (interest in the organisation) and 'performance' (capacity to do the job). Evaluation indicated that candidates would benefit from exposure to the work environment ('is this right for me?') before making a decision to progress to pre-employment training. Pre-employment training design needs to include 'non-technical' aspects such as job readiness or employment preparation.
Learning and development: Better practice example			
Company: Deutsche Bank **Sector:** Banking **Project:** Age Diversity	**Ageing:** Workforce ageing **Skills shortages:** In core business areas **Strategic:** Transfer of critical skills and knowledge	Four working models were identified: 1. Intergenerational project teams 2. Knowledge capture programs – highly skilled, older employees spend 2-4 hours per week with an external service provider. 3. Partnering of older, experienced employees with less experienced (usually younger) colleagues.	A systematic and sustained commitment to knowledge transfer ensures that service levels are maintained and the impact when older, experienced employees leave is minimised. Job satisfaction and teamwork is positively impacted by well planned and implemented knowledge transfer programs. Transfer of implicit knowledge requires a sustained commitment over time.

Learning and development: Better practice example			
		4. 'Know-how tandems' in customer contact & acquisition areas to optimise the process of customer handover.	
Reward and recognition: Better practice example			
Company: St George Bank **Sector:** Banking and Finance **Size:** Approx. 8,500 **Project:** Grandparents leave	**Skill shortages:** Need to attract people with relevant skills **Retention:** Staff losses through retirement **Attraction:** Majority of future labour market growth is in the over 45 groups **Customer needs:** A workforce profile that reflects their customer base	Launched in June, 2007, this initiative provides for 12 months' leave without pay, which can be taken in one block or periodically before the child's 2nd birthday. Grandparenting leave is not an entitlement and must be balanced against operational requirements. It has been introduced in a suite of new leave options, including paid volunteer leave, flexible work for over 50s and career breaks (e.g. four years on, one year off with pay spread over five years).	St George sees grandparenting leave as part of a bigger attraction and retention effort, which helps differentiate the bank in a highly skilled, competitive sector. There are no costs apart from those associated with backfilling roles during leave periods. However, this is also seen as an investment as people stay longer and become very strong advocates for the organisation. The initiative is too new to be evaluated, but early indicators will include patterns of management approval, being monitored to ensure that leave is being granted or denied on sound business grounds

Source: Adapted from Victorian State Services Authority, 2008.

The relative 'newness' of age diversity as an issue requiring organisational interventions means that academic analysis of outcomes from a management, human resource or employee perspective are limited. The main concerns of initiatives to address ageing workforces are the extent to which they meet the needs of older workers without further alienating them within the workforce. An additional issue is the extent to which initiatives genuinely value the contribution of older workers and whether older workers perceive their contributions to be valued.

Ageing, public policy, and strategic HRM

For OECD governments, the consequences of an ageing population have arguably been considered more in economic terms than any other diversity issue.

The case for social justice

In many countries the social justice case has received significantly less consideration than that addressing discrimination against persons on the basis of gender, race, and religion. Across the OECD, legislation concerning age discrimination has been unevenly introduced and to a far more limited extent. Where introduced, age discrimination legislation contains loopholes providing employers with the opportunity to use business case arguments to protect them from charges of discrimination on the basis of age.

Age discrimination legislation

There are clear links between nationally driven and legislated policy directed at ageing populations and ageing workforces and the impact at social, economic and workplace levels. In Japan, for example, where there are no separate age discrimination laws and no penalties for failure to meet what limited legislation exists, employers remain free to specify age in job advertisements. Such practices have on-flow effects on the employment opportunities and work experiences of older workers.

In countries with anti-discrimination legislation in place, the intent of such legislation may backfire, creating a working environment for older workers that is not only unsupportive but which has a detrimental effect on their well being. Furthermore, policy is often formulated with only limited consideration or understanding for the realities of 'how age operates in organisations: the normative and prescriptive rhetoric and policies have developed faster than evidence-based knowledge' (Brooke & Taylor 2005, p. 427).

Economic focus of policy initiatives

The focus of most policy initiatives across the OECD has been to address the economic impact of increasing old-age dependency ratios where fewer tax-paying workers support a growing dependent and inactive older population.

Governments have primarily sought ways to discourage older workers from retirement rather than positive responses (such as financial incentives to workers and employers) to encourage employment. There have been only limited direct financial incentives (such as tax concessions) to actively encourage older persons to stay in the workforce longer and, across the OECD, very little policy activity to motivate employers financially to employ older workers.

Issues faced by older workers

In addition, pro-active policies to improve the employability and work experiences of older workers through training, job restructure and workplace reform have been very limited. Policy has therefore not comprehensively addressed the issues faced by older workers and, as a consequence, older workers continue to be differentiated from their middle-aged and younger counterparts in that:

- they are more experienced, but on average less educated and receive less training;
- they appear to be more productive than younger workers, but slightly less so than middle-aged workers;
- they are less likely to become unemployed than other age groups, but once unemployed take longer to find a new job;
- in any given year, they tend to change jobs less often and are less willing or able to move jobs to another location; and
- they tend to have a greater incidence of disability and ill health, and suffer some general physical and cognitive declines.

Productivity Commission (2005, p. 48)

These characteristics of older workers, however, are not fixed or consistent. Over time, the generalised characteristics of older workers may well change. Currently there are many who do not fit this profile.

Changes in the characteristics of older workers

Changes to the characteristics of older workers over time are especially significant. By mid-century, current younger and middle-aged workers with increased educational attainment will be older workers. As these workers move into older age brackets it may well be the case that more will choose to continue in the workforce longer and that projections based on current statistics may underestimate future productivity (Productivity Commission 2005).

These potential changes in the profile of older workers highlight the weaknesses associated with stereotyping older workers. Such stereotypes may lead to an alienation and underutilisation of valuable human resources within organisations. Such underutilisation and stereotyping has already been evidenced in findings from studies into the employment of older workers (Brooke & Taylor 2005).

Interface between workforce ageing, public policy and SHRM

There are two questions fundamental to the understanding of the interface between workforce ageing, public policy and Strategic Human Resource Management (SHRM). These are:

- government motivations to encourage the employment of older workers; and
- employer motivations to employ older workers.

Government motivations

From a policy perspective, if a government's motivation is to build a larger tax base, reduce the expenditure on aged pensions, or present a social justice case, the message sent to employers is 'do the right thing for the economy and society'.

There is, however, a clear disjuncture between this policy motive and the aims of SHRM. SHRM is concerned with the alignment of business and human resource management strategies and involves a consideration of how to adapt human resources to meet organisational long-term goals (Boxall & Purcell 2000). SHRM is not primarily concerned with national economic or social considerations and, where the policy response is aimed at such goals, it may lead organisations to devalue the skills and contributions of older workers with consequences for the self-esteem of those workers.

Employer motivations

If, on the other hand, the motivation for the employment of older workers is to address shortages in labour, knowledge, and skills, then the employment of older workers becomes a response to organisational need more in line with SHRM objectives. Under this scenario there may be a greater valuing of older workers.

This latter situation is, however, tenuous. Past experience has demonstrated that where labour market conditions loosen and there is a ready availability of labour, it is often older workers who are 'retired off'. For employers, this is often stimulated by SHRM considerations. Not only do older workers generally cost more but, as Lyon, Hallier and Glover (1998) cogently argue, there is a fundamental mismatch between the older workforce and general HR principles:

> 'On the one hand, its [HR's] investment principle is, in part, predicated on employers' commitment to long, single-employer service. On the other, the pursuit of organisational adaptability largely excludes older employees from any real core membership' (Lyon et al. 1998, p. 58).

Reasons for the non-employment of older workers

As a result, the principal reasons given for the non-employment of older workers are their lack of flexibility—both geographic and role, and their non-adaptability to change.

A key HR concern is that the employment of older workers may pre-date the implementation of new organisational practices. Management may consider older workers to have values at odds with what their organisation is now trying to achieve (Taylor 2008).

Furthermore, Lyon *et al.* (1998) propose that HRM is inherently ageist in its preference for younger workers who are more readily adaptable to existing organisational cultures. The perceived difficulty in aligning older workers with the strategic objectives and culture of the organisation implies that the principles of SHRM are at odds with the employment of older workers. The result is the observable reticence of many organisations to actively seek to employ older workers.

Re-employment of older workers

A consequence of this reticence is that, once out of work, older workers face much greater difficulties finding a job.

While it is estimated that the 2008/09 international financial crisis will affect youth unemployment more than that of older workers, statistics suggest that it will be more difficult for older workers to re-enter the workforce than their youthful counterparts.

In 2004, the average duration of unemployment for persons aged 55 and over in Australia was 130 weeks—twice the long-term unemployment rate for the population as a whole. This trend occurred despite relatively comprehensive anti-discrimination legislation. Policy is therefore not actively or effectively responding to the stereotyping and labour segmentation of older workers within the workplace. At best, organisational responses have been ad hoc; at worst, they have been actively hostile to the attraction, employment, retention and training of older workers.

Organisational case study ANZ

Valuing mature workers: Our approach

At ANZ we aim to create a culture where mature-aged workers and their experience are valued. We want to retain skills and experience, increase our talent pool, and build a workforce that reflects our customers and the community.

We were the first Australian company to introduce a Career Extension Policy guaranteeing part-time work for employees aged 55 and over, and in 2006, we were recognised as a mature-age champion by the federal government.

Career extension program

We recognise that the traditional approach to retirement—stopping full-time work to become a full-time retiree—may not be the right solution for everyone. Drawing on flexibility options available to all staff, we have identified three options to assist mature-age lifestyle decisions:

- **rejuvenate** your career with flexible leave options such as lifestyle leave, flexible long service leave and career breaks;
- **rebalance** your work to suit your life with options such as job sharing, working offsite, and working part-time or on a cyclical or seasonal basis; and
- **reshape** your career, taking a gradual approach to retirement and changing pace through exploring different roles.

Diversity progress in 2008

We continue to track globally the number of employees aged 55 years or over.

ANZ employees over 55 years of age:

	Australia	New Zealand	Asia	Pacific	India	EMEA
Employees over 55 years of age	6.61%	10.66%	1.30%	2.30%	0.25%	11.40%
Employees 55+ who are full time	57.43%	69.80%	1.30%	2.10%	100.00%	10.80%
Employees 55+ who are part time	40.76%	29.73%	0.00%	0.30%	0.00%	0.30%

	Australia	New Zealand	Asia	Pacific	India	EMEA
Employees 55+ who are temporary	1.81%	0.47%	0.00%	0.00%	0.00%	0.30%
Annual turnover of 55+	15.92%	12.69%	21.05%	10.64%	51.06%	9.20%

Source: Extract from - ANZ Banking Group – Diversity Strategy <http://www.anz.com/about%2Dus/corporate%2Dresponsibility/employees/diversity%2Dculture/diversity/age/>.

Case study questions

1. What evidence is there that ANZ values the contribution of older workers?
2. What strategies has ANZ introduced both to attract and retain older workers?
3. Do you think other organisations could adopt similar strategies to those introduced by ANZ? If yes, why? If no, why not?

References

ANZ Banking Group 2009, *Diversity Strategy 2009*, accessed November 20, <http://www.anz.com/about%2Dus/corporate%2Dresponsibility/employees/diversity%2Dculture/diversity/age/>.

Boxall, P & Purcell, J 2000, 'Strategic Human Resource Management: Where have we come from and where should we be going?', *International Journal of Human Resource Management*, 2, 183-203.

Brooke, L & Taylor, P 2005, 'Older Workers and Employment: Managing Age Relations', *Ageing and Society*, 25:415-429.

DEEWR n.d., Case Studies and Success Stories - Flexible Work Practices, accessed October 23, 2009, <http://www.deewr.gov.au/Employment/Programs/Jobwise/Employers/Pages/case03.aspx#02>.

Encel, S 2008, 'Looking Forward to Working Longer in Australia', in *Ageing Labour Forces: Promises and Prospects*, ed., Philip Taylor, Edward Elgar, Northampton, Ma.

International Labour Organization 2003, *Promoting Decent Work for an Ageing Population: Actors, Partners and Corporate Social Responsibility*, Background Paper Delivered by the ILO to the G8 High Level Meeting on Employment, Paris, 12-13 May.

Lyons, P Hallier, J & Glover, I 1998, 'Divestment or Investment: the Contradictions of HRM in Relation to Older Employees', *Human Resource Management Journal*, 8(1): 56-66.

OECD 2002, Work Force Ageing: Consequences and Policy Responses, Working Paper AWP 4.1, OECD, Paris.

OECD 2006, Live Longer, Work Longer, OECD, Paris.

OECD 2007, Ageing and the Public Service: Human Resource Challenges, OECD.

Oka, M 2008, 'Japan: Towards Employment Extension for Older Workers' in Ageing Labour Force: Promises and Prospects, ed. Philip Taylor, Edward Elgar, Northampton, Ma.

Ministry of the Premier and Cabinet Western Australia 1999, 'The Ageing Workforce: Trends and Issues in the Western Australia Public Sector', Ageing Workforce Discussion Paper Series, Perth, W.A.

Productivity Commission 2005, 'Economic Implications of an Ageing Australia', Productivity Commission Research Report, Productivity Commission, Canberra, ACT.

Riach, K 2009, 'Managing 'difference': Understanding Age Diversity in Practice', *Human Resource Management Journal*, 19(3): 313-335.

Sakuraba, R 2009, 'The Amendment of the Employment Measure Act: Japanese Anti-age Discrimination Law', *Japan Labor Review,* 6(2): 56-75

Sergeant, M 2007, *Age Discrimination in Employment*, Gower Publishing, UK.

Statistics New Zealand 2004, 'National Population Projections 2004 (base) to 2051'.

Taylor, P 2008, 'Conclusions. The Prospects for Ageing Labour Forces' in *Ageing Labour Forces: Promises and Prospects*, ed., Philip Taylor, Edward Elgar, Northampton, Ma.

Victorian State Services Authority 2008, 'Attracting and Retaining an Ageing Workforce: A Guide for Victorian Public Sector Managers', Victorian State Services Authority, Melbourne.

Walker, A 1999, 'Managing an Ageing Workforce: A Guide to Good Practice', European Foundation for the Improvement of Living and Working Conditions, Office for Official Publications of the European Communities, Luxembourg.

Westpac Banking Corporation n.d., 'Submission by Westpac Banking Corporation to the Parliamentary Standing Committee on Employment and Workplace Relations: Inquiry into Employment – Increasing Participation in Paid Work, accessed October 23 2009, <http://www.aph.gov.au/house/committee/ewrwp/paidwork/subs/sub97.pdf>.

Chapter 12

MANAGING DIVERSITY, SOCIAL INCLUSION AND CHANGE IN THE WORKPLACE

Christina Kirsch & Charmine E J Härtel

OBJECTIVES

This chapter discusses the impact of workforce diversity on HRM practice. By the completion of the chapter you should be able to:

1. identify the key issues associated with managing diversity and achieving social inclusion in the workplace;
2. outline the main dimensions regarding workforce diversity in Australia;
3. provide examples of the challenges for strategic HRM posed by workforce diversity;
4. discuss some of the organisational responses to workforce diversity and the need for effective workforce diversity programs and work design for diverse workforces; and
5. outline differences in the management of change in diverse cultures.

DEFINITIONS

Diversity: Ways in which people differ (such as age, race, gender, ethnicity, mental and physical abilities and sexual orientation) and acquired characteristics (such as education, income, religion, work experience, language skills, geographic location, and family status).

Diversity management: A process intended to create and maintain a positive work environment where the similarities and differences of individuals are valued, so that all can reach their potential and maximize their contributions to an organisation's strategic goals and objectives.

Discrimination: Discrimination is often used to mean illegal discriminatory acts. Illegal discrimination is the unfavourable treatment of a person, or a group of people, by category, class, or group rather than objective treatment on the basis of merit. Under EEO law, it is illegal to discriminate on the basis of race, colour, national or ethnic origin, sex, pregnancy or marital status, age, disability, religion, sexual preference, trade union activity or some other characteristic specified under anti-discrimination or human rights legislation.

Workplace discrimination can occur in: recruitment and selection; terms, conditions and benefits of employment; training opportunities; promotion and career opportunities.

Equal Employment Opportunity (EEO): The goal of laws that make some types of discrimination in employment illegal. Equal employment opportunity will become a reality when each citizen has an equal chance to enjoy the benefits of employment. EEO is not a guarantee of employment for anyone. Under EEO law, only job-related factors can be used to determine whether an individual is qualified for a particular job.

Equal Employment Opportunity Laws: The laws that prohibit discrimination on the basis of race, colour, religion, sex, national origin, age, or handicap in any terms, conditions, or privileges of employment. In Australia, the following laws operate at a federal level and are administered by the Australian Human Rights Commission: *Age Discrimination Act* 2004; *Australian Human Rights Commission Act* 1986; *Disability Discrimination Act* 1992; *Racial Discrimination Act* 1975; *Sex Discrimination Act* 1984.

Workforce diversity: Refers to ways in which people in a workforce are similar to and different from one another. In addition to the characteristics protected by law, other similarities and differences commonly cited include background, education, language skills, personality, sexual orientation and work role.

Introduction

'The need to preserve the diversity of cultures in a world which is threatened by monotony and uniformity has surely not escaped our international institutions. They must also be aware that it is not enough to nurture local traditions and to save the past for a short period longer. It is diversity itself which must be saved, not the outward and visible form in which each period has clothed that diversity, and which can never be preserved beyond the period which gave it birth ... We can see the diversity of human cultures behind us, around us, and before us. The only demand that we can justly make ... is that all the forms this diversity may take may be so many contributions to the fullness of all the others.' Claude Levi-Strauss (1952) Race and History

Growing diversity of workforces

With more of the population participating in employment, organisations operating internationally, and employees migrating around the globe, the diversity of workforces is growing (Ashkanasy, Härtel & Daus 2002; Asis 2005). Consequently, the differences in backgrounds, norms, belief systems, capabilities and skills that come with diversity are shaping the way in which organisations operate (Cox 2001).

Diversity can be a boon for the organisation if managed appropriately, but it can also come at a cost and be detrimental to organisational performance if managed badly (Härtel & Fujimoto 2000; Simsarian Webbera & Donahue 2001).

The meaning of diversity

In order to delve into the challenges and processes of managing a diverse workforce, first we need a better understanding of what we mean by 'diversity' and the characteristics of the workforce relevant to the management of human resources.

Some academics incorporate a large array of potential differences in their discourse on diversity—from leadership style and personality traits to demographics differences (Thomas 1996; Thomas & Ely 1996). Aspects that are included under the umbrella of diversity include:

- language;
- race;
- ethnicity;
- age;
- disability;
- gender;

- faith;
- sexual orientation;
- social and community responsibilities;
- family and family responsibilities;
- political views; and
- aboriginality.

Diversity also refers to differences in education, experience, socio-economic background, personality and marital status.

Focus on discrimination

Other authors argue in favour of a more parsimonious approach and focus on groups that have faced systematic discrimination and oppression at work—for example:

- women;
- indigenous populations;
- ethnic minorities;
- individuals with disabilities,
- older employees;
- overweight employees;
- gay, lesbian or bisexual employees (Hays-Thomas 2004; Linnehan & Konrad 1999).

They argue that diversity is mainly relevant in regards to those aspects that have been systematically discriminated against or that provide challenges in regards to the management of differences:

- gender;
- age;
- body weight;
- sexual orientation;
- race; and
- ethnicity.

Group identity v. individual differences

In this chapter, we follow Härtel and Fujimoto (2000) in adopting an integration of the definitions based on group identity and individual differences. We emphasise the importance of the diversity arising from historically disadvantaged and advantaged social groups, at the same time recognising the individual diversity which occurs within such groups. In other words, individuals' experiences are shaped partly by the social group they are identified with and partly by their unique personal characteristics.

Managing diversity

The effective management of diversity requires the establishment of an organisational culture that values and encourages contributions by people with different backgrounds, experiences and perspectives. Thus, human resource managers need to develop strategies that not only accommodate these differences, but harness the tremendous potential inherent in a diverse workforce.

Organisational culture

In order to successfully manage a diverse workforce, management needs to create an inclusive culture that:

- embraces people's individual differences;
- adjusts to differences in employees' needs; and
- provides opportunities for all staff to achieve their full potential.

This requires promoting open attitudes to diversity within individual employees, workgroups and the overall organisation (Härtel & Fujimoto 2009).

Social inclusion

Effective diversity management is all about social inclusion, but there is little agreement on the measures that are to be applied to ensure a workplace is inclusive.

The management of diversity has, in the past, primarily focused on the recruitment and retention of employees that belong to different social and cultural groups. This approach, however, neglects the fact that the whole of a person's lifespan is affected by the characteristics of their diversity and the responses of others to them.

Need for a holistic, lifespan perspective

Effective diversity management, therefore, requires a holistic, lifespan perspective on potential and incumbent employees. This means taking an enlarged view of what constitutes human resources management. It involves not only a broader range of HR activities in diversity management—e.g.

- workforce planning;
- work design;
- optimisation of the employment value proposition;
- recruitment;
- selection;
- training; and
- exit management;

but novel ways of enacting such activities to meet the needs of a diverse population (see Figure 12.1).

Figure 12.1 Diversity within the context of Strategic HR Management

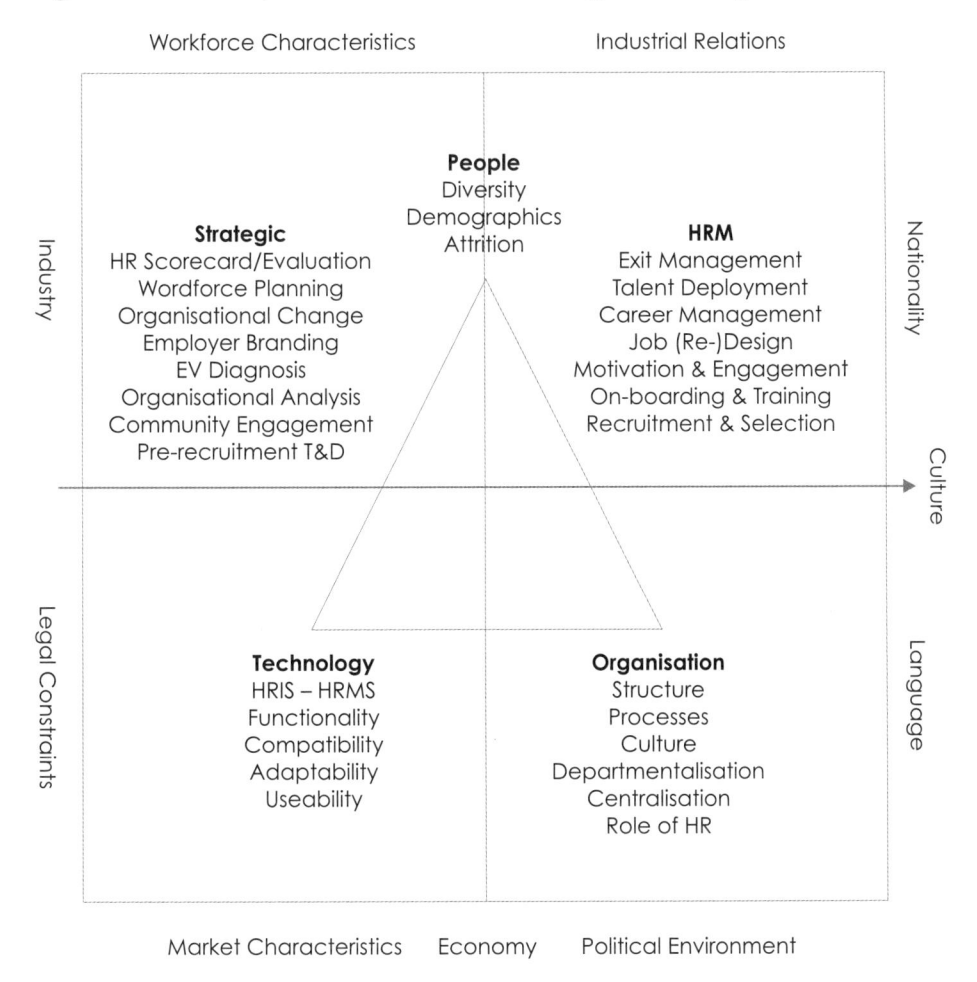

```
                Workforce Characteristics        Industrial Relations

                                    People
                                    Diversity
                                    Demographics
                    Strategic       Attrition       HRM
                    HR Scorecard/Evaluation         Exit Management
                    Wordforce Planning              Talent Deployment
          Industry  Organisational Change           Career Management          Nationality
                    Employer Branding               Job (Re-)Design
                    EV Diagnosis                    Motivation & Engagement
                    Organisational Analysis         On-boarding & Training
                    Community Engagement            Recruitment & Selection
                    Pre-recruitment T&D
                                                                                Culture

          Legal
          Constraints
                    Technology                      Organisation               Language
                    HRIS – HRMS                     Structure
                    Functionality                   Processes
                    Compatibility                   Culture
                    Adaptability                    Departmentalisation
                    Useability                      Centralisation
                                                    Role of HR

                Market Characteristics    Economy    Political Environment
```

Benefits of diversity in the workforce

Diversity is potentially beneficial to both the organisation and its employees.

Organisation benefits

A diverse workforce with a broad spectrum of experiences and perspectives can:

- contribute to an organisation's overall sustainability;
- create economic benefits from the variation in experiences and skills (Kochan *et al.* 2002);

- understand the firm's clients better, and be able to provide better service (Konrad, Prasad & Pringle 2006).

Empirical studies show that successfully managed heterogeneous teams consistently out-perform homogeneous teams on a variety of tasks (Horwitz 2005). They generate a broader range of ideas and innovation and achieve a better understanding of the needs of an organisation's various stakeholders.

The business case for diversity in an era of globalisation and increasing competition is that greater diversity enhances the potential for greater innovation and adaptability (Linehan & Konrad 1999).

Employee benefits

The successful management of employee diversity allows organisations to provide productive and fulfilling workplaces that attract and retain employees. Managing diversity goes beyond the elimination of discrimination and the provision of equal opportunity. It entails the creation of a culture that accepts and accommodates inter-individual differences that facilitate:

- learning;
- growth;
- collaboration;
- inclusion; and
- involvement (Härtel & Fujimoto 2009).

A climate of openness that embraces diversity leads to:

- social inclusion;
- increased employee engagement and commitment;
- savings in recruitment and training costs; and
- the maintenance of corporate knowledge and expertise (Härtel & Fujimoto 2009).

Country perspective on diversity – diversity in Australia

A key source of Australia's cultural diversity is migration. The 2008 Census released by the Australian Bureau of Statistics (ABS 2006) estimated the resident population of Australia at 21.4 million people with one quarter (5.5 million people) being born overseas.

Composition of Australia's overseas-born population

The makeup of Australia's overseas-born population has been greatly affected by successive waves of migration to Australia since the Second World War.

Persons born in the United Kingdom continued to be the largest group of overseas-born residents, accounting for 5.4% of Australia's total population, those born in New Zealand accounted for 2.3%, followed by persons born in China (1.5%), India (1.1%) and Italy (1.0%).

The proportion of immigrants born in North-West Europe has been in decline in recent years, falling from 8% in 1998 to 7.2% in 2008. The share of Southern and Eastern Europe migrants is also in decline, falling from 4.7% in 1998 to 3.9% in 2008. Conversely, the proportion of migrants from North-East Asia and Southern and Central Asia to Australia is greater than ever (Birrell & Betts 2001).

Over the past decade migrants from all other global regions increased within Australia's population, indicating that Australia is becoming increasingly diverse (Australian Bureau of Statistics 2008a). That said, Aboriginal Australians and Torres Strait Islanders are amongst some of the most disadvantaged people in Australia's labour market (Richardson, Roberston & Ilsley 2001) and are viewed as 'culturally diverse' in light of Australia's mainstream Anglo-Saxon culture.

Language diversity

The diversity of cultures in the Asia Pacific region also comes with growing diversity in languages.

Collectively, Australians speak over 200 languages. In 2006, Italian (with 316,895 speakers) was the most popular language spoken at home other than English, followed by Greek (252,226), Cantonese (244,553), Arabic (243,662) and Mandarin (220,600) (Australian Bureau of Statistics 2008a). There were 55,698 people who reported speaking an Australian Indigenous language at home, an increase of 9.4 per cent over the 2001 Census (Australian Human Rights Commission 2008).

Women in the workforce

In August 2007, women represented 45% of all employed people in Australia, with more than 1.06 million more men employed in Australia than women. Unemployment among women (4.8%) was higher than the national unemployment rate of 4.4% and the unemployment rate for men (4%). Of the 10,469,900 people employed in Australia, women are far more likely to be working part-time than men, with almost 45% of women working part-time compared with just 15% of men. In 2007, 25% of employed women, compared with 16% of employed men, did not receive paid leave entitlements (Australian Bureau of Statistics 2008b).

An aging population

Demographic changes due to increasing life expectancy and declining birth rates after the introduction of the birth control pill have resulted in an aging population in Australia. Recently, the Australian government announced an increase in retirement age from 65 to 67 and further increases of the retirement age to 70 are being discussed (Abbott 2009) to address expected skill shortages. Hence, overall the workforce participation of mature age workers is increasing and will continue to do so. *(For more information on the ageing workforce see chapter 11 in this book)*.

Challenges for managing diversity

There are many challenges to managing a diverse workforce. Managing diversity is more than simply acknowledging differences in people. It involves:

- learning to value differences;
- overcoming personal biases and discriminatory practices; and
- creating a culture of mutual learning and growth (Härtel & Fujimoto 2009).

Due to increased communication requirements and potential for conflict and misunderstanding the benefits of workforce diversity will come at a cost unless it is managed successfully, (Baer, Niessen & Ruenzi 2009). Diversity needs to be managed appropriately in order to avoid increased personnel turnover and lower work productivity.

In this chapter, we focus on three key challenges in the management of workforce diversity:

- discrimination against women in terms of pay equity and equal career opportunity;
- the necessity to reconsider work design to accommodate the needs of mature age workers; and
- working conditions to suit diverse workforces and cultural diversity (Kramar 1998; Simsarian Webbera, Donahue 2001).

Women in the workforce — Still the short straw?

Diversity related guidance in Australian companies has tended to focus strongly on equal opportunity for women in the workforce. This is mainly due to a history of feminist movement and the resulting changes to legislation focusing on eliminating the gap between female and male workers. Despite increased workforce participation, however, women still often draw the 'shorter straw' with less pay for equal work and fewer career opportunities (Strachan, Burgess & Sullivan 2004).

Hourly earnings

Research commissioned by the Australian Fair Pay Commission, based on data from the 2006 ABS Employee Earnings and Hours Survey, found that, on average, women earn only 90% of the hourly earnings of men (Austen, Jefferson, Preston & Seymour 2008; Healy, Kidd & Richardson 2008, p. 242.).

Salaries of top earners

A recent AMP Financial Services report (AMP.NATSEM 2009) revealed that Australian men have the potential to earn about $1 million more over their lifetime than women. Moreover, a study conducted by the Equal Opportunity for Women in the Workplace Agency that compared the salaries of top earners in ASX 200 companies found that female chief operating officers and chief financial officers are receiving only about 50 per cent of the median wage of their equivalent male colleagues (EOWA 2008).

The *Workplace Relations Act* 1996

Under the *Workplace Relations Act* 1996 the Australian Industrial Relations Commission (AIRC) has the power to ensure that men and women receive equal remuneration for work of equal value. Female employees who suffer discrimination can apply to the federal Human Rights and Equal Opportunity Commission and if the commission decides that discrimination has occurred, it can make orders to ensure that equal rates of remuneration for work of equal value will apply (Australian Workplace 2009).

Accommodating the needs of mature workers

One of the challenges of the industrialised world is an aging workforce. Due to demographic changes the median age of our population — and henceforth the labour market – is increasing and companies need to adjust to the aging workforce.

Needs and preferences of mature-age workers

Mature-age workers are a great resource in times of economic growth. They are a highly educated, experienced pool of potential employees. Mature-age workers, however, have specific needs and preferences that need to be taken into account. Research commissioned by the Diversity Council Australia (2007) showed that the average hours mature-age people would prefer to work is 35 hours, but the actual hours worked was 40 hours. Having a job with flexibility, including hours of work, was important for 97% of those not currently employed. Employed mature-age workers indicated their top two ideal employment practices approaching retirement involve:

- flexibility in start and finish times; and
- phased retirement.

Mature-age people not currently working indicated their top employment practices would involve:

- work from home;
- limited travel requirements; and
- flexible working hours.

Around 80% of mature-age people not currently employed said working for an organisation that was supportive of their learning and development needs and careers was important or very important in influencing their decision to remain in the workplace. Some 97% of mature-age people indicated working for an organisation that was inclusive and supportive of older workers was important in influencing their decision to remain in the workplace (Diversity Council Australia 2007).

Challenges in managing a culturally diverse workforce

Despite Australia's growing economic dependence on skilled immigrants, research indicates that employment opportunities for refugees and migrants from non-English speaking backgrounds are not on parity with the that native-born Australians and English-speaking migrants (Colic-Peisker & Tilbury 2006; Richardson, Roberston & Ilsley 2001).

Collectivist cultures v. individualist cultures

A study of 14 multinationals in Australia (Fujimoto, Härtel & Panipucci 2005) indicated that tensions exist between employees from collectivist cultures (e.g. Eastern cultures) and individualist cultures (e.g. Australia). These findings underscore that close attention to cultural of diversity is warranted in the Australian context.

Social exclusion

Cultural diversity brings with it different communication styles, interaction patterns and belief systems. Consequently it is often considered to be the most challenging type of diversity for organisations to manage (Foldy 2004).

Research indicates that individuals can face social exclusion on the basis of one or more of their diverse characteristics (Trau & Härtel 2004). To achieve social inclusion and reap the potential of culturally diverse workgroups, it is essential that group members possess the attitudes and skills to understand and integrate each other's ideas and contributions (Härtel & Fujimoto 2000; Maznevski 1994; Shaw & Barrett-Power 1998). When such intercultural competencies are lacking, discrimination, power imbalances and exclusion are likely to result (Kelsey 2000).

Putting it all together—
Challenges of a multi-faceted diverse workplace

Increasing globalisation, labour mobility and demographic changes combine to make a multi-faceted diverse workforce. The challenges for human resource managers are further exacerbated by a continuing low level of unemployment, despite the recession following the global financial crisis (GFC) in 2008/2009.

The underlying dynamics of the labour market imply that organisations need to brace themselves for the next 'war on talent' and secure talent from previously untapped sources. Indigenous Australians, women, mature-aged workers and migrants are important constituents of the Australian labour force, but current work practices impede the full utilisation of this valuable resource.

Organisational responses are needed to ensure that:

- organisational structures and processes allow for a work design that suits a diverse workforce; and
- workplace diversity programs eliminate discrimination or disadvantage to anyone based on personal characteristics.

Moreover, for organisations operating across borders, there is a need to recognise and accommodate cross-cultural differences in responses to change.

In the sections that follow, we first discuss the principles for managing workforce diversity within an organisation and then present findings of a large scale study having implications for the management of diversity across national borders.

Organisational responses to the management of diversity

Recruitment and selection

Traditionally, human resource managers have focused on EEO issues in the recruitment and selection of employees (Ashkanasy, Härtel & Daus 2002). This compliance perspective places a premium on:

- thorough job analysis; and
- determination of potential employees' required skills, aptitudes and knowledge

in order to fulfil selection criteria and eliminate the potential for bias.

Diversity in teams

The composition of teams within the organisation has also been an important aspect in the selection of employees. Diversity in teams has numerous potential benefits including broader perspective-taking and idea generation (Härtel & Fujimoto 2000).

Achieving diversity in teams can be problematic, however, if the selection process encourages the team to pick new members on the basis of perceived 'fit'. If team members have not been prepared attitudinally to value and embrace diversity, they are likely to reject what is perceived as 'different' and select individuals they perceive as similar to themselves.

Similarly, as the diversity in a team grows, if unmanaged or managed ineffectively, it can often make for destructive conflict (Härtel & Fujimoto 2000). Careful attention to fostering diversity and open attitudes in individual employees, workgroups and the organisation is essential to ensuring that an organisation is hiring and nurturing 'true' diversity rather than just creating the appearance of diversity (Härtel & Fujimoto 2009).

Work design and working conditions

Although the importance of fair recruitment and selection procedures in managing a diverse workforce cannot be underestimated, work design and working conditions are the main determinants of inclusiveness and fairness. One of the main issues is the need to adjust work design to a diverse workforce.

No 'one best way'

The increased variance in needs and expectations of a diverse workforce requires relinquishing the idea of 'one best way' to design work. It requires flexible and dynamic work structures that can adjust to the needs and requirements of the workforce (Ulrich 1983).

Empirical studies shown that the assumption that there is one-best way for the accomplishment of a task has been a fundamental error in traditional work design with far-reaching consequences (Zink 1978). Inter-individual differences need to be taken into account in the planning and design of work processes and technologies in order to ensure that work design allows for different, flexible and adaptable approaches to the accomplishment of tasks.

Principles of work design

The focus required for today's diverse workforce is aptly captured by Ulrich's (1978; 1983) principles of work design—namely:

- flexible work design; and
- differential work design.

Flexible work design

The first principle, referred to as the principle of flexible work design, takes inter-individual differences into account in the design of jobs, technologies, work structures and processes. Here the notion of flexibility is referred to as accommodating both a diverse workforce and dealing with variances in the internal and external environment.

Differential work design

The second principle, referred to as the principle of differential work design, advocates the need to offer employees a choice of work structure and work design options.

In doing so, organisations are able to draw on the potential benefits of a diverse workforce. It allows an optimisation between work design and individual characteristics, facilitating the development and growth of the individual in the accomplishment of tasks.

Differential work design offers the option to work either in a team or individually. It accommodates inter-individual differences. A highly extroverted employee or someone from a collectivist background, for example, will generally prefer teamwork more so than an introverted employee or someone from a highly individualistic culture.

Need for both flexible work design and differential work design

In order to accommodate intra-individual differences, and take into account the process of individual development, learning and growth, the principle of flexible work design (Ulrich 1978) needs to be complemented with the principle of differential work design (Ulrich 1983).

Individual needs, expectations and demands change over time. Work design, therefore, needs to adjust to changes in skills, aptitudes, knowledge, personal and family situation, and commitments outside of work. It needs to accommodate intra-individual differences.

Employees' needs with regard to working hours and flexibility, for example, will change with the birth of their first child. Unless the organisation is capable of adapting to these changes, and adjusts to intra-individual differences, it will lose those employees if their needs cannot be met.

Establishing workplace diversity programs

Workplace diversity programs are aimed at preventing discrimination and using diversity in the workplace to the best advantage of the organisation and its employees. Such programs provide a structured and efficient means to ensure that diversity within the organisation is well managed and that challenges are successfully dealt with. The process of developing a workplace diversity program involves:

- analysis;
- planning:
- implementation;
- monitoring; and
- evaluation (Härtel & Fujimoto 2009).

Each of these elements is discussed in turn.

Analysis

In order to develop a workplace diversity program the organisation needs to assess its current workforce characteristics—for example:

- the demographic profile of employees;

- the organisational culture;
- business requirements;
- performance objectives;
- previous workplace diversity;
- EEO performance, work design and human resources policies and practices such as recruitment and selection practices, anti-harassment strategies and performance management schemes.

This information provides a baseline for evaluation and a starting point for setting the program's objectives.

Planning

The planning of an effective workplace diversity program involves determining the intended outcomes and objectives and devising the steps and interventions required in order to get there.

It is important to clarify the intended outcomes of workplace diversity strategies and to link those to corporate goals. Potential objectives can range from increased awareness of and commitment to workplace diversity principles to the integration of workplace diversity principles in business and human resources practices and systems.

Based on the objectives, strategies and interventions are devised which address the identified issues and move the organisation forwards towards the intended outcomes. Employees and managers should be involved in the planning and implementation of the program. Demonstrated support and commitment from the senior leadership team and consistent modelling of workplace diversity principles by senior executives are essential to the success of a diversity program. Programs need to have measurable outcomes and clear accountability.

Implementation of workplace diversity programs

Challenges in implementing a workplace diversity program include the need to:

- sustain interest and energy;
- provide resources;
- allocate accountability;
- ensure employee involvement; and
- address potential resistance from managers or employees, especially those perceiving a threat to their social status or power.

For these reasons, careful and ongoing monitoring of the implementation of a diversity program is important in order to determine if and where a program might be going off track and to ensure that adequate actions and decisions are taken to achieve successful implementation over time.

Monitoring

Performance indicators can provide the basis for tracking the progress of the program implementation. Measurements can include:

- employment status;
- patterns of recruitment and retention;
- absenteeism; and
- complaints about bullying and harassment.

Assessment should include factors that impact on the implementation of the diversity program—for example:

- leadership skills;
- available resources; and
- the emotional energy of people within workplace teams.

Evaluation

The evaluation process will establish the effectiveness of workplace diversity strategies and help assess why particular outcomes occurred. Data gathered during and prior to program implementation can be compared with information gathered for evaluation. The results can then be used either to modify existing strategies or to develop new strategies.

Managing organisational change in diverse cultures

Cross-cultural transfer of approaches to organisational change

The globalisation of our industries has led to increasing numbers of organisations operating internationally in a variety of countries and cultures (Ashkanasy, Härtel & Daus 2002). One of the emerging issues in managing across cultures is the question of management concepts and approaches to the management of change and whether they are cross-culturally transferable (see chapter 8 in this book).

Diversity in single cultures

As previously discussed, cultural diversity brings with it different communication styles, interaction patterns and belief systems. Within a single cultural context, management attention is needed to foster social inclusion and equal opportunities. This requires awareness, openness and integration of the different cultural dimensions within an organisation's workforce.

Diversity between cultures

When we change our level of analysis from within a given culture to looking across cultural contexts, we see diversity at the country level, manifest as variations in the mix of cultural dimensions. Accordingly, a number of authors (Adler 1997; Chang 2002; Hall 1960; Hofstede 1980; Hofstede 1993; Kirsch 1997; Schneider & Barsoux 2003) have questioned the cross-cultural transferability of management practices such as:

- reward systems;
- performance management systems;
- teamwork and collaboration;
- organisational structure; or
- leadership style (Walumba, Lawler & Avolio 2007).

In other words, the diversity of national cultures means solutions to organisational problems in one country may not be effective in another country.

Impact of cultural dimensions on organisational change projects

Resistance to change

There is empirical evidence that cultures characterised by:

- high power distance;
- low individualism; and
- high avoidance of uncertainty

will display the strongest resistance to change (Harzing and Hofstede, 1996). These cultures include most Latin American countries, Portugal, Korea, Japan, France, Spain, Greece, Turkey and Arab countries.

Countries low on power distance, high on individualism, and low on uncertainty avoidance will tend to have lower levels of resistance to change. These countries include the Anglo and Nordic countries, the Netherlands, Singapore, Hong Kong and South Africa.

PDI, UAI and IDV

Harzing and Hofstede suggest that both power distance (PDI) and uncertainty avoidance (UAI) increase the resistance to change, while individualism (IDV) reduces it. They presume that uncertainty avoidance has the strongest influence (p. 315) and calculate a resistance to change index giving two points to a large UAI and one each to a large PDI and a small IDV.

CTRE cross-cultural comparison of change projects

In 2009, ChangeTracking Research (CTRE) conducted a cross-cultural comparison of change projects in order to:

- identify the ways in which change is managed in various countries; and

- determine how these relate to cultural dimensions.

The comparison was based on a database of over 111,000 responses to an employee survey (begun by CTRE in 1998) across a large variety of cultures and industries (Kirsch & Parry 2009). The survey investigated the relationship between Hofstede's (1993) cultural dimensions and the characteristics of change projects (Parry 2008).

Figure 12.2 The Impact of cultural dimensions on characteristics of change projects

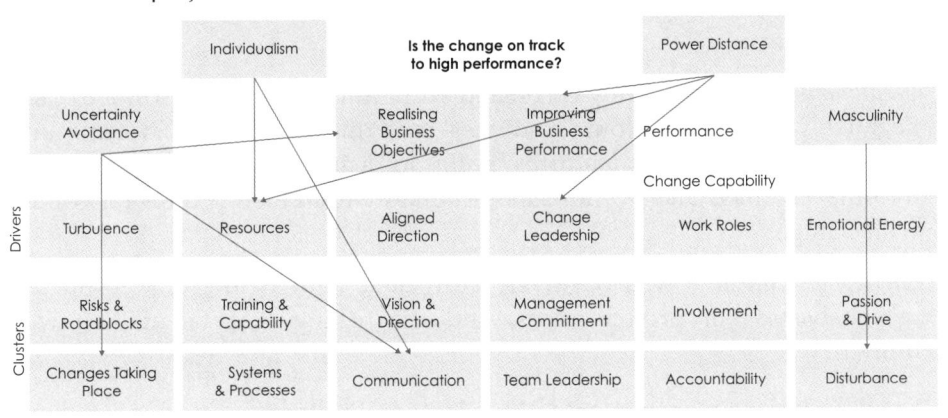

Source: Kirsch & Parry 2009.

Differences between countries

The survey findings indicated that the relationship with the direct supervisor and the emotions experienced during organisational change showed little difference between cultures.

Significant differences were found to exist between countries with respect to the:

- amount and pace of change;
- availability of resources;
- level of employee involvement; and
- responsiveness of the teams.

Large differences between countries and the database norm were found for 'Improvements in customer service', 'Stage of change', and 'Understanding of the company vision'.

Correlation between cultural dimensions and change management

The analysis of the correlation between cultural dimensions (Hofstede 1993) and change management characteristics revealed that cultural dimensions significantly correlate with certain aspects of change management (Figure 12.2).

Uncertainty avoidance was negatively correlated with:

- the amount, pace and stage of change;
- confidence in change management;
- confidence that the change project will succeed; and
- the amount of information received.

It was also related to higher role clarity and less 'anger' expressed by team members.

Masculinity was found to be related to a higher level of expressed anger within the team.

Individualism was positively correlated with 'Information from rumour' and negatively with workgroup resources in terms of staffing, systems and processes. Individualist cultures seem to learn about change through informal channels and overall lack resources within their groups for coping with change.

High power distance was positively correlated with workgroup resources, responsiveness of project teams, and the feeling that talents are well utilised.

Need for change management to be adapted to culture

The observed cultural differences indicate that change management interventions need to be adapted to suit the specific cultural characteristics of the organisational and national environment. Most approaches to organisational change, however, have been developed in highly individualistic cultures that are characterised by low power distance. Cultural dimensions need to be considered and the change management approach adapted to culturally diverse environments or to cultures that have different characteristics than the western 'home' cultures.

Public policy and legislation on diversity

Diversity, discrimination and the legal framework in Australia

The main issues in the management of a diverse workforce relate to:

- the potential for discrimination; and
- the requirement to guarantee equal opportunity.

Equal opportunity

Equal opportunity means that everybody has an equal and fair chance to compete for employment, promotion, training, career development, or other opportunities. It means that that nobody is discriminated against on the basis of individual characteristics—for example

- gender;
- race;
- religion; or
- sexual preferences.

Direct discrimination

There is a distinction between direct or indirect discrimination, with direct discrimination defined as the unfair treatment of a person on the grounds of particular attributes such as:

- race;
- colour;
- sex;
- sexual preference;
- age;
- disability;
- medical record;
- impairment;
- marital status;
- pregnancy;
- family responsibilities;
- criminal record;
- trade union activity;
- political opinion;
- religion;
- national origin; or
- social origin.

For example, direct discrimination would be occurring if a selection panel decided not to employ a person because of their gender and age, and concerns about a potential pregnancy and related maternity leave.

Indirect discrimination

Indirect discrimination includes practices which might look fair, but which can have discriminatory side effects. It applies when an apparently neutral provision, criterion, or practice disadvantages members of a specified group relative to others. An example of this is where the design of a workplace prevents a person with a disability from accessing the equipment needed to do the job.

Anti-discrimination legislation in Australia

It is unlawful in Australia to discriminate even when there is no proven intention to discriminate (Syed 2006). Companies need to ensure that employment practices, especially recruitment and selection, do not favour people based on specific attributes unless those attributes are indispensable for the job on offer. A beauty parlour, for example, might be able to prove that gender is a crucial job requirement.

Workplace Relations Act 1996

The importance of preventing discrimination is stressed in the *Workplace Relations Act 1996*, which refers to respecting and valuing the diversity of the workforce by helping to prevent and eliminate discrimination on the basis of race, colour, sex, sexual preference, age, disability, marital status, family responsibilities, pregnancy, religion, political opinion, national extraction or social origin. There are a number of Acts which address discrimination. These are listed in *Appendix 1*.

Case study

Diversity management in the Australian public sector

The Australian Public Sector (APS) is at the forefront of combating discrimination and working towards successful management of diversity in the workplace. It can provide valuable lessons and examples for private sector companies operating in Australia. Two exemplary approaches include the policy for developing and reviewing diversity programs and the introduction of a Workforce Diversity Coordinator role.

The *Public Service Act 1999* and associated legislation establishes a framework that reflects the expectations of government and the community about a fair, inclusive and productive public service. Under section 18 of the *PS Act*, agencies in the public sector need to:

- establish workplace diversity programs;
- annually evaluate and report on the effectiveness and outcomes of the program; and
- review their program at least once every four years (Steger & Erwee 2001).

An example of the implementation of this act is the Employment and Capability Strategy for Aboriginal and Torres Strait Islander Employees.

In August 2005, the Prime Minister announced an APS Employment and Capability Strategy for Aboriginal and Torres Strait Islander Employees in order to counteract the declining percentage of employees with Aboriginal heritage in the Australian public service. The directions allow an agency head to identify opportunities for employment as open to indigenous Australians as long as these vacancies:

- comply with Commonwealth law;
- are notified in the Gazette and advertised widely;
- are identified as open to indigenous Australians; and
- are open to all members of the community who are indigenous Australians.

There are two avenues for addressing the issue:

- identified criteria, and
- special measures.

Identified criteria

Identified criteria can be used to emphasise some of the skills, attributes or experience considered essential or desirable for the effective performance of the duties of a particular job. They may include an understanding of the issues affecting Aboriginal and/or Torres Strait Islander people and an ability to communicate sensitively and effectively with Aboriginal and/or Torres Strait Islander people.

Special measures

Special measures provisions are authorised under section 8 of the *Racial Discrimination Act 1975*. It is therefore not unlawful to limit certain employment opportunities to a particular ethnic or racial group if that group has an identified history of disadvantage and the use of the limiting measure would help to redress the employment outcome imbalance.

Workplace diversity coordinator

Another exemplary practice in the APS is the appointment by many public service agencies of a workplace diversity coordinator. The role involves:

- advocating and actively promoting the benefits of diversity;
- gaining an understanding of the workplace diversity needs of staff;
- increasing awareness of workplace diversity issues;
- advocating the inclusion of equity and diversity issues on strategic planning agendas;
- promoting the integration of workplace diversity issues in human resource policies and practices;

- developing and monitoring compliance with relevant laws and regulations;
- developing, implementing and monitoring the workplace diversity program; and
- keeping senior executives informed about workplace diversity issues and about the effectiveness of the workplace diversity program.

Conclusion

In this chapter we demonstrated that for organisations to be fair and productive, it is essential to ensure that the workplace culture and practices value and encourage contributions by people with different backgrounds, experiences and perspectives.

We provided examples of such differences and the HR strategies and adaptive practices that can accommodate these differences. By recognising that the whole of a person's lifespan is affected by their diversity characteristics and the responses to them, and taking a holistic and lifespan perspective of potential and incumbent employees, the tremendous benefit to organisations and society inherent in a diverse population can be realised.

Discussion questions

1. What is diversity?
2. What are the key issues associated with managing diversity and achieving social inclusion in the workplace?
3. How has the population in Australia changed over time and what are the corresponding implications of these changes for strategic HRM?
4. Provide some specific ways in which work design can be used to address the diversity of needs which may arise due to cultural diversity and age diversity in the workplace.
5. What are the characteristics of an effective workforce diversity program?
6. What are the HR considerations of managing change in diverse cultures?

References

Abbott, T 2009, *Battle lines*, Melbourne, Melbourne University Press.

Adler, N 1997, *International dimensions of organizational behaviour*, Cincinnati, South-Western.

AMP. NATSEM 2009, 'She works hard for the money', AMP, NATSEM Income and Wealth Report, available at http://media.amp.com.au/.

Appo, D & Härtel, CEJ 2003, 'Questioning management paradigms that deal with Aboriginal development programs in Australia', *Asia Pacific Journal of Human Resources*, 41(1): 36-50.

Asis, MMB 2005, 'Recent Trends in International Migration in Asia and the Pacific', *Asia-Pacific Population Journal*, 20(3), 15-38.

Ashkanasy, NM, Härtel, CEJ & Daus, CS 2002, 'Diversity and emotion: The new frontiers in organizational behavior research', *Journal of Management*, 28(3), 307-338.

Austen, S, Jefferson, T, Preston, A & Seymour, R 2008, 'Gender Pay Differentials in Low-Paid Employment (Women in Social and Economic Research, Curtin University of Technology)', Australian Fair Pay Commission, www.fairpay.gov.au.

Australian Human Rights Commission 2008, 'Face the Facts. Some Questions and Answers about Indigenous Peoples, Migrants and Refugees and Asylum Seekers', http://www.hreoc.gov.au/

Australian Bureau of Statistics 2006, Census Data by Topic, Commonwealth of Australia, http://www.censusdata.abs.gov.au.

Australian Bureau of Statistics 2008A, Migration March 2008, ABS Cat. No. 3412.0, located at http://www.ausstats.abs.gov.au/Ausstats/subscriber.nsf/0/F15E154C9434F250CA2574170011B45B/$File/34120_2006-07.pdf, accessed 09.07.09.

Australian Bureau of Statistics 2008b, Australian Labour Market Statistics July 2008, ABS Cat. No. 6105.0, accessed 26.07.09, <http://www.ausstats.abs.gov.au/ausstats/subscriber.nsf/0/C13A89556EEE7941CA25747A00116F59/$File/61050_jul%202008.pdf>.

Australian Workplace 2009, accessed 28.07.09, <http://www.workplace.gov.au/workplace/Organisation/Employer/EmployerResponsibilities/Avoidingdiscriminationinemployment.htm>.

Baer, M, Niessen, A & Ruenzi, S 2009, 'The Impact of Team Diversity on Mutual Fund Performance', Working paper, available at SSRN: http://ssrn.com/abstract=1343472.

Birrell, B & Betts, K 2001, 'Australians' Attitudes to Migration', *Public Affairs*, December, 3-5.

Chang, L 2002, 'Cross-cultural differences in international management using Kluckhohn-Strodtbeck framework', *The Journal of the Academy of Business*, September, 20-27.

Colic-Peisker, V & Tilbury, F 2006, 'Employment niches for recent refugees: Segmented labour market in twenty-first century Australia', *Journal of Refugee Studies*, 19(2): 203-229.

Cox, T 2001, *Cultural Diversity in Organisations*, San Francisco, Barrett-Koehler Publishers Inc.

Diversity Council Australia 2007, 'Grey Matters: Engaging Mature Age Workers'.

EOWA 2008, 'Equal Opportunity for Women in the Workplace Agency's Gender Income Distribution of Top Earners in ASX200 Companies', available at http://www.eowa.gov.au/Australian_Women_In_Leadership_Census/2006_Australian_Women_In_Leadership_Census/Top_Earner_Report/FINAL_REPORT.pdf.

Foldy, EG 2004, 'Learning from diversity: A theoretical exploration', *Public Administration Review*, 64(5): 529-538.

Fujimoto, Y, Härtel, CEJ & Panipucci, D 2005, 'Emotional experience of individualist–collectivist workgroups: Findings from a study of 14 multinationals located in Australia', in CEJ Härtel, WJ Zerbe & NM Ashkanasy (Eds), *Emotions in Organizational Behavior*, Lawrence Erlbaum Associates, Mahwah.

Hall, E 1960, 'The silent language of overseas business', *Harvard Business Review*, 38(3), 87-96.

Härtel, CEJ & Fujimoto, Y 2009, *Human Resource Management: Transforming Theory into Innovative Practice (2nd edition)*, Pearson Education Australia.

Härtel, CEJ & Fujimoto, Y 2000, 'Diversity is not a problem to be managed by organisations but openness to perceived dissimilarity is', *Journal of Australian and New Zealand Academy of Management*, 6(1), 14-27.

Harzing, A-W & Hofstede, G 1996, 'Planned change in organizations: The influence of national cultures', in Bamberger, PA, Erez, M & Bacharach SB (Eds), *Research in the Sociology and Organizations: Cross-Cultural Analysis of Organizations*, Vol 14, pp. 297-340, Greenwich, Conn, JAI Press.

Hays-Thomas, R 2004, 'Why now? The contemporary focus on managing diversity', in M Stockdale & FJ Crosby (Eds), *The psychology and management of workforce diversity*, pp. 3-30, Malden, MA, Blackwell.

Healy, J, Kidd, M & Richardson, S 2008, 'Gender pay differentials in the low-paid labour market', National Institute of Labour Studies, Flinders University of South Australia 2008 Minimum Wage Research Forum, Australian Fair Pay Commission, www.fairpay.gov.au.

Hofstede, G 1980, 'Motivation, leadership, and organization: Do American theories apply abroad?', *Organizational Dynamics*, 9(1), 42-63.

Hofstede, G 1993, 'Cultural constraints in management theory',. *Academy of Management Executive*, 7(1), 81-94.

Hofstede, G 2001, *Culture's consequences: comparing values, behaviors, institutions, and organizations across nations*, 2nd edn, Thousand Oaks, Sage Publications.

Horwitz, S K 2005, 'The Compositional Impact of Team Diversity on Performance: Theoretical Considerations', *Human Resource Development Review*, 4 (2): 219-245.

Kelsey, BL 2000, 'Increasing minority group participation and influence using a group support system', *Canadian Journal of Administrative Science*, 17(1): 63-75.

Kirsch, C 1997, 'Analyse von Gruppenarbeit in der Fertigung schweizerischer und japanischer Unternehmen, Versuch einer Integration von arbeitspsychologischer und kulturvergleichender Perspektive', Dissertation, Institute of Psychology, Faculty of Philosophy II, University of Potsdam.

Kirsch, C & Parry, W 2009, 'Cross-cultural differences in Organizational Change – The Impact of Cultural Dimensions on the Management of Change Projects', Insight Article, ChangeTracking Research CTRE, http://www.changetracking.com.

Kochan T, Bezrukova, K, Ely, R, Jackson, S, Joshi, A & Jen, K 2002, ,The effects of diversity on business performance', Report of the Diversity Research Network, Building Opportunities for Leadership Development Initiative, Alfred P Sloan, Foundation and the Society for Human Resource Management.

Konrad, AM, Prasad, P & Pringle, JK 2006, *Handbook of workplace diversity*, London, Sage.

Kramar, R 1998, 'Managing diversity: beyond affirmative action in Australia', *Women in Management Review*, 13 (4): 133 – 142.

Linnehan, F & Konrad, AM 1999, 'Diluting diversity: Implications for intergroup inequality in organizations', *Journal of management inquiry*, 8, 399-414.

Maznevski, ML 1994, 'Understanding Our Differences: Performance in Decision-Making Groups with Diverse Members', *Human Relations*, 47(5): 531-552.

NSW – Department of Premier and Cabinet. Equal Employment Opportunity. http://www.eeo.nsw.gov.au/.

Parry, W 2008, 'Achieving exceptional performance across times of change', Insight Article CT0108, ChangeTracking Research CTRE http://www.changetracking.com.

Richardson, S, Roberston, F & Ilsley, D 2001, 'The labour force experience of new migrants', National Institute of Labour Studies, Finders University, Adelaide.

Schneider, S & JL Barsoux 2003, *Managing across cultures*, Essex, Pearson Education Limited.

Shaw, JB & Barrett-Power, E 1998, 'The Effects of Diversity on Small Work Group Processes and Performance', *Human Relations*, 51(10): 1307-1325.

Simsarian Webbera, S & Donahue, LM 2001, 'Impact of highly and less job-related diversity on work group cohesion and performance: a meta-analysis', *Journal of Management* 27(2): 141-162.

Steger, M & Erwee, R 2001, 'Managing Diversity in the Public Sector: A case study of a small city council', *International Journal of Organisational Behaviour*, 4(1), 77-956.

Strachan, G, Burgess, J & Sullivan, A 2004, 'Affirmative action or managing diversity: what is the future of equal opportunity policies in organisations?', *Women in Management Review*, 19 (4): 196 – 204.

Syed, J 2006, 'What is the Australian model of managing diversity?', proceedings of the 20th ANZAM (Australian New Zealand Academy of Management) Conference on "Management: Pragmatism, Philosophy, Priorities", 6-9 December 2006, Central Queensland University, Rockhampton, http://library-resources.cqu.edu.au:8888/access/detail.php?pid=cqu:932.

Thomas, R 1996, *Building a house for diversity*, Boston, Harvard Business School Press.

Thomas, DA & Ely RJ 1996, 'Making Differences Matter – a new paradigm for managing diversity, *Harvard Business Review*, Sept-Oct.

Trau, RNC & Härtel, CEJ 2004, 'One career, two identities: An assessment of gay men's career trajectory', *Career Development International*, 9(6/7), 627-637.

Ulich, E 1978, 'Uber das Prinzip der differentiellen Arbeitsgestaltung', *Industrielle Organisation*, 47, 566-568.

Ulich, E 1983, 'Differentielle Arbeistgestaltung – ein Diskussionsbeitrag', *Zeitschrift fur Arbeitswissenschaft*, 37, 12-15.

Walumba, F, Lawler, J & Avolio, B 2007, 'Leadership, individual differences, and work related attitudes: A cross-cultural investigation', *Applied Psychology*, 56(2), 212-230.

Zink, K 1978, 'Zur Begrundung einer zielgruppenspezifischen Organisationsentwicklung', *Zeitschrift fur Arbeitswissenschaft*, 32, 42-48.

Appendix 1—Acts related to diversity in the workplace

The *Racial Discrimination Act* 1975 makes it unlawful to discriminate in employment on the grounds of race, colour or national or ethnic origin.

The *Sex Discrimination Act* 1984 makes it unlawful to discriminate in employment on the grounds of a person's sex, marital status, pregnancy or potential pregnancy or to sexually harass another person.

The *Human Rights and Equal Opportunity Commission Act* 1986 provides for the rights of people with physical or mental disabilities and addresses issues of discrimination in employment.

Under the *Occupational Health and Safety (Commonwealth Employment) Act* 1991 all employers and employees must maintain a secure, healthy and safe working environment. An employer must take practical precautions to prevent harassment.

The *Disability Discrimination Act* 1992 makes it unlawful for an employer to discriminate against a person on the grounds of disability, including a disease.

The *Workplace Relations Act* 1996 prohibits discrimination in awards and agreements and in the termination of employment.

The *Age Discrimination Act* 2004 aims to eliminate, as far as possible, discrimination against persons on the ground of age in work, education, access to premises, the provision of goods, services and facilities. It also intends to remove barriers to older people participating in society, particularly in the workforce and to change negative stereotypes about older people.

Chapter 13

PERFORMANCE MANAGEMENT OF EXPATRIATES IN CHINA

Susan McGrath-Champ, Anthony Fee & Xiaohua Yang

OBJECTIVES

By the completion of the chapter you should be able to:

1. present a holistic framework for the management of international assignees' (expatriates') performance, linking internationalisation with HR functions of training, development, and mentoring;

2. discuss the international HRM function as a strategic management practice in China and in Chinese and foreign MNEs within a global context; and

3. analyse and evaluate expatriate performance management as a strategic international HRM mechanism that achieves change and contributes to cultural transformation, and discuss what this means in relation to strategic HRM (SHRM) in China in a broader sense.

DEFINITIONS

International human resource management (IHRM): 'The HRM issues and problems arising from the internationalization of business, and the HRM strategies, policies and practices which firms pursue in response to the internationalization of business' (Scullion 1995 cited in Scullion & Lineham 2005, p. 4).

Strategic HRM (SHRM): One of the key features that characterises strategic HRM is the concern with 'models and studies which link HRM to performance' (Boxall & Purcell 2003, p. 6).

Strategic international HRM (SIHRM): SIHRM is a more wide-ranging and complex counterpart of SHRM in the context of organisations' internationalised operations.

Expatriate performance management (EPM): EPM includes four components (consistent with Dowling, Festing & Engle 2008):

- goal setting, which acts as a formal control mechanism when integrated with performance appraisal, and as an informal control mechanism by directing attention and motivating and sustaining performance (Latham 2004);
- performance appraisal (PA) or performance evaluation[5] may be defined as 'a process that identifies, evaluates and develops employee performance to meet employee and organizational goals' (Dessler, Griffiths & Lloyd-Walker 2004, p. 258);
- training and development, including pre-departure and in-country training for the expatriate; and
- mentoring, a commonly overlooked component of EPM, which contributes directly and indirectly to performance management through monitoring and feedback by the mentor, as well as knowledge, skill and value transferral to the protégé.

Table 13.1 draws on a range of (primarily Western) literature to summarise the key features of each of the four components considered necessary for effective EPM.

Introduction

In recent times economic change and growth in China has been fast and vast. With 2008 GDP of US$3.86 trillion (ranking only after the US and Japan) and GDP growth rate in excess of 7% even in the global economic meltdown (World Bank 2009), issues of work, employment and people management—the strategic management of human resources—are vital.

This chapter provides an overview of the role of international human resources in strategic management within contemporary China. It explores the manner in which IHRM (in particular expatriate performance management—EPM) contributes to driving change within organisations in China. The core of the chapter addresses the management of expatriates.

---

[5] The terms 'performance evaluation' and 'performance appraisal' are used interchangeably in the literature (see Dowling *et al.* 2008).

The chapter is distinctive in that it connects EPM with firm internationalisation, emphasising the strategic role of the HRM function in a global context.

Moving beyond a narrow notion of EPM as solely performance appraisal to a more holistic and integrated definition recognises that functions other than just evaluating employees' performance are essential to supporting and promoting good practices in overseas ventures (Cascio 2006). Used holistically, these components provide MNEs with both formal and informal control mechanisms.

Table 13.1 Overview of literature—Features of effective expatriate performance management components (EPM)

Activity	Features for effective EPM
Goal setting	A combination of qualitative and quantitative, and individual and team, goals (Clause & Briscoe 2008; Gregersen, Hite & Black 1996) that are specific, challenging and measurable (Knight, Durham & Locke 2001), and formalised in writing (Suutari & Tahvanainen 2002). Host-country managers and/or the expatriate should be involved in setting goals (Suutari & Tahvanainen 2002).
Performance appraisal	Clear performance appraisal procedures and measures (Martin & Bartol 2003) which are formalised (Suutari & Tahvanainen 2002) and incorporate regular appraisals from a range of stakeholders familiar with the expatriate's work, from both the parent- and host-culture (Black, Gregersen & Mendenhall 1992; Cascio & Bailey 1995; Ward 1997).
Training	Both pre-departure and in-country training for the expatriate, aligned with (in-country) performance appraisal and goals (e.g. Brewster & Scullion 1997; Linehan & Scullion 2001; Wright & Geroy 2001).
Mentoring	Formalised mentoring partnership for the expatriate facilitated and supported by the organisation (Carraher, Sullivan & Croccito 2008).

Goal-setting and performance appraisal for expatriates can be used to intervene directly in the activities of subsidiaries so their goals will align with the parent firm's overall strategy. At the same time, structured support for expatriates through training and mentoring allows firms to promote values and behaviours consistent with the parent firm's goals and strategies (Kobrin 1988).

A critical outcome of this informal EPM is that the firm's cultural control can be extended through the expatriate internalising and disseminating corporate values, norms and strategy within the subsidiary. As Dowling *et al.* (2008, p. 271) point out, *'(i)t is through formal and informal control mechanisms that the multinational achieves the consistency, coordination and compliance of desired behaviour and outcomes to implement its global strategy'.*

A country perspective: HRM in China

A brief background to HRM in China is necessary to understand EPM in that country. This section provides a brief historical overview of domestic HRM in the Chinese context, outlines key changes in business practices accompanying the transformation of the Chinese economy, canvasses the nature of strategic HRM in China (i.e. HRM-performance links), and concludes with a brief overview of PA in China.

Historical overview

As Cooke (2004, p. 17) observes, 'HRM in China is as new as its market economy'. From 1949 (when the People's Republic was founded) to 1978 (when Deng's reforms were introduced) and beyond to the 21st century, there have been major changes in workplace people management.

It is common nowadays to distinguish between HRM in enterprises of different ownership type in China since distinct differences have emerged amongst contrasting businesses types (see Table 13.2).

Table 13.2 Characteristics of human resource practices in Chinese enterprises

Business type	Research findings
State-owned enterprises (SOEs)	Generally reliant on traditional Chinese personnel practices, limited use of strategic human resource management and so have the greatest potential benefit to derive from increased use of HR practices.
Collective-owned enterprises (COEs)	Have begun employing more mainstream HR practices, although traditional Chinese personnel practices are still more prevalent.
Private-owned enterprise (POEs)	Generally less constrained by the need for traditional personnel practices that SOEs or COEs, especially newly developed POEs.
Foreign-invested enterprises (FIEs)	In general, not bound by traditional rules and so have more opportunities for quicker adoption of western-style HR practices. Usually take home strategy to China based on the experience that 'humanistic' concerns benefit the organisation in the longer term.

Sources: Ngo, Lau & Foley 2008; Wang, Bruning & Peng 2007.

Changes in business practices accompanying the transformation of the Chinese economy

HRM in China

The closed economy and dominance of SOEs and COEs until the late 1970s meant only a basic system of personnel administration existed, involving:

- life-long employment;
- separation of workers from 'cadres';
- worker immobility;
- dependence on the work unit for 'cradle to grave' social security; and
- non-existence of a labour market (Zhao 1994; Zou & Lansbury forthcoming).

Enterprises lacked autonomy to make HR-related decisions. The single trade union (All China Federation of Trade Unions) functioned as an extension of government as a conveyor of social welfare (Cooke 2004). Personnel allocation, training, compensation and other HR decisions were controlled by the government (Wang et al. 2007).

During the 1990s this system waned. By the 21st century the 'iron rice bowl' employment system had been substantially replaced, though with differences in HRM practices between different types of enterprises. These are outlined in Table 13.2 (Ding, Goodall & Warner, 2000; Zhu, Thomson & de Cieri 2008).

By the mid to late 2000s, China's labour market had become fiercely competitive (e.g. turnover rate of 12–17%; a ratio of 10:1 management positions to qualified Chinese applicants). This pressure gave rise to HR departments taking charge of recruitment, training, and performance appraisal, and acquiring increased autonomy over promotion and even dismissal (Wang et al. 2007).

Strategic integration of HRM and firm performance in China

Chinese firms, like Western firms, are able to reap higher financial and operational performance when HRM is strategic (Ngo et al. 2008). Zheng et al.'s (2006) research in small and medium enterprises supported the existence of both

- an HR practices/HR performance link; and
- an HR performance/organisational performance link.

More generally, however, and contrary to Western countries, because provision of social security schemes in China is associated with the old regime, enhancing social security is ineffective in improving the HR practices/HR performance link.

Holistic performance evaluation is not widespread, so has little influence on HR performance. Training/development lacks impact on HR performance due to the ineffectiveness of training programs for low-skilled employees in a context of deep skill deficiencies. Employee commitment is more important than employee competence in the HR performance/organisational performance link. Ngo *et al.* (2008) propose that focusing narrowly on increasing staff competency via training and development may not help firm performance. Rather, it should be combined with other motivational instruments which, together, can enhance organisational performance.

Performance appraisal in non-foreign firms in China

From 1949 to 1978, PA was more commonly used for cadres (equivalent to white-collar employees) than for workers. The purpose of appraising cadres was mainly for promotion or transfer, and the criteria were heavily reliant on political loyalty and seniority. Cultural values around 'saving face' and China's high 'power distance' ran counter to open expression and discussion of views regarding performance. Management saw 'seniority' as an easy way out when appraising workers (Zhu & Dowling 1998).

By the mid 1990s, PA had begun to be used for administrative, but not for communication or development purposes. Little feedback from PA was given to the person being appraised; sometimes PA results were kept confidential. There was little emphasis on development, since employees were historically expected to remain in one work unit ('danwei' or 工作单位) throughout their life-time employment. There are contrasting findings about the extent to which results of PA are communicated to staff (e.g. Shen 2008, Bai & Bennington 2005).

While cultural factors like the desire to reduce interpersonal conflict and maintain face may be limiting its use, it is likely that the type of firm, as well as industry and institutional factors all influence the extent to which PA is implemented in organisations.

Strategic HRM in China

Some studies of HRM in China take up a theme, now common in Western literature, of the *strategic* role of HRM — that is, whether and how improved HRM practices contribute to enhanced HRM outcomes and the manner in which this augments organisational performance. The premise is that when HRM is strategically integrated with organisational goals, it can be a source of competitive advantage (Boxall & Purcell 2003; Huselid 1995).

Accompanying this are discussions concerning 'bundles' of HR practices that promote optimal HR (and thus firm) performance, and the HRM underpinnings of 'high performance work systems' (e.g. Arthur 1992; Frenke, Tam, Korczynski & Shire 1998).

Despite controversy within the 'Western' setting around the exact nature of the HRM/organisational performance link, a number of theoretical models have been devised, accompanied by empirical studies in numerous countries (summarised in Zheng, Morrison & O'Neill 2006). The outcome of these studies is a broad consensus that the adoption of HRM practices, and particularly specific packages of HR practices, enhance organisational performance. Research concerning the link between HR practices, HR performance and organisational performance are summarised under the earlier heading 'Strategic integration of HRM and firm performance in China'.

Performance appraisal in China

In studies of HRM in China, research on performance appraisal (PA) is quite scarce (Cooke, 2009) and research addressing a holistic notion of performance management (PM) is even more so.

Currently, although institutional factors and cultural heritage still impede the full play of Western PA practices in Chinese SOEs, PA systems and practices have undergone rapid changes responding to market and reform influences. Research findings are summarised under the earlier heading 'PA in non-foreign enterprises in China'.

Global perspectives on performance management

An understanding of PM globally can be obtained from at least two of the three approaches to international work and management outlined above.

A 'comparative/ country studies' approach yields a sense of the nature and differences in domestic PM from country to country such as provided by Budhwar and Debrah (2001), and Varma, Budhwar and DeNisi (2008). Alternatively, and consistent with the focus of this chapter, the 'international HRM' approach focuses attention on PM of expatriates and/or local ('host country') employees in foreign MNEs operating in various parts of the globe. Accordingly, this section briefly outlines what Shen (2004, 2005, 2006) terms 'international performance management' in Chinese MNEs, followed by a more detailed discussion of EPM in foreign MNEs in China.

Most researchers agree that expatriates, especially expatriate managers, are central to the internationalisation objectives of MNEs and thus their performance should be managed carefully (Suutari & Tahvanainen 2002). Given this, there is a surprising dearth of research looking specifically at EPM (e.g. Bonache, Brewster & Suutari 2001; Suutari & Tahvanainen 2002).

A recent review concludes that the academic literature has 'paid only scant attention to the PM of expatriates' (Claus & Briscoe 2008, p. 17). Of the small body of research, most studies have tended to focus on a limited number of components of EPM in isolation, with a bias in the literature toward the 'hard' aspects of EPM like goal setting and performance evaluation (e.g. Gregersen *et al.* 1996; Suutari & Tahvanainen 2002; Tahvanainen & Suutari 2005).

International PM in Chinese MNEs

Growth of Chinese MNEs

Along with greater market openness within China, a significant new development is the growth and expansion of Chinese MNEs. By 2004, made-in-China MNEs could be found in virtually every corner of the world (Yang, Lim, Sakurai & Seo 2009). Among the 2009 BCG 100 New Global Challengers, 36 Chinese MNEs are contenders for global leadership (The Boston Consulting Group 2009).

IPM of non-expatriate and 'third-country' staff

Jie Shen and Miao Zhang have been foremost in examining HR practices in Chinese MNEs. Amidst a broad-ranging examination of HR practices, Shen's work (2004, 2005, 2006) includes scrutiny specifically of international performance appraisal deploying a broad notion, 'international performance management' (IPM) which encompasses EPM plus performance management of non-expatriate (local/host), and 'third-country' staff.

Shen's research reveals that PA in Chinese multi-nationals entails a mix of:

- home and local appraisal systems;
- traditional Chinese personnel management and modern Western HRM concepts; and
- host-contextual and firm-specific factors.

There is a 'blending' of HR practices in domestic and international firms, with home country HR practices generally (and performance management practices specifically) influencing how MNEs undertake performance management.

Performance appraisal

Shen's study of leading Chinese MNEs showed that headquarters set and administer performance appraisal criteria for senior management (executives/deputy executive managers) but executive managers of subsidiaries are allowed to take responsibility for appraisals of non-executive employees including both HCNs and expatriates in their operations.

Senior management are appraised annually with bi-annual delegations sent by headquarters for appraisal purposes via self-assessment and peer-opinion mechanisms, procedures that are the same in home operations. PA procedures for non-executive HCNs are host-based and include self-assessment and assessment by direct managers or executives.

Shen (2005) notes a lack of transparency and feedback in PA processes in Chinese MNEs. Reluctance of appraisers to pass negative evaluations on to appraisees limits the effectiveness of PA as a mechanism to enhance performance, is seemingly a remnant of the non-transparency of older-style PA practices in China, and is considered by Shen 'an area in Chinese international performance appraisal that needs to be improved' (Shen 2005, p. 554).

IPM v. domestic PM

IPM differs from domestic PM in China through PA criteria being primarily concerned with tangibles including:

- the firm's (past) performance record;
- compliance; and
- regulations.

Aspects such as political and moral correctness in IPM take a lower priority than in the domestic context. However, PA is a largely static/retrospective undertaking rather than a forward-looking, strategically-focused process.

Of particular relevance to the further study of PM in MNEs was Shen's finding that less internationalised companies deploy more home performance appraisal systems in operations abroad than more highly internationalised operations which 'try to achieve global integration and national responsiveness ... by employing adaptive performance appraisal systems' (Shen 2005, p. 557).

Two sets of comparisons can be drawn in respect to Chinese MNEs — namely:

- with PM in Western MNEs and,
- with PM in domestic Chinese organisations.

PM in Chinese MNEs v. Western MNEs

In contrasting PM in Chinese and Western MNEs, Shen (2005, p. 559) notes that:

- Chinese MNEs adopt different performance approaches to employees holding different managerial positions and different nationalities rather than deploying a universal PA policy for all employees;
- the focus of IPM in Chinese MNEs is short-term business achievement (particularly concerning how much to pay employees) rather than organisational development; and
- Chinese and Western MNEs use different types of PA criteria.

PM in Chinese MNEs v. domestic organisations

There are several contrasts between PM in Chinese organisations operating in the international and domestic domains (Shen 2005, p. 560) including:

- less emphasis in Chinese MNEs on political attitudes and harmonious relations than their domestic counterparts;
- less 'group-meeting' input to non-executive PA processes in Chinese MNEs than domestic firms; and
- greater variation in the procedures and criteria deployed by Chinese MNEs than their domestic counterparts.

Overall, Shen (2005, p. 561) concluded that:

- PA in Chinese MNEs is more 'progressive' than the domestic system in terms of adopting Western HRM;
- the current practices of PM in Chinese MNEs is more convergent with home practices than with Western MNEs; but
- there is an apparent tendency for Chinese IPM to westernise based on Chinese MNE managers' expressed desire to reach 'international' HRM standards.

Reverse diffusion

Zhang found that Chinese MNEs engage in 'reverse diffusion' — that is, the transfer of Western HRM practices from developed-country foreign subsidiaries to developing-country domestic plants in China (Zhang 2003; Zhang & Edwards 2007).

Performance management was one of several HRM practices (along with competency-selection processes, performance-related pay, training and development and western work organisation systems) where, through the influence of their UK-based subsidiaries, there was some 'uptake' of Western practices within China. Zhang and Edwards found that reverse diffusion (UK as a source of 'best practice') was a strategic priority for the Chinese MNEs included in their study, but that the impact of reverse diffusion on the home firm was not as large as expected and was 'evolutionary' rather than 'transformative' in nature.

EPM in foreign MNEs: The importance of internationalisation

While research has tended to focus on components of EPM in isolation rather than holistically, the research is unambiguous in its view that using 'standard' PM approaches are ineffective for expatriate staff. The cultural and geographic distances between head-office and an international subsidiary make each component of EPM more challenging, and the need to integrate these with each other and with the firm's strategic objectives more important.

EPM and level of internationalisation

A small number of recent studies have begun to suggest a link between EPM and a firm's level of internationalisation (e.g. Gong 2003; Suutari & Tahvanainen 2002), primarily as a way to solve 'agency' problems (e.g. Roth & O'Donnell 1996) where a parent firm and the subsidiary have divergent interests in the principal–agent relationship (Jensen & Meckling 1976). This is especially true in situations where a large cultural distance exists between the parent and the subsidiary (Gong 2003).

While none of these studies has incorporated all four components of EPM (i.e. goal setting, performance appraisal, training and development, and mentoring), they do suggest that as firms become more internationalised (that is, as MNEs open subsidiaries in more geographically dispersed regions and their international operations take on greater strategic importance) they need to develop more robust, comprehensive and formalised EPM procedures.

As firms internationalise, the extent of direct control that head office can exert on foreign subsidiaries is reduced; hence 'agency costs' increase (e.g. Roth & O'Donnell 1996) and so highly internationalised firms must employ more comprehensive and formalised control mechanisms to limit the risk of expatriate managers acting against the organisation's interests.

Similarly, subsidiaries operating in countries with very different cultural and institutional environments find it more difficult and expensive to access, interpret, and evaluate information (e.g. Gregersen *et al.* 1996; Orr & Scott 2008; Zaheer & Mosakowski 1997). Consequently, firms can use EPM as a mechanism to promote knowledge transfer between parent and subsidiaries, thus offsetting the liability of 'foreignness' and building competitive advantage (Bonache *et al.* 2001; Kogut & Zander 1993).

In short, the literature suggests that as MNEs' international operations take on greater significance and extend the reach of their subsidiary offices to more diverse cultures, EPM systems are likely to take on greater importance. These firms are more likely to use EPM for both bureaucratic and cultural control. Consequently, their EPM systems would be expected to reflect the characteristics of EPM systems outlined in Table 13.1. This relationship was examined in a recent study of foreign MNEs in China, summarised in the following section.

EPM in foreign MNEs in China

This section outlines the methodology, findings, and case studies undertaken by the authors from a detailed study of EPM in foreign MNEs operating in China.

Methodology

To examine the proposition that as firms become more internationalised they develop more comprehensive EPM systems, the relationship between the level of internationalisation of a firm and its EPM systems was explored[6]. The study deployed a multi-site case study methodology. Data were collected through in-depth interviews with 17 expatriates from 16 foreign ventures operating in China and Hong Kong in 2004/5. The firms came from a range of industries, including manufacturing, financial services, retailing, and technology. All but one of the firms was based in Australia. Although there were variations, the typical expatriate interviewed was an Australian male, aged in his thirties, working in a top management position.

Using measures drawn from the literature, each firm was categorised into 'high', 'medium' or 'low' based on its level of:

- internationalisation[7];
- comprehensiveness of goal setting;
- comprehensiveness of performance evaluation;
- comprehensiveness of training systems; and
- formality of mentoring system.

Where applicable, interview data was triangulated with publicly available records.

Findings

It was found was that distinct variations existed in EPM and a visible link was observable between EPM and the level of internationalisation existing across firms in the study. Figure 13.1 charts the level of comprehensiveness/formality for each EPM component for all 16 firms.

Companies with a high degree of internationalisation tended to have more comprehensive and robust EPM systems, particularly in relation to goal-setting and performance-evaluation systems. All four highly internationalised companies in the study (firms A to D in Figure 13.1) had highly comprehensive goal-setting and performance-evaluation structures.

---

[6] A more detailed discussion of the research methods used in this study can be found in Yang, X, McGrath-Champ, S & Fee, A 2009, 'Minding the minders: The relationship between a firm's level of internationalization and its expatriate performance management system', Academy of International Business Annual Conference, San Diego, United States, 30 June.

[7] 'High internationalisers' were defined as firms with a foreign sales to total sales (FSTS) ratio of greater than 50%, *and* with operations in all world regions. By contrast, 'low internationalisers' are those with a FSTS of less than 20%, and with limited geographic spread in their operations.

They tended to use a more systematic goal-setting approach in their business planning (for example, annual and five-year plans) and in establishing goals for managing expatriates' performance, such as quantifiable six-month and 12-month targets. In some instances, business targets and timeframes were integrated with expatriate's performance appraisal.

In contrast, the less internationalised firms (firms I to P in Figure 13.1) tended to use more variable approaches with less specific and less quantifiable goals, often expressed in vague terms such as 'establish a financial base' or 'develop new business.' While highly internationalised companies had performance evaluation arrangements that were standardised and comprehensive, companies with a low and medium degree of internationalisation were less comprehensive; for instance, there were commonly different performance management practices within the same company for management (expatriates) and less senior (usually local) employees.

What was most surprising, however, was that even highly internationalised companies with comprehensive goal setting and performance appraisal lacked comprehensive training or formalised mentoring systems. In fact, none of the highly internationalised companies provided any formal training, either pre-departure or in-country training. Of the 16 firms, only two provided extensive training, one from the medium internationalisation category and one in the low category.

Logically, while more pre-departure training would seem to prepare employees better for the commencement of their assignment and on-assignment training ensure that needed skills are maintained or honed throughout an assignment, there was wide variation in terms of the perceived need for either type of training. Moreover, no firm in any category had a comprehensive mentoring system, with the highly internationalised firms being worst of all. Only one company (company L with a low level of internationalisation) had established formal mentoring structures.

The lack of consistent and comprehensive training and mentoring programs across-the-board is puzzling. The data suggest that parent firms, and especially the highly internationalised companies, tend to prefer 'hard' control mechanisms like goal-setting and performance appraisal over 'soft' control mechanisms like developmental programs such as training or mentoring. Thus, while there appears to be a greater recognition of the need for EPM among the highly internationalised firms, they are not taking advantage of opportunities for 'cultural' control that might reduce agency costs and improve competitiveness. Among the less internationalised firms no discernable pattern emerged, suggesting a more ad hoc and less strategic approach to control and coordination.

Chapter 13 – Performance Management of Expatriates in China

Figure 13.1 Degree of internationalisation and performance management by firm

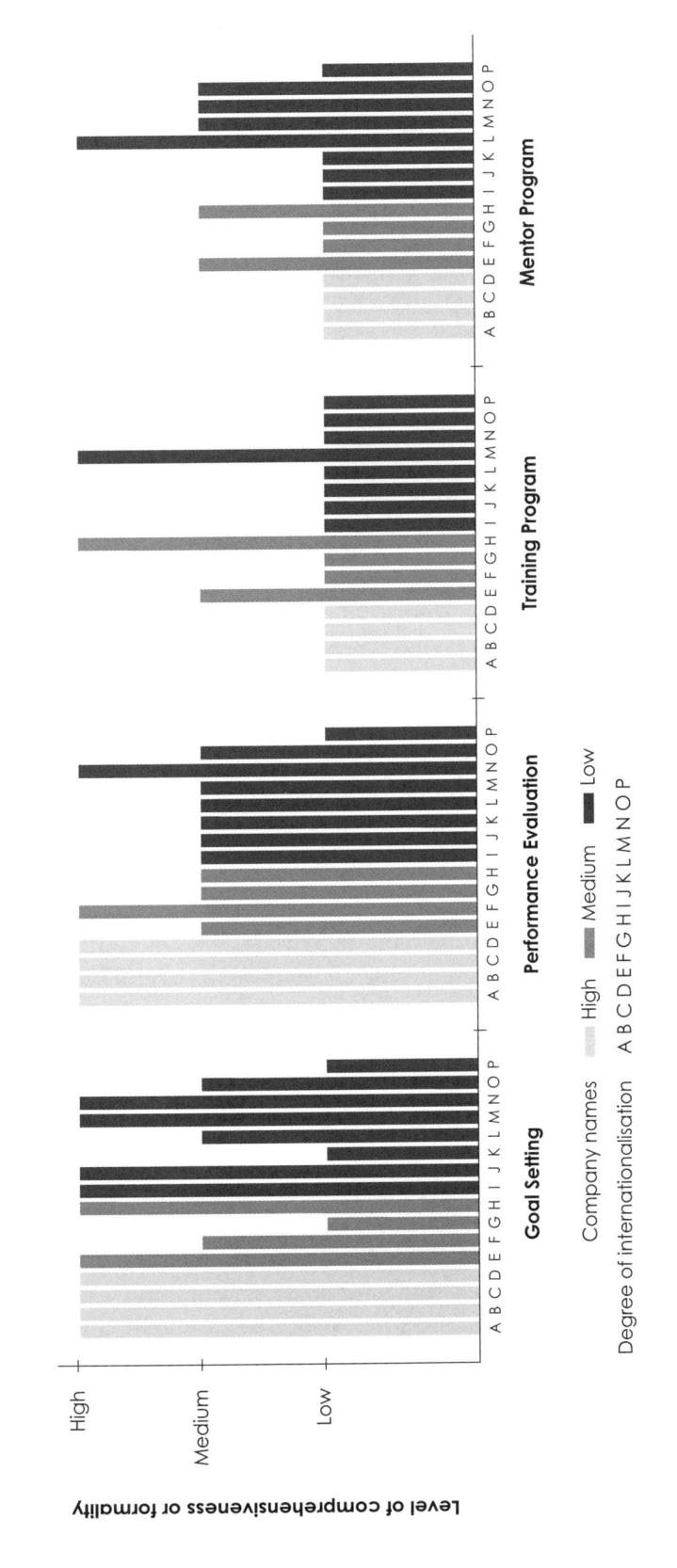

Case studies

Two in-depth contrasting case studies are outlined from the authors' multi-site field work:

- one highly internationalised company; and
- another company with a low level of internationalisation.

The two companies deploy different approaches to managing the performance of their expatriates. The cases illustrate the link between expatriate performance management and the level of internationalisation of the firm.

Mining Giant International

Mining Giant International is a global conglomerate in the resource sector with extensive experience overseas. With annual revenue in excess of US$23 billion it has production and sales facilities in 25 countries across all major continents. Worldwide, it employs over 30,000 people.

The company generally produces in the southern hemisphere and sells in the northern hemisphere. The sales function of the company was established in China in the 1970s, but the production function is at an 'entry' phase in that market. The company's business in China takes the forms of wholly-owned subsidiaries, contractual joint ventures and representative offices.

The interviewee was a 'career expatriate', with ten previous international assignments spanning 25 years with several companies. This was his first assignment in China—as a specialist upper middle-level manager. Originally from the United Kingdom, he was selected internally to develop new (production) business in China.

The company sets the following goals for its employees worldwide:

- win-win relationship with customers;
- high safety standards; and
- investment in the environment.

Details about performance management are set out in the expatriates' contracts. Performance management processes are generally similar throughout the company, with adaptation to suit different business units. Specifically, the firm uses a balanced score card system:

- goals are set out at the beginning of the year by expatriates' supervisors, accepted by expatriates, and assessed at the end of the year, usually with an interim review;

- performance goals are identified by expatriates' supervisors and accepted by the expatriates.

The performance evaluation criteria include:
- behavioural and outcome indicators;
- financial indicators (40% on firm-level and 60% on individual-level performance);
- health and safety; and
- personnel management.

The hard figures are applied across a range of business activities including:
- new business development as part of the company's global human management system; and
- a control system for achieving global corporate strategic goals.

As one interviewee articulated, however, there is difficulty in applying numerical outcome criteria to his work which is not well suited to this type of appraisal.

While the expatriate had no Chinese language skills, the company did not provide any form of pre-departure or post-departure cultural training to the expatriate. The company had no formal mentoring programs for its expatriates. It is up to the individual expatriate to set up mentoring relationships. In this case, this expatriate had no independent mentoring relationship other than the self-initiated informal mentoring relationship with his immediate supervisor.

Oz Construction

Oz Construction is a small, project-based construction company with limited international business. The firm started internationalising its business 15 years ago and has operations in Malaysia and Indonesia It entered the Chinese market only four months prior to the interview.

The company was at an entry stage of business in China and this current contract was the company's first project in that market. The company had not established formal performance goals and basically relied on informal performance goals. In this expatriate's case, these informal performance goals included finishing the nine-month project and developing new business, without specifying any targets.

This was the first expatriate assignment for the young, unmarried Australian who was deployed as a project manager for the purpose of managing a construction project. He had worked with the company previously in Australia and also had overseas (UK) work experience outside the firm.

Oz Construction had no formal performance appraisal process. The evaluation criteria were vague:

- an implicit expectation of on-time completion of the project; and
- establishment of new business.

The expatriate did not receive any training prior to departure or during the project in China. He could not speak Chinese upon arrival and expressed a desire for assistance of an interpreter to enhance communication.

Four months into his assignment, cultural adjustment was still a challenge to him, but the probability of cultural training was non-existent. There was no formal mentoring; instead the expatriate sought advice informally from two Australia-based mentors in light of a lack of rapport with his immediate (also Australian-based) superior 'who expected deliverables should be the same as in Australia [when] they just can't be'.

Case study questions

1. Using Table 13.1, how would you evaluate the different components of EPM for the two companies?
2. Based on the case company profiles, what recommendations regarding improvements to the current EPM approach would you make?
3. Mining Giant International and Oz Construction are both Western companies head-quartered in Australia with operations in China. What changes to your recommendations might be needed if the firms were operating in the following contexts:
   - a Western-based subsidiary of a Chinese MNE;
   - a domestic Chinese state-owned enterprise (SOE).

Conclusion

This chapter has outlined some issues concerning performance management and HRM in China, in both Chinese MNEs and foreign MNEs operating in China. In doing so it goes beyond the focus of studies of performance that are commonly restricted to goal setting and/or performance appraisal.

In our empirical study, we approached performance management as integrated and situated within a suite of management activities and objectives. Amongst other things, this chapter establishes that highly internationalised companies operating in China tend to have more comprehensive, formalised and robust goal setting and performance evaluation systems for their expatriates than firms with low levels of internationalisation. The effectiveness of such companies' overall EPM systems, however, may be problematic because they tend to overlook other EPM activities such as training and mentoring.

The empirical findings presented in the chapter provide insights of potentially wider relevance. As Tung (2007) suggests, in its transformation to the fastest growing economy in the world and its quest for global expansion, China has to confront one of the biggest business challenges— namely, effectively deploying human resources. As they become even more internationalised[8], Chinese MNEs would be wise to pay equal attention to 'hard' *and* 'soft' control levers to avoid the 'mistakes' that the firms in our study appear to have made. These mistakes include linking performance appraisal with only a limited range of related and supporting HR activities, thus limiting the effectiveness of their performance management systems.

As Chinese HRM practices continue to evolve, the greater internalisation of Chinese MNEs raises a number of questions. These include:

- the effect of internationalisation on HRM domestically and internationally;
- the risks associated with the present tendency to ignore 'soft' performance criteria in favour of 'hard' criteria of Western EPM.
- the incorporation of seemingly incompatible aspects of Chinese culture into Western EPM methods.

Our study suggests that foreign MNEs could contribute to the build-up of a human powerhouse in China diffusing PM 'best practices' within China.

The mirror image of this 'reverse diffusion' (Zhang & Edwards 2007) also works towards disseminating a more developed and comprehensive PM system within China. As Chinese MNEs realise the need to develop structured and comprehensive EPM systems, further spillover of best practice may occur in HR in China, both domestically and in China's growing realm of firms that engage in global business.

Finally, in augmenting HR capacities, more robust PM systems could well contribute to addressing the 'talent deficit' that presently limits China's capacity to manage overseas operations. Such an approach may facilitate a

---

[8] Given the large size of the domestic market, many Chinese firms with an international presence would still qualify as having low foreign sales to total sales, and thus as having a 'low' level of internationalisation.

subtle shift from one of 'brain drain' (where individuals leave their home countries to work overseas) to 'brain circulation' whereby individuals return to serve in their home countries whilst maintaining ties with their former host countries (Saxenian 2005; Yang & Terjerson 2007).

For researchers, this opens a number of areas for future studies. These include:

- examining how local Chinese firms benefit from the spillover of best practice from foreign MNEs in China;
- the link between brain circulation and changes to human resources practices;
- investigating the influence of adoption of best practices on the management of expatriates and the success of internationalisation processes.

References

Arthur, J 1992, 'The link between business strategy and industrial relations systems in American steel minimills', *Industrial and Labor Relations Review*, 45(3): 488-506.

Bai, X & Bennington, L 2005, 'Performance appraisal in the Chinese state-owned coal industry', *International Journal of Business Performance*, 7(3): 275-287.

Black, J, Gregersen, H & Mendenhall, M 1992, *Global Assignments: Successfully expatriating and repatriating international managers*, Jossey-Bass, San Francisco, CA.

Bonache, J, Brewster, C & Suutari, V 2001, 'Expatriation: A developing research agenda', *Thunderbird International Business Review*, 43(1): 3-20.

Boxall, P & Purcell, J 2003, *Strategy and Human Resource Management*, Palgrave Macmillan, New York.

Brewster, C & Scullion, H 1997, 'A Review and Agenda for Expatriate HRM', *Human Resource Management Journal*, 7(3): 32-41.

Budhwar, P & Debrah, Y (eds) 2001, *Human Resource Management in Developing Countries*, Routledge, London.

Carraher, SM, Sullivan, SE & Crocitto, MM 2008, 'Mentoring across global boundaries: An empirical examination of home- and host-country mentors on expatriate career outcomes', *Journal of International Business Studies*, 39(8): 1310-26.

Cascio, WF 2006, 'Global performance management systems', in GK Stahl, I Bjorkman, A Ot & R Cebula (eds) *Handbook of Research in International Human Resource Management*, Edward Elgar, Cheltenham, UK.

Cascio, WF & Bailey, E 1995, 'International HRM: The state of research and practice', in Shenkar, O (ed) *Global Perspectives of Human Resource Management*, Prentice Hall, Englewood Cliffs, NJ.

Claus, L & Briscoe, D 2008, 'Employee performance management across borders: A review of relevant academic literature', *International Journal of Management Review*, 10(2): 1-22.

Cooke, FL 2004, 'HRM in China' in PS Budhwar (ed) *Managing Human Resources in Asia-Pacific*, Routledge, London and New York.

Cooke, FL 2009 'A decade of transformation of HRM in China: A review of literature and suggestions for future studies', *Asia Pacific Journal of Human Resources*, 47(1): 6-40.

Dessler, G Griffiths, J & Lloyd-Walker, B 2004, *Human Resource Management*, 2nd edn, Pearson Education Australia, Frenchs Forest.

de Cieri, H & Dowling, PJ 1997, 'Strategic international human resource management: An Asia-Pacific perspective', *Management International Review*, 37(1): 21–42.

Dowling, P, Festing, M & Engle, AD 2008, *International Human Resource Management: Managing People in a Multinational Context*, 5th edn, Thomson Learning, South Melbourne.

Ding, DZ Goodall, K & Warner, M 2000, 'The end of the "Iron rice-bowl": whither Chinese human resource management?', *International Journal of human Resource Management*, 11(2): 217-236.

Frenkel, S, Tam, M, Korczynski, J & Shire, K 1998, 'Beyond bureaucracy? Work organization in call centres' *International Journal of Human Resource Management*, 9(6): 957-79.

Gong, Y 2003, 'Subsidiary staffing in multinational enterprises: Agency, resources, and performance', *Academy of Management Journal*, 46(6): 728-39.

Guest, D 1999, 'Human resource management – the workers' verdict', *Human Resource Management Journal*, 9(3): 5-25.

Gregersen, HB, Hite, JM & Black, JS 1996, 'Expatriate performance appraisal in U.S. multinational firms', *Journal of International Business Studies*, 27(4): 711-38.

Harris, H, Brewster, C & Sparrow, P 2003, *International Human Resource Management*, Chartered Institute of Personnel and Development, London.

Huselid, M 1995, 'The impact of human resource management practices on turnover, productivity, and corporate financial performance', *Academy of Management Journal*, 38(3): 635-672.

Jensen, MC & Meckling, WM 1976, 'Theory of the firm: Managerial behavior, agency costs and ownership structures', *Journal of Financial Economics*, 3: 305-60.

Knight, D, Durham, CC & Locke, EA 2001, 'The relationship of team goals, incentives, and efficacy to strategic risk, tactical implementation and performance', *Academy of Management Journal*, 44(2): 326-38.

Kobrin, S 1988, 'Expatriate reduction and strategic control in American multinational corporations', *Human Resource Management*, 27(1): 63-75.

Kogut, B & Zander, U 1993, 'Knowledge of the firm and the evolutionary theory of the multinational corporation', *Journal of International Business Studies* 24(4): 625-45.

Latham, GP 2004, 'The motivational benefits of goal setting', *Academy of Management Executive*, 18(4): 126-9.

Linehan, M & Scullion, H 2001 'Factors influencing participation of female executives in international assignments', *Comportamento Organizational e Gestao*, 6(2): 213-26.

McGrath-Champ, S 2006 'A spatial perspective on international work and management', Hearn, M & Michelson, G (eds) *Rethinking Work: Time, Space and Discourse,* Campridge University Press, pp. 165-186.

Martin, DC & Bartol, KM 2003, 'Factors influencing expatriate performance appraisal system success: an organizational perspective', *Journal of International Management*, 9(2): 115-32.

Ngo, HY, Lau, CM & Foley, S 2008 'Strategic human resource management, firm performance and employees relations climate in China', *Human Resource Management,* 47(1): 73-90.

Orr, RJ & Scott, WR 2008, 'Institutional exceptions on global projects: A process model', *Journal of International Business Studies*, 39(4): 562-88.

Roth, K & O'Donnell, S 1996 'Foreign subsidiary compensation strategy: an agency theory perspective', *Academy of Management Journal*, 39(3): 678-703.

Saxenian, A 2005, 'From Brain Drain to Brain Circulation: Transnational Communities and Regional Upgrading in India and China', *Studies in Comparative International Development*, 40(2): 35-61.

Scullion, H & Linehan, M 2005 (eds), *International Human Resource Management: A Critical Text*, Basingstoke, Palgrave.

Shen, J 2004, 'International performance appraisals: policies, practices and determinants in the case of Chinese multinational companies', *International Journal of Manpower*, 25(6): 547-63.

Shen, J 2005, 'Effective international performance appraisals: easily said, hard to do', *Compensation and Benefits Review*, 37(4): 70-79.

Shen, J 2006, 'International performance appraisal', in J Shen & V Edwards (eds) *International Human Resource Management in Chinese Multinationals*, Routledge, London and New York.

Shen, J 2008, 'HRM in Chinese privately owned enterprises', *Thunderbird International Business Review*, 50(2): 91-104.

Stroh, LK 2006, 'Appraising: Determining if people are doing the right things', in LK Stroh, JS Black, ME Mendenhall & HB Gregersen (eds) *International Assignments: An integration of strategy, research, and practice,* Routledge, London.

Suutari, V & Tahvanainen, M 2002, 'The antecedents of performance management among Finnish expatriates', *International Journal of Human Resource Management*, 13(1): 55-75.

Tahvanainen, M & Suutari, V 2005, 'Expatriate performance management in MNCs', in H Scullion, & M Linehan (eds), *International Human Resource Management: A Critical Text*, Palgrave, Basingstoke.

The Boston Consulting Group 2009, BCG Report: The 2009 BCG 100 new global challengers: How companies from rapidly developing economies are contending for global leadership, Boston, MA.

Tung, RL 2007, 'The human resource challenge to outward foreign direct investment aspirations from emerging economies: the case of China', *International Journal of Human Resource Management*, 18 (5): 868-889.

Varma, A, Budhwar, P & DeNisi, A (eds) 2008, *Performance management systems: A global perspective*, Routledge, London.

Wang, X Bruning, N & Peng, S 2007, 'Western high-performance HR practices in China: a comparison among public-owned, private and foreign-invested enterprises', *International Journal of Human Resource Management*, 18(4): 684-701.

Woods, P 2003, 'Performance management of Australian and Singaporean expatriates', *International Journal of Manpower*, 24(5): 517-34.

World Bank 2009, *World Development Indicators Database*, viewed 1 July 2009, <http://web.worldbank.org/data>.

Wright, PC & Geroy, GD 2001, 'Changing the mindset: The training myth and the need for world-class performance', *International Journal of Human Resource Management* 12(4): 586-600.

Yang, X, Lim, Y, Sakurai, Y, & Seo, S 2009, 'Comparative analysis of internationalization of Chinese and Korean firms', *Thunderbird International Business Review*, 51 (1): 37-51.

Yang, X, & Terjesen, S 2007, 'In Search of Confidence: Context, Collaboration, and Constraints', *Asia Pacific Journal of Management*. 24: 497-507.

Zaheer, S & Mosakowski, E 1997, 'The dynamics of the liability of foreignness: A global study of survival in financial services', *Strategic Management Journal*, 18(6): 439-63.

Zhao, S 1994, 'Human resource management in China', *Asia Pacific Journal of Human Resources*, 32(2): 3-12.

Zhang, M 2003, 'Transferring human resource management across national boundaries: The case of Chinese multinational companies in the UK', *Employee Relations*, 25(6): 613-26.

Zhang, M & Edwards, C 2007, 'Diffusing "best practice' in Chinese multinationals: the motivation, facilitation and limitations', *International Journal of Human Resource Management*, 18(12): 2147-2165.

Zheng, C, Morrison, M & O'Neill, G 2006, 'An empirical study of high performance HRM practices in Chinese SMEs', *International Journal of Human Resource Management*, 17(10): 1772-1803.

Zheng, C, O'Neill, G & Morrison, M 2009, 'Enhancing Chinese SME performance through innovative HR practices', *Personnel Review*, 38(2): 175-94.

Zhu, CJ & Dowling, P 1998, 'Performance appraisal in China' in J. Selmer (ed) *International Management in China: Cross Cultural Issues*, Routledge, London.

Zhu, CJ, Thomson, B & de Cieri, H 2008, 'A retrospective and prospective analysis of HRM research in Chinese firms: Implications and directions for future study', *Human Resource Management*, 47(1): 133-156.

Zou, M & Lansbury, R (forthcoming) 'Multinational corporations and employment relations in China: The case of Beijing Hyundai Motor Company', *International Journal of Human Resource Management*.

Chapter 14

THE ETHICS OF WORKFORCE DRUG TESTING AND HRM

Edward Wray-Bliss

OBJECTIVES

By the completion of the chapter you should be able to:

1. discuss international evidence concerning drug usage and alleged associations with workplace accidents and poor productivity;
2. discuss the positioning of HR with regard to workplace drug testing;
3. explore the legitimacy of, and rationale for, workforce drug testing; and
4. discuss the ethics of the widening managerial prerogative embodied in contemporary HR practices.

DEFINITIONS

Workforce drug testing: Workforce drug testing is the testing of an employee, or prospective employee's, blood, urine, hair, sweat or saliva and oral fluids for traces of previously consumed illicit drugs (for instance cannabis, amphetamines, cocaine, opiates, methamphetamines) and certain licit (prescription) drugs.

Workforce drug testing can be conducted at a number of stages in the employment cycle:

- pre-recruitment;
- on suspicion of drug use;

- post-incident or accident; or
- randomly, during employment.

Introduction

This chapter examines the practice of workforce drug testing and comments on the ethics of the widening managerial prerogative embodied in contemporary HRM.

The spectre of employee drug use enables a rhetorically powerful link to be made between workforce drug testing and health and safety at work. This evocative rhetorical couplet is evidenced widely in material produced for, and by, management and policy makers—including a body of material traceable to organisations with a commercial interest in drug testing.

An examination of international evidence, both on the nature of drug use in wider society and on the purported link between workplace accidents and employee drug use, fails to support the assertion of a widespread, credible threat to workplace health and safety from employee drug use.

Without such support, the invasiveness of workforce drug testing and the potentially severe disciplinary effects of positive drug tests are argued to be ethically problematic. It is presented as part of a wider, ethically questionable, move by HR professionals to seek to intervene in ever more areas of an employee's private life.

Global perspectives

Global growth of workforce drug testing

Much of the current push for workforce drug testing in the Asia Pacific region and elsewhere can be understood to originate from the US, where the practice is widespread.

Workforce drug testing in the USA

It has been estimated that somewhere between 67% and 80% of the larger US organisations have some form of workforce drug testing regime (IIDTW 2004). Mandatory testing for all federal organisations has been US policy since 1986. The passing of the *Drug Free Workplace Act* 1988 prohibited 'the manufacture, distribution, possession and use of controlled substances in the workplace' (AIVL n.d.).

The practice of workforce drug testing has filtered down to other nations through a combination of:

- US international companies requiring their subsidiaries to mirror home policy (Nolan 2008);

- the commercial push of the larger US drug testing organisations (IIDTW 2004); and
- processes of translation and mimicry that often sees business and management practitioners and academics in the rest of the world adopting US management practices.

Workforce drug testing in the Asia Pacific region

Reliable data on the extent of workforce drug testing in the Asia Pacific region is very limited—though two available estimates suggest that 8% of medium to large New Zealand organisations (Harr & Spell 2007) and a similar number of Australian organisations (Watts 2008) have adopted the practice.

In other countries in the region it is likely that workforce drug testing will be limited either to the subsidiaries of large US corporations or adopted piecemeal by a small number of individual organisations, particularly those in industries such as mining or oil and gas exploration.

Workforce drug testing in the UK

When considering the rest of the world, the UK is possibly the next most prevalent user of workforce drug tests with an estimated 13% of organisations implementing some form of testing. There is, however, considerable momentum building for more widespread workforce drug testing both in the UK (IIDTW 2004) and elsewhere.

Rhetoric and evidence

HR rationale for workforce drug testing

At a surface level the practice of and momentum for drug testing of employees seems to have a strong HR rationale. Advocates of workforce drug testing have argued, for instance, that drug users:

- are more likely to be absent from work;
- present a greater health and safety risk;
- have lower productivity;
- are more likely to be involved in criminal activities in the workplace; and
- tend to be more violent to co-workers and customers (see e.g. ADCA 2008; Ghodse 2005).

Links between drug use and high-risk employees

It has therefore been presented as a legitimate, even essential, HR concern to seek to intervene in employees drug use: to screen, detect, treat, and eventually exclude, such risky individuals from the workplace (Russell

2004). These claims are rhetorically powerful and appeal 'to simple logic as a solution to the issue of drug use in the workplace' (Pidd n.d., p. 2).

Evidence and credibility

Evidence for negative effects of employee drug use

An examination of international academic, governmental and published organisational research, however, generates little compelling evidence to support the claimed links between employee drug use and serious negative effects, either in relation to health and safety, criminality or productivity in organisations (Draper 1998; Harris 2004; IIDTW 2004; Pidd n.d.).

Effectiveness of workforce drug testing

Further, there is markedly little international evidence of the effectiveness of workforce drug testing in reducing employee drug use (Jardine-Tweedle and Wright 1998). Perhaps, somewhat surprisingly, there is also little evidence that organisations conduct any cost-benefit analysis of these drug testing programs (Easter-Bahls 1998; Eckersley 1995; Fine 1992; Martinson 1999), despite the considerable costs of implementation.

The testing process

Without the support of a credible and extensive body of evidence behind it, deciding to embark upon a program of requiring employees to provide samples for testing may be regarded as a very significant, and quite controversial, step for HR professionals to take.

Urine testing

Urine testing, as the most common form of workforce drug testing, illustrates the controversy.

Personal privacy

The process of taking and testing a sample of urine can be highly intrusive and embarrassing for the employee. To minimise various possibilities of 'cheating' on the test, the 'collector' remains physically close to the employee during the collection of the specimen, controlling such things as the employee's access to water, soap etc. Some, minimal, individual privacy may be allowed during the actual passing of urine—for instance the employee might be allowed to step behind a curtained off area—but for the remainder of the process the employee's urine sample is tested for temperature, inspected for colour, labelled and processed in the presence of the employee.

Other privacy issues

Moreover, this is not the only possible intrusion into the privacy of the employee that drug testing represents. An employee's use of many prescription drugs, including anti-depressants, medically prescribed opiates (e.g. morphine), or amphetamine-based licit drugs (e.g. prescriptions for attention deficit disorder), can be detected by the test. Further, though this would be in breach of most testing guidelines, there has also been some suggestion that urine samples have been used to discover whether a female employee is pregnant (Cheng & Henry 2005).

Dubious value of workplace drug testing

Recency of drug use

Even a properly conducted test, and one that yields a positive result for drug use, does not indicate an employee's current level of on-the-job impairment, nor can it detect use that may have occurred within the last few hours. Rather, the test indicates that the substance was consumed sometime in the past, between 3 to 28 days prior to the test. This means that an employee who tests positive for drugs may well have consumed them recreationally, in their private, non-work time and that the intoxicating effects of these drugs did not carry over into their workplace.

Recreational drug use

Indeed a sustained body of sociological research by UK academics (Measham *et al.* 2001; Parker *et al.* 2002; Hammersley *et al.* 2002; Makhoul *et al.* 1998) suggests that the vast majority of drug use in contemporary society is of recreational nature.

In other words, most users of illicit drugs use them in their 'private' leisure time, to enhance their leisure pursuits, and do so in a way that is cognisant of their work, study, family or other responsibilities. Yet, it is precisely such recreational users of 'softer' drugs such as cannabis who are the most likely to be 'caught' by the tests (NCETA 2006).

The consequences of a positive test for an employee are potentially severe. They may include:

- disciplinary action;
- enforced drug treatment;
- dismissal;
- criminal prosecution; and
- the disruption of the domestic sphere and child custody (Lucas 2005).

These consequences may be initiated by management for drug use that has little or no bearing on an employee's behaviour within the workplace.

Random drug testing

Clearly, therefore, workforce drug testing is in general a controversial practice. Some workforce drug testing programs, however, generate additional concerns. Random testing is the most contested pattern of testing. This is because it is divorced from any behavioural cues on the part of the employee (such as apparent intoxication at work) or incidents in the workplace (such as an unexplained accident) that might warrant the belief that the employee was impaired by drugs.

As such, random testing of employees is the most likely to harm the employment relationship (Pidd n.d.). It may also engender the suspicion that 'random' testing may not be random at all, but may in fact be used punitively to target selected employees. Consequently, random testing may generate a low morale environment at work, whereby employees perceive they are not trusted by management (Pidd & Roche 2006).

Behind the momentum for testing

If, then, a review of available research does not support the implementation of workforce drug testing on either health and safety or performance and productivity grounds, how else may we explain what appears to be an increasing momentum for the use of workforce drug testing? A number of possible explanations can be gleaned from wider academic studies of management (see Warren & Wray-Bliss 2009).

Non-instrumental reasons

Cavanaugh and Prasad (1994, p. 268), for instance, remind us that 'organizations frequently take actions that do *not* have immediate efficiency payoffs and in fact do so for a number of *non-instrumental* reasons'. They use this idea to explore symbolic reasons for managers to target drug use. They argue that for organisations 'rationality is the core principle that shapes their form and actions ... leading to their emphasis on impersonality, instrumentality and rule-like behaviour'.

Preservation of rational order

Management is the group charged with the authority and responsibility to maintain this rational order. Drug use however, threatens to undermine organisational rationality, and by implication, management control in the eyes of organisational stakeholders 'by symbolising an oppositional consciousness rooted in disorder' (Cavanaugh & Prasad 1994, p. 268) and signalling apparently hedonistic, deviant or excessive behaviour on the part of organisational members.

Drug testing, therefore, may be regarded in part as the reassertion of the managerial prerogative and part of the maintenance of the power 'myth' of managed, rational, ordered organisation. It does so by restoring an image of control, offering a seemingly scientific or rational response, and shoring up the moral legitimacy of management and organisation in the eye of its beholders.

Managerial anxiety

Readings of developments such as workforce drug testing in symbolic terms finds further purchase when we consider the nature of managerial work and managerial identity more generally.

In contrast to the image of management as calmly rational and operating through carefully thought through strategic plans, empirical studies of managerial work show us that management is defined by:

- high levels of ambiguity over the formal and informal markers of one's performance;
- uncertainty of the effectiveness of one's actions; and
- an ever-pervasive feeling of anxiety (Jackall 1988; Watson 2004).

Anxiety is no stranger to HRM professionals either. Since its inception, HRM has struggled to convince an often sceptical senior managerial cadre of its strategic importance and 'bottom line' contribution (Legge 1995). For those with HR responsibilities, the 'normal' anxieties of managing in the complex, ambiguous world of large, formal organisation are coupled with a more particular anxiety of continually striving to prove one's organisational contribution and importance to peers and superiors.

Commercial providers of workforce drug tests

These conditions of managerial anxiety constitute a context ripe for exploitation. Consultants, management advisers and providers of specialist and technical HR services are ever ready to sell HR managers a range of what have been derided as 'faddish' or 'fashionable', products, advice and services (Abrahamson 1991; Huczynski 1993; Shapiro 1998) with questionable efficacy (Collins 2001; Grint 1991; Guest 1992).

The emergence of a lucrative and growing multi-billion dollar market for the provision of employee drug testing by specialist commercial organisations and laboratories fits this model rather well. Previous research has found that much of the international 'evidence' regarding the dangers and costs of employee drug use can be traced to those organisations with a commercial interest in drug testing (ACLU 1999; IIDTW 2004).

The spectre these organisations evoke of intoxicated workers breaching health and safety rules, flouting organisational policies, and disregarding the sober, productive orientation required of today's workers helps cultivate a managerial anxiety over risk, organisational order, performance and legal liability for public safety. Once sufficient managerial and wider media attention is generated regarding the 'risks' of employee drug use, professional managerial bodies and governmental agencies begin to reflect these concerns in their publications and advice to industry.

Hard-pressed HR managers and directors do not, of course, have the academic's luxury of time to trace the source of such evidence and arguments. For them, the implementation of workforce drug testing may be akin to 'fashion' following behaviour, whereby a new found anxiety over employee drug taking is assuaged by following what other organisations seem to be doing—namely, contracting-in commercial providers of workforce drug tests.

How then do the preceding arguments and issues pertain to the Asia Pacific region, and in particular the context of Australia?

Country and sector perspective: Australia

National Drug and Alcohol Household Survey 2007

According to the federal government's most recent National Drug and Alcohol Household Survey (2007, published 2008), approximately 13.4% of surveyed Australians aged 14 years and older had used an illicit drug in the previous 12 months. As a contrast, 82.9% of surveyed Australians had recently used alcohol. Cannabis was the illicit drug most commonly used, with 9.1% reporting some use of this in 2007, with ecstasy the next most commonly used at 3.5% of the population.

Compared to previous years, illicit drug use in Australia is in decline and has been since 1998. It is currently at the lowest level since 1993 when the National Drug and Alcohol Surveys began.

Workforce drug testing in Australian organisations

Though figures are less reliable for the prevalence of workforce drug testing in Australian organisations, one of the larger commercial laboratories has estimated that 8% of workplaces have already implemented drug testing (Watts 2008). However, in an intriguing contrast to the consistent pattern of *declining* illicit drug use in Australian society, there is *increasing* interest in (Pidd & Roche 2006) and momentum building for (AIVL n.d., p. 2) further drug testing of more Australian employees. Why might this be the case?

Legal obligations

A number of organisations (including BHP, Westrail, and Shell) have claimed in industrial relations commissions that drug testing of their employees is necessary to meet their legal obligations in Australia (Nolan 2000).

Indeed, federal and state laws governing such areas as:

- occupational health and safety;
- road traffic;
- anti-discrimination;
- vicarious liability;
- criminal legislation; and
- specific legislation covering health and safety in mining, aviation, and rail transportation

are all relevant to the issue of drugs and alcohol at work (see NCETA 2006; Nolan 2000).

Position of the Australian Industrial Relations Commission

However, while strongly upholding the responsibility for health and safety of both the employee and employer, the Australian Industrial Relations Commission has not tended to support the argument that there is a legal *compulsion* to test in most industries. Further, a review of the decisions of the Commission suggests that, compared to the American courts which have tended to strongly uphold the right to test and discipline or dismiss positively tested employees (Gilliom 1994), the Australian Industrial Relations Commission is 'likely to be more sympathetic to employees' (Nolan 2000) in disputes over these matters.

Why the momentum for increased drug testing by Australian employers?

In the light of the equivocal legal situation with regard to workforce drug testing in Australian organisations, the consistent pattern of decreasing illicit drug use in Australian society, and what Pidd (n.d.) at the *National Centre for Education and Training on Addiction* has argued is an extremely limited landscape of research on drug use and its relation to the Australian workplace, how are we to make sense of the apparent momentum for increased drug testing by Australian employers?

Management 'fads' and 'fashions'

Part of an answer to this question could usefully recall the above mentioned research into the promotion and uptake of management 'fads' and 'fashions'. The ongoing creation of a 'market' for employee drug testing in Australia would seem to have some of the familiar features identified — namely:

- a managerial anxiety is cultivated;
- the anxiety is widely disseminated; and then
- assuaged by the purchase of a particular product or service.

As previously highlighted, much of the evidence for employee drug use and arguments supporting the increased use of drug testing at work in relation to both the US market (ACLU 1999) and the UK market (IIDTW 2004) was found to be traceable to those organisations with a commercial interest in the area.

Tainted evidence

This is a pattern that we are beginning to see in Australia also (Pidd n.d.). A pertinent case in point would be the following extract from a national media story (Watts 2008), printed in the *Daily Telegraph* in March 2008, with the dramatic headline DRUG USE RIFE IN AUSTRALIAN WORKFORCE.

> *'One in eight Australians are testing positive to drugs at work – a rate that has more than doubled over the past decade. More than 5% of employees are also abusing illicit drugs in high-risk jobs, according to new statistics obtained by The Daily Telegraph. The number of positives is expected to soar up to a quarter of employees in some industries, drug experts also warned yesterday, with cannabis abuse accounting for more than 90% of positive results.'*

The article went on to state that 'a lot of employers' are now drug testing their staff, as well as to report demands that the federal and state governments make employee drug testing mandatory. The source of such arguments and evidence is the commercial drug testing organisation *Medvet Laboratories*. Needless to say, basing HR policy for Australian organisations in such a significant and controversial area on the evidence and arguments of an organisation with a commercial interest in promoting drug testing might be considered poor HR strategy.

We consider next a case of contested policy in this area that was recently presented to the Australian Industrial Relations Commission.

Case study

Shell Refining (Australia) Pty Ltd, Clyde Refinery v Construction, Forestry, Mining and Energy Union (CFMEU)

The following case study considers a recent Australian Industrial Relations Commission decision (August 2008) in the case of *Shell Refining (Australia) Pty Ltd, Clyde Refinery* v *Construction, Forestry, Mining and Energy Union (CFMEU)* and review of that decision (May 2009).

The dispute between Shell Refining (Australia) and the CFMEU centred on the union's concerns with several aspects of the revised drug and alcohol policy that Shell wished to apply to workers at the

Clyde Refinery and Gore Bay Terminal.

Shell applied to have a binding, dispute resolution process conducted by the Commission under Division 3 of Part 13 of the *Workplace Relations Act* 1996. Of particular concern for this case study was the CFMEU union's opposition to the use of urine samples as the basis of random workforce drug tests and its insistence on the use of oral fluid testing in these circumstances instead.

By way of background, urine testing has a significantly longer window of detection than oral fluid samples, with a positive result possible for drugs that were used between two and 28 days earlier. Urine testing is not capable of detecting very recent drug use or actual impairment due to drug consumption.

Oral fluid testing cannot detect actual impairment due to drug or alcohol use either. It can, however, detect more recent drug use than urine testing and this, combined with the fact that oral fluid testing also has a much shorter window of detection—typically 12 to 24 hours—makes it much more likely than urine testing to indicate recent rather than past drug use.

Mr Neil McKenzie, Shell's Country Health Safety Security and Environment Manager, provided the following description of the objectives of Shell's drug and alcohol policy:

> *'Shell is committed to providing a safe work system and a safe and productive workplace by eliminating conditions and work practices that could lead to personal injury and equipment and other damage.*
>
> *People whose fitness for work may be impaired by alcohol or the use of drugs (such as cannabis, amphetamines, cocaine, opiates, and other narcotics), the use of prescription drugs (such as benzodiazepines, barbiturates or methadone), or the misuse of non-prescription drugs (such as codeine) can pose a risk to themselves and other people. Shell's objectives are that employees recognise the threat that alcohol and other drug consumption can present and that the associated risks to people, property and Shell's business are eliminated.'*

The disputed drug testing policy proposed:

- testing as a condition of employment for designated safety and environmentally sensitive positions and designated management positions;
- continual random urine sample drug testing of workers in designated safety and environmentally sensitive positions; and

- testing in circumstances where there is a reasonable belief that a person's fitness for work may be adversely affected by alcohol or drugs.

The company's disciplinary procedures were to be instigated for those employees who tested positive, with three positive tests being cause for dismissal. Policy documentation described the policy as intending to:

- assist in identifying people who may be either unfit for work or at risk of being unfit for work;
- discourage people from coming to work when they may be impaired by alcohol or other drugs; and
- raise awareness about the effects of alcohol and other drugs in the workplace.

Acknowledging that although the historic focus of a urine test does not indicate that the employee is intoxicated at work, Shell's legal representative Mr Adrian Morris, Partner at Blake Dawson, argued that the longer window of detection offered by urine testing was necessary as Shell was

'... interested more in influencing the behaviour of people around the use of drugs and alcohol to eliminate the risk, whether it's acute impairment, it's a lingering ongoing impairment or whether it's a chronic effect. So a responsible employer professing a policy like Shell's must be interested in more than whether X comes to work intoxicated.'

For the CFMEU, the prevention of employees being actually intoxicated at work was a legitimate health and safety concern for employees and managers. They argued, however, that the historic gaze of urine testing was a gross invasion of privacy and an unwarranted extension of managerial control and discipline outside of the boundaries of the workplace and into a person's private time. Witness for the CFMEU, Professor Olaf Drummer, Head of Forensic and Scientific Services, Victorian Institute of Forensic Medicine, expressed it thus:

'In general, drugs can be detected in urine well beyond the time the drug is having a significant biological effect. For example, cannabis, when smoked, the behavioural and physiological effects are generally no longer detectable after four hours.'

However, the biological trace of this past consumption can, for heavy users, linger and be detectable in the body for *'weeks following the last consumption.'* Therefore while urine testing is

> 'a perfectly adequate specimen to determine past use of drug ... it does not provide any proof of recent use; use that might render the worker unsafe to perform their duties.'

Whereas oral fluid testing provides

> 'a valid alternative specimen to detect drugs used much more recently at a time when drug use might render a person unsafe to perform their duties'.

The question for the Industrial Relations Commission to decide upon then became:

> '... whether it would be unjust or unreasonable for the company to implement a urine-based random testing regime with its wide 'window of detection', with all that implies for interfering with the private lives of employees, when a much more focused method is available, where a positive test is far more likely to indicate actual impairment, and is far less likely to detect the use of drugs at a time that would have no consequential effect on the employee's performance at work.'

The conclusion and verdict of the Commission, given by Senior Deputy President of the AIRC Jonathan Hamberger, was

> '... that the implementation of a urine-based random drug testing regime in these circumstances would be unjust and unreasonable'.

After application by Shell, a subsequent review of the decision of the Commission was undertaken and the verdict published in May 2009. President of the Commission, Justice Giudice, Senior Deputy President, Harrison and Commissioner Larkin, upheld the earlier decision, summarising the key conclusions and principles as follows:

> '...the Senior Deputy President did not disregard the importance of detecting drug use. It is equally apparent that he regarded drug use during non-working hours as something which was not the employer's business unless there was a risk that the drug user was impaired at work. His preference for oral fluid testing rather than urine testing was based on the finding that oral fluid testing was more likely than urine testing to detect recent use and therefore impairment. This is not to deny the possibility that a positive urine test might be an indication that the employee would at some time constitute an actual risk to health and safety. But, as we understand the decision, His Honour did not think that possibility justified the intrusion into the privacy of the employee which a urine test involves and which an oral fluid test does not. This reasoning is cogent and the conclusion was one of a number clearly open to him. In our view no error arose from it'.

> The CFMEU welcomed the verdict against urine testing at the Clyde Refinery and Gore Bay Terminal as a 'significant decision in protecting employees' privacy and improving drug and alcohol testing standards throughout the workforce' (CFMEU 2009). This case was reported nationally (*Sydney Morning Herald*, 25 May 2009) and internationally (*Reuters Press Digest*, 25 May 2009; *UK Trades Union Congress Bulletin*, 30 May 2009) as a significant verdict in favour of employee privacy.
>
> **Case study questions**
>
> On the basis of the case you should now be able to answer the following questions:
>
> 1. Why was the CFMEU union insisting on oral fluid testing rather than urine testing of staff?
> 2. What were Shell's stated goals with regard to their drug and alcohol policy?
> 3. What was the 'more' that Shell's legal representative, Mr Adrian Morris, was referring to when he said that 'a responsible employer professing a policy like Shell's must be interested in **more** than whether X comes to work intoxicated'?
> 4. Explain the distinction the Commission made between 'private' time and 'work' time. What limits does this distinction suggest for the legitimate reach of an organisation's HR practices?

Summary

This chapter has considered a contemporary and controversial HR issue reported to be gathering momentum both internationally and locally. Thus far, credible evidence in support of drug testing employees — for instance:

- evidence of significant deleterious effects of employee drug use on workplace health and safety, on productivity, on violence at work; and
- evidence that workforce drug testing reduces accidents, increases productivity or reduces employee drug use

has been shown to be weak. This is despite the practice being widespread in the US since the mid 1980s, despite the serious ramifications of the practice for employees, and despite the considerable financial and employment relation costs where drug testing has been implemented.

This chapter has highlighted the tendency of the evidence and arguments in support of drug testing to originate from organisations with a commercial interest in supporting workplace drug testing. Drawing upon organisational research into management fads and fashions, it has been suggested that, in part, the momentum for further workforce drug testing may be regarded as a product of:

- people responsible for commercial drug testing successfully cultivating and exploiting legitimate managerial anxieties with regard to legal liability;
- wider societal anxiety around illicit drugs; and
- the seemingly exact and scientific solution of workforce drug tests.

Final comments relate to the issue at stake in the case study—namely, the encroachment of drug testing into the private lives and bodies of employees. For some, the practice of workforce drug testing has been judged as stepping too far from legitimate managerial concerns with workplace behaviour and into areas of individual employees' private lives.

For a growing number of critics, such encroachment is also symptomatic of a more general movement in contemporary HR practices to seek to intervene in areas of an employee's

- private life;
- sense of self; and
- personal identity

that were hitherto regarded as private and outside the scope of a legitimate managerial prerogative.

Critics have argued that:

- employee health programs (Goss 1997);
- the management of employee smoking (Brewis & Grey 2008);
- limitations on employees' freedom of speech (Barry 2007);
- attempts to manage the views and values of employees through the manipulation of corporate cultures (Willmott 1993); and
- recent burgeoning interest in the management of 'everyday life' issues (Hancock & Tyler 2009) such as employees' sleep (Hancock 2008)

represent elements of an unwarranted extension of managerial discipline, discourse and surveillance.

In their recent article on the management of employees' smoking, Brewis and Grey (2008, p. 983), drawing upon Jackson and Carter (1998), make the morally disquieting argument that the regulation of employee smoking may be regarded as

> 'a 'discipline' or 'taming' of employees who smoke, not for reasons of enhancing productivity but rather 'for the satisfaction of the controller

and as a public display of compliance, obedience to discipline' (Jackson & Carter 1998, p. 54). All such 'non-useful' forms of regulation, Jackson and Carter suggest, can be understood as contributing to the inculcation of submissiveness amongst workers, as well as demonstrating to interested onlookers — shareholders, say — that all is as it should be in the moral universe of the organization.'

In certain aspects of contemporary HR practice there is almost an imperialist aspiration, an attempt to redraw the boundaries of the employment relationship so as to render the employee an object of management discipline both in work and out of work. This would seem to evoke an ideal of the modern individual as one who is continually and constantly attuned to the demands of their employer: reduced to ordering their life according to a narrow, work-oriented, rationality (Hancock & Tyler 2008).

HRM has long attracted questions with regard to its efficacy and ethics (Legge 1998; Watson 2007). The movement into areas (such as workforce drug testing) that extend management control explicitly into the out-of-work choices of employees, however, generates some of the most pressing questions yet regarding the scope of the managerial prerogative embodied in contemporary HRM.

Discussion questions

1. Why is workforce drug testing *not* a straightforward means of assessing an employee's intoxication at work?

2. Explain the argument that HR practices, such as workforce drug testing, may be the result of 'fashion following' behaviour rather than arising from careful scrutiny of the available evidence.

3. Explain the argument that the practice of workforce drug testing extends the managerial prerogative outside of the workplace and into an employee's private life.

4. Why, given your answer to question 3, might workforce drug testing encourage us to question the ethics of contemporary HR practice more generally?

References

Abrahamson, E 1991, 'Managerial fads and fashions: the diffusion and rejection of innovations', *Academy of Management Review*, 16(3): 586-612.

ACLU 1999, 'Drug testing: a bad investment', American Civil Liberties Union, www.aclu.org.

ADCA 2008, 'Improve drug and alcohol management at work', *Alcohol and Other Drugs Council of Australia*, 22 February, www.adca.org.au.

AIVL n.d, *Policy position: workplace based drug testing*, www.aivl.org.au.

Barry, B 2007, 'The cringing and the craven: freedom of expression in, around, and beyond the workplace', *Business Ethics Quarterly*, 17(2): 263-296

Brewis, J & Grey, C 2008, 'The regulation of smoking at work', *Human Relations*, 61(7): 965-987.

Cavanaugh, JM & Prasad, P 1994, 'Drug Testing as Symbolic Managerial Action', *Organization Science* 5, 2, 267-271.

CFMEU 2009, 'CFMEU's major win in Shell random drug testing case', *Construction Forestry Mining Energy Union*, www.cfmeu.com.au.

Cheng, W & Henry, J 2005, 'Ethical, Legal and Practical Aspects of Testing' in H Ghodse (Ed) 2005a, *Addiction at Work: Tackling Drug Use and Misuse in the Workplace*, Gower Publishing:

Collins, D 2001, 'The fad motif in management scholarship', *Employee Relations*, 23(1): 26-37.

Draper, E 1998, 'Drug Testing in the Workplace: The allure of management technologies', *International Journal of Sociology and Social Policy*, 18, 5/6, 62-103.

Easter-Bahls, J 1998, 'Dealing with Drugs; keep it legal', *HR Magazine*, 43, 3, 104-111.

Eckersley, K 1995, 'Dealing with Drugs - Part 2: Lightening the employer's latest burden', *Employee Counselling Today*, 7 (4) pp. 20-22.

Fine, C 1992, 'Video tests are the new frontier in drug detection', *Personnel Journal*, 71 (6): 148-157.

Ghodse, H 2005, 'Drugs and Alcohol in the Workplace', in H Ghodse (Ed) 2005, *Addiction at Work: Tackling Drug Use and Misuse in the Workplace*, Gower Publishing, Aldershot, pp. 3-10.

Gilliom, J 1994, *Surveillance, Privacy and the Law: Employee drug testing and the politics of social control*, Michigan, University of Michigan Press.

Goss, D 1997, 'Healthy discipline? Health promotion at work', *Electronic Journal of Radical Organization Theory*, 3(2).

Grint, K 1994, 'Reengineering History: Social Resonances and Business Process Reengineering', *Organization*, 1(1): 179–201.

Guest, D 1991, 'Right enough to be dangerously wrong' in G Salaman, S Cameron, H Hamblin, P Iles, C Mabey & K. Thompson (Eds), *Human Resource Strategies*, London, Sage, pp. 5-19.

Hammersley, R, Khan, F & Ditton, J 2002, *Ecstasy: and the rise of the chemical generation*, Routledge, London.

Hancock, P 2008, 'Cultures of sleep: organization and the lure of dormancy', *Culture and Organization*, 14(4): 411-424.

Hancock, P & Tyler, M (Eds.) 2009, *The Management of Everyday Life*, Hampshire, Palgrave.

Hancock, P Tyler, M 2008, 'Beyond the confines: management, colonization and the everyday', *Critical Sociology,* 34(1): 29-49.

Harr, J & Spell, C 2007, 'Factors affecting employer adoption of drug testing in New Zealand', *Asia Pacific Journal of Human Resources,* 45(2): 200-217.

Harris, M 2004, 'Alcohol and Drug Use in the Workplace' in R Griffin & A O'Leary-Kelly (Eds) 2004, *The Dark Side of Organizational Behaviour,* 341-372, San Francisco, Jossey Bass.

Huczynski, A 1993, 'Explaining the succession of management fads', The *International Journal of Human Resource Management,* 4(2): 443-463.

IIDTW 2004, *Drug Testing in the Workplace: The Report of the Independent Inquiry into Drug Testing at Work,* York/London, Joseph Rowntree Foundation/Drugscope.

Jackall, R 1988, *Moral mazes: the world of corporate managers,* Oxford, Oxford University Press.

Jackson, N & Carter, P 1998, 'Labour as dressage' in A McKinlay & K Starkey (Eds), *Foucault, management and organization theory: From Panopticon to technologies of self,* London, SAGE, 49–64.

Jardine-Tweedie, L & Wright, P 1998, 'Workplace drug testing: avoiding the testing addiction', *Journal of Managerial Psychology,* Vol 13(8) pp. 534 – 543.

Legge, K 1998, 'Is HRM ethical? Can HRM be ethical?', in Parker, M (Ed) *Ethics and Organizations,* London, Sage: 150-172.

Legge, K 1995, *Human Resource Management: Rhetorics and Realities,* Basingstoke, Palgrave.

Lucas, G 2005, 'Policy design and implementation' in H Ghodse (Ed) 2005a, *Addiction at Work: Tackling Drug Use and Misuse in the Workplace,* Gower Publishing, Aldershot, pp. 109-123.

Makhoul, M, Yates, F & Wolfson, S 1998, 'A Survey of Substance Use at a UK University: Prevalence of Use and Views of Students', *Journal of Substance Misuse,* 3: 119-24.

Martinson, J 1999, 'Drugs testing 'a waste of money' *The Guardian,* 2 September.

Measham, F, Aldridge, J & Parker, H 2001, *Dancing on Drugs: Risk, Health and Hedonism in the British Club Scene,* Free Association Books, London.

NCETA 2006, 'Responding to alcohol and other drugs in the workplace: useful information', *National Centre for Education and Training on Addiction* (NCETA), Flinders University, Adelaide.

Nolan, S 2008, 'Drug-free workplace programmes: New Zealand perspective', *Forensic Science International,* 174: 125-132.

Nolan, J 2000, 'Employee privacy in the electronic workplace Part 2: drug testing, out of hours conduct and references', *Privacy Law and Policy Reporter,* 61, www.austlii.edu.au.

Parker, H, Williams, L & Aldridge, J 2002, 'The Normalisation of 'Sensible' Recreational Drug Use', *Sociology,* 36, 4, 941-964.

Pidd, K (n.d.), 'Drugs and alcohol 'abuse' and testing workers for the presence of drugs and alcohol', *National Centre for Education and Training on Addiction* (NCETA), Flinders University, Adelaide.

Pidd, K & Roche, A 2006, 'Drug testing as a response to alcohol and other issues in the workplace', *National Centre for Education and Training on Addiction* (NCETA), Flinders University, Adelaide.

Russell, T 2004, 'Drugs and alcohol: testing issues', *Human Resources Leader*, May 29, www.humanresourcesmagazine.com.au.

Shapiro, E 1998, *Fad surfing in the boardroom*, Capstone, Oxford.

Warren, S & Wray-Bliss, E 2009, 'Workforce drug testing: A review, critique and reframing', *New technology, Work and Employment*, 24(2): 163-176.

Watson, T 2007, 'HRM, ethical irrationality, and the limits of ethical action', in A Pinnington, R Macklin, T Campbell (Ed), *Human Resource Management: ethics and employment*, Oxford, Oxford University Press.

Watson, T 2004, *In Search of Management*, London, Routledge.

Watts, B 2008, 'Drug use rife in Australian workforce', *Daily Telegraph*, March 24.

Willmott, H 1993, 'Strength is ignorance, slavery is freedom: managing culture in modern organizations', *Journal of Management Studies*, 30(4): 515-552.

Glossary

Aged Dependency Ratio: Ratio of the population 65 years and over as a percentage of the population aged 20–64 years. (Chapter 11)

Ageing workforce: A changing demographic composition of the workforce where the average workforce age is increasing. An ageing workforce reflects an underlying ageing of a general population. (Chapter 11)

Anglo-Saxon capitalism: Typical of English-speaking economies, Anglo-Saxon capitalism is a liberal free-market model of capitalism characterised by deregulated labour and financial markets and low taxation. It is at the centre of the debate on 'varieties of capitalism'. (Chapter 4)

Discrimination: Discrimination is often used to mean illegal discriminatory acts. Illegal discrimination is the unfavourable treatment of a person, or a group of people, by category, class, or group rather than objective treatment on the basis of merit. Under EEO law, it is illegal to discriminate on the basis of race, colour, national or ethnic origin, sex, pregnancy or marital status, age, disability, religion, sexual preference, trade union activity or some other characteristic specified under anti-discrimination or human rights legislation.

Workplace discrimination can occur in: recruitment and selection; terms, conditions and benefits of employment; training opportunities; promotion and career opportunities. (Chapter 12)

Diversity: Ways in which people differ (such as age, race, gender, ethnicity, mental and physical abilities and sexual orientation) and acquired characteristics (such as education, income, religion, work experience, language skills, geographic location, and family status). (Chapter 12)

Diversity management: A process intended to create and maintain a positive work environment where the similarities and differences of individuals are valued, so that all can reach their potential and maximize their contributions to an organisation's strategic goals and objectives. (Chapter 12)

Employment relations: The formal and informal rules which regulate the employment relationship and the social processes which create and enforce these rules. (Chapter 3)

Employment relations institutions: Rule-making bodies that create and enforce the rules of the employment relationship. (Chapter 3)

Equal Employment Opportunity (EEO): The goal of laws that make some types of discrimination in employment illegal. Equal employment opportunity will become a reality when each citizen has an equal chance to enjoy the benefits of employment. EEO is not a guarantee of employment for anyone. Under EEO law, only job-related factors can be used to determine whether an individual is qualified for a particular job. (Chapter 12)

Equal Employment Opportunity Laws: The laws that prohibit discrimination on the basis of race, colour, religion, sex, national origin, age, or handicap in any terms, conditions, or privileges of employment. In Australia, the following laws operate at a federal level and are administered by the Australian Human Rights Commission: *Age Discrimination Act* 2004; *Australian Human Rights Commission Act* 1986; *Disability Discrimination Act* 1992; *Racial Discrimination Act* 1975; *Sex Discrimination Act* 1984. (Chapter 12)

Expatriate performance management (EPM): EPM includes four components (consistent with Dowling, Festing & Engle 2008):

- goal setting, which acts as a formal control mechanism when integrated with performance appraisal, and as an informal control mechanism by directing attention and motivating and sustaining performance (Latham 2004);
- performance appraisal (PA) or performance evaluation[9] may be defined as 'a process that identifies, evaluates and develops employee performance to meet employee and organizational goals' (Dessler, Griffiths & Lloyd-Walker 2004, p. 258);
- training and development, including pre-departure and in-country training for the expatriate; and
- mentoring, a commonly overlooked component of EPM, which contributes directly and indirectly to performance management through monitoring and feedback by the mentor, as well as knowledge, skill and value transferral to the protégé.

Table 13.1 draws on a range of (primarily Western) literature to summarise the key features of each of the four components considered necessary for effective EPM. (Chapter 13)

Global responsibility: Global responsibility (Antal & Sobczak 2004; Perez 2003; Thevenet 2003) is a concept that recognises that the effects of decision making within an organisation go far beyond its walls. Organisations now have capacities that are potent enough to leverage the effects of internal decisions around the world.

---

[9] The terms 'performance evaluation' and 'performance appraisal' are used interchangeably in the literature (see Dowling *et al.* 2008).

This raises a second meaning of 'global'. Decision making is more global if it is more inclusive. This means that leaders recognise the wider range of stakeholders whose lives are affected by decision making and consider the implications for those stakeholders as they make their decisions. Anatal and Sobczak (2004) also point out that the concept of global responsibility surpasses its conceptual antecedent—'corporate social responsibility'—which tended to focus on the responsibilities of large, private sector entities. Global responsibility can also be exercised by small organisations, not-for-profit organisations and NGOs. This element is particularly salient in this chapter where we see the concept of global responsibility applied in our case study of PricewaterhouseCoopers, particularly with respect to that company's interactions with stakeholders across the three sectors. (Kramar & Jones - Chapter 5)

Globalisation: Globalisation refers to the increasing economic, technological and cultural interdependence across national borders. (Chapter 4)

Globalisation: Globalisation is a phenomenon 'driven by many factors, of which technology, the related mobility of people, goods and ideas, and a liberal trading environment are perhaps the most obvious' (McKenna 2000, p. 75). It emphasises a 'freeing up of labour and capital flows' (Floyd 2001, p. 109) at the global scale to achieve a competitive advantage through 'efficiency and low cost labour' (Floyd 2001, p. 111). Globalisation is marked by:

- trade liberalisation;
- international economics integration;
- the formation of regional economic communities such as North America, Europe and the Asia Pacific;
- cultural homogeneity; and
- political universalism. (Chapter 8)

Globality: Globality is a term coined in 2008 by Sirkin, Hemerling and Bhattacharya to capture the rapid rise of developing economies and the reshaping of global competition. They developed the phrase 'competing with everyone from everywhere for everything' to describe the nature of future global competition. (Chapter 4)

HR outsourcing: In common with other aspects of the outsourcing business, HR outsourcing places 'responsibility for various elements of the HR function with a third-party provider' (Turnbull 2002, p.11). (Chapter 7)

HR shared services: HR shared services is a system of providing well-defined services for internal customers that consist of more than one unit. According to Oates (1998), although shared service centres remain within the organisation concerned, they have a high degree of independence that allows them to act in a manner similar to an external outsourcing provider. (Chapter 7)

Human capital: Human capital refers to the sustainability of people management systems which are likely to have an impact on the share price of a firm. (Chapter 6)

Human capital metrics: Human capital metrics can be seen broadly as a component of a firm's risk management, which is an essential component of management particularly since the GFC corporate collapses. (Chapter 6)

Human capital v. employee engagement: While the literature concerning the concept of 'employee engagement' is increasingly compelling, it is an incomplete proxy for human capital *per se*. Human capital is broader than employee engagement, and incorporates management systems of recruitment, retention, training, performance management and knowledge management. (Chapter 6)

Human capital v. social capital: The term 'human capital' is used here to define the practices used in organisations which work towards the long-term sustainability of organisations. It is distinguishable from the more commonly used term 'social capital' which is defined by Dunphy *et al.* (2000, p. 6) as human sustainability, which implies building human capability and skills for sustainable high level organisational performance, and for community and societal well being. (Chapter 6)

Intangible assets: Human capital is a subset of the concept of intangible assets. The International Accounting Standards (IAS) Board defines intangibles as an identifiable non-monetary asset without physical substance, held for use in the production and supply of goods or services, for rental to others or for administrative purposes. One International Accounting Standard (Number 38) prescribes that an intangible asset is a resource controlled by an enterprise as a result of past events, from which future economic benefits are expected to flow to the enterprise (Pitkanen 2006). (Chapter 6)

International human resource management (IHRM): 'The HRM issues and problems arising from the internationalization of business, and the HRM strategies, policies and practices which firms pursue in response to the internationalization of business' (Scullion 1995 cited in Scullion & Lineham 2005, p. 4). (Chapter 13)

Offshoring: The term is sometimes related to outsourcing but is often incorrectly used interchangeably with it. Offshoring can be defined as the process of outsourcing business activities or services to a third party overseas and/or an employer moving its business activities or services to another country directly or indirectly. In other words, offshoring may not always involve the services of an external provider. (Chapter 7)

Glossary

Organisational units: In the context of MNCs, organisational units are the headquarters and/or other subsidiaries in the corporation. (Chapter 8)

Outsourcing: The term here refers to assigning one or more business processes to an external service provider who takes over the responsibility of owning and managing these processes and delivering the envisaged service as per the terms of the agreement. Outsourcing thus enables an organisation to shift its responsibility for certain operations and/or processes to another entity. (Chapter 7)

Multinational enterprises: MNEs are organisations with production, trading or service operations in more than one country. (Chapter 4)

Receiving unit: The receiving unit is the focal subsidiary. (Chapter 8)

Reflective practice: Reflective practice is a concept introduced by Donald Schon (1983, 1987). More recently it has been linked to the engagement of staff in thinking and acting in ways that enhance sustainability (Tilbury & Wortman 2004). Schon initially distinguished between 'reflection *on* action' and 'reflection *in* action'. Reflection *on* action is a kind of postmortem reflection after the action has been executed; reflection *in* action could be described as critical self reflection—it is a process of considering action while the individual is in the process of taking that action. The latter requires not only a cognitive ability to assess basic assumptions at the same time as those assumptions are driving actions, but has more recently been recognised as the capacity to deploy a highly developed affective competence enabling the actor to recognise the feelings that come into being during the action, take responsibility for those feelings and recognise their influence on judgement (Taylor 2007, p. 86). (Chapter 5)

Regime competition: Regime competition works from a belief that different countries compete for foreign direct investment (FDI). It is suggested that countries will promote a lowering of labour market conditions as part of their competitive strategy to attract FDI. (Chapter 4)

Regime shopping: Regime shopping is a process whereby MNEs compare different employment relations systems as part of their location decision-making processes. (Chapter 4)

Risk management: Risk management is defined by Standards Australia (1999, p. iii) as follows:

> *'To be most effective, risk management should become part of the organisation's culture. It should be integrated into the organisation's philosophy, practices and business plans rather than be viewed or practiced as a separate program. When this is achieved, risk management becomes the business of everyone in the organisation.'*

It is this underlying principle which informs this chapter's approach to human capital metrics. (Chapter 6)

States: The entire apparatus of formal roles and public institutions that exercise political authority over populations within a given territory (Bell & Head 1994, p. 3). (Chapter 3)

Strategic HRM (SHRM): One of the key features that characterises strategic HRM is the concern with 'models and studies which link HRM to performance' (Boxall & Purcell 2003, p. 6). (Chapter 13)

Strategic international HRM (SIHRM): SIHRM is a more wide-ranging and complex counterpart of SHRM in the context of organisations' internationalised operations. (Chapter 13)

Sustainability: 'Sustainable' human resource management systems are those which are internally consistent with a firm's strategy and with the broader context in which the firm is operating (Royal & O'Donnell 2005a, p. 3). (Chapter 6)

Sustainability: Sustainability is often thought of as focusing on the three elements of Elkington's (1997) triple bottom line: economic outcomes, social impacts, and environmental impacts. The definition is limited, however, in that it focuses the attention of managers on their external impacts, without looking inwards to the internal dynamics that contribute to those impacts. For example, the HR focus tends to be limited to factors that make the organisation a good employer, factors which are then grouped under the social dimension. (Chapter 5)

Talent: The sum of a person's knowledge, skills, ability and experience as well as their ability to learn and grow. (Chapter 10)

Talent pipeline: Talent pipeline is a strategy organisations employ to identify and engage with a pool of potential talent for future positions. (Chapter 4)

Talent management: The ability to attract, retain and utilise the human resource talent available to the organisation. (Chapter 10)

Talent management: Talent management refers to the strategies that organisations employ to identify, develop and promote potential within existing employees. (Chapter 4)

Transfer of HRM policies and practices: The transfer of HRM policies and practices between organisational units is 'a process that covers several stages starting from identifying the knowledge to the actual process of transferring the knowledge to its final utilization by the receiving unit' (Minbaeva, Pedersen, Bjorkman, Fey & Park 2003, p. 587). The transfer process can occur not only from the headquarters to the subsidiary and from one subsidiary to another, but also from the subsidiary to headquarters (through a reverse diffusion process). (Chapter 8)

Unions: Continuous associations of employees that seek to advance the economic, social and sometimes political interests of their members. (Chapter 3)

Workforce diversity: Refers to ways in which people in a workforce are similar to and different from one another. In addition to the characteristics protected by law, other similarities and differences commonly cited include background, education, language skills, personality, sexual orientation and work role. (Chapter 12)

Workforce drug testing: Workforce drug testing is the testing of an employee, or prospective employee's, blood, urine, hair, sweat or saliva and oral fluids for traces of previously consumed illicit drugs (for instance cannabis, amphetamines, cocaine, opiates, methamphetamines) and certain licit (prescription) drugs.

Workforce drug testing can be conducted at a number of stages in the employment cycle:

- pre-recruitment;
- on suspicion of drug use;
- post-incident or accident; or
- randomly, during employment. (Chapter 14)

Work-life balance: A more holistic term that includes your ability to balance your overall life, including your responsibilities to yourself, your community, and your many priorities, which may or may not have to do with family. (Chapter 9)

Work-family balance: Refers to how you manage your family responsibilities towards children, ageing parents, a disabled family member, or a partner/spouse. (Chapter 9)

Work-life initiatives: Those strategies, policies, programs and practices initiated and maintained in workplaces to address work-family conflict, quality of work and life, and need for flexibility. (Chapter 9)

INDEX

A
activities, core v. periphery, 142
adaptive approach, 173
affective competence, 87, 97, 98, 105, 331
age discrimination, 237, 240, 241, 242, 243, 245, 249
ageing workforce, 4, 11, 234, 235, 236, 243, 244, 245, 246, 247, 264
ageing workforce, definition, 233, 327
annual pay, 29, 34
arbitration, 46, 52
Asia-Pacific Talent Index, 226
auditing, 38

B
Balanced Scorecard, 122
best practices, 13, 36, 37, 39, 114, 128, 144, 162, 166, 293, 301, 302
business measurement theory, 116
business strategy, 4, 142, 169, 174, 197

C
call-centre approaches, 144
capital mobility, 68
capitalism, 61, 63, 66, 70, 163, 166, 176, 327
collaborative learning, 98
collective bargaining, 49, 52, 53, 54, 55
collectivist cultures, 187, 266
commitment-maximising strategy, 30
contingency, 37, 38, 163
convergence, 35, 36, 37, 38, 75, 161
core competences, 28, 32
corporate citizenship, 199, 200
corporate social responsibility (CSR), 90
corporate venture capital (CVC), 31
corporate venturing programs (CVP), 31
country of origin perspective, 165
critical thinking, 97
culturalist perspective, 161, 163
culture change, 95, 199

D
Democratic Party of Japan (DPJ), 54
differential work design, 269
direct discrimination, 275
discrimination, definition, 257, 327
dismissal, 30, 32, 52, 288, 311
dispute resolution, 52
diversity management, 260
diversity management, definition, 257, 327
diversity, definition, 256, 327
dominance effect, 165, 166
Dow Jones Sustainability Index (DJSI), 90, 91

E
economic and labour market, 6, 19, 22, 33
economic interdependency, 72
economic protectionism, 71
employee retention, 30, 40, 226
employment arrangements, 51, 243
employment contracts, 51, 53, 54
employment discrimination, 55
employment mode, 39
employment relations, 6, 7, 45, 46, 47, 48, 49, 50, 53, 56, 60, 331
engagement scores, 113
environmental management system, 93
environmental sustainability, 93, 98
environmental turbulence, 35
Equal Employment Opportunity (EEO), definition, 257, 328
equity in the workplace, 30
ethical leadership, 100
European business excellence model, 120
expatriate performance management (EPM), definition, 285, 328
exportive approach, 173

F
foreign direct investment (FDI), 61, 64, 69, 72, 73, 331

G
generic orientations, 172, 176
geographical challenges, 71
geographical fragmentation, 68
global competition, 61, 63, 68, 69, 76, 77, 162, 329
global financial crisis, 7, 10, 11, 12, 47, 50, 53, 55, 56, 63, 73, 89, 112, 202, 213, 215, 227, 266
global industries, 168
global integration, 73, 75, 292

335

global job pacts, 67
global managerial capacity, 89
Global Reporting Initiative (GRI), 90
global responsibility, 87, 329
global responsibility, definition, 86, 328
global terrorism, 63, 65
globalisation, 36, 61, 65, 66, 69, 159
globalisation thesis, 67, 161, 162
globalisation, definition, 60, 159, 329
globality, 61, 63, 329
goal setting, 285, 291, 294, 295, 296, 300, 301, 328

H

host country perspective, 166
HR interventions, 140
HR metrics, 8, 91, 119, 134
HR performance index, 38
HR policies, 4, 91, 92, 95, 143, 201
HR scorecard, 38, 123
HR service providers, categories, 141
HR shared services model, 144
HR shared services, definition, 140, 329
HRM content, 3
HRM function, 3, 12, 13, 169, 177, 286
HRM practices
  emerging, 27
  key, 27, 32
  traditional, 27
HRM, key elements of, 23
human capital (HC) metrics, 8
human capital analysis, tools
  analysing, 128
  change management matrix, 129
  mapping, 128
  rating, 128
human capital indicators, 112
human capital measurement, 115, 116, 117
human capital metrics. *See* human capital (HC) metrics
human capital metrics, definition, 111, 330
Human Capital Monitor, 120, 124, 125
Human Capital Scorecard, 128, 130, 131
human capital, definition, 111, 330
human resource outsourcing (HRO), 8, 140, 141, 143, 147, 148, 151, 152

I

individualist cultures, 266
industrialisation, 21, 23, 48, 54, 161, 167
insamangsa, 6, 20
insamansa, 6, 20

institutional perspective, 163, 164
Intangible assets monitor, 124
intangible assets, definition, 111, 330
integrative approach, 173
Intellectual Capital Index, 125
intergenerational equity, 89
International HRM (IHRM), 7, 12, 79, 285
international human resource mgmt. (IHRM), definition, 284, 330
isomorphism, 36, 170

K

knowledge workers, 219

L

labour laws, 7, 32, 46, 47, 49, 50, 51, 52, 54, 55, 57
labour markets, 2, 23, 29, 30, 48, 57, 77, 78
labour policies, 234, 237
labour policy, 11, 234
labour supply, 30, 193, 237
Leadership and Management Systems Matrix, 128, 131, 132
legislation
  Age Discrimination Act 2004, 242, 257, 283, 328
  Australian Human Rights Commission Act 1986, 257, 328
  Disability Discrimination Act 1992, 257, 283, 328
  Drug Free Workplace Act 1988, 308
  Employment Act 1968, Singapore, 55
  Employment Measure Act 1966, Japan, 240
  Employment Protection Law, China, 51
  Equal Opportunity Act 1995 (Vic), 196
  Fair Work Act 2009, 196, 242
  Human Rights and Equal Opportunity Commission Act 1986, 283
  Industrial Relations Act 1960, Singapore, 55
  Labour Contract Act, Japan, 53
  Labour Contract Law (LCL), China, 51, 52
  Labour Mediation and Arbitration Law, China, 51
  Law on Protecting Dispatched Workers 1998, Korea, 32
  Occupational Health and Safety (Commonwealth Employment) Act 1991, 283
  Racial Discrimination Act 1975, 283

Sex Discrimination Act 1984, 257, 283, 328
Workplace Relations Act 1996, 242, 265, 276, 283
Workplace Relations Act 1996 (Cwth), 196
Workplace Safety and Health Act 2006, Singapore, 55

M
Malcolm Baldrige Criteria for Performance Excellence, 120
managerial anxiety, 313, 315
market for capital, 48
McKinsey report, The, 76, 77, 217
mediation, 52
mentoring, 30, 31, 222, 284, 285, 286, 294, 295, 296, 301, 328
Montreal Protocol, 89
morale, 92, 198, 312
multidomestic industries, 167, 168
multinational enterprise (MNE), 7, 63, 68, 69, 70, 77, 293
multinational enterprises, definition, 60, 331

N
new venture units (NVU), 31
numerical flexibility strategy, 30, 35, 40,

O
Open-door Policy, China, 50
organisational competencies, 4, 8
organisational culture, 260
organisational resilience, 7, 88
organisational transformation, 41
organisational units, definition, 160, 331
outplacement programs, 32
outsourcing, definition, 140, 331

P
paradoxes, 39, 41
performance appraisal, 285, 286, 288, 290, 291, 292, 294, 296, 300, 301, 328
performance evaluation, 285, 289, 291, 295, 296, 301, 328
performance-based system, 29, 33, 34, 35, 40, 41
privacy during drug testing, 310, 311
product markets, 22, 40, 47
promotion, 53, 57, 66, 96, 200, 237, 246, 257, 274, 288, 289, 315, 327
protective labour regulation, 53, 54, 57

R
random drug testing, 312
receiving unit, definition, 160, 331
recruitment processing outsourcing (RPO), 151, 155
redundancies, 32
reflective practice, definition, 87, 331
regime competition, 61, 69, 331
regime shopping, definition, 60, 331
resistance to change, 272
resource-based view (of a firm), 5, 10, 11, 88, 141, 213, 215, 218
restructuring, 40, 46, 68, 75, 96, 218, 245
retention strategies, 30, 31, 234
reverse diffusion, 160, 172, 293, 301, 333
rewards, 30, 40, 92, 94, 116, 128, 131, 199, 200, 220
risk management, definition, 111, 331
ROI, 41, 119, 120, 121, 140
role of leaders and managers, 96
role-related responsibilities, 190

S
Samsung, recruitment, 28, 29, 30, 32
seniority, 21, 27, 29, 32, 33, 34, 35, 40, 53, 289
sentiment against offshoring, 152
Shared Services Centre, 144
Skandia Navigator, 120, 123
skill supply, 142
social and cultural factors, 6, 19, 21, 33, 161, 167, 202, 260
social and human objectives, 92
social inclusion, 256, 260, 262, 266, 271
socialist market economy, 50
Sovereign Wealth Funds (SWFs), 64
stakeholder management, 94
states, definition, 45, 332
strategic capability, 5
strategic choice, 35
strategic HRM (SHRM), definition, 285, 332
strategic international human resource management (SIHRM), 60, 61, 62, 63, 73, 74, 76, 78, 285, 332
sustainability, definition, 86, 111, 332
sustainable development, 88, 89, 90
sustained competitive advantage, 5, 37, 40, 75, 91, 141, 216
systemic thinking, 99

T

talent management, 4, 7, 10, 11, 61, 62, 74, 76, 77, 151, 198, 199, 202, 212, 213, 214, 215, 221, 224, 332
talent pipeline, 61, 332
talent, definition, 212, 332
trade barriers, 9, 48, 160
trade unions, 48, 49, 51, 92

U

uncertainties for management, 41
union density, 53, 54
unions, definition, 45, 333
United Nations Principles for Responsible Investment (UNPRI 2009), 114
urbanisation, 191, 193

V

vision, 94, 98, 99, 273

W

war for talent, 11, 28, 40, 56, 217, 220, 227
Warwick model of strategic change, 2, 3
Watson Wyatt's Human Capital Index, 91, 112, 120
William Mercer's Human Capital Wheel, 121
women in the workforce, 192, 194, 263
work design, 226, 256, 260, 264, 267, 268, 269, 270
work-family balance, definition, 185, 333
workforce diversity, 12, 235, 236, 256, 257, 264, 267, 333
workforce drug testing in Australia, 307, 314, 333
work-life balance, definition, 185, 333
work-life initiatives, definition, 186, 333
work–life issues, 186, 187, 188, 191, 193, 201, 202
work–life management, 4, 10, 188
workplace diversity programs, 267